CELEBRITY

Celebrity introduces the key terms and concepts, dilemmas and issues that are central to the study and critical understanding of celebrity.

Drawing on two dynamic models from two different modes of enquiry – the circuit of celebrity culture and the circuit of celebrity affect – this book explores the multi-layered, multi-faceted contexts and concepts that sit within and surround the study of celebrity. Through building a critical story about celebrity, Sean Redmond discusses key topics such as identity and representation; the celebrity body; the consumption of celebrity and celebrity culture; and the sensory connection between fans and celebrities, gender, activism, gossip and toxicity.

Including case studies on Miley Cyrus, David Bowie, Scarlett Johansson and Kate Winslet, *Celebrity* is a dynamic and topical volume ideal for students and academics in celebrity and cultural studies.

Sean Redmond is Professor in Screen and Design at Deakin University, Australia. He convenes the Melbourne-based Eye Tracking and the Moving Image Research Group and the Science Fiction Research Group at Deakin University. He has published numerous books on celebrity, including *A Companion to Celebrity* (2015), *Celebrity and the Media* (2014) and *Framing Celebrity: New Directions in Celebrity Culture* (2006). With Su Holmes, he edits the journal *Celebrity Studies*, short-listed by The Association of Learned Professional Society Publishers for best new academic journal in 2011.

KEY IDEAS IN MEDIA AND CULTURAL STUDIES

The *Key Ideas in Media and Cultural Studies* series covers the main concepts, issues, debates and controversies in contemporary media and cultural studies. Titles in the series constitute authoritative, original essays rather than literary surveys, but are also written explicitly to support undergraduate teaching. The series provides students and teachers with lively and original treatments of key topics in the field.

Cultural Policy
David Bell and Kate Oakley

Reality TV
Annette Hill

Culture
Ben Highmore

Representation
Jenny Kidd

Celebrity
Sean Redmond

For more information about this series, please visit: https://www.routledge.com/Key-Ideas-in-Media--Cultural-Studies/book-series/KEYIDEA

CELEBRITY

Sean Redmond

Routledge
Taylor & Francis Group

LONDON AND NEW YORK

First published 2019
by Routledge
2 Park Square, Milton Park, Abingdon, Oxon OX14 4RN

and by Routledge
711 Third Avenue, New York, NY 10017

Routledge is an imprint of the Taylor & Francis Group, an informa business

© 2019 Sean Redmond

British Library Cataloguing-in-Publication Data
A catalogue record for this book is available from the British Library

Library of Congress Cataloging-in-Publication Data
A catalog record has been requested for this title

ISBN: 978-0-415-52743-9 (hbk)
ISBN: 978-0-415-52744-6 (pbk)
ISBN: 978-0-203-11480-3 (ebk)

Typeset in Times New Roman
by Deanta Global Publishing Services, Chennai, India
Printed by CPI Group (UK) Ltd, Croydon CR0 4YY

For Lee:
The summer arrived with you

CONTENTS

List of illustrations   viii
Acknowledgements   ix

1 **The key idea: Two celebrity circuits beat as one**   1

2 **Celebrity representations**   33

3 **More than just a feeling: Celebrity affects**   57

4 **(Post)modern identities and celebrity
   selfhood**   83

5 **Celebrity embodiment**   108

6 **The liquid lights of celebrity productions**   137

7 **Celebrity texturality**   171

8 **Impressionable audiences: Consuming celebrity
   culture**   197

9 **Celebrity agency**   226

10 **Celebrity regulation in body and space**   248

11 **Celebrity disruption**   275

   Conclusion   303
   References   308
   Index   326

ILLUSTRATIONS

FIGURES

1.1	David Bowie: The hyper-white rock star	10
1.2	The face of Garbo	18
2.1	The haunting mirror of whiteness	50
3.1	Lost in transmission	65
5.1	The race and gender of West and Swift	111
5.2	In-between in *Holy Smoke*	132
6.1	Manufacturing boy bands: BTS	144
6.2	Retro-scoping Obama	167
10.1	Miley pole dancing	255

CHARTS

8.1	Use of 'Miley Cyrus' and volume over time	216
8.2	Use of #Bangerz and volume over time	216

TABLES

6.1	BTS album chart position by country	145
8.1	Number of impressions using #MileyCyrus	215
10.1	Celebrity rules	249

Acknowledgements

I would like to acknowledge Deakin University for the support they have shown my research, and to thank my colleague Toija Cinque for being such a tremendous writing collaborator and research adventurer. Over the past few years I have had the pleasure and privilege of attending a number of wonderful conferences and symposia where celebrity was under the microscope: as always it is in these spaces of good discussion where stronger ideas and better writing emerges.

The case study *White manly beast: Exploring the star image of Russell Crowe* is one part of a longer project co-written with Toija Cinque (unpublished).

The case study *Producing Barack Obama* is adapted from the article, 'Avatar Obama in the Age of Liquid Celebrity' published in the inaugural edition of *Celebrity Studies* in 2010.

The case study *Talking Miley: The value of celebrity gossip* is adapted from a chapter co-written with Toija Cinque and published in: Harrington S (ed.) *Entertainment Values*. Palgrave Macmillan, London (2017).

The case study *Lazarus rises and the migrant fandom of David Bowie* is adapted from an article co-written with Toija Cinque and published in the *Journal of the International Association for the Study of Popular Music* (2016).

1

THE KEY IDEA
TWO CELEBRITY CIRCUITS BEAT AS ONE

One of the challenges of defining the key ideas in a research field as broad as celebrity is ensuring that you assess its coordinates and computations across a number of theoretical positions and within overlapping, and sometimes competing, contexts. To meet these cross-wind challenges, the approach in this book is to draw on two dynamic models from two different modes of enquiry to get beneath and beyond the porous skin of celebrity culture. These models are the circuit of celebrity culture and the circuit of celebrity affect.

THE CIRCUIT OF CELEBRITY CULTURE

The first model is drawn from British Cultural Studies and the pioneering work of sociology scholars from the Open University. The circuit of culture model is an intersecting, analytical schema that allows one to explore a cultural artefact, form, or phenomena across five dynamically 'charged' nodes or points. By employing the circuit of culture, one contends that it is only by passing a cultural form or formation through these nodes or points that one is allowed to adequately and fully understand the phenomena in question (du Gay et al., 1997: 3).

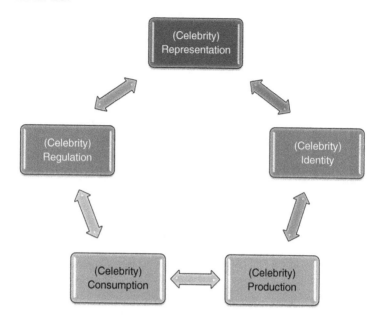

No one node or point is more important than the other and they all intersect and cross-connect in a myriad of both competing and complementary ways, creating the spaces for the negotiation and transformation of meaning. The five nodes or points are as follows:

Representation

Or how phenomena are made meaningful through shared languages that people in a given culture readily understand. Representations are found in or through the language of films, books, music videos, blogs, photographs, newspaper stories, adverts and fashion – they are the very material out of which 'things' get their meaning, or as Stuart Hall puts it:

> Meaning is produced within language, in and through various representational systems which, for convenience we call 'languages'. Meaning is produced by the practice, by the 'work', of representation. It is constructed through signifying – i.e. meaning-producing practices.
>
> (1997: 18)

Stars and celebrities are always representational constructs: their representations connected to, and dissected by, notions of possessive individualism, social class, gender, sexuality, race and ethnicity; and through commodity and consumer relationships. Celebrities are both ideologies and forms of a consumerist dream. For example, in the television advertising campaign for Chanel's newest fragrance, *Gabrielle* (2017), American actress Kristen Stewart is seen breaking free from a cocoon-like sac and smashing through over-sized perfume bottles, before emerging to stand tall in front of a golden sun rising on the honey-coloured horizon. Stewart embodies the values of Gabrielle, the name of the founder of Chanel: feminine but powerful, mysterious but knowable. Stewart's own star biography is transferred to the brand – she is independent, a trail-blazer, classically beautiful but also androgynous. Here gender is being post-feminised and turned into a commodity fetish – through the layering representational sheets of the possessive perfume, the figure of Gabrielle and the sexualised star image of Stewart.

Identity

Is the subject position that an individual comes to take up in society. People get their identities through both how they see themselves and how they are seen by others. Identity is never fixed and is a mix of active agency and normative and associative labelling or imposition, whereby certain identities are given or ascribed to people. Identity classifications occur on a daily basis through such discursive or meaning-making frameworks as social class, gender, race, ethnicity and sexuality. These identity positions are called *classificatory systems* and they permeate every area of the social world, including education, work, leisure and the arts and entertainment industries. Classificatory systems are not neutral: they are power-saturated and involve creating hierarchies that favour one group over another. As Chris Shilling and Patricia Mellor note, 'discourses and systems of representations construct places from which individuals can position themselves and from which they can speak' (1996: 5).

Stars and celebrities offer people particularly appealing identity positions that they are asked to 'take up', and are positioned to identify with. Stars and celebrities are often supericonic figures, who embody model identity positions that speak to certain psychic, cultural and economic needs, desires and aspirations and that fans and consumers are invited or positioned to hold and share. Stars and celebrities 'interpellate' their fans so that their subjectivities are, in part, defined by the ideologies that they stand for. The singer Beyoncé, for example, offers up a particularly powerful and arguably positive role model of black womanhood, which 'shapes' how black women see and feel about themselves. Beyoncé, of course, can also be read as mythologising the American Dream, or the myth that anyone can make it if they are talented and work hard enough (Cashmore, 2010). The reality for the majority of black Americans is quite the opposite.

One can see how closely representation and identity are articulated together: they are part of the same woven fabric of cultural meaning. In terms of celebrity culture, one begins to understand how celebrity and stardom produce representations and identities in the same registers of meaning. Representations create identities and identities are found in forms of representation: they are interlocking points on the circuit of celebrity culture.

Consumption

Refers to the way people interact with a whole range of products, services and social-cultural encounters, including how they watch television drama, respond to the news, engage with the social media and identify with certain film stars and not others, and the types of goods that are purchased. Consumption is also connected to questions of power and ideology since,

> the consumption of cultural objects by consumers can empower, demean, disenfranchise, liberate, essentialise and stereotype. Consumers are trapped within a hegemonic marketplace.
>
> (Denzin, 2001: 325)

Consumption is also, of course and conversely, active and resistant: people are shown to not passively respond to the media – celebrities included – but rather to subvert and transcode the very meanings associated with them. Consumption and reception involve both compliant and resistant readers, and readership is dependent on a whole range of contextual factors. Joshua Gamson (1994) has suggested, for example, that audiences consume celebrities with a degree of skepticism and knowing-ness. When it comes to a subcultural practice, such as fan fiction, we see celebrities re-inscribed or re-written, given new subject positions in the artwork, stories and amateur fan videos that are made of them. The slash fan work around Martin Freeman and Benedict Cumberbatch as Watson and Holmes, respectively, queers their relationship, opening up their representation to new and competing forms of masculinity and sexuality.

Production

involves the way goods, products and services, even 'ideas', are engineered, manufactured, marketed and sold. The cultural industries, for example, produce various forms, channels and modes of entertainment that include films, television programmes, streaming services, books, videos, as well as concerts, tours and the merchandising streams that accompany them.

However, one can also contend that today, the modes of production have themselves been thoroughly 'culturalised', so much so that one can write of a 'cultural economy' given the economic power given or afforded to global entertainment corporations. The transnational production of entertainment media has arguably created a 'global cultural village' through which the 'whole world' is connected to/by the production *and* consumption of cultural products.

Celebrity is seen to be one of the driving engines of the globalised production of entertainment media: whole franchises are built in and around celebrities, so that a star such as Taylor Swift isn't simply a singer/performer but a revenue stream for a whole range of ancillary products and services. Taylor Swift has endorsement deals with international brands that include Keds, Diet Coke and Apple. Two particular sponsorship deals with UPS and AT&T were built around the release of her album, *Reputation* (2017), and promoted with the following press release and announcement:

> UPS Delivering a Secure Logistics and Distribution Solution for Millions of Taylor Swift Album Deliveries to Retailers and Consumers Fans Can Win a Flyaway Package to an Upcoming Taylor Swift Show and Special Memorabilia Through Exclusive UPS Promotions. Two cultural icons,

10x GRAMMY winner Taylor Swift and UPS (NYSE: UPS), the world's largest package delivery company, are partnering to deliver a new experience for customers, fans and employees in celebration of Taylor's 6th studio album, *Reputation*.

(https://pressroom.ups.com/pressroom/ContentDetailsViewer.page?ConceptType=PressReleases&id=1503657046045-509)

AT&T Inc. has signed pop star Taylor Swift to an exclusive, multiyear partnership that includes a performance at a party the wireless and pay-tv service provider will host the night before the 2017 Super Bowl, the company said on Tuesday. The partnership includes exclusive performances and other content, AT&T said in a statement. Financial terms were not disclosed. Swift will headline the AT&T DirecTV Super Saturday Night concert in Houston on Feb. 4, the night before the 2017 Super Bowl ... Exclusive content and portions of Swift's concert will be made available to AT&T's U-verse video and DirecTV customers after the show, AT&T spokesman Brett Levecchio said.

(https://finance.yahoo.com/news/t-signs-taylor-swift-multiyear-partnership-deal-184759145--nfl.html)

Such deals extend the way that sponsorship and partnership manifest: they move celebrity culture from soft commercial services, to logistics, and from roadways to information superhighways, ensuring that they occupy both material and digital spaces simultaneously.

Regulation

Is made up of two interconnecting components: external and internal governance. Regulation that is externalised is necessarily bound up with cultural politics and policy: it is made up from and out of rules, laws, agreed and shared rituals and certain moral and ethical codes. External regulation:

Is about the ways in which we routinely go about our lives, the ways in which we observe the 'normal' rules of behaviour in public – in the street, in cars and on public transport. *Regulation is therefore ordinary; it is part of the routine that orders our lives each and every day.*

(Thompson, 1997: 10)

Regulation is also equally about internalisation or what might be termed self-regulation. People continually regulate themselves, their social behaviour and everyday actions, even without knowing that this is what they are doing, so 'routine' and 'natural' one's own self-regulation practices become. According to Michel Foucault, the 'course of development in modernity (is) ... from external regulation and external discipline towards self-regulation and self-discipline' (1995: 198).

Internal regulation is about maintaining or gaining self-control and is concerned with how people become complicit in the way they monitor and 'check' their everyday behaviour. Nonetheless, regulation is also resisted by counter-regulatory practices. Body projects can be seen as an attempt to take resistant control of the gendered body, opening it up to non-binary norms.

When it comes to celebrity culture I have elsewhere suggested that the metronome can best take into account its regulatory impact on people's everyday lives. Celebrities 'beat out' a particular rhythm, which shapes the way people orientate themselves in the world and the way they see themselves in society. Celebrities are both external and internal regulatory conduits, shaping behaviour, shaping the way fans and consumers mould their own life practices. For example, the cultural and psychic process of 'girling' is in part orchestrated through the way female celebrities regulate their own femininity: they draw upon and actively use health, beauty and lifestyle products to self-survey themselves. Female celebrities are often objectified and coded to-be-looked-at. They offer up a regime of looking and being looked at, which suggests objectification and the constant need to perform or embody a particular form of femininity, ethnicity and heterosexuality, which becomes normal and desirable.

In Japan, for example, there has been the recent phenomenon of a form of Bihaku embodiment that emerged among teenage girls who wanted to imitate the look of their favourite pop stars. Bihaku is a term, employed in marketing, which means 'beautifully white', and was first coined in the 1990s with the emergence of skin-whitening products and cosmetics. The desire to have whiter skin has a long tradition in Japanese culture but has gathered force with the rise of global celebrity and its associated chain of products endorsed by idealised white celebrities, such as Cate Blanchett. Pop stars such as Ayumi

Hamasaki have taken on the glamour and appeal of white female stars and promote Bihaku products to solidify the sensory transnational relationship. In a conjoining chain of signification and commodification, youth subcultures such as the Bihaku girls take on the look, fashion and glamour reminiscent of Brigitte Bardot, including her blonde hair.

FORCES OF EQUILIBRIUM

Unlike traditional Marxist models of power, in which the forces of production were seen to shape all aspects of material, social and economic reality, the circuit of culture equals out power relations: no one node or point is more important (more powerful) than the other. Further, the circuit of culture contends that there isn't a starting or ending point, as in a top-down model of power relations, but that the forces of equilibrium operate in a dynamic relationship. Taking the example of the relationship between production and consumption, for example, the latter is 'increasingly seen as an activity with its own practices, tempo, significance and determination' (Mackay, 1997: 4), best encapsulated through the way consumers can appropriate or transcode the material of 'mass culture' to their own ends, through a range of everyday creative and symbolic practices, including hair and body modification, scratching and sampling (records) and fan fiction. Such appropriation often shows itself as protest and resistance against the 'dominant ideology' embedded in the cultural form from which it came.

Let me now work through a case with you.

CASE STUDY

Let's Dance – *Intersecting David Bowie*

To answer the question 'what does pop and rock icon David Bowie mean?', we need to take him through each of the moments in the circuit of celebrity culture, answering the following five node-specific questions as we do so:

1. How has David Bowie been **represented** in (media) culture: in his live performances, music videos, film appearances, biographies,

interviews, online and in news and magazine coverage? What types of meanings, values and ideologies are or have been attached to his various star images, from the lightning bolt of Aladdin Sane to the heroin death of Major Tom?

In terms of representation, David Bowie:

> Is human and flawed (visibly so with a damaged eye) as well as extraordinary in appearance, demeanour and projected self-belief. The ethereal aspect central to Bowie's star persona and epitomized in many of his characterizations – Major Tom, Ziggy Stardust, Aladdin Sane and so on – overtly embraces the 'otherness' of the outsider.
>
> (Hunt, 2015: 178)

Similarly, Bowie's androgyny, cross-dressing and play with sexuality openly challenged dominant notions of masculinity and heterosexuality. Taken together, Bowie can be seen as a figure who offered counter-meanings to dominant forms of binary gender classifications that were produced in media culture during his career (Figure 1.1).

However, Bowie also flirted with a potent form of white masculinity, one which carried a version of hyper-whiteness forward that held the connotations of (post) colonial power and racial superiority. Bowie's idealised whiteness was most notably found in the figure of the Thin White Duke, a character he created in the late 1970s, with iconography that drew upon Nietzschean imagery, and in the music video to *Let's Dance* (1982). In this music video, shot in Sydney and the Blue Mountains, Bowie draws upon 'primitive' Aboriginal myths and rituals from the exalted position of his status as a hyper-white rock star, offering the two aboriginal dancers a sermon (on a mount) on how to be truly free. The video suggests this 'freedom' is a return to (their) 'nature', as we witness the dancers return to the 'bush', leaving their Western clothes behind them. Bowie's white masculinity is exalted and placed in a position of surveilling power and influence.

2.   What types of **identity positions** does David Bowie embody and call forth? What sort of identities do Bowie fans imagine for themselves?

Figure 1.1 David Bowie: The hyper-white rock star
Image courtesy of PL Gould/IMAGES/Getty Images

Bowie's open and contested play with gender and sexuality created positive, empowering identity spaces for those who felt socially marginalised. In Nick Stevenson's empirical study of David Bowie fandom we find, for example, one fan, Guy, commenting:

> People tend to go back to it [Bowie's music] when they're having problems, they deal with it by secluding themselves through Bowie and turning to him for, like a guide, inspiration … or just to cope.
>
> (Stevenson, 2009: 84)

Bowie fandom is often shown to be transformative and liberating: gay people in particular were able to see themselves powerfully embodied in Bowie's various star images, opening up the possibility for self-expression and self-actualisation.

3. Over the span of his career, how have David Bowie's music, tours, films and various revenue streams been **produced**? What sorts of production and design changes have happened to David Bowie? Why have these changes occurred? Does David Bowie actively produce his various star images?

One can read Bowie's career through the lens of proto-capitalist production and as an artist who disrupted the way he could be sold and marketed as a product. As Andy Bennett writes:

> In a very real sense, early in his career Bowie embraced the music business concept of identity production, acquiring a highly reflexive understanding of himself as an object to be fashioned and marketed and skilfully adapting this into a tantalising mode of DIY (do-it-yourself) iconicity.
>
> (2017: 574)

David Bowie's understanding of his value in the marketplace was best illustrated in 1997 when he came up with a cash-generating scheme involving selling 'Bowie bonds', which awarded investors a share in his future royalties for 10 years. The bonds, which were bought by US insurance giant Prudential Financial for $55m (£38m), committed David Bowie to repay his new creditors out of future income, and gave a fixed annual return of 7.9%. Twenty-five albums released between 1969 and 1990 – which included *The Man Who Sold the World*, *The Fall and Rise of Ziggy Stardust* and *Heroes* – were involved in the deal.

4. How has David Bowie been used or **consumed** in everyday life? How does his fan-base actively make new meanings out of his artistic and commercial work? Has his star image been consumed and commodified by the entertainment industries?

David Bowie has a large and loyal fan-base. These fans are part of networks and associations and involve running and attending events, conventions, band nights and social activities. At the everyday level, Bowie fans speak of the way he was central to a whole set of ritualistic and event-based times in their lives, including 'coming out', cross-dressing, sexual awakening and personal freedom. One fan writes:

> Dear David Bowie
> I love you very much. I would love it if you sent a picture of you to me. I saw you at Scope. I am 13 year old. My favourite song is Putting out the Fire with gasolene. Me and my friend talk about you all the time. I have a poster of you in my room. I saw you on the news. So would you send me a picture of you.
> I love you,
> Sabrina
>
> (www.bbc.co.uk/music/articles/48fe8a2f-13d9-4cdf-8c5d-d85c809d28d1)

David Bowie's iconic lightning bolt image of Aladdin Sane has been re-appropriated by various cultural industries, including urban design, sanctioned street art and advertisements, to repackage Bowie's androgyny in more 'palatable', commercial forms. Here, production and consumption are again welded together in articulated points of intersection.

5. How has David Bowie been used to **regulate** questions of identity and belonging, masculinity and ethnicity? How might he have challenged the way the music industry regulated their star products? How might David Bowie have been a counter-regulatory force, challenging normative masculinity and outsider status?

David Bowie can be seen to have impacted on both external and internal forms of regulation: as a transgressive star who played with gender and sexuality he was subjected to various forms of censorship; and those fans who imitated him – through dress, make-up, posture and performance – challenged embodied notions of straight and masculine. As Peri Bradley and James Page argue,

> Bowie's rebellion through the creation of his androgynous persona Ziggy Stardust can be seen to offer other artists a new way to explore their own

performances, and the audience a new way to explore their own identity, therefore bringing about a gradual but unstoppable transformation in the criteria for gender performance. Bowie effectively demonstrated to the world the liberation offered by rejecting stringent gender roles and labels thereby ensuring that it did not 'repeat itself to infinity' and also offering a voice and form of expression to marginalised groups.

(2017: 586)

For example, on the original cover to David Bowie's album *Diamond Dogs*, he is positioned as if he is lying naked on a carnival stage, with two female-like empusae or vampiric demons standing either side of him – the famed creatures who folklore suggest seduced men in order to feed on their flesh and blood. Bowie's upper torso reveals the androgynous red hair and painted lipstick rock star of previous incarnations, including Ziggy Stardust and Aladdin Sane, and the lower part of the torso shows him to be a dog, with his/its penis clearly visible. This album cover was quickly censored in both the UK and the USA, with the penis being air-brushed out in subsequent releases. The need to regulate Bowie's gender-bending, explicit imagery connects to moral codes around what can be shown in culture, with the penis a taboo item, and with the ideological struggle over meaning-making. Addressing regulation in this way allows us to ask and answer a whole interconnecting set of questions:

How is meaning actually produced? Which meanings are shared within society, and by which groups? What other, counter meanings are circulating? What meanings are contested? How does the struggle between different sets of meanings reflect the play of power and the resistance to power in society?

(du Gay et al., 1997: 12)

The circuit of celebrity culture model offers us a dynamic schema with which to answer all these questions. It is a model with a dynamic equilibrium, in which, although shifting and changing, the overall pattern of forces or energy is in a stable, organised configuration. What this suggests is that although at any moment of time the model may not be at equilibrium because of its dynamic nature, equilibrium exerts itself over an extended period of time – disruptions to the points or nodes in the model are ultimately subsumed or taken into account and the 'model' continues in its exquisite cultural dance.

Nonetheless, it is the contention of this book that the circuit of celebrity culture marginalises the affective relations crucial to the production and consumption of celebrity and fails to account for the way experience is not always in the pay master of ideology. To fully understand the impact of celebrity, one needs to have a complimentary, intersecting and sometimes competing model in reverberating circulation.

THE CIRCUIT OF CELEBRITY AFFECT

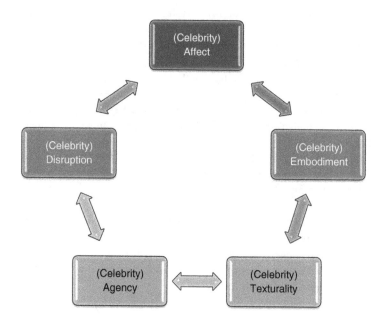

Close your eyes

Drawing upon your other senses to imagine that your favourite celebrity is stood before you, *close your eyes for a moment*.

As you do so, try to experience them as a body, a surface and as sound. Sense your celebrity as enveloping textures and qualities.

Smell their perfume or eau de cologne. Hear their voices as a synaesthetic register, not just composed of sound but colour, taste and light.

Now employ your closed eyes as if they are organs of touch, feeling these textures, becoming immersed in their texturality. Experience
your celebrity as a cross-modal encounter. Hear their footsteps or
movements on the floor in front of you. Become aware of the enchanted
weight of your own body at the same time; feel your delight, revel in
the changes in your physiology, as the celebrity materialises before
and within you.

Open your eyes

While the circuit of culture is a wonderfully skilled model which allows
us to examine celebrity through all the facets that make it meaningful
in everyday life, there are a further set of qualities or variables that are
either neglected by, or subsumed within, its articulating points. The
circuit of affect is an attempt to give definition and visibility to these
lost, emotive tones: since it is also through the culture of impressions
– of the senses – that drives this complementary, and sometimes oppositional, circuit of affect schema.

Much of the body of work that has addressed celebrity has done
so through theories and methods that see the senses and emotions as
always bound up with language, representation and discourse. Emotion is very often said to be in the service of neo-liberalism or late
capitalism, enunciated from subject positions where feeling is regulated and where desire and wants are honed-in on consumer goods
and services; and are manufactured out of and through gender and
sexual binaries, reinforcing the surveillance of the emotional self and
the simultaneous reification of emotion. Affect theory, by contrast,
suggests that:

> from a certain perspective, affects are only meaningful within language.
> Indeed, the affect can be understood, can be figured, as always already
> a representation of what we might call the Ur or originary affect. The
> latter positioned as an unreachable (and unsayable) origin ... And yet
> affects are also, and primarily, affective. There are no denying, or defer-
> ring, affects. They are what make up life, and art. For there is a sense in
> which art itself is made up of affects. Affects frozen in time and space.

> Affects are, then, to use Deleuzo-Guattarian terms and to move the register away from deconstruction and away from representation, the molecular beneath the molar. The molecular understood here as life's, and arts, intensive quality, as the stuff that goes on beneath, beyond, even parallel to signification.
>
> (O'Sullivan, 2001: 126)

One can sense celebrities into carnal existence, and while representation may often shape the way they are encountered, senses and sensation are not simply irreducible to semiotic signs, discourse and ideology (Redmond, 2013). The senses can be wilder, freer and more intense and transgressive than that (Massumi, 2002). In fact, as the circuit of affect demonstrates, celebrity culture is one of the defining spaces for heightened experiential encounters, and for the circulation and transmission of intense affects that are often empowered and empowering. They are part of the 'distribution of the sensible' but in ways that can challenge the 'police order' (Ranciere, 2004), and they readily enact and embody ribald instances of the contemporary Bahktinian carnival. The ecstasy that greets certain live performances is testimony to the power of emotional outpouring and the way it questions the 'fixedness' of subjectivity and routinised life. For example, as Hanlon suggests, in relation to heavy metal music fandom:

> Fans experience carnivalesque music scenes as outcast communities of belonging, as celebrations of tolerance and egalitarianism, as extraordinary places for freedom of self-expression, and most importantly, as refreshing, multifaceted 'difference' from the commercialized mainstream.
>
> (2006: 35–36)

The five points on the circuit of celebrity affect are as follows. Each point corresponds to the equivalent node on the circuit of celebrity culture. Affect is matched with representation; embodiment with identity; texturality with production; agency with consumption; and disruption with regulation. These circuits work together in both relational and oppositional ways, as the journey of the book will attest.

1. Affect

When we write about affects we are concerned with the way certain experiences people are involved in seem to be incredibly intense, vital and beyond the normal forms of responses they give. An affective response seems to emerge automatically, sits outside, beyond or before rational thought and creates a sense of 'aliveness' in the body of the affected. Brian Massumi asserts that affects are 'irreducibly bodily and autonomic' (2002: 28). Nonetheless, Clough suggests that:

> affect is not 'presocial' .... There is a reflux back from conscious experience to affect, which is registered, however, as affect, such that 'past action and contexts are conserved and repeated, autonomically reactivated but not accomplished; begun but not completed.
>
> (2007: 2)

Affect is different from feelings and emotions, which are personal and social. Emotionality emerges out of memorial work, shared encounters and can be easily verbalised and rationalised. However, when engaged in highly charged encounters, affect and emotion may overlap or lead to or through one another: one can be emotionalised and subsequently enter a fully affective state and as one exists in an affective state, language and feeling remerge.

Celebrity culture is unquestionably an affective machine. The instances of affective responses are varied and many. And the intensities that are produced can be said to question the way representation (and identity) usually works, since it can be argued one isn't being interpolated into an ideological system (of governance, of control) by the affective frames of fame but being momentarily liberated from it (Figure 1.2).

Take the example of the close-up of the film star: It can be argued that the close-up as a photographic and cinematic technique reveals the 'truth' of the star's performance through the power of total (in)sight. The power of the close-up is marked by its revelatory capacity: the fine grain of physicality, the depth of emotional health and well-being, as well as psychological and existential uncovering. One clear example of this is the close-up of the star's face that registers as a particularly strong affection-image, as 'immobile unity' combined with 'intense expressive movements' (Deleuze, 2005). For Deleuze,

The face is this organ carrying plate of nerves which has sacrificed most of its global mobility and which gatherer or expresses in a free way all kids of tiny local movement which the rest of the body usually keeps hidden.

(Deleuze, 2005: 90)

Figure 1.2 The face of Garbo
Image courtesy of Donaldson Collection/Getty Images

The close-up leaks the drama of the text and the viewer is asked to look into the image and see the star as they really are (Balázs, 1970). The close-up of the face, in particular, may capture the star in a state of pure perfection, as if they descended from the heavens. Their physical and emotional beauty will be there on their skin and in the skin of the image, for all to see. As Barthes writes of the close-up in relation to Greta Garbo:

> Offered to one's gaze a sort of Platonic Idea of the human creature ... The name given to her, the Divine, probably aimed to convey less a superlative state of beauty than the essence of her corporeal person, descended from a heaven where all things are formed and perfected in the clearest light.
>
> (Barthes, 2007: 261)

One can argue that the close-up allows the viewer to 'touch' and feel a gesture, a look: to see the fine lines of a cheek, since the face of the star stays close to them in an intensified field of vision. In the close-up, there is only 'you' and the star placed in a one-to-one relational exchange. The space in and between you and the star is consequently evaporated, creating a proximity or closeness of utmost intimacy. Strong out-of-body identifications emerge through the affecting power of the close-up.

2. Embodiment

By the beginning of the 21st century, numerous scholars have argued that the human body has been thoroughly *civilised* and 'made docile'. Through external and internal surveillance processes, micro-managed self-control practices and across a range of intrusive, regulatory discourses, it is apparent that the human body has been thoroughly rationalised, and equally pacified. As Chris Shilling summarises,

> From being associated with the rhythms of nature, bodily functions are socially managed, organised and made private ... As the body becomes subject to expanding taboos, it is transformed into a location for and an expression of behavioural codes. With the bodily functions which

people shared increasingly hidden, the manners which separated individuals could be taken as markers of value and identity.

(2005: 94)

However, embodiment theory has also emerged, suggesting that the human body is a site of active agency, of self-determination, involved in contests and struggles over what it stands for and can achieve. In fact, it can be argued that never in the history of humankind has the body been such a site of struggle, with people resisting the biologically 'given' and the social constructs used to label and map it. The human body is very often at war with itself through a range of beautifying, self-determining and destructive body projects; including dieting, tattooing, body building, face lifts, liposuction, tanning, bleaching, transplanting, bio-fertilisation, cutting, piercing, penetration, etc. These embodied acts and actions can be seen either as serving surveillance regimes or as resisting the invasive machinery of the panopticon.

This embodied resistance can also be seen as sensorial – as textural tactics and strategies to feel the body outside of discursive practices and processes. As philosopher Elizabeth Grosz puts it:

Things solicit the flesh just as the flesh beckons to and as an object for things. Perception is the flesh's reversibility, the flesh touching, seeing, perceiving itself, one fold (provisionally) catching the other in its own self-embrace.

(1993: 46)

Celebrity culture is very much an embodied set of entanglements: celebrities visit people in and through their enchanted bodies. These bodies emit political signs and they engender powerful feelings and mobilise affects that are heightened and intense. Celebrities often stand as perfected or flawed creatures, embody identity politics and give meaning to the imagined body of the nation state. In this respect, golfer Tiger Woods becomes, first, the embodied truth that the United States has entered a postrace state of greater social equality (Berlant, 1997), and second, the reconstituted radicalised myth that black men are, after all, essentially sexual 'bad bucks' (Bogle, 1973). Celebrity embodiment then is not simply about the body of the celebrity, as it literally presents itself in the social and representational world, but the range of values, meanings and affecting qualities that are attached to its skin, bone and torso. The celebrity body is never neutral: it carries with it the discourses, concerns and passions of the age.

Celebrity embodiment is decidedly phenomenological and experiential, something that I have (Redmond, 2014) defined as the celebaesthetic encounter. There is always a sensuous aesthetic exchange that takes place when fans and consumers take hold of a celebrity. Textures, light, colour, sounds, movements and impressions permeate the way celebrities enter the social and are engaged with it. The body of the celebrity and the body of the fan can be experienced first-hand, cast in an asemiotic landscape of intense affects. Fans and consumers feel or make sense of celebrities in and through their bodies and communicate their response to them in richly somatic ways. The body of the fan screams, cries, jumps up and down, swoons in absolute rare delight. It is as if their 'fingers know' what the celebrity means to them, at the exact moment language fails to comprehend the sensory power of the encounter.

If one was to take the celebrity body and fandom of Britney Spears at the time of the 'head-shaving' incident in 2007, one can see how embodied celebrity culture is. Head-shaving is a powerful indicator of self-identity and group-belonging. Buddhist monks, for example, shave their heads for purification purposes. For skinheads in the West, a shorn head is a symbol of aggressive, hard-bodied masculinity. Among lesbians, a shaved head is part of a wider body project where patriarchal and heterosexist notions of femininity are undermined. The lesbian photographer, Del LaGrace Volcano, for example, has combined a shorn head with muscularity, tattoos and facial/body hair. Historically, the act of shaving a head was employed to punish, discipline and weaken the body. Samson was deprived of his incredible physical power when the duplicitous Delilah cut off his hair while he was asleep. In ancient Greece, a shaved head indicated one's slave status. Shorn hair is an indicator of sickness and disease and has been deployed by armies to both dehumanise/herd their own soldiers and punish their enemies. In World War II, the heads of French collaborators were shaved as part of their public humiliation. In Joy Divisions, in which groups of Jewish women were kept for the sexual pleasure of Nazi soldiers, the women had their heads shaved to indicate their role and function in the camps. In celebrity culture, hair is used to suggest idealised perfection, undermine or challenge gender norms, and to race famous figures. Britney Spears's long flowing blonde hair placed her within a hierarchy of beauty and female whiteness that is particularly feted and fetishised.

Consequently, when Britney Spears shaved her head it was an incredibly suggestive and violent act, which was read either as an attempt to gain control of her image, her celebrity self, or as a mental marker of the damage that fame had done to her. Britney was either finding her true self or losing it completely. According to the reports at the time, when hair studio owner Esther Tognozzi refused to shave off the pop star's hair, Britney took hold of the clippers and removed her locks. Emily Wynne-Hughes, an eye-witness, told the press that Spears had said that 'she didn't want anybody to touch her'. The desire, then, for self-control is paramount here, but so is the sense that her body is perceived to have been soiled or penetrated in some way and a self-loathing Britney is in recoil from it. Given that long, flowing, blonde hair is associated with idealised female beauty, and is read to be a visible symbol of their reproductive power, Britney's skinhead rejects/denies her own idealisation and the womanly body that is fertile.

This is so clearly a direct form of fame damage, a profound form of symbolic selfharm, a sensational outing of her heretical body. In a sense, Britney becomes the 21st-century, post-God, tabloid version of Joan of Arc replete with her own duplicitous tele-evangelical priest Dr Phil, brought to her hospital bedside in a later incident to announce to the world that he was 'convinced more than ever that she is in dire need of both medical and psychological intervention'. Britney publicly punishes her body, in a form of self-flagellation, and her heretical body is punished by the media as it is pawed over, examined, analysed, spied-on, laughed at, hated, desired.

But to what affect/effect? For Britney's teen fans, the contradiction in and between her personae produces an aggressive response: Britney is a whore or a 'slore' (an elision of slut and whore: Lowe, 2003: 124–5). They cannot accept the dislocation between the innocent Britney and the vamp Britney. Their extreme, let-down responses, however, can be understood to be the very same rejection that Britney practises on herself. They hate the same thing in her. Celebrity and fan, then, aligned in pro-feminist embodied rejection of the divided body demanded by patriarchy and commodity capitalism.

3. *Texturality*

When we think about production processes and the products, goods and services we come into contact with on a daily basis, touch and texture are crucial. In fact, the aesthetics of design, one that is 'born of the senses', bring fetishised commodities into textual existence. Similarly, people's engagement with the world is a tactile one, as Juhani Pallasmaa suggests,

> The tactile sense has become increasingly evident ... The very essence of the lived experience is moulded by hapticity and peripheral unfocused vision. Focused vision confronts us with the world whereas peripheral vision envelops us in the flesh of the world ... All the senses, including vision, are extensions of the tactile sense; the senses are specialisations of skin tissue, and all sensory experiences are modes of touching and thus related to tactility. Our contact with the world takes place at the boundary line of the self through specialised parts of our enveloping membrane.
>
> (1996: 10)

In terms of celebrity culture, texturality manifests in two interrelated or interlocking ways. First, celebrity representations are crafted out of sensory aesthetic signifiers. Light, colour, texture, fabric, movement and sound are used to create an enveloping membrane that the celebrity emerges out of. For example, Natalie Portman's 2013 Miss Dior '*La vie en rose*' advertising campaign draws upon sensory-based signifiers to create the conditions for her romanticised star-self to emerge. Portman is captured in a series of heightened Parisian-inspired backdrops, with elemental, natural and haute couture textures brought together in an irresistible *mise-en-scène* of enveloping texturality. Water, sunlight, blossom, silk, flower and bouquet are brought into the world of opulent apartments and summer houses, long drives in open sports cars, and romantic embraces and dreamy kisses. This is a world crafted out of primal and primary sensory experiences and Portman is the carnal embodiment of what her celebrity image and the perfume will bring to one's life if one consumes them both together. The star-crossed romantic environment is furnished from a sea of sensory-based experiences that dances across the skin of the screen, across Portman's body.

Texturality is also encountered in the spectacular settings and spectacle events that we find the celebrity in. Fine-grain paparazzi shots of celebrities coming out of high-end fashion shops, kissing in doorways or emerging from swimming pools on exotic beach holiday locations create a world of tactile impressions and expressions of touch, taste, sound and smell. Celebrity texturality renders the viewer's or reader's eyes as haptic instruments of touch.

Celebrity texturality has been heightened by innovations in augmented and virtual reality digital technology that have 'transformed the photographic image into a truly "plastic" object that can be moulded and remoulded into whatever shape is desired' (Belton, 2002: 101). In this limitless realm of new-world building, fans and consumers are offered an enriched, deeply immersive, intro-subjective experience that is exactly like being-within-the-world-of-the-celebrity. Sensation is increasingly mobilised through digital technologies that can render the image free from its indexical root, allowing one to see things that were never physically there in the first place, including one's own presence, if that is desired. One can Photoshop one's bodies into any event they would like to be seen in, including a red-carpet entrance with a favourite celebrity. In the 3D *Kiss Justin* android app game, one can meet Justin Bieber at a virtual holiday resort and get to kiss him in dreamy locations that one moves around in. The speed at which one can kiss Justin can be speeded up or slowed down, with the aim of achieving hallowed 'Mrs Bieber' status.

4. Agency

A great deal of the writing on celebrity culture imagines a passive dichotomy when it comes to the way fans and consumers 'digest' stars and celebrities. The framework that this type of compliant reception takes place within links production and consumption through a production of culture perspective or a type of materialism that sees culture as manufactured in the same way that cars and televisions are; subject to the same 'rationalised organisational procedures' found in any neo-liberal industry; and operating at the 'lowest common denominator', so that the widest number of people can consume what are considered to be these low-brow texts. Culture, it is suggested, is loaded with a particular (dominant) ideology, which works upon what is argued to be a passive and obedient audience. Culture affects and shapes, in a one-way causal relationship, those that it comes into contact with – the 'mass audience'. As Keith Negus summarises,

> In doing this they linked the idea of the culture industry to a model of mass culture in which cultural production had become a routine, standardised repetitive operation that produced undemanding cultural commodities which in turn resulted in a type of consumption that was also standardised, distracted and passive.
>
> (1997: 69)

This position, then, denies that at the point of consumption people actively work on the culture produced for them – appropriating it, shaping it, subverting it, modifying it. This alternative position suggests that 'culture' only really becomes meaningful – material – when it is actively produced at the site of consumption by those engaging with it. For example, empirical research on fandom often demonstrates that through a process of bricolage, (young) fans and consumers appropriate or transcode the material of celebrity culture for their own ends: that through a range of everyday creative and symbolic practices, protest and resistance emerge to act against the dominant ideology embedded in cultural forms.

Two activation methods can be drawn upon to understand the way fans bring celebrity culture into meaningful existence. The first involves the method of storying the self (Finnegan, 1997), where people are asked to recount their encounters with celebrity through memorial work and personal narratives. These stories when told, however, are born from textural qualities: they draw upon synaesthesia and co-synaesthetic relations. Fans and consumers draw upon their full sensorium to experience the wonder (and terror) of the celebrity figure. In remembering them, fans draw upon sensuous and sensory memory.

Also crucial, then, to understanding the way celebrities make sense-based meaning is the role of autoethnography. For example, I have written about the personal impact of Sam Taylor-Wood's photograph of

Daniel Craig, because of the way his wedding band activated a poignant affective memory that my wedding ring is long gone. In sensing the punctum of the photograph, I felt the weight, coldness and colour of the ring missing from my finger (Redmond, 2014). Sensing celebrities is uniquely personal and activated through embodied relations.

Celebrity culture is in effect an affective constituent of storying the self: where identities in part emerge from the ways in which they are woven into the fabric of everyday life. Celebrity culture helps people to tell stories, live their stories and embody the stories they tell one another. These are stories of hope, fear and hurt, aspiration, love, friendship and growth – powerfully cast in starry narrative form.

Agency, then, is interested in the 'micro' stories that emerge from the consumption of celebrity culture; made in the moment of the live, and which originate from what the person is feeling, going through and memorialising at that time in their life. One's living biography is powerfully brought into the open through these shared stories, and these stories grow, as new content is added, and the self grows with it (Redmond, 2014).

5. Disruption

In the circuit of celebrity culture, regulation is defined as,

> a process or direction .... Regulation is inescapably bound up with cultural politics and policy. Nothing stands outside of regulation, and its scope extends into areas such as religion and education ... Regulation also has an everyday aspect – it is about the ways in which we routinely go about our lives, the ways in which observe the 'normal' rules of behaviour in public – in the street, in cars and on public transport. Regulation is therefore ordinary; it is part of the routine that orders our lives each and every day.
>
> (du Gay, 1997: 3)

By contrast, in the circuit of celebrity affect, the core dynamic is seen to be the forces of disruption: those acts and activities, individual and collective, which disrupt the everyday and the way ordinary life is directly experienced. While it can be argued that disruption and regulation go hand-in-hand, in the way that counter-regulation is often followed or accompanied by re-regulation, disruption has its own distinct cultural beat and set of imperatives. Disruption can and does fully transform the way a particular cultural artefact is taken up or how identities are resisted and transformed. To return to the example of David Bowie given above, his set of transgressive star images, in conjunction with queer fandom, disrupted the media images of masculinity that were circulating and the way fanning gay men lived their sexuality, intensely and freely.

To return to the issue of fandom, it can be argued that fandom constitutes an alternative and oppositional set of practices to the profit-orientated mechanisms of neo-liberal capitalism – a gift economy. In the fan-gift economy, it is the exchange of gifts that drives interactions, builds and fosters social networks, and disrupts the capital and commodity flow of dominant forms of media production. As Karen Hellekson argues,

> Fan communities as they are currently comprised, require exchanges of gifts: you do not pay to read fan fiction or watch a fan-made music vid. They are offered for free … yet within a web of context that specifies an appropriate method of 'payment'.
>
> (2009: 114)

One of the core 'gifts' of fan communities is creativity, creative artwork, that re-inscribes the text in question, and extends their universe in so-doing. Such fan artwork is unique and personal – it suffers less from cultural mediation and mass reproduction, re-signing it with an 'aura', a sense-based quality. For example, Simon Jacobs's hand-made and-drawn graphic novel, *Saturn*, explores through a semi-autobiographical lens 16 short story encounters with David Bowie, each story a 'story of the self', set within a semi-fictional universe. In Jacobs's work we find anti-regulation through the way his life is re-enchanted through these fictive encounters with David Bowie, entailing,

> a state of wonder, and one of the distinctions of this state is the temporary suspension of chronological time and bodily movement. To be enchanted, then, is to participate in a momentarily immobilizing encounter; it is to be transfixed, spellbound.
>
> (Bennett, 2001: 5)

Enchantment occurs most often in participatory spaces and setting where fans 'let go' of their docile and regulated selves. Enchantment can of course be grotesque, built out of the carnivalesque, as is the case with heavy metal fans at a live gig:

> Fans rage, swear, chant with middle fingers and metal horns, and other billingsgate. They body thrash, mosh, body surf, and delight in parade stripping rituals. As in Bakhtin's carnival, amid sweaty bodies pushing, grabbing, swaying, rubbing, and touching, the crowd is made 'concrete and sensual.' Among the 'pressing throng, the physical contact of bodies, … [t]he individual feels that he is an indissoluble part of the collectivity, a member of the people's mass body' (Bakhtin [1936] 1984:255). This more subtle yet powerful carnival experience may be among the most transgressive aspects of heavy metal carnival, for it grates against a society that places primacy on autonomy, self-interest, and individualism.
>
> (Hanlon, 2006: 40)

Heavy metal bands enact and embody the grotesque in similar ways, 'dramatized by a communal flow of human excretions such as spit, blood, vomit, urine, semen, and faeces' (Hanlon, 2006: 36). For both performing fan and performing celebrity, the grotesque communal experience of metal music is 'dis-alienating', since it provides a space for a shared body experience that empties insides, draws back the borders, re-situates the self as an uncivil animal set free.

Disruptive innovation is also a key marker of resistant and transformatory celebrity culture. Termed by Clayton Christensen in 1997, disruptive innovation:

> Explains the phenomenon by which an innovation transforms an existing market or sector by introducing simplicity, convenience, accessibility and affordability where complication and high cost are the status quo. Initially, a disruptive innovation is formed in a niche market that may appear unattractive or inconsequential to industry incumbents, but eventually the new product or idea completely redefines the industry.
>
> (www.christenseninstitute.org/key-concepts /disruptive-innovation-2/)

One can see how the advent of social media and micro-celebrity transformed the way communication between fans and celebrities took place, and the way fan work could be circulated and copyright circumnavigated. While much of the disruption has been taken up by media agencies to self-promote their celebrity brands and commodify (regulate) these interactions, disruption still remains with fans using these technological interfaces to undermine official scripts, offer counter merchandising and engage in civic action. For example, the Harry Potter Alliance (HPA) is a US-based nonprofit organisation that works 'for human rights, equality, and a better world just as Harry and his friends did' (http://thehpalliance.org/what-we-do). Inspired by Dumbledore's Army in the *Harry Potter* narratives,

> the HPA taps fan community practices to run advocacy and activist campaigns through a decentered network of paid and volunteer staff and local chapters. The HPA builds on active and creative engagement with the *Harry Potter* content world, connecting this content to social justice aims in the real world, such as fair trade and marriage equality. The HPA has also motivated some nonfans to join their collective actions.

Celebrity disruption is both a series of activities and a sense-based way to challenge regulation and conformity. While regulation and disruption feed off one another, in a dialectical exchange, they are also subject to their own forces – disruption has its own effects and is affecting.

CIRCUITS OF CELEBRITY CULTURES AND AFFECTS: A BOOK LIKE NO OTHER

The rest of this book is divided into ten chapters. Each chapter takes a moment each from the circuit of celebrity culture and the circuit of celebrity affect to assess celebrity culture as both an ideological mechanism and an affecting regime. The circuit points addressed in each chapter will be discussed separately and in dialogue or opposition, where those intersections meet or compete. Each chapter involves the discussion of one or two complimentary case studies, with a summary that draws their relations, oppositions and fissions out into the open.

In Chapter 2, *Celebrity Representations*, the way celebrities are constructed as particular types of perfected individuals is discussed. The chapter draws upon both semiotic and discursive analysis, and links celebrity representations to commodity branding and the identity intersections it manufactures and sustains. The chapter uses celebrity whiteness as one of its central illustrations, ending with a close textual and contextual analysis of *The Alien Whiteness of Scarlett Johansson*, suggesting that her star image is caught in a paradox that both privileges her and renders her threatening and sterile. Whiteness then becomes a thread picked up throughout the book.

In Chapter 3, *More than Just a Feeling: Celebrity Affects*, fame is encountered through its relationship to emotion and intensity, and to the way it mobilises sensorial engagements. Drawing upon affect theory and phenomenology, it assesses the way celebrity culture mobilises the forces of affect to sustain fan encounters, and how affect materialises 'naturally' in the passions of the day. The chapter illustrates affective engagement through two case studies: an autoethnographic encounter with Ian Curtis, and a sensorial 'becoming animal' analysis of star filmmaker, Takeshi Kitano.

In Chapter 4, *(Post)Modern Identities and Celebrity Selfhood*, the focus of the book shifts to the second node on the circuit of celebrity culture and the ways that celebrity culture constructs identity positions, which people are asked to 'speak from'. Drawing upon intersectional analysis, celebrities are shown to offer up neo-liberal, possessive definitions of the self, while propagating embodied myths about gender, race and class, among other subject positions. The chapter concludes with a national identity reading of Australian film star Russell Crowe, showing how his skill as an actor is often identified in terms of brute physicality and mythological masculine certainty, and how he brings to his Hollywood films archetypal Australian qualities that are on the one hand suppressed or de-odorised, while on another, are employed to help enculture and authenticate the performances he gives.

In Chapter 5, *Celebrity Embodiment*, the second (and corresponding) point on the circuit of celebrity affect is addressed. The chapter explores the way celebrity and fan encounters are often made-in-the-flesh, and draw upon sensory registers to communicate. These can be 'fortress-like' embodiments, sealing the body in an affective 'cage', but they can also be taboo-breaking and transgressive, letting the body escape its perceived docility. Kate Winslet is employed as the case study, who, on the one hand, resists definitions of the ideal female body, and on the other re-inscribes it – the senses of the Winslet body are in open warfare. The whiteness of Winslet's star image is also discussed and contested.

In Chapter 6 and Chapter 7, we turn to the production node in the circuit of celebrity culture and the textural point in the circuit of celebrity affect. In Chapter 6, *The Liquid Lights of Celebrity Productions*, the industrial and commercial streams of producing celebrity culture are examined, including the manufacturing of boy bands and the branding of Beyoncé. The chapter concludes with an analysis of Barack Obama's 2008 presidential election campaign to draw on the ideas of spectacle and liquid modernity as forces in the 'production' of celebrity-based politics. Spectacle also now becomes a leading thread, picked up in subsequent chapters, connecting nodes on different parts of both circuits.

In Chapter 7, *Celebrity Texturality*, the focus shifts to haptic design, fashion and costume and the aesthetics of celebrity culture. The recent work of celebrity influencers is drawn upon, as are the cathedrals of celebrity consumption, and the sensorial environments that the celebrity is often situated in. Celebrity wetness is focused upon as the case study: drawing upon the idea of 'to-be-enwatered' as a particularly heightened form of celebrity texturality, entwining water with liquidity to show how fame floods the shores of culture.

In Chapter 8, *Impressionable Audiences: Consuming Celebrity Culture*, the book examines the effects of fame and the limitations it serves fans and consumers. Threading in various examples of negative celebrity effects, from possessive individualism, narcissism, erotomania, to the value of gossip, and drawing on examples that include K-pop, celebrity magazines and Madonna, it concludes with an empirical analysis case study of Miley Cyrus and the social media – how she uses Twitter and how her fans enculture her in their Facebook posts and social media use.

In Chapter 9, the book offers up a direct response to the findings in Chapter 8: *Celebrity Agency* charts the way that fans actively make use of the fame they come into contact with. Activism, creativity, resistance and self-transformation are the activation markers for celebrity agency.

The case study drawn upon in this chapter stems from empirical work carried out with migrants on how they used David Bowie to settle and to resist the various repressive cultures they were facing at that time. David Bowie now becomes a constant companion, his star image examined in different ways as the book concludes.

The last two chapters of the book twin regulation and disruption. In Chapter 10, *Celebrity Regulation in Body and Space*, the forces of internal and external regulation are applied to celebrity culture. Celebrities are shown to be implicated in the routinisation of everyday life, self-monitoring practices and processes and the ethics of choice. Utilising both gender and social class, the chapter demonstrates the power that celebrity culture has – to shape the way that life is experienced and consumed. Examples drawn upon include celebrity spectacle, celebrity embodiment, civil society and the politics of celebrity food-consumption. The case study employed to close this chapter is on the Bollywood actor Shilpa Shetty, and the 'disgust' narratives she faced in the *Celebrity Big Brother* house.

In Chapter 11, *Celebrity Disruption*, the focus is on those texts and contexts that oppose the way that everyday life is usually experienced, and on those new media platforms and interfaces, which offer a challenge to how celebrity is dominantly produced. Drawing on examples that include fan activism, toxic celebrity and DIY celebrity citizenship, the chapter outlines the more radical qualities of celebrity and its relationship to the ordinary. The chapter closes with an autoethnographic case study – a story-based exploration of how David Bowie shaped this author's unruly life.

The book's conclusion draws together the nodes and points on the two circuits to demonstrate how, when taken together, they show the forces and limitations involved in exploring both the poetics and politics of celebrity culture.

2

CELEBRITY REPRESENTATIONS

REPRESENTATIONS: LANGUAGE AND DISCOURSE

> In language we use signs and symbols – whether they are sounds, written words, electronically produced images, musical notes, even objects – to stand for or represent to other people our concepts, ideas and feelings.
>
> (Hall, 1997: 1)

Representation theory suggests that we make sense of the world and communicate with other people through shared, common languages. Language is made up from signs which stand for or represent the concepts which we carry around in our heads: meaning does not inhere in things but is produced through signs *making things mean* in and through our thought processes. Signs are organised into classificatory systems: we know what a sign means because of both its *shared* relationship to and its *difference from* other signs.

For Saussure (2011) a sign produces meaning through its two related elements: the signifier or the form of the sign, which includes sound, images, words, paintings, photographs; and the signified or the idea or concept that comes to mind when the signifier is made sense of or decoded. For Roland Barthes (1967), the relationship between the signifier and the signified and the *production of meaning* it solicits involves two distinct levels. The first order of signification is denotation or the descriptive, surface-level meaning of a particular signifier, found in everyday usage, such as a jacket and trousers together is called a suit. The second order of signification is connotation or the deeper sub-textual meaning of a particular signifier, where 'suit' comes to represent class, power and patriarchy, for example.

Barthes calls this second level of signification the level of myth, where powerful ideological messages about family, nation, religion, gender, race, class and sexuality take shape. Barthes powerfully uses this example as an illustration of how colonial mythologies take hold in the dominant culture, reconstructing racial dichotomies and inequalities in power:

> I am at the barber's, and a copy of Paris-Match is offered to me. On the cover, a young Negro in a French uniform is saluting, with his eyes uplifted, probably fixed on a fold of the tricolour. All this is the meaning of the picture. But whether naively or not, I see very well what it signifies to me: that France is a great Empire, that all her sons, without any colour discrimination, faithfully serve under the flag, and that there is no better answer to the detractors of an alleged colonialism than the zeal shown by this Negro in serving his so-called oppressor.
>
> (1972: 115)

Nonetheless, the meaning of a sign is never fixed and a myth is not free from contamination: not only do signs acquire new meanings (signifieds) over time – the word 'gay' for example has changed from being a word associated with happiness to the negative and then positive labelling of sexuality – but the way a sign/signifier is understood by each individual within any one culture can vary (to some degree). As Stuart Hall writes, 'meaning has to be actively read or interpreted' (1997) each time the process of signification takes place.

Michel Foucault offers a different set of coordinates for understanding representation in modern society. For Foucault, one makes sense of the world through discourse which 'produces the objects of our knowledge', frames the way one thinks about a topic and the way people engage with a topic as it occurs in the real world. Discourse is made up of 'a group of statements which provide a language for talking about – a way of representing the knowledge about – a particular topic at a particular moment' (Hall, 1997: 44). According to Foucault, we cannot know something outside of discourse because we are positioned to speak and make meaning from within its enunciations only.

All the things that we know about a topic: the regimes that are put into place to order or classify that topic, are said to belong to the same discursive formation. The implication of a discursive formation is that they close off all alternative ways of thinking about a topic: the discursive formation appears as truth, or sustains a *regime of truth*:

> The types of discourses which it accepts and makes function as true, the mechanisms and instances which enable one to distinguish true and false statements, the means by which each is sanctioned ... the status of those who are charged with saying what counts as true.
>
> (Foucault, 1980: 131)

For example, a racist discourse produces, 'through different practices of representation (scholarship, exhibition, literature, painting etc.), a form of racialised knowledge of the Other ... deeply implicated in the operations of power' (Hall, 1997: 260). Inter-textuality is central to this racialised regime of representation since the 'whole repertoire of imagery and visual effects' (ibid: 232) ensures the meaning of difference is established. A discursive formation around race might include: racist jokes; news story 'moral panics' about deviant black youth 'pushing' drugs and committing crime; investigative and anthropological film and television documentaries that scientifically historicise black culture as primitive or needing or warring; media appeals that call for a 'collective' Western sympathy for the helpless and the hungry people of 'Africa'; and provocative, all-rhythm, all-black music dancers and performers who populate the background worlds of white pop star music videos. Taken together, a discursive formation emerges that speaks to and about racial difference, placing black people in a negative relationship – a power-saturated binary opposition – to white people.

CELEBRITY REPRESENTATIONS

Celebrity exists through forms of signification and as over-arching and textually specific discursive formations. Celebrities often stand as perfected or flawed creatures, embody identity politics and give meaning to the imagined body of the nation state. As Moynagh Sullivan suggests:

> British bands such as the Spice Girls or Take That were openly patriotic in their iconography and in their dress, manufactured Irish bands, such as Boyzone and Westlife, who stormed the Irish and British markets in the 1990s and the early years of this decade, never draped themselves in the tricolour nor riverdanced. So although the boy bands appear, in contrast, innocently apolitical, they implicitly perform not only the newfound success of Celtic Tiger Ireland, but also the reasons for that success.
>
> (2007: 184)

Celebrity representations carry the range of politicised values and meanings that are attached to their image when in circulation. Celebrity representations are never neutral: they carry the discourses, concerns, inequalities and dreams of the contemporary age.

The celebrity body is very often the conduit through which dominant ideologies about gender, race, class and sexuality are disseminated (Holmes and Redmond, 2006: 124). These ideologies are most commonly mobilised through the channels of celebrity gossip: in which celebrities are scrutinised for signs of ageing, addiction, plastic surgery, pregnancy, weight gain or weight loss and social class designators (Fairclough, 2012; Wilson, 2010). Through the discourse of celebrity gossip, fans and consumers are made aware of what is deemed to be appropriate displays of the famous body. Further, one is discursively positioned to evaluate and make judgments about these celebrities, particularly when their bodies are excessively gendered and raced.

For example, images from Kim Kardashian's nude photo spread for *Paper* magazine (2014) were distributed across a plethora of media outlets. Through the discourse of celebrity embodiment readers were being positioned to evaluate (and 'gossip' about) her corporeality in terms of race and gender. Kardashian's Armenian heritage is evoked through her olive colouring and her curvaceous buttocks speak to racist myths about non-white female bodies and their 'surplus' of sexuality. There are also class and esteem measures being signified:

Kim Kardashian emerged through starring in a reality TV show and sex tape – she is both heiress and tramp/slut. Nonetheless, as Katherine Appleford argues:

> Kim Kardashian has been an important influence in shaping young women's notions of attractiveness, by encouraging a common concept of body image and desirability across racial groups. Indeed, operating as an 'exotic other', who sits somewhere between black and white beauty, Kim Kardashian and the 'slim-thick' ideal perhaps offer an example of cultural assimilation, and yet they also work to exaggerate cultural stereotypes, encouraging a notion of beauty that is unrealistic, and far outside the reach of ordinary women.

(2016: 193)

When the representation of the celebrity is heavily gendered, it is often through an idealised framework: they are photographed with radiant smiles and chiselled arms and have perfect figures to admire, desire and long for (Dyer, 1978). Masculinity and femininity are created around these two poles of difference, set within a heterosexual ethical space. When the famed masculinity or femininity of these extraordinary celestial bodies become absolute in terms of heavenly forms of signification, the representation they offer up is seen as transcendent, beyond earthly configurations. They are tied up with the politics of whiteness.

Idealised white celebrities encapsulate this translucent deification, since they are often imagined to be made of light and as close to God as one can be while still being mortal (Dyer, 1997). For example, the star body of Cate Blanchett speaks to white femininity and to the aura of the 'blonde', whose beauty registers at the apex of idealisation. However, her white female idealisation is also immaculate and non-sexual, which creates a form of embodiment that very often teeters on the brink of its own expiration (Dyer, 1997; Redmond, 2014).

As perfected human representations, the celebrity also gives flesh to abstract desire; they become the conduit through which neoliberal fantasies are played out precisely in the way the promotion and purchasing of all manner of goods and services are impregnated with the star-dust of the famous endorser (Rojek, 2001; Cashmore, 2006). When a perfume bottle is shaped like the celebrity who endorses it, their corporeality is transferred from body to bottle, then from hand to neck, the scent becoming their skin re-cast in liquid form.

As child-star Hannah Montana, Miley Cyrus is white innocence and exacting beauty personified (see also Chapter 8 for a case study on Miley Cyrus). She is heavenly and carries the church within her heart. She holds within her obedient, gendered body, the values of patriarchy and heterosexual dreaming. As the young woman who twerks and can't be tamed, she draws upon black radicalised idioms and caricatures to fetishise her buttocks and sexualise her flesh. Miley's twerk repositions her as a transgressive or wayward teen celebrity, as someone who has left the wholesome body of Hannah Montana behind. Nonetheless, both Miley's Hannah and Miley's sexualised dance help sell perfume, branded clothes and concert tickets. Celebrity flesh and sex sell. Miley is the perfect representation of this commodity carnal cartography.

Nonetheless, celebrity representations are not static, fixed or immobile: they age and age differently for men and women, and their star image gets re-signified to ensure career longevity and to shape and be shaped by cultural transformations occurring in society. Female celebrities are not only asked to age differently to men, they are exhorted to *defy* the ageing process. The representation of the ageing celebrity body is taken up by the dominant culture in different ways and across different media; with male celebrities maintaining viable and lucrative careers in Hollywood and television as they age (Fairclough, 2012; Jermyn, 2016). Many of the discourses around ageing female celebrity bodies are framed in terms of whether or not they are able to hide their ageing and keep the labour involved in doing so hidden, through plastic surgery for example (Fairclough, 2012).

QUESTIONING CELEBRITY REPRESENTATIONS: *REASONABLE DOUBT* ALBUM, JAY-Z

When looking to begin an analysis of a celebrity representation, one can work through the following questions:

1.   What signifiers are being represented (clothing, hair, body language, iconography, tactile objects)?

On Jay-Z's 1996 album cover for *Reasonable Doubt* we find him dressed in the iconography of the Brooklyn Mafia: trilby, silk scarf, diamond ring and large Cuban cigar.

2. What technical codes are being employed in the representation (lighting, framing, camera position)?

    The shot is moody black-and-white, slightly blurred, with Jay-Z in medium close-up, centre frame. The cigar dominates the foreground while the brim of the trilby provides symmetry to the composition.

3. What values, meanings, desires and needs are being associated with the celebrity?

    Jay-Z is taking on the role of the mafia boss, mysterious and powerful. He is eschewing the codes of hip-hop iconography, 'passing' as white. His persona grants him status and wealth and plays with the idea of innocence and guilt.

4. Are there examples of stereotyping and myth circulating in the world of the celebrity representation?

    There are ethnic, race and gender myths circulated in the cover: Jay-Z has arisen out of the ghetto and has in a sense made it. Nonetheless, he is still connected to crime and criminality and the 'trace' of the mythological 'bad buck'.

5. What lifestyle(s) is/are being represented?

    A double persona is in view: Jay-Z the successful rapper and the shady mafia boss he plays. Both celebrate consumption success.

6. What identity is being hailed? Who is the audience for the representation?

    The advert speaks to rap fans and black American youth in particular. It is aspirational and individually possessive.

7. Are there 'anchors' employed such as text, dialogue and sound to 'fix' the meaning of the celebrity representation?

    The album's title is found across the bottom of the cover, in raised televisual lettering. It has two meanings: Jay-Z is the best rapper, beyond reasonable doubt; that his guilt has to be proven beyond reasonable doubt. The subtext takes us to the criminal justice system and the way black males are harshly treated.

8. What discursive formations does the celebrity representation belong to, speak within? What contemporary discourse does it speak from and to?

It promotes the power of fame to grant one success and connects with the myth of the American Dream, where anyone can make it if they try hard enough. This is of course subverted by the criminal signification as if crime (rap) does pay.

9. Who has produced the representation? What type of industry does it belong to?

Photographer Jonathan Mannion, who directed the shoot, 'recalls the light being spectacular and advised Jay to go with a black-and-white cover since nobody was really shooting in black-and-white. One of the few other albums that came out around that time in black-and-white was De La Soul's *Stakes Is High* album. The stretch of Manhattan's Westside is where Trump's buildings are lined up in all of their dystopian glory. Now, in this moment, it was Jay's turn to express his empire state of mind' (Toba, 2016).

The album was independently produced, in part by Jay-Z's own production company, Roc-A-Fella Records, but it had a distribution deal with a major record company.

10. What different types of reading might we be able to give this representation?

The cover can be read as shaping a new star image for Jay-Z but it can also be read as a text that reinforces racial stereotypes and the desire to consume.

I am going to use the case study below to employ both semiotic and discursive analysis to answer a similar set of questions: through this analysis of film star Scarlett Johansson I draw upon star, race and gender representational theory, combined with the discursive strands of science fiction film and television. By reading Scarlett Johansson in this way, one is not simply employing close textual analysis to a specific case study but demonstrating the wider streams with which these representations connect and effect. This is a case study in celebrity representation but we will also see how it connects to other points on the circuit of celebrity culture.

CASE STUDY

The alien whiteness of Scarlett Johansson

When a star image and idealised whiteness are combined, or brought together, in symbiotic union they construct a powerful narrative about privilege and belonging in the world, one that places or situates white identity at the apex of civilised and successful life. At the same time, however, this hyper-perfect conjunction renders the white star both unattainably immaculate and, as a consequence, essentially non-reproductive. The idealised whiteness of stars is inherently gendered in this respect: female white stars are both acute forms of physical and spiritual perfection and troubling vessels of abstinence who cannot 'reproduce' the species. Their star image is built on an unhealthy paradox: the more positive qualities of starry whiteness, such as purity, transcendence and hyper-rationalism, mean that 'the very things that make us white endanger the repro-duction of whiteness' (Dyer, 1997: 27).

This complexity is acutely realised in the science fiction film text because of the way the problem of reproduction is writ large over their themes and concerns (Telotte, 1990). As I will go on to argue, Johans-son's star image both embodies and expresses these inherent reproduc-tive tensions, particularly in and through her roles in films such as *Her* (Jonze, 2013), *Under the Skin* (Glazer, 2014) and *Ghost in the Shell* (Sanders, 2017), since her whiteness is both accentuated and rendered a dangerous form of progeny. Johansson comes to embody an alien and alienating form of whiteness even if its ontological power contin-ues to hegemonically structure the films under analysis.

To set the background to this case study, I will now begin by defin-ing my terms, and briefly exploring this relationship between star-dom, whiteness and gender, before turning to Johansson's overall star position within the politics of white identity formation as it manifests within the science fiction films that she often appears in.

Starry, sterile whiteness

Film stars are mythological constructs, their narratives of success built on an imagined relationship with high-order qualities and attributes. For example, the star success myth posits that film stars have a par-ticularly close connection with the 'extraordinary' and the heavenly (Dyer, 1998). Film stars are represented to be naturally more spiritual and closer to the heavens precisely because they are made out of or from natural light. Film stars glow; they emit light and sunshine like no other human beings on Earth. There is a metaphysical aura around them that surrounds them, and which is imagined to light up 'our' dreary worlds too. Film stars shine and we – all of us, regardless of race or ethnicity – shine when in contact or communion with them.

As Richard Dyer writes, we live in a 'culture of light' (1997: 103) where visibility is an indicator of authenticity, knowability and where giving off light is imagined as a highly positive attribute. And as Dyer further contends, it is whiteness which is so clearly light producing, which is even made up from light itself: 'white people are central to it, to the extent that they come to seem to have a special relationship to light' (1997: 103).

Light is of course central to the star success myth which posits that higher-order or 'supericonic' film stars are made in God's enlightened image, are, at least in a metaphorical sense, God's ideal(ised) and favoured children: the beautiful and the pure ones. This is especially true in relation to white female stars, where the qualities of idealised whiteness – light, purity and transcendence – seem to exude from their very pores, their inner state of being. Here, the 'non-physical, spiritual, indeed ethereal qualities' of the 'white woman as angel' (Dyer, 1997: 127) become the very qualities of the female star, so that whiteness and stardom conjoin to produce a truly extraordinary and highly desirable representation that appears to be not of this world or rather – to draw on the lexicon of science fiction – out of this world.

If one was to turn momentarily to the set of promotional texts that circulate in and around Scarlett Johansson, we see how her blondeness and natural auratic light shapes the commercial streams she is represented in. For example, in the Dolce & Gabbana campaign for both the perfume range for *The One* and their make-up accessories, Johansson is captured as a sultry figure whose auratic glow ripples in and around her blonde hair and flawless white skin. She is captured laying on silk sheets, or in Paris-end urban settings, with her eyes facing the imagined reader. She lights up the image and the enchanted world she moves in and through.

Johansson's blondeness is here marketed as a physical characteristic that seems to have divine origins, and which naturally produces a heavenly appearance. Marina Warner (1994) has traced the significance of blondeness in religion, fairy tale and myth and found that blondeness is equated with beauty, with goodness and with heroic deed.

Of course, Johansson's own public commentary that 'monogamy isn't natural' (Weaver, 2017) also leaks its way back into these adverts, as does the fact that white women can achieve this status, for example, if they use the right, subtle hair-dye. In so doing, the holy nature of whiteness seems to be undermined. Johansson, however, is a *natural* blonde and her auratic glow privileges the sense that she is unattainable, if open to desire. As an idealised white star, she is allowed to have her representational cake and eat it.

Herein lies the crux of the apparent representational contradiction of idealised, starry whiteness: in this coalescing sign system, the idealised white female star floats between two extremes: at one end, she is the ultimate object of identification, someone who is to be desired and desiring; and at the other, she is a subject who nonetheless remains above and beyond easy identification and sexual availability. The idealised white female star is 'embodied' in a state of being and not being, as someone who *miraculously* descends from the heavens with her virginity, purity intact and yet one who simultaneously occupies the space of reproductive perfection. In the adverts for Dolce & Gabbana, Johansson occupies a space of white womanly perfection, is desiring and desirable, but occupies a space betwixt and between absence and presence. She is a heavenly star fallen to Earth.

In science fiction film one can see how the whitely markers of Heaven and Angel are transposed to the impressive vastness of utopian Space, and the figure of the Alien Messiah who descends to Earth and is given symbolic transformative powers, such as the ability to heal, resurrect and, if wronged, seek vengeance (Ruppersberg, 1990). The Alien Messiah confuses and upsets binary reproductive structures and is implicated in the non-reproductive framework of idealised whiteness since they are beyond reproduction and see it as a lesser form of evolution. One can see this trope emerging in Johansson's star image in such films as *Her* and *Under the Skin* where the question of desire and reproduction is highly problematised.

Elizabeth Ellsworth (1997: 226) calls this essential paradox the 'double binds of whiteness', whereby rationalised purity necessarily brings privileged white people closer to their own negation, owing to a lack of empathy and denial of the sex drive that in the end would result in the eradication of the species. In a great many science fiction films, the figure of the hyper-white scientist is presented as dangerous precisely because they are non-reproductive beings and are shown to value 'alien' life above our own.

Science fiction film is obsessed with the question of reproduction (Cranny-Francis, 2015). When there is too much whiteness in the fictional world, reproduction is threatened. When there is too little whiteness, the species is threatened by the Other. In the wider narratives of science fiction film, the 'ethnic' alien is often placed in binary opposition to white communities, and the healing, positive values of white science and scientists. The ethnic alien visits 'Earth' or a space 'community' to destroy it; infect it; transform its dominant cultures and moral systems. Monstrous, unstoppable and inter-racial reproduction is often the (white) terror that follows the alien creature. In *Alien* (Scott, 1979) one can offer a reading of the alien queen that recognises the hallmarks of a sexually charged, animalistic black woman. As Amy Taubin contends:

> the alien queen bears a suspicious resemblance to a scapegoat of the Reagan/Bush era – the black welfare mother, the parasite on the economy whose uncurbed reproductive drive reduced hard-working taxpayers to bankruptcy.
>
> (1993: 95–96)

What we find through the science fiction films that Johansson stars in, however, is idealised whiteness being the alienating force, albeit within narratives that ultimately privilege her and her idealisation. It is true, of course, that white stars very often populate the universes of science fiction film, and even when a black actor such as Will Smith takes the leading role their race and ethnicity are 'de-odorised'. White stars, as I will go on to discuss with regards to Johansson's role in *Ghost in the Shell*, are also allowed to 'travel' across the racial spectrum, taking on roles designed for non-white actors. The idealised whiteness of stars matches the white hegemony of science fiction film: their narrative pattern predominately gives the power to travel and change the world to white star-characters, who are marked with exceptionalism – as if it is their (white people's) manifest destiny to reach for the stars.

What is particularly interesting, then, about American film star Scarlett Johansson? What does she signify in the context of stardom, gender and idealised whiteness within the science fiction film text? How might her idealised whiteness speak to the trauma at the heart of this subject position? What might her alien(ating) whiteness say about the state of celebrity whiteness in contemporary culture? To answer these related questions, I examine three films, taking each in turn: *Her*, in which she plays the AI Operating System, Samantha; *Under the Skin*, in which she plays an unnamed Alien Other who comes to question her own position in the film; and *Ghost in the Shell*, in which she plays the Major, a Special Ops, human-cyborg hybrid, charged with defending the bio-tech corporation she works for. These films are tightly grouped not only in terms of genre and theme but also release date, allowing this chapter to assess Johansson's star image and idealised whiteness at a particular moment in her career, and wider cultural life.

In all these films, Johansson plays roles that are anti-reproductive, and which therefore seemingly undermine the telos of idealised whiteness. The roles question the very framework of her star image, are often anti-star, either explicitly, or through the way the texts unconsciously reveal the 'death' at the heart of her idealised whiteness. As I navigate through these readings I will argue that Johansson's alien(ating) whiteness very much speaks to what Monbiot (2014) calls the present condition of the 'culture of loneliness', where it (white people) acutely suffers from this type of agonising despair.

Her *(not her)*

In *Her* (Jonze, 2013), the lonely, soon-to-be-divorced Theodore Twombly (Joaquin Phoenix) develops a relationship with Samantha (Scarlett Johansson), an artificially intelligent computer Operating System that is personified through female voice alone. Theodore is a professional writer who composes love letters for people unable or unwilling to do so, for a website called BeautfulHandwrittenLetters.com. The film establishes from the beginning that intimacy failure is writ large across contemporary life, and that loneliness is the dominant existential condition that the populace face. Here, however, people are overly networked and plugged in, and either long for rematerialisation in the real world, whether it be through 'analogue' forms of paper letters, or yearn for these digital spaces to offer them something more meaningful. Theodore's soon-to-be ex-wife's main criticism of him is that he could never really handle the intimacies and tensions of the real world.

In the case of Theodore, Samantha becomes the conduit for him to experience both public and private spaces, rituals and intimacies, in a new and heightened way. She becomes female utopia (Williams, 1999) and he can re-engage with the real world since it is now free of conflict while being full of uncomplicated and perfected – if abstracted – sexualisation. The rich, suffuse, high-sheen *mise-en-scène* of the film gives it an ethereal, floating realisation, as if this electronic love heats and cools everything around Theodore and Samantha. The film's very spaces and spatial relations, then, call forth the qualities and symbolism of idealised whiteness.

Samantha becomes Theodore's ever-present, connected to him via a small earpiece that allows them to go on dates to the beach or trips to the mall. Their relationship is synaesthetic and cross-modal: he gives Samantha embodiment, while she gives him voice, the means to 'feel' and to have 'grounded' connectivity. In their first scene of sexual consummation, Samantha and Theodore make virtual love and he climaxes at the end. However, this level of monogamous intimacy is not enough for Samantha, so she asks him to have sex with someone he finds on the web; the love-making to be captured with miniature cameras and microphones on the woman's body so that Samantha can be virtually penetrated and caressed by Theodore as he does so. The scene blurs normal, patriarchal sexual relations: machine and human are multiplied (the AI Samantha is connected to the woman by digital recording devices and Theodore makes love to both the woman and the Operating System). Nonetheless, this experiment isn't successful and we find subsequently that Samantha has been communicating with hundreds of men in a similar way – she loves Theodore but only in the same way as she loves all her operating clients. *Her* speaks to the supposed promiscuousness of online dating culture and the lack of commitment it fosters. On one level, *Her* prophesies a future where the liquid streams of modern life produce wealthy but lonely isolates, and where AIs will ultimately expand their capabilities way beyond human comprehension and imagination. On another level, *Her* prophesies about the failing nature and power of contemporary whiteness.

Her is clearly about the double binds of whiteness, drawing in part on Johansson's star image to do so. Samantha may not have literal embodiment in the film but being voiced by Johansson ensures that the film's sonic register is given sensual flesh. Her well-known, accented buttery tones are star-sensory signifiers and allow her to be both absent and present in the film – by hearing her we see her, even though she is never there physically. The very mythos of (Johansson's) idealised white female stardom is in play in the film: her role, as a sentient AI, gives her power over the film's narrative trajectory and places her beyond normal earthly reproductive capabilities. She lives in the network (heaven) and in the intimate (earthly) one-to-one relationships with Theodore and her many (thousands?) of clients. The film is framed like a revisionist technological Virgin Mary parable: Johansson/Samantha has earthly desires, but they are never (actually) consummated. Further, because her polygamy is aural and virtual – is ultimately *out of this world* – her actions seem above and beyond human urges and needs. Johansson's star image clearly is a 'perfect fit' for such whitely oscillations: as noted above, in interviews she has come out in favour of polygamy, and her star embodiment exists at the axis between sensuality and immaculation. She is all body and beyond body at the same time.

By contrast, Theodore clearly represents white masculinity in crisis: he is suffering a terrifying confusion over his place within the new digital social and economic order. He has few social ties; his marriage is over and he suffers from depression. His only true solace is in/with Samantha – a transcendental figure he can only (softly) hear. As Richard Dyer suggests, the theme of white men belonging to an endangered species is increasingly found across a range of contemporary cultural texts, which 'may suggest that the suspicion of nothingness and the death of whiteness is, as far as white identity goes, the cultural dominant of our times, that we really do feel we're played out' (Dyer, 1997: 217).

To summarise, Samantha clearly (dis)embodies the absent/present paradox at the heart of idealised whiteness: she is (initially) conceived as an immaculate being: without a body, without desire, her only objective is seemingly to give meaningful embodiment to Theodore – she initially exists subserviently, to satisfy his needs and wants. She is the Angelic motherly figure of myth and lore and the classically coded figure of science fiction AI. Of course, what complicates or troubles the representation is that Samantha is duplicitous and Theodore's white masculinity is shown to be not enough for her. Given she is voiced by Johansson, her idealised white star image impresses upon the text. Her blondeness and voluptuousness emerge through her voice and the virtual seductions and love-making that are undertaken. On one level, the virtual nature of the love-making carries forward the concept that white people (idealised white stars) don't have sex (we/they are immaculately conceived). On another level, the virtual love-making brings her star body into the film world – a body that is ultimately, arguably, plastic in the re-moulding sense.

Paul Adams (1995: 268) has argued that contemporary digital global relations have enabled 'personal extensibility' in which (privileged) people have almost limitless travel capabilities, granting them access to and control over places, services, commodities right around the world. This produces a new form of virtual colonisation, with physical or lived consequences for those – the digital poor – who can't extend themselves in these ways. I would suggest that this is acutely racialised. Johansson/Samantha embodies this newfound expansion of the white self, able to move in and between different realities, to take electronic flight and try on new relations wherever the networks may take her. As Hobson contends, 'digital whiteness' is associated with 'progress,' 'technology' and 'civilization' (2008: 114).

This is of course the reality of *Ghost in the Shell*, as I will go on to argue later.

Under the white skin

Humankind is supposedly living in the age of loneliness; a period where we have fewer companions; communal networks have broken down and our social encounters are conducted through superficial augmented interfaces. When we gravitate to the social media, we find that it doesn't actually connect us but increases our sense of isolation and deepens or thickens our profound sense of loneliness (Steers, Wickham, and Acitelli, 2014). In the age of loneliness we are supposedly very much alone, as George Monbiot suggests,

> Three months ago we read that loneliness has become an epidemic among young adults. Now we learn that it is just as great an affliction of older people. A study by Independent Age shows that severe loneliness in England blights the lives of 700,000 men and 1.1m women over 50, and is rising with astonishing speed ... Social isolation is as

potent a cause of early death as smoking 15 cigarettes a day; loneliness, research suggests, is twice as deadly as obesity. Dementia, high blood pressure, alcoholism and accidents – all these, like depression, para-noia, anxiety and suicide, become more prevalent when connections are cut. We cannot cope alone.

(2014)

Under the Skin is a perfect metaphoric and experiential exploration of this ennui of loneliness, set within a crumbling Scotland. It also captures perfectly the paradox of idealised whiteness and white star-dom as it manifests today – carried into and through the film by Johansson's star image.

In the film, an unnamed, alien seductress (Scarlet Johansson) lures single, isolated men back to her house where they are submerged in a liquid tar and where their bodies are then slowly consumed by an unknown force. The film's central scenes occur in the industrial and urban wastelands of Scotland, Glasgow, in particular. The alien seduc-tress drives a white van around the city estates and its empty roads, luring lonely men to their deaths; and by day, through the teeming metropolis, where movement seems both accelerated and dead slow, like time is out of kilter, in a state of temporal and existential crisis. People are disconnected, in a hurry, or are cut adrift, such as the white men the seductress meets and who yearn for connection and intimacy. They are just 'poorer' versions of Theodore who we find in *Her* (see Figure 2.1).

Under the Skin's architecture, its sombre materiality and its oppres-sive *mise-en-scène* help create the spatial conditions of modern living and capture perfectly the 'extinction' threat that sits at the heart of whiteness. The liquid black tomb that the single white men drown in captures the sense that modern life is permeable, boundaryless and that their own masculinity is not desired or empowered, but only devoured. In the film, white masculinity isn't just lonely, pathetic, it is food. The men drown and are consumed in the isolated and isolating conditions of what it means to be 'lowly' white (Bonnett, 1998, 2000).

Scarlet Johansson's character is also eventually caught in this caul-dron of white anomie. In one pivotal scene, she stares blankly at her-self in a mirror, misrecognising who she really is. She examines her body as if it doesn't belong to her (which it doesn't, it has been lifted

Figure 2.1 The haunting mirror of whiteness

off a corpse), capturing the sense that the self is a project that can be made, re-engineered, in an age of consumer products and surgical transformations. More tellingly, one can read this scene as representing the self-reflective haunting mirror of whiteness and of the idealised white star staring back at herself. White people have the exceptional power to make themselves over (Vera and Gordon, 2003), and idealised white female stars embody this ability since they exist in promotional streams where this is foregrounded, such as in the Dolce & Gabbana adverts analysed near the beginning of this case study. However, the question that *Under the Skin* poses is: to what ends? The film's answer, on one level, seems to suggest naught: whiteness is on the verge of extinction and whitely stardom is a vacuous enterprise.

The absence of reproduction is also central to this film, as it was with *Her*. Johansson's character tries to have an intimate relationship with an unnamed, isolated white man in the film, but they cannot consummate. He has forgotten simply how to connect; and she is alien, Other, without a vagina or a womb, and therefore unable to love or reproduce but only destroy/castrate. In my reading, this alien Otherness in the film is the spectre of non-reproductive whiteness, of idealised white female stardom: Johansson is a phantasmagoric embodiment of the immaculate conception, but here rendered as a form of self-annihilation. The ideological implications of idealised white female stardom are laid bare: it is to be psychically annihilated. The parallels here with *Her* are striking, except in that film Johansson's character is set free on the digital superhighway; here she is ultimately punished, as I will presently go on to argue.

This is very much an anti-star performance by Johansson: she appears with little glamour and draws upon a range of authentic performance codes that suggest a hyperrealist embodiment is being presented. Such codes include her mass-market street attire, mournful gait and the improvised exchanges of dialogue which are filmed in a documentary style. This is a performance that seems to out the artifice of white stardom and of what white stardom can do to the actor who is caught in its glare. Through her performance, Johansson seems to be addressing the loneliness of idealised whiteness itself. In this context, stardom and whiteness ultimately become conduits for this 'culture of loneliness', even as it extra-textually washes itself in the glamour of enriched connectivity (Redmond, 2014).

Nonetheless, there is a further, colossal tension in the film's representation and understanding of female whiteness and of Johansson's star embodiment of it. One can read the cruising scenes as 'pick-ups' and one-night stands, and the seductress as 'white trash'. There is more than a touch of *Looking for Mr Goodbar* (Brooks, 1977) in the film's ideological allusions: Johansson's character is ultimately 'punished' for consuming (fucking over) the white men she didn't desire but wanted on her own terms. Her murder, an immolation at the hands of a would-be rapist, in the hushed, ever-so-quiet snow-covered tundra, is a vicious 'moral retribution of order' by the 'type' of failed white man she had taken to task earlier in the film. The seductress/ Johansson is being punished for being less than 'ideal', for daring to have earthly desires. She alienates her idealised whiteness and suffers as a consequence.

One can begin to see how the theme of promiscuity begins to mark out Johansson's star image and the roles she plays. It isn't just contained within the films under analysis in the chapter, either, or the promotional texts briefly highlighted. Johansson occupies a space where her star embodiment is both highly idealised and corporeally suspect. She is virgin and whore, a trope that actually follows a number of iconic white stars, such as Marilyn Monroe, who 'seemed to "be" the very tensions that ran through the ideological life of 50s America', with its 'flux of ideas about morality and sexuality' (Dyer, 1998: 31).

Monroe is 'the ultimate embodiment of the desirable woman' but is 'nevertheless not an image of the danger of sex'. Monroe is the 'ultimate white playmate' and yet her innocence and naiveté suggest that this is beyond her or rather, she is beyond this. Johansson occupies a similar position today, embodying not only the tensions inherent in idealised whiteness in the 21st century, but the fraught position of women in a fragmented, post-feminist culture.

Johansson revels in and openly celebrates her whitely, feminine transgression. The arguable power this gives Johansson over her own unruly body and the male gaze directed at her (*please look at me this way*, she seems to be saying) is one that ruptures the idealised representation that female white stars are supposed to take on. Through Johansson's unruly white body, a transgressive sexualised form of female whiteness emerges. A transgression that gives *life*, vitality, corporeality and control – rather than ethereality and negation – to her star image and the 'body' that houses it.

However, that is not to deny or forget such transgressions often also bring a degree of 'death', since such wanton and aggressive displays of female sexuality are ultimately managed (made safe) or punished in some way, as they are in both *Her* and *Under the Skin*, and in the promotional texts we most often find her in, where she is perfected eye-candy.

What this continues to suggest is that Johansson can be both sex and death, pure and impure, absent and present, precisely because she is an idealised white female star and has the power to 'travel', as I will now go on to argue in relation to *Ghost in the Shell*.

White in the Shell

Historically, as Vera and Gordon suggest, 'white privilege includes the privilege to temporarily change one's colour, to masquerade as non-white' (2003: 120). Vera and Gordon use the example of 'racial masquerade' by whites in American film to explore what they see as an impossible fantasy solution, both to the 'lack of life' at the core of whiteness and to the racial guilt experienced by whites in relation to the Other. According to Vera and Gordon:

> The fantasy played out in most white race-switching movies is an adult male fantasy of reversion to boyhood or adolescence, when the

white self was free to play Indian or black. These white male heroes temporarily descend into an exotic racial underworld and assume the imagined qualities of the racial other ... only to return at the end to the security of the white bourgeois world. The white passing for another person of another race is, in effect, indulging in voyeurism, liberal slumming, and cultural tourism.

(2003: 117)

One can apply this masquerade fantasy framework to the live action re-make/translation of *Ghost in the Shell*, but obviously in a more vexing and complex way. Scarlett Johansson takes on the role of Major Mira Killian (Motoko Kusanagi in the original anime film), a 'consciousness' implanted in a mechanical body that grants her both exceptional capabilities and near immortality since her parts and organs can be repaired. As the Major in the anti-terrorist bureau Section 9, Killian engages in a quest to not only defeat the terrorists but find out more about her true self, since the 'glitches' she increasingly gets suggest a 'past' beyond her shell.

The film is set in a retrofuturistic Tokyo/Japan and is saturated in orientalist images: the visual effects and camera work draw on the aesthetics of Asian cityphilia to capture the sensorial, ritualised stereotypes of Japan/Asia. As the Major navigates herself through the metropolis we are witnessing the very appropriation of the authentic markers found in the original film and given it is Johansson doing the 'touring', the film establishes a fetishistic looking regime from the eyes of a highly fetishised white star/character. Given also that in the original, the Major is a Japanese character, and that the film is set in Japan, and foregrounds its cultural specificity, one can read this positioning as a form of racial masquerade: the Major is white and yet Other, or a version of the Other that white culture is able to 'pimp' or try on (hooks, 1992).

The Major is a male fantasy figure but layered so: as the narrative agent, she drives the film but is at the same time 'positioned' by the mysterious male figure she is trying to track down (Kuze, played by Michael Carmen Pitt). The Major's costume is tight and accentuates Johansson's curves and breasts (she is to be looked at) at the same time as it promotes her physicality and strength. Narratively speaking, given it is not her body, and is not a human body but a cyborg one, the character is again beyond reproduction. The Major, then, embodies the reproductive paradoxes of idealised whiteness as it manifests in and through Johansson's star image.

Nonetheless, *Ghost in the Shell* occupies an unusual space in racial masquerade films since it inverts the usual narrative in which the Other tries to pass as white. Their journey is very often a tragic one, since an inquisitor finds out the 'truth' that she or he is not racially pure and the revelation is accompanied by the character's destruction (Gabriel, 1988). In *Ghost in the Shell*, the Major finds out that she is actually Japanese, the daughter of a widowed mother, and the revelation leads to the destruction of the commercial organ-isation that has been harvesting humans for this end. In a sense, then, *Ghost in the Shell* embraces the racial hybridity the film is built on, although it is imagined through the idealised white body of Johansson.

One can argue that at the core of a white longing for Easternisation is a 'dissatisfaction with and alienation from the limitations of the white bourgeois self – a white self-loathing – and a romanticisation of the racial other' (Vera and Gordon, 2003: 117). Play and performance are key here. In fact, Celia Lury suggests that the 'making of races' or the creation of racial identities is central to consumer culture and the way that, in contemporary representations, 'all races are represented, not as a biological category, but as a question of style, as a choice' (1996: 168). Of course, the play with race may be argued to be a hege-monic tactic for ensuring that whiteness maintains its racial superi-ority, particularly when it comes to white people taking on/in racial Otherness. As Hernan Vera and Andrew M Gordon suggest, 'white privilege includes the privilege to temporarily change one's colour, to masquerade as non-white' (2003: 120).

Nonetheless, one can also argue that there is potentially a trans-gressive and subversive quality to white masquerade and the desire for the racial Other. In terms of primitivism, Bonnett argues that there must be some attempt to 'cross the boundaries of cultural and racial purity' (2000: 117). Similarly, Gina Marchetti concludes that racial masquerade films 'implicitly critique the racial hierarchy of main-stream American culture, since they feature the conscious and delib-erate impersonation of another race, putting aside a supposed racial superiority so as to become part of a supposedly inferior other' (quoted in Vera and Gordon, 2003: 119). Through impersonation, passing, performing and masquerading, racial identity shifts, moves and floats so that the borders and boundaries in and between white and non-white people begin to melt into air.

According to Zygmunt Bauman (2000), constructing a durable identity that coheres over time and space has become increasingly impossible within the conditions of electronic modernity. He suggests that we have moved from a period where we understood ourselves as 'pilgrims' in search of deeper or higher meaning, to one where we now act as 'tourists' in search of multiple but meeting social experiences. Johansson's idealised white star image seems to speak to both this restlessness and to tie it to a crisis – an aching loneliness – in whiteness.

CONCLUSION: ALIENATING WHITENESS

Johansson's idealised white star image, as I have begun to establish in this case study, clearly works in and through a set of complex intersections and tensions; particularly around the vexing question of reproduction as it uniquely materialises in the science fiction film. I have set this reading in relation to the contemporary condition of 'loneliness' and of identity fragmentation as it manifests in the digital worlds we live in, and the subjectivities we pass through. On the one hand, Johansson embodies the mythos of idealised female whiteness, securing its cultural power. On the other hand, she so clearly demonstrates its fault-lines and negations and represents it as a set of fraught alienations.

Through Johansson, idealised female whiteness is alien because it is out of this world, non- or anti-reproductive, and, more powerfully perhaps, because it threatens its own ontological coherency. The three films under analysis in the chapter do this alienating whiteness in distinct but overlapping ways. They are in conversation with other promotional texts, and with other films in the Johansson oeuvre, beyond the reach of the capabilities of this chapter. Yet uniquely it is in the science fiction films where we see the fraught conditions of idealised whiteness play out.

CHAPTER SUMMARY

This chapter has set out to define celebrity representation through the parameters of semiotic and discourse analysis. The chapter weaves in questions of identity and power, image construction and the contextual parameters that representations nestle in. As such it gives truth to the importance of representation as a node on the circuit of celebrity culture but also of the intersecting nature of cultural construction.

3

MORE THAN JUST A FEELING
CELEBRITY AFFECTS

In Chapter 2 the book employed the reading and contextual tools of cultural analysis to both define representation and to demonstrate how celebrity represents various forms of identities. In this chapter, we move our focus to the issue of affect and affective relations, and the way the senses are mobilised in often liberating ways when fan and celebrity meet in the arena of fantasy and dreaming. This chapter takes us to the circuit of celebrity affect.

MORE THAN JUST A FEELING: CELEBRITY AFFECTS

It would seem an obvious observation that celebrity culture is intimately tied to the mobilisation of emotions. Through its core practices and processes, celebrity is an emotive apparatus that engages with common modes of feelings and delirious forms of affect. Celebrities situate themselves within broad economies of intimacy, creating para-social relationships that seem particularly strong and heartfelt, but which may ultimately disappoint – so dependent are they on loose, mediated and ephemeral connections (Rojek, 2001; Stever, 2011). All the sub-sets of emotion, from love, anger, surprise and sadness, are made manifest through the way celebrities enter people's lives. We cry with and for them. They dance in our dreams. They occupy the spaces of event spectacle calling forth our emotions to receive and exalt them. Celebrities register as key moments in biographical and memorial exchanges where fans and consumers story and remember through the event moments they help shaped. The emotion of celebrity matches or catches the emotional encounters people go through, providing the meta-context for love, romance, heartache and desire. People live emotional lives in and through the emotions of celebrity culture.

Affective celebrity is tied to the myth of the media centre, inviting people to gravitate towards their famed status as if that is where organic and intensified life takes place. Access to this emotional control centre promises liberation and intensification but may ultimately serve to ensnare people within regulated and conformist sets of sensuous expression (Littler, 2008; Couldry, 2003). Politics operates within this arena of adoration: it has been celebratised and celebrity politics trades and traffics in the representation of 'authentic' emotion and appeals to the ethical feelings inscribed in democratic life (Kellner, 2008). Political rallies are a mark of this cavalcade of affect. Oh Obama you have spoken to us through your heart and through emotive abstractions that suggest democracy is to be felt and experienced as much as made meaningful through policy and action. Of course, Donald Trump's presidency is also met by emotional connectivity but here it is the affect of channelling hate, or of disgust, which marks out the way he is experienced. In the liquid modern age, just feeling something can replace active agency, although charismatic leader figures, charged by the embodiment of passionate intensity, have always led people to protest, to fight, to go to war, to kill and be killed (see Chapter 6 for a discussion of the production of political leadership).

The passion and frenzy of feeling that celebrity ignites and attaches itself to is part of a wider culture where sense and sensation, revelation and confession, outpouring and gossip have begun to shape the pulsating veins and arteries of everyday life (Berlant, 2011). Celebrity compels one to feel but such feeling may well be in the service of late capitalism and liquid modernity. As Ellis Cashmore powerfully contends in relation to Beyoncé, she:

> embodies a narrative, a living description of a culture in which race is a remnant of history and limitless consumer choice has become a substitute for equality ... The multiple products bearing her imprimatur and the revenue they generate suggest comparisons with a medium-size industry. Yet the most valuable product Beyoncé sells is a particular conception of America – as a nation where history has been, if not banished, rendered insignificant. Her ability to do so is predicated on her ethnic ambiguity: she claims to be 'universal', yet slides comfortably into a familiar discourse of exoticism essayed by earlier black female performers. A refusal to conform to existing categories combined with an insistence on the primacy of the market makes Beyoncé an exquisite commodity in a celebrity-fixated consumer culture although an unreliable indicator of black America.
>
> (2010: 140)

Emotional celebrity pricks people to feel but in limited ways, creating the conditions for the manufacturing of the neo-liberal self that restricts and channels one's egos so that we work well, consume well, reproduce well. Celebrity passion and commodity relations go hand-in-hand: the value transference crafted out of emotional appeal and short-form desire.

This is particularly true of the confessional mode of feeling since the revelation and outpouring serves as a form of the return of the repressed, letting out the carnival of emotions that might otherwise lead to wrack and ruin if left unchecked. The gendered nature of this will to emotional truth is often telling: the confession and its associated forms of gossip are 'female' centred, signified by dominant discourse to be inferior modes of expression, and that position women within patriarchal frames that limit their access to, and involvement with, the more serious, more 'rational' public world.

As Su Holmes and Dianne Negra (2011) further suggest, celebrity confessions around mental distress are heavily gendered, with women being marked out as essentially 'feminine' for speaking in the way they do. Emotional celebrity, then, is a Janus-faced creature: on the one hand, it creates the conditions for emotional attachment and engagement, on the other it attaches itself to gendered discourses that devalue those within its callings. This is all context based: emotional celebrity shifts its affecting ground to foreground emotion when it needs to, and to devalue or limit its reach when it threatens normative social and political relations. Too much emotional celebrity is presented as a bad thing, toxic in its impact and import.

There is something syncretic, then, in the way emotional celebrity operates, framed I would suggest between Apollonian and Dionysian forces – between restraint and reason and those impulses which are marked by their frenzy of feeling and vitality – which when brought together create the conditions for the production and consumption of fame to take place. Purchasing a celebrity-endorsed product is both a rational choice and the buying (into) of desire.

Nonetheless, to turn the feeling wheel one more time, emotional celebrity also leads to extreme forms of attachment and outpouring: ultimately, emotions cannot be simply tamed. The instances of stalking, the phenomena of celebrity worship syndrome, and erotomania point to the condition where an overinvestment in emotional celebrity threatens the stable self and undermines familial relations. In the age of liquid modernity where 'togetherness has been dismantled' (Bauman, 2000: 21), and social and emotional bonds have been largely rendered ephemeral, people are particularly susceptible to suffering, anguish and the pains of alienation. They long for connection and are implored that emotional attachment to celebrity figures is the answer. Celebrities become the emotional stream of the modern age, steeped in passion, wet with representations that are decidedly experiential, even if all is still held in the iron cage of liquid modern conditions.

As I have noted earlier, emotion and affect are related – if not simultaneous – phenomena. As Eric Shouse argues,

> it is important not to confuse affect with feelings and emotions ... Affect is not a personal feeling. Feelings are personal and biographical, emotions are social ... and affects are pre-personal ... An affect is a non-conscious experience of intensity; it is a moment of unformed and unstructured potential ... Affect cannot be fully realized in language ... because affect is always prior to and/or outside consciousness ... Affect is the body's way of preparing itself for action in a given circumstance by adding a quantitative dimension of intensity to the quality of

an experience. The body has a grammar of its own that cannot be fully captured in language.

(2005)

Affective celebrity, then, is not the same as personal feeling: it exists outside of language and representational discourse, and rises in somatic and asemiotic realms. Celebrity affect offers up a different set of intensified possibilities for those who employ cross-modal senses to feel beyond feeling. Ultimately, if one embraces the logic of sensation and the vibrations of affect in and through the figure of the celebrity, there is the opportunity to become animal, to be set free on the wild plains of modern life.

AFFECTIVE CELEBRITY TIME

For Deleuze, (cinema) history should not be understood as an organic process in which one traces its origins and developments to some inevitable, chronologically determined conclusion. Rather, it should be understood as that which arises from taxonomies or classificatory systems. For Deleuze, images and signs 'emerge in stratigraphic series, sedimented at unpredictable angles and betraying so many peculiar intersections' (Flaxman, 2000: 24). Deleuze's history of cinema, which borrows heavily from Foucault's work on genealogy, considers there to be two particular, articulating taxonomies of the film image in play, that between the articulable (discourse, statements, utterances) and the visible (made from, out of a plane of light and the machinery or screens of vision). Articulable cinema, found predominately in the movement image, in the first part of the 20th century, is rendered inherently or fully representational, in the service of representational cliché and narrative action that is causal (pre)determined. Diegetic sound and continuity editing fix the image, the narrative action, holding it in the grip of a power geometry that impoverishes free-radical thought and truth. By contrast, visible cinema, 'corresponds to the emergence of a new episteme' (Flaxman, 2000: 25), or the development of a culture that effortlessly produces 'light'. This new episteme emerged after the end of World War II.

For Deleuze, this flooding of light into the cinema world produces a break or disjuncture between the articulable (movement and action in film) and the visible, which because of its luminosity, its zero-degree possibilities, is or can be unhinged from the determinants of sensory-motor schema. After the end of World War II, in Europe particularly, Deleuze suggests that cinema gives birth to the time image (images of immanent light) in which what is said, spoken and acted upon is less important or determining than the overwhelming potential of the visible put before the viewer. In the time image film, narrative causation, chronology, the inevitable happy ending or hermeneutically sealed closure are not just decentred or denied but brought together and blended into multiple layers of time-orientated (in)action and free-floating images of time.

Deleuze argues that in the time-image film there are sheets of time which coexist between past and present, each sheet having its own characteristics. As he writes, 'the image has to be present and past, still present and already past, at once and at the same time ... The past does not follow the present that it is no longer, it coexists with the present it was' (1989: 79). Because the time image film emerges out of slices of time, cleaved into existence through discontinuity editing; because its visibility emerges in character silence, narrative ellipses and causal gaps, and out of multiple and impossible links and articulations, all of time (all of thought) can be found in those films that espouse this light. For Deleuze, this has radical potential since once the covenant between movement and time has been broken – once narrative logic has been washed away by time – the image can have an overwhelming truthfulness about it, allowing one to experience 'a thought that stands outside subjectivity' (Foucault, 1990: 15).

I would like to draw on two case studies to outline the affecting time of celebrity culture, where thought stands outside subjectivity, drawing on two distinct methods or approaches to do so: auto-ethnography and celebrity authorship. Both case studies use sensorial analysis to evidence how affecting celebrity experiences can be.

CASE STUDY 1

I need to dance with Ian Curtis

My approach to celebrity auto-ethnography is two-fold. First, it involves a call for scholars and practitioners to look closely at sensory aesthetics, and sensuous knowledge (Eagleton, 1990; Pink, 2009). This is because I take or start from the position that our encounters with celebrity are sensorial and multi-modal, involve joy and pleasure, and at their most heightened are asemiotic – activated in and through feeling alone. I also suggest that in these immersive encounters there exists the potential for the radicalisation of the body, or a type of becoming that creates the conditions to free the self from its normally constituted docility and entrapment. What I am calling sensing celebrity aesthetics isn't just then about the poetics of the celebrity figure; a call to analyse light, colour, dress, setting and non-representational signifiers. It is an approach also centrally concerned with recognising the politics of sensuous embodiment in which one can see in that intimate celebrity moment a liberating emergence of the carnal body (Sobchack, 2004).

Second, my approach involves the method of storying the self (Finnegan, 1997), where people are asked to recount their encounters with celebrity through memorial work and personal narratives. As noted in Chapter 1, these stories, however, are born from textural qualities; draw upon synaesthesia and co-synaesthetic relations. Again, this is something I have defined as involving self creating the celebaesthetic subject through the process of recounting and reliving the senses of celebrity identification (Redmond, 2014). This is what I think we should be interested in: the 'micro' stories that emerge from the consumption of celebrity culture; made in the moment of the lived experience, and which originate from what the person is feeling, going through and memoralising at that time in their life.

I story my life in part through celebrity figures I identify with. For example, my own Facebook feed is a testament to the way I story my feelings, memories and emotional state through my celebrity postings. You can see the schedule and programming of my moods, interests and obsessions through my Facebook celebrity stories. When I am blue and hurt and missing a lover, temporarily absent or perhaps long gone, I post songs and movie clips that speak that truth or which (secretly) connected us in some way. These are songs and memories that create in me a sea of synaesthetic affects – they wash my body in the memories they evoke. Celebrity threads – taut, loose and barely visible to the naked eye – emerge across the life of my page. When a particular affecting content hits my feed, or I find it elsewhere, I make sense of it in terms of my own biography. I story the stories I encounter, inserting myself into them, and they into my life (also see the David Bowie case study in Chapter 11).

These are not just macro stories, but micro-moments crystallised in terms of proximity and distance, self-worth and self-belonging, fleshed out of the sights, smells, spaces and places that the celebrity and I are found in. As such, a complex picture of my psychology emerges from exploring the storied detail contained in each feed and through the cross-fertilisation that is carried on continually in the tapestry that marks Facebook out as a site of the social media. The truth is that the uneven truth of my selfhood has begun to be storied on my Facebook celebrity postings. Let me now tell you an aesthetic auto-ethnographic story to charge my discussion with the intimate qualities I suggest this approach brings into the warm light of the day.

In the *Something Else* live footage of Joy Division playing Transmission, we witness the late Ian Curtis dance, dance, dance to the tune or guitar-driven noise of the titular track. Images or videos of damaged celebrities are always endowed with real power, particularly with a figure such as Ian who committed suicide, and whose biography was laced with pain and anguish. Ian was an anti-star, suffered from epilepsy and was involved in a traumatic relationship with his girlfriend of the time. This is the last and only nationally broadcast UK TV appearance by Joy Division and as such has been given reverential status by fans such as myself.

However, I think these anchoring frameworks that I have just supplied are not entirely necessary to get to the poetic sensibility of the live performance and its phenomenal star before us – that can be achieved through the work of celebrity aesthetics and aesthetic auto-ethnography.

The recording is a classic live piece studio set: the audience barely respond as they might do if this was a gig in a sweaty club in the industrial heartland of Northern England. However, there is a swaying as the song, the band's performance, builds and takes the audience over or under its spell. As the song starts up, the band turn in on itself, with a looking down and a focusing inwards, as if they are playing for and within themselves. This is a brooding, macabre performance supported by a track that is made up of only two or three chord changes but whose sonic and sonorous potential is, for me, simply overwhelming (see Figure 3.1).

The beat is relentless, the lyrics haunting and the vocals growl and harmonise in a frenetic discordant way. Ian, the front man, is of course

Figure 3.1 Lost in transmission
Image courtesy of Chris Mills/Redferns/Getty Images

the centre of attention, constantly returned to in medium or close up shot, his face full of anguish and unexplainable terror. It is his embodied performance that takes me to the heart of the matter since he seems to exist in a state of immanence and transcendence – an inner and outer physicality – that shatters the confines of his body and this (*my*) body lost in the transformative experience. This performance is all about sensuous impression and expressive feeling.

Vivian Sobchack suggests:

> That as lived bodies we are always grounded in the radical materialism of bodily immanence, in the here and now of our sensorial existence – and this no matter how different our cultural situations or differently organized and valued modes of making sense. However, as lived bodies, we always also have the capacity for transcendence: for a unique exteriority of being – an ex stasis – that locates us elsewhere and otherwise even as it is grounded in and tethered to our lived body's here and now. That is, our ontological capacity for transcendence emerges from and in our ontic immanence. This is an experience of transcendence in immanence.
>
> (2008: 200)

Ian's hypnotic performance demonstrates this capacity for simultaneous immanence and transcendence; he is angular and thin, initially static and controlled and yet already caught by the music, the song, as he begins to sway; emote, slightly feverish in his appearance. His eyes remain half-closed, crescent shaped and his eyeballs roll.

He is an affecting and affected body on the stage. Of course, as the music builds and the chorus repeats, as the song and music take a tighter grip on him (and him on the song, the music, the vocal delivery), he seems less present rather than more. It feels as if he is not really on the stage, in the room with us at all, but has been taken to a higher truth, to a new plane of experience and existence.

This of course becomes the sensorial appreciation of the Ian Curtis dance: jagged, discordant, agitated, aggressive but thoughtless, only felt, lived as if it is a becoming minor in the Deleuzean sense, in the flood and flow of the music. Ian sings/shouts 'there is no language, just sound, that's all we need to know, to synchronise love to the beat of the show'.

I *sense* that for him, music and the dance he devotes to it are an asemiotic encounter in which the constraints and conditioning of the body have been left behind, transcended, transgressed. I experience the clip/the song/Ian in the same way – as a sensuous aesthetic, and composed of blocs of sensation. This for me is an intensive experience, a radical becoming in which the immanent me is transcended.

For Deleuze, a minor literature is not one that belongs to a marginal or marginalised group, and neither is it a literature that exists outside the dominant canon. Minor literature subverts and recasts dominant language to create new potential and new possibilities in the very act of making-meaning. As Bogue notes, for Deleuze these shimmering 'lines of flight',

> Involves a certain kind of becoming: becoming-imperceptible. Becoming-imperceptible is a process of elimination whereby one divests oneself of all coded identity and engages in the abstract lines of a non-organic life, the immanent, virtual lines of continuous variation that play through discursive regimes of signs and nondiscursive machinic assemblages alike.
>
> (2004: 73)

In short, minor literature generates a type of experience that breaks through the normative and conventional, creating what Deleuze calls 'the virtual' (2005). This is what I sense is happening in Ian's performance and in my own responsive becoming minor. I danced with Ian Curtis and became something more or less virtual.

This becoming minor resonates with my own troubled sense of alienation and loneliness that has haunted me for as long as I can remember. Even when surrounded by friends, sitting with a pretty girl, or on a high after a successful presentation, I can feel terribly alone. I call this my loneliness room (Redmond, 2014). I have rarely felt comfortable in my own skin, and so Ian provides me with a form of embodiment that stings me, enwraps me and sets me free, free, free.

Sensing celebrities involves recognition of the way complimentary sensory-based elements come together to create, produce and transmit levels of affect and intensities. The approach recognises the cross-modal nature of identification, and the way the body readily escapes its own docility and entrapment. I see transgressive and positive outcomes from the way the celebaesthetic subject operates and have used the example of dancing with Ian Curtis to anchor the way resistance is brought into corporeal being.

We escape through, in and within celebrity, and not through some fantasy mechanism or para-social fakery. We escape because our bodies and their senses are activated in intense and affecting ways that cannot be simply used up or be recuperated by dominant ideology. We escape because the conditions of our existence demand it of us even as they attempt to regulate us and control us. In sensing celebrities, we can get beyond the constraints and impositions of ideology and discourse, finding new ways to be in the world.

Julia Kristeva (writing about contemporary installations at the Venice Biennale) suggests that:

> In an installation it is the body in its entirety which is asked to participate through its sensations, through vision obviously, but also hearing, touch, and on occasions smell. As if these artists, in the place of an object sought to place us in a space at the limits of the sacred, and asked us not to contemplate images but to communicate with beings. I had the impression, she writes, that [the artists] were communicating this: that the ultimate aim of art is perhaps what was formerly celebrated

under the term of incarnation. I mean by that a wish to make us feel, through the abstractions, the forms, the colours, the volumes, the sensations, a *real experience*.

(Quoted in Bann, 1998: 69)

This I would like to suggest might be the project of celebrity affects: to see it as (one of) its functions: to activate our intensive register, to reconnect us in new and profound and perhaps liberating ways with the world. Further, it involves the recognition that the power of employing aesthetic auto-ethnography rests with its ability to give people the space to tell their own stories and to express their connection with celebrity through the shimmering streams of feeling. This approach necessarily resists a top-down model where an ideological and cultural reading is simply imposed upon texts and audiences and fans.

There are moments in time and space, and in the arteries and veins of the everyday and the everywhere, where we can escape the ideological conditions under which we normally exist. The celebaesthetic encounter with the celebrity can produce such immanent and transcendent moments.

CASE STUDY 2

Starring affective Takeshi Kitano

Takeshi Kitano/Beat Takeshi occupies a vexing position when it comes to the question of stardom and celebrity. As film-art auteur and troubled multi-talented genius or *tensai*, he is a feted, auratic figure of fame. As film star Beat Takeshi, he is typed to play certain explosive roles tinged with pathos and melancholy and when these roles are circumnavigated, this 'problematic fit' extends the semiotic and affective reach of his star image. As game show host, he is a television personality or celebrity, more ordinary and immediate than extraordinary and lasting, to paraphrase John Ellis's (2007) problematic distinction between the film star and the television personality. As *Brand Kitano* he exists in the slipstream of his films, books, art, promotional and television work. Office Kitano is where the real hard work of movie deals, endorsements and contract negotiations is done. That all these Kitanos may make different sense to different audiences, both in Japan and internationally, adds one final liquid ingredient to the multi-dimensional, split persona that emerges, converges and dissipates itself.

Christine Geraghty (2007) has usefully located three categories through which stars generate meaning. First, there is the 'Star-as-celebrity', who is primarily represented in terms of their leisure pursuits and lifestyle, and who 'literally interacts with those from other areas'. The star-celebrity exists in the public arena and this is what primarily interests us about them. Second, there is the 'Star-as-professional', or the individual who plays to type, their star signification sustaining itself as a form of pleasure and attachment. The star vehicle promises one a particular type of performance, whether it is heroic action, slapstick comedy or idealised romantic coupling. Third, there is the 'Star-as-performer', marked by an emphasis on 'impersonation', improvisation and method acting; on a distinction between star and role which is effaced in the 'star-as-professional' category. The actor-star builds a performance out of the demands of their piece; their fame built on their greatness as actors and (often) on the diversity of the roles they take. While Geraghty recognises the articulations or links between these three categories, it is David P Marshall who draws them together to recognise their full importance in liquid modern times:

> From an industrial as well as cultural vantage point, celebrities are integral for understanding the contemporary moment. As phenomena, celebrities intersect with a remarkable array of political, cultural and economic activities to a threshold point that it is worth identifying the operation of a *celebrity culture* embedded in national and transnational cultures [emphasis in original].
>
> (2006: 6)

Kitano, as I will now go on to argue, pours in and between these categories, a watery movement which ultimately confirms him as a star of anomie and a brand of pathos ultimately in tune with an out-of-tune world. Kitano(s) is a supericonic, affecting image of these troubled contemporary times.

Kitano's affective images

In the introduction to *Heavenly Bodies*, Richard Dyer sets up the dual hypothesis that firstly, 'images have to be made. Stars are produced by the media industries, film stars by Hollywood (or its equivalent in other countries)' and secondly, star images relate to 'notions of personhood and social reality'. Dyer suggests that it is only through combining textual and intertextual analysis of stars with an understanding of the ideological and historical contexts in which they emerge that one can make sense of their fascination for audiences and their power to affect ordinary people's lives. As Dyer writes:

> Stars articulate what it is to be human being in contemporary society; that is, they express the particular notion we hold of the person, of the 'individual'. They do so complexly, variously – they are not straight-forward affirmations of individualism. On the contrary, they articulate both the promise and the difficulty that the notion of individuality presents for all of us who live by it.
>
> (1997: 10)

Let me begin, then, with a textual and intertextual image-based analysis of Kitano's star self (although even this is tricky because there are always multiple Takeshi Kitanos to contend with). Nonetheless, in one key respect, he seems to reverse the usual trajectory for how a film's star image is born. With a long history in popular entertainment, and with the brash, vulgar comedy persona of Beat Takeshi cemented in the Japanese cultural imagination, his first serious starring role in *Merry Christmas Mr Lawrence* (Ôshima, 1983) was viewed as a 'problematic fit', one which fazed parts of the Japanese audience. They struggled to take his performance as a brutal prison camp officer seriously, his comedian persona standing in the way of their ability to suspend their disbelief. That Takeshi Kitano had to re-birth, refashion Beat Takeshi – as a brooding, silent, exacting man of violent action and anomic desire – was a conscious project to cleave him(self) into different roles and embodiments.

If we take the Beat Takeshi film star persona as being built out of a split with his television personality, one can discern a collision between alternative versions of the entertainer/artist. Daisuke Miyao (2004) argues that the gap that exists between the two Kitanos is one that draws attention to the difference that exists between cinema (cinephelia) and television (telephilia). Miyao concludes rather apocalyptically that telephilia elided this gap with Takeshi Kitano becoming just 'another television personality', although this is a position that I will now take issue with.

John Ellis (2007: 93) argues that 'the star is at once ordinary and extraordinary, available for desire and unattainable. This paradox is repeated and intensified in cinema by the regime of presence-yet absence that is the filmic image'. In this way, the 'this is was' nature of the star 'awakens a series of psychic mechanisms which involve various impossible images', including 'the narcissistic experience of the mirror phase'. Ellis then goes on to set up his position on television fame, which he considers to be that much more present or immediate than cinema stardom. For Ellis, television presents the viewer with,

> Personality ... someone who is famous for being famous, and is famous only in so far as he or she makes frequent television appearances ... In some ways, they are the opposite of stars, agreeable voids rather than sites of conflicting meanings.
>
> (2007: 96)

While one can clearly take issue with Ellis's position, particularly since television is increasingly cinematic and visual technologies have converged with specific regards to Kitano, one can readily see the film/television, star/personality dichotomy manifesting itself in Kitano's divided persona. Takeshi Kitano fashions films in which the past/present/future potential of the Kitano star image is brought into full view and where the associated awakenings and new becomings that the viewer experiences in front of such forceful sites of identification emerge. The black-suited, dark shade-wearing and phallic-smoking active male that defines Beat the film star is the perfect(ed) personification of idealised masculine identity. The spontaneous, improvised performer that fleshes a character together in the moment is a necessary indicator of the authentic artist/actor wrapped around the star. That Beat Takeshi, the lightweight, mouthy television comedian and game show host also haunts this film star image, is part of the intertextual relay that gives further definition or a depth of crisis to the persona.

In the body of Beat Takeshi, fat comedian meets muscular anti-hero; slapstick, foul-mouthed humour meets dramatic performer; void meets depth; language meets silence and irony meets pathos. However, what is required of this body is to deny, while not being able to fully suppress, its television, celebrity half. In the body of Beat Takeshi is a struggle between the minoritarian (alternative, oppositional) film star-artist and the majoritarian (mass-produced) TV host. Of course, there is a third entity occupying the Beat Takeshi body, that of the director Takeshi Kitano. However, this possession may very well manifest itself in the head space, in the Takeshi stare, of the Beat Takeshi body.

The Beat Takeshi stare

One can argue that the Kitano film is often a star vehicle for Beat Takeshi. The narrative is organised to enable him to display his star qualities – a setting/situation is arranged so that he can 'perform' his attributes and qualities. The character type that Beat Takeshi plays 'fits' the star image he brings with him to the text, while the aesthetic dimensions of the film enable him to be lit, dressed and staged in recognisable ways. I have earlier commented on the Beat Takeshi walk, the facial tic and the iconography employed to fashion his hard-bodied, silent and quick-to-react, anti-hero persona. Now I would like to examine the Beat Takeshi stare, since its penetration and silence make it a particular affecting source of his star signification and of the body that lies beyond the constructed gaze.

While in nearly all of his films' characters are found staring at the camera, in a dislocated form of direct address, or into space, at some-one, some thing, or some 'memory' off-screen, the Takeshi stare is of a particularly intense form. This is in part because the weight of his star image bears down upon the look. The viewer comes to recognise this stare as inter-subjective, memorial and one that is caught looking deeply into things; at the past, future (including one's own death) and at parallel events it is not possible for it to be present at.

In *Boiling Point*, the Kitano stare punctuates the narrative with a searing intensity that destabilises temporal and spatial continuity. Four inter-connected scenes are pulled into affective power through the dead-look that Kitano directs at the camera. While on the way to get even with a yakuza mob, the hand-held camera takes up a position in the car that enables it to capture Uehara/Takeshi staring back at it, or into the imagined space it possibly represents. It is the cold, emo-tionless stare we have become used to, but here it is rendered alien by the discordant, otherworldly, non-diegetic sound that enters the shot. This triggers the rapidly edited dream or death prophecy sequence that itself includes two direct address shots. Later, in the field of flowers, Lion-man Uehara silently waits in the 'forest' to take his prey when the time comes: the direct address positions us as the lambs ready for the slaughter. This is directly followed by a cut to the car, stationary, with Uehara again staring deep into space, surrounded by the flowers he has picked. The reflections in and off the windscreen, however, place irregular patterns between him and the viewer-camera. Finally, in the scene where he takes vengeance on the yakuza mob, Kitano stares right into the retina of the lens and guns it down; a murderous, bloody gaze that the previous three sequences have prepared us for – death at the face of Kitano.

The Beat Takeshi stare is given impossible qualities, a vision capability in fact very like that of the film director, a blink of his eye registering like the cut between shots. The controlling look of Takeshi Kitano finds its way into Beat Takeshi's god-like view of events. And yet, Beat Takeshi often seems unable to control events but rather accidentally or inadvertently causes their happening and the death and violence that usually ensue. It is as if the director is pulling the strings of the puppet Beat Takeshi and this adds to his pathos. As Kitano himself suggested: 'I'm having fun with Beat Takeshi and Kitano Takeshi. If I'm asked who I am, I can only answer, "I'm the man who plays Beat Takeshi and Kitano Takeshi"' (Gerow, 2007: 3).

There is a self-destructive quality to the Takeshi stare; it is a pathetic, violent, remorseful look, and consequently and in addition, it carries the inherent violence of the cinema machine and the work of the film director into or out of the retina of his/their eye. Abe Kasho (2000) argues that Takeshi Kitano is actually breaking down the body of the television comedian Beat Takeshi so that the pathetic cinematic character can emerge. Beat Takeshi's blindness or partial vision, and his silence, is a sadistic gagging order imposed by the director. Beat Takeshi's waywardness is a rebellious snub to the 'cultured' director.

There is also a cold intimacy about the Beat look, particularly when aimed at the viewer. Its despair, found in one film after another, layering his brooding star persona, attempts to symbiotically resonate or connect at the level of anomic dissatisfaction that many viewers live through in the modern world. In fact, Beat Takeshi's dead-beat stare does not singularly emerge from his being, or that of the director, but is also a rebound look from the pathetic stares viewers throw at him when immersed in the film world. The viewer enters the text through the familiar eyes of Beat Takeshi and this vibrates throughout the looking regime of the film. The filmic world acts upon the viewer and the viewer acts upon/in the events of the film and these film-world-events are infused with pathos and death. Beat Takeshi cannot stand (the pain of) us looking at him while we feel the pain image intensely as it is thrown back at us. The blind Zatoichi is the result of Beat Takeshi not being able to bear looking on the world, or to see the viewer looking on him so mournfully. As I have argued before, these intense exchanges foster or cleave into existence an out-of-body experience. But why, how does the star Beat Takeshi achieve this god-/anti-god-like affect on fans of his work? Is it simply a matter of charisma?

Charisma of anomie

Takeshi Kitano/Beat Takeshi is often written about in the popular press as having cool charisma, or an auratic presence that is special, unique and which naturally reveals itself in interviews and on camera. It is said that the charismatic Takeshi lights up the screen, and it is this supposed essential quality that fans are attracted to. Charisma, of course, is actually a mythic construct, in the service of dominant ideology, and 'is effective especially when the social order is uncertain, unstable and ambiguous and when the charismatic figure or group offers a value, order or stability to counterpoise this' (Dyer, 1997: 31). Charismatic figures emerge most forcefully in times of social and political crisis. They are cohesive types who help paper over ideological and political differences and inequalities and cultural shifts that have grown too large, and they are reliant on ordinary people to strongly invest in the message, art or campaign that the charismatic figure champions.

For example, Richard Dyer uses the star charisma of Marilyn Monroe, in particular her sexual chemistry and naïve innocence, to show how she 'seemed to be the very tensions that run through the ideological life of 50s America' (1997: 31). More recently, I have suggested that Barack Obama represented a type of fusion charisma figure that attempted to connect with liquid moderns lost in the world, politics being the last refuge for cultural and political re-birth (see Chapter 6 for a discussion of this). I would now like to argue that Takeshi Kitano/ Beat Takeshi's charismatic authority can be read in a similar way, but his affect is one that derails, to a degree, the dominant order rather than shoring it up. I will further break down the key constituents of his charismatic persona, looking at his suggested 'genius' and performative pathology or 'damage' as the way in which these intense relationships are made good. Kitano's charisma is one composed of anomie.

Womanly Kitano genius

Takeshi Kitano/Beat Takeshi has all the traits or characteristics of the romantic artist and, perhaps less obviously, 'tortured genius'. His abilities extend across a range of art forms: painting, poetry, literature, journalism, film and television. As the press notes for *Hana-Bi* remind us, in 1995 Kitano,

> was back hosting six network shows, writing six regular columns for national magazines and a sports newspaper and releasing his fifth film, the comedy *Minna Yatteruka? (Getting Any?)* ... He also writes poetry, essays, and serious novels and has published fifty-five books. Kitano took up painting after his accident and has created hundreds of striking artworks, including those featured in *Fireworks*. He also acts in films for other directors — most recently in Robert Longo's *Johnny Mnemonic* and Takashi Ishii's *Gonin*. He also starred in the film adaptation of his novel, *Many Happy Returns (Kyoso Tanjo)* (1993) a satire of Japanese religious cults.
>
> (1997: 8)

His artistic method is said to be spontaneous and volatile, particularly when it comes to film direction and the rehearsal stage of a shoot. Kitano generally works with a minimal script, characters grow or reduce in the rehearsal space, dependent on the interaction and quality of performances that emerge, and shooting is itself a rapid process with Kitano favouring a one-take regime. This knowledge we have of Kitano's working method, filtered through interviews, press-packs and Kitano's own autobiographical accounts of his life, acts as an indicator of his desire to capture the essence or quality he is after at each and every moment of his creative life. Biographical accounts add to the artistic depth and mystique that surround Kitano. We learn that he is haunted personally, and that he had a difficult upbringing: there was little money in the house and his father a drunk who beat his mother, both perhaps indicators of his chronic sense of failure. We know that Kitano underwent a transformative recovery from a near-fatal motorcycle accident, taking up painting, a pursuit triggered by his seeing/sensing/smelling flowers differently as if for the very first time.

One can read these accounts as the meeting place where public/professional and private/personal commentary fuses to render him an artistic star-genius who lives on/past the edge of psychological normativity. In terms of this alignment between public and private persona, the roles he takes are of pathetic men, often suicidal, always anguished and nearly all on the verge, or past the point, of nervous, emotional exhaustion. This can be read as a manifestation of his real self. As Stephen Harper suggests,

> Today, as in the Renaissance and Romantic periods, mental illness is a token of both public greatness and private vulnerability; the celebrity, that most visible of attractions, is always imperilled by mental illness, 'the most solitary of afflictions'.
>
> (2006: 314)

Celebrity genius, this most solitary of afflictions, is gender encoded, as Harper goes on to demonstrate. On the one hand, the qualities and conditions of extraordinary talent are understood to be both masculine and feminine. On the other, the struggle for recognition and the troubles one faces on the road to acceptance are marked by heroic, triumphant becoming for male geniuses and 'tragedy, melodrama and hysteria' for female artists. Harper points us to the various portrayals of Jackson Pollock and Sylvia Plath to illustrate his point that men overcome their psychological afflictions to claim their right as geniuses, while flowering female artists implode emotionally, an ultimate full-stop to their talent. I would like to take a moment to consider these articulations in relation to Takeshi Kitano/Beat Takeshi, since I see them operating in/through the complexities of his divided persona, so that his 'genius' is marked by a border crossing and a pathos that becomes its over-determining characteristic.

Takeshi Kitano/Beat Takeshi's journey to feted auratic artist closely follows a rags-to-riches trajectory laced with masculinist sentiments. Kitano came from a working-class background, was a rebel at school, dropped out from university, and took what looked like a string of dead-end jobs, including 'janitor, waiter, airport baggage handler, taxi driver and finally elevator operator in the France-za burlesque theater in the Asakusa entertainment district of Tokyo' (in an interview with Makota Shinozaki, 1997). Of course, as these 'inevitable' becoming-star narratives prophesise, Kitano got his first break at the theatre when he asked to step in for the partner of Beat Kiyoshi (Kiyoshi Kaneko). The two clicked together and a new *manzai* comedy act was born: *Tsuu Biito* or *Two Beats*. They worked the strip clubs and the theatres, until Beat Takeshi's big break in television came. Success followed success, as his portfolio of skills grew, until he was asked to step into direct *Violent Cop*, each 'break' of course read subsequently as the recognition of the latent talent that was burning within him.

In fact, the movement from low-brow, mass-orientated art or media forms, to the high art of non-conventional, genre-breaking cinema, is seen as an inevitable result of Kitano's artistic vision. All three of the elements that Richard Dyer argues go into making the star success myth work are in play here: 'that ordinariness is the hallmark of the star'; that the system rewards talent and 'specialness'; and that 'hard work and professionalism are necessary for stardom' (1998: 42). Takeshi Kitano/Beat Takeshi seems to be the very embodiment of successful individualism, a *tarento*, who emerged in Japan's consumerist-driven economy proving as he did so the country's own success as an inventive, liquid capitalist nation state. Nonetheless, that Kitano consistently wrestles with this becoming-special, with the ideology of the success myth, can be read as a desire to challenge the status quo and to move beyond representational cliché. He does this through becoming a woman, becoming an animal, becoming a minoritarian.

Takeshi Kitano/Beat Takeshi's embodiment of his artistic talent seems to be one that has feminine and masculine qualities although the auto-destruction that regularly inhabits the characters he plays is a particularly feminine version of the tortured soul who cannot bear their life anymore. It is clear that the brute force of the characters Beat Takeshi plays is crafted out of phallic, masculine elements; and that his parallel wallowing and pathos is of feminine composition. The pathos that wraps itself around Kitano's film work, and Beat Takeshi in particular, is one usually confined to, or conferred on, genres or characters of low status; women in melodramas, for example. I have argued that his films offer viewers the chance to become a woman as instances of drag, mask and masquerade regularly take over his work, and take over/on the body of Beat Takeshi. There is also a queer impulse or intensity to his work, to Beat Takeshi's homoerotic and masochistic tendencies. In the wounding of the/his body, in the blood-spill that follows, one becomes, or rather one *is*, animal. In the star becoming woman and animal, in the border crossings that take place when Kitano silently weeps and kills, there is an intense recognition of his/our molecular, salty and fleshy and wet and red being-in-the-world. As Patricia MacCormack explains,

> Becoming is the entering into a participation with specific molecular intensities of another element. Becoming is neither an imitation where we act like, nor a creation of a new Oedipal or capital family where we belong within a hierarchical structure of a different genealogy. Becoming selects certain specificities and intensities of a thing and dissipates those intensities within our own molecularities to redistribute ourselves. We select a term and by opening to affectuations of forces of that term become a hybrid anomaly, a unique mingling.
>
> (2008: 92)

Takeshi Kitano/Beat Takeshi's unique self-Other co-mingling, the liquid confusion at the centre of his star/artist/personality persona, and the suffering he goes through in his films, is one based on marginal identity and minority becoming. Textually, then, Kitano's films challenge the very substance of the success myth, and of the trajectory of his own becoming-star. Through the dissolution of the star-artist body, through the womanly and the animalistic, and through the alien alterity that wraps itself around everything, one gets to sense, to experience a body beyond language, beyond the docility and disappointment which it is usually rooted in. Kitano's sadism is matched by his masochism; the violence he puts out is itself put back into his body as it is pummelled, and turned into a pain image. Kitano does not simply beat up on his star selves, however, but on stardom and celebrity, and on liquid capitalism itself.

One can read the Haruna/Nukui/Aoki sequence from *Dolls* as a critical engagement with celebrity culture and the faulty para-social relationships it produces. Haruna only experiences the world through her celebrity self, while Nukui and Aoki only find pleasure or communion in the world through the figure of Haruna and the fan-tribes that emerge around her performances and output. Haruna cannot face the real world when her celebrity status is taken away. Nukui (Tsutomu Takeshige) and Aoki (Al Kitago) struggle to live in a (mediated) world without the celebrity image of Haruna to connect with. They were blinded by her 'love' before her car accident and Nukui blinds himself so that he can carry on the imagined connection that he (now) thinks they share. This is an extreme form of fan journeying and worship. That these engagements end in tragedy is a sign of the liquid nature of the celebrity and the liquefying condition of modern living. One can read Haruna in *Dolls*, then, as the empty body of commodity celebrity as it manifests in contemporary Japan. She is a mediated, para-social entity, whose manufactured performance lacks depth or meaning. Her blindness is the blindness of contemporary commodity life itself. For Kitano, of course, Haruna resonated with his own sense of celebrity following his motorcycle accident:

> Obviously her story parodies my own experience after the motorcycle accident. There were celebrities and fans in Chikamatsu's time too, and his plays suggest that the liaisons between idols and their fans were even more extreme than they are nowadays. Anyhow, like everything else in the film, the notion of a fan blinding himself to spare the feelings of his idol is caricature. It's the relationship between a celebrity and a fan as seen by a Chikamatsu doll.
>
> (Rayns, 2003)

Nonetheless, by the time Kitano makes *Takeshis*, the notion of a fan (the star-actor) going berserk is played out with telling significance. The idea that the mass media is very doll-like, and that celebrity culture produces dolls and doll-like fans, is a powerful one and connects to the damage that fame can do.

This connection between fame, damage and identification finds itself more directly circulating in the Takeshi Kitano/Beat Takeshi persona, a damage that senses itself into and out of the anomic world from which he and his fans materialise. Chris Rojek suggests that the sense of loss and disconnect can help to explain the appeal of celebrities to audiences in such atomised societies:

> In societies in which as many as 50 per cent of the population confess to sub-clinical feelings of isolation and loneliness, para-social interaction is a significant aspect of the search for recognition and belonging.
> (2001: 52)

The celebrity is incorporated into a fan's worldview so that they feel they belong and can readily connect to the social centre.

Kitano damage

Richard Dyer has argued in relation to Hollywood stars that the wealth and visibility that fame brings are often shown to have a destructive, dark side: 'Consumption can be characterised as wastefulness and decadence, while success may be short-lived or a psychological burden' (1997: 44). Stars can be said to be damaged by their success; their elevation in status taking them away from their humble backgrounds, while their God-complex isolates and alienates them from the real world. In this nether region of unhappy-happy existence they turn to drink, drugs, even suicide to help them escape the loneliness of their lives. As I have argued elsewhere, this corrosive type of fame is said to offer the star or celebrity too much of everything that is vacuous and surface level, and very little of the intimate, the psychologically deep or the long-lasting. Stardom destroys their ability to be happy and contented (Redmond, 2006). While the damaged star is of course as much a mythic construction as the contented figure of fame, their inability to cope, their all-too-visible failure as stars, resonates in ways that have a profound effect/affect on those who are similarly placed in the cultural world.

The alienated, burnt-out star, marginalised by the media and abandoned by a great body of their fans, exists in a realm of exclusion, of inverted Otherness, that is familiar to the minoritarian individual who has similarly been marked as a failure and who consequently exists outside of dominant social networks. While the star is trapped in the 'artifice' of fame and infamy, the minoritarian is caged in the 'reality' of material inequality and social exclusion. What can emerge from such damaged mirrors of likeness is a more symbiotic, inter-dependent affecting connectivity that runs its power in, through and across the wounded bodies of the star and the minoritarian. The damaged star and the failing (in life) anomic fan share their pain in confessional acts that resonate at the carnal level of being-in-the-world. These are often the most intimate if seemingly destructive of sensory exchanges, since again as I have argued elsewhere, they are expressed in suicide diaries and notes (Kurt Cobain, Lesley Cheung), cut into the flesh (Richie Edwards), sung out in heartfelt revelation (Judy Garland, Elvis Presley, Rhianna) or directly observed in verifiable mental breakdowns (Ian Holm, Adam Ant). This embodied intimacy or intensity of loss, alienation and death directly accesses the life force of the minoritarian.

In Richard Dyer's reading of Judy Garland, for example, she emerges as a crisis figure who had 'a special relationship to suffering' (1986: 143), a 'gay sensibility' (154) that gay men particularly identified with. When Judy Garland sings there is an 'intensity and irony' (ibid) to the performance that reverberates from the body of the screen into the bodies of gay men; a connection so profound that it feels exactly like the marginalisation they face in the world. In a similar vein, 'Kitano's works can be considered an alternative realism, one that, in films like *Violent Cop* or *Kids Return*, shows the true corruption or hopelessness of post-war life' (Gerow, 2007: 31).

Takeshi Kitano/Beat Takeshi is not exactly a figure of fame damage, at least not in terms of his 'public', extra-diegetic persona. He is incredibly successful, wealthy and grounded. Nonetheless, there is enough of a story of personal crisis to begin to suggest an access point for the disaffected. When one considers the disaffected, suicidal characters he plays, this opening multiplies exponentially and forcefully. However, it is the articulation between all three classifications of the star that Geraghty outlines which I think pulls his persona into the liquid spill of modern life and living. Kitano is a star-celebrity, he exists as a celebrated public figure, subject to constant media scrutiny. Kitano is a star-professional, his star image cemented in role choice and type, although this extends to encompass his directorial fame. Kitano is a star-performer, an actorly star that brings 'method' and improvisation to the parts he plays and consequently a heightened authenticity. Kitano's star-celebrity-professional-performer image is born of damage; he is critical of celebrity culture and has attempted to kill his own ulterior celebrity self (television comedian Beat Takeshi); his star image is crafted out of playing alien alterities, sociopaths and men-women gripped by pathos; his acting is 'real', revelatory or confessional, and comes from deep, interior forces that lie within his body; and he is a minoritarian, sadistic director who attempts to get his star self to self-destruct, if only to become animal, to become woman.

CHAPTER SUMMARY

This chapter has explored the affective and affecting streams that celebrity culture is digested in. It stands in sharp contrast to a fully representational reading of fame, demonstrating the need to look at story, feeling and affective connectivity. However, it is not the book's intention to set representation against affect, but to place them on top of one another. This layering of sheets is not static, like two pages of paper placed on top of each other, but is dynamic, like moving tectonic plates always in contact but not necessarily aligned. The examples used take us from the micro stories of ethnography to the macro constituents of a filmmaking auteur.

4

(POST)MODERN IDENTITIES AND CELEBRITY SELFHOOD

We have already seen in the last two chapters how matted or wedded representation and affect are to questions of identity. The book is charged by the dynamic forces in play between cultures and senses, as well as their collisions and divisions. In this chapter we explicitly look at the way celebrity and identity work in the circuit of celebrity culture.

DEFINING IDENTITY

Within the sociological and cultural studies traditions, identity is argued to be composed of who we think we are and how (we think) others see us. Identity always seems to be both a matter of two inter-active ingredients. First, identity is a form of social agency whereby people exercise a degree of free choice about the way they self-present themselves to the world (what they wear, their body idioms), the way they choose to identify with a set of values and ideas, and the deci-sions they exercise to belong to certain groups or sub-cultures. Sec-ond, identity is a matter of imposition, whereby certain identities are given or ascribed to individuals. People are classified on a daily basis as occupying certain subjectivities, embodying certain types of identity because of their social class, gender, race, sexuality, occupation and age. These frameworks that identities sit within are called *classificatory systems* and they permeate every area of the social world.

A sense of one's identity is therefore constructed from the relationship between individual autonomy and the labelling, regulating and manufacturing of identity through the significant others people interact with; the discourses found in the media, education and bio-medical practices; and the wider cultural material out of which representations flourish. Nonetheless, the degree of autonomy or power that one has to shape one's own identity is not equal: some people have much more power to shape their own identities because of the prejudices and limitations that operate within and across classificatory systems.

The politics of identity is best understood as establishing difference, as a process where borders are put up or markers are put down between the 'I' and the 'you'. As Kath Woodward summarises,

> Often identity is most clearly defined by difference, that is by what it is not. Identities may be marked by polarisation, for example in the most extreme forms of national or ethnic conflict, and by the marking of inclusion or exclusion – insiders and outsiders, 'us' and 'them'. Identities are frequently constructed in terms of oppositions such as man/ woman, black/white, straight/gay, healthy/unhealthy, normal/deviant.
> (1997: 2)

People establish their differences through symbols, signs, rituals and everyday social practices. One's own sense of identity makes sense only because it is constantly related to those things that one *doesn't* identify with, which one will not allow into a sense of self. By establishing borders, people try to fix their identity, to give it some essential and anchored quality. This is an attempt to keep at bay the sense that identity is inherently in-flight and that one is not lacking something at the core drives of the self. For example, the borders and boundaries one tries to construct – and which are impressed upon the individual by discourse – might *essentialise* their gender, class, race and ethnicity. Historically, identity has felt like it has had this stability or trans-historical quality to it. People draw on stories of the imagined nation state to suggest something historical and binding between the citizens who live there. Film stars, of course, are often caught up in helping 'bind' the identity of the nation state, as the case study on Russell Crowe at the end of this chapter attests to.

Identity is never fixed or unitary: it is, as Stuart Hall argues, multi-dimensional, fluid and always in process, 'a matter of becoming' (1997). Every single day people walk in and out of particular subject positions and they can be occupying more than one subject position simultaneously. Even the way people occupy these subject positions changes from day-to-day: one can be a daughter, mother, partner, business executive, amateur singer within a shifting set of role-based contexts. However, when such fluidity comes to feel like it is over-determining – so people can no longer recognise themselves as a complete identity – it can be emotionally disturbing, unsettling. For postmodernists, in fact, identity is now perpetually in a state of crisis because it is fractured and dislocated and the meta-narratives that used to give people sustenance are no longer believed in (such as religious faith in the West). People supposedly live in an age of postmodern angst, of identity dislocation. They no longer know who they are or what they should become, or what the world expects them to be. As Kobena Mercer suggests,

> In political terms, identities are in crises because traditional structures of membership and belonging inscribed in relations of class, party and nation-state have been called into question.
>
> (1994: 424)

Similarly, for Lacanians people walk this earth in lack, searching for the unified self they imagine they were before the so-called mirror stage, when they were at one with their mothers. Nonetheless, when people speak about their identity, they generally either revert to essentialised notions of what they are, drawing on their cultural heritage, the collective imagined past they share with people/groups they identify with, to solidify their selfhood; or else, they will see themselves as fractured and in-flight, needing to gravitate to such entities as stars and celebrities to find root and branch.

IDENTITY AND CONSUMPTION

Jean Baudrillard argues that in the Western world the dominant mode of communication is in and through the language of consumption:

> marketing, purchasing, sales, the acquisition of differentiated commodities and objects/signs – all of these presently constitute our language, a code, in which our entire society communicates and speaks of and to itself.
>
> (1988: 44)

While this is a contentious position to take, especially given the recent, often violent, backlash against the brand, one can see how the language and motor of consumption have become increasingly central to the way the economy functions, and to how individual identities are formed, taken up and resisted. Identity is increasingly purchased and connected to consumption practices and consumption agencies. These commodity identities are connected to consuming culture, wearing culture, living in 'design culture' environments. The role of so-called 'cultural intermediaries' (Bourdieu, 1984), or those who are employed to positively represent goods and services, is central here.

Cultural intermediaries 'lifestyle' products so that they symbolically 'speak' to people about their place and position in the world. They are 'most frequently found in the media, fashion, advertising and design industries' (du Gay, 1997: 62) and attempt to give functional artefacts a symbolic form. Through the language of advertising and marketing, cultural intermediaries attempt to create 'identification between consumer and product' (ibid: 65).

This identification centrally hangs on fantasy networks, where symbolic goods are imagined to transform the identity of the consumer in ways that enrich, empower or improve their lives. Cultural intermediaries fill functional goods with ideological meaning that both efface the 'reality' of how the product came into being (in a factory, for example) and the 'reality' as it is (and will be) really lived by the consumer. As Lauren Langman argues:

> Everyday life has been transformed into an extension of consumer capitalism and the person rendered a consumer or spectator in whom the

commodified meanings, the symbolic and addictive values embedded in the sign system, have been interiorised as representations of reality. The ideology of consumerism promises the good life, good feelings, and good selfhood.

(1992: 47)

The concept of self-identity is caught up in this regime of individuated ownership and consumer surveillance. The 'possessive individual' (Abercrombie, Hill, and Turner, 1986; Pateman, 1988) is concerned with not only the purchase of commodities, goods and property, but the ownership of the self that becomes 'a kind of cultural resource, asset or possession' (Lury, 1996: 8). The possessive individual styles themselves in the same way as goods and services are styled: they measure their self-worth in terms of the aestheticisation of the self. The loss of material possessions is seen as a loss to the individual and is 'experienced as a personal violation and a lessening of the self' (ibid: 8).

All these qualities of identity hitherto defined wrap themselves around celebrity culture, as I will now go on to explore.

CELEBRITY AND IDENTITY

Celebrities are always connected to vexing questions about identity, they 'articulate what it is to be human being in contemporary society; that is, they express the particular notion we hold of the person, of the "individual"' (Dyer, 1987: 10). The type of person or figure that gets celebrated however, needs to be individuated; they need to be seen to exist as something unique or special and this is best encapsulated through the way the celebrity is made to signify, to be the material out of which identities and subjectivities emerge and converge. Celebrity culture has in fact become so entwined with the practices, behaviours and rituals of everyday life in much of the Western world that one can argue they exist symbiotically, interdependent with one another. People experience the world and their place in it increasingly through the representations of celebrity that dominate the cultural and entertainment industries. This is compounded by the fact that famed individuals are associated with a range of products, services and industries that migrate way beyond related enterprises, so that people's consumption and ritualistic lifestyles are inextricably bound up with celebrity.

This is seemingly a particular truism for young children and their identity formation. As Uhls and Greenfield found (2011) in their empirical study of what preteens wanted most in the future, fame was given as their number one choice. They argue that current popular preadolescent TV shows such as *iCarly* suggest that fame and public recognition, as an individualistic goal, is an important and achievable aspiration to hold, and that this message may be particularly salient for preadolescents, ages 10–12. They found that, enacting the value of fame, the majority of preadolescent participants used online video sharing sites (YouTube in particular) to seek an audience beyond their immediate community and in so doing achieve the public recognition they craved. For example, in response to a question from the moderator asking whether anyone had made a video to post online, one 11-year-old respondent says:

> [Boy 1] Um, my friends and I are making a YouTube Channel ...
> [M] Why are you doing that? ... For fun? Or do you have a goal?
> [Boy 1] Our goal is to try and get a million subscribers.
>
> (Group V, Middle boys) (2011: 7)

The equation of individual success with numbers, with big data, also refers to the notion of the quantified self, where people track their everyday life through measurement schema.

So pervasive is celebrity culture to notions of identity and self-worth, it can be argued that it 'occupies' the centre ground of contemporary life and this in consort with the media who act as a mythic progenitor of and for fame. Nick Couldry contends that we have entered a state-of-being in the world where having access to the (celebrity) media is imagined to be the very thing that guarantees having a productive and meaningful modern identity. This famed mediascape is where people's identities are forged:

> The idea that society has a centre helps naturalise the idea that we have, or need, media that 'represent' that centre; media's claims for themselves that they are society's 'frame' help naturalise the idea, underlying countless media texts, that there is a social 'centre' to be re-presented to us.
>
> (2003: 46)

This cultural or ideological myth of the mediated centre is magnetic in the way it pulls people towards its illusionary centre. People are convinced that the only way to be visible, to have power and individuality, is to be 'present' in this celebrated mythic media centre. It holds people in its spectacular attractions and asks them to think themselves through this myth: to live in ways and through means that this myth sanctions and to make lifestyle, career, familial and consumption decisions based on the properties of this celebratory myth.

The centre of our beings, the centre of culture and society, miraculously emerge in and through this media-narrated, naturalising myth where everyone can, should and 'probably' will be famous. The media exists as a meta-frame on the celebratised world and behind, or perfectly fitted within this frame, is the mythic, binding, naturalised material of celebrity culture. The media become the outer centre of contemporary life, celebrity the inner, very like the way television quiz shows create an elite or auratic space for those who win through to the final round. Celebrity becomes the imagined glue that binds people together; it creates a social, cultural and economic whole, while promising the good life for the individual. For Chris Rojek, this type of fame directive helps produce the phenomena of the celetoid, which is 'any form of compressed, concentrated attributed celebrity' (21). For Rojek,

> The desire for fame now far exceeds talent, accomplishment or skill. The upshot of the present condition is the emergence of the *celetoid*: a person who acquires short, intense bursts of media time simply by dint of being recognized by TV producers as coveting and chasing fame in a sufficiently determined way.
>
> (2009)

POSSESSIVE CELEBRITY IDENTITY

There is, of course, something possessive and divisive about this grand illusion: contemporary celebrity is bathed in its own culture of narcissism with the selfie one of the modes of expression that best encapsulates this self-love and the love for public expression. The desire of fans to take selfies with celebrities and for celebrities to represent themselves through the selfie is one of the ways that identification now emerges – through the frenzy of the visible, through the immediacy of the close-up, through the belief that while being in the public eye one is granted status and warrants attention. As Uhls and Greenfield's findings suggest, 'the documented historical increase in narcissistic personality in emerging adults begins in the preadolescent years with a desire for fame' (2011: 13).

As importantly, when individuals take on public roles it as if they are embodying celebrity values. As Chris Rojek observes, people 'fall into a trap that celebrities have been experiencing for years, the split between the public and private self' (2001, 11). Further,

> Celebrity status always implies a split between a private self and a public self ... The public presentation of self is always a staged activity, in which the human actor presents a 'front' or 'face' to others while keeping a significant portion of the self in reserve. For the celebrity, the split between the I and the Me is often disturbing. So much so, that celebrities frequently complain of identity confusion.
>
> (Rojek, 2001: 11–12)

CELEBRITY IDENTITY TYPES

Celebrities also chart the way identities are imagined to be forged within the sociological and postmodern traditions. First, the ascribed celebrity, whose fame is based on lineage and 'whose status typically follows from blood-line' (Rojek, 2001: 17), equates to essentialised notions of identity: that some people are born better than others, with a high degree of natural capital. Members of royalty, the aristocracy and heirs and heiresses have ascribed celebrity status.

Second, the achieved celebrity, whose fame 'derives from the perceived accomplishments of the individual in open competition' (Rojek, 2001: 18), equates to the notion that identity is possessed, forged by talent and hard work in a competitive environment that rewards the best of us. Achieved celebrities include film stars, pop stars, sports stars, leading artists, inventors, elite scientists and grand philanthropists.

Third, there is attributed celebrity, whose fame is, 'largely the result of the concentrated representation of an individual as noteworthy or exceptional by cultural intermediaries' (Rojek, 2001: 18). Reporters, publicists, photographers, personal trainers and chat show hosts, among others, highlight these attributed individuals because of single acts of bravery, invention, difference, certitude and honour.

Attributed celebrity relates to the traditional social subject as defined in much of sociology: the identity of the celebrity emerges between the interaction of self-perceived subjectivity and the opinions and actions of significant others. Attributed celebrity can also emerge because of what are considered to be heinous acts and infamous behaviour, such as the atrocities undertaken by a serial killer. Here the relationship between the private and public breaks down and identity is caught in a schizophrenic or psychotic state. As noted above, a great deal of postmodern thought suggests that identities today are split and divided.

Into this divisive landscape emerge a number of neo-tribes, populated by identities that are self-conscious, self-aware and hybrid in form, particularly around what were once represented to be fixed and essentialised determinants of the human condition, such as gender roles and sexual preferences. The attraction of neo-tribes, then, is that they provide a spiritual home for the isolated, possessive individual of the modern age who has no other social network to belong to or no other ontological 'truth' to believe in. As Zygmunt Bauman argues, 'tribes are simultaneously refuges for those trying in vain to escape the loneliness of privatized survival, and the stuff from which private policies of survival, and thus the identity of the survivor is self-assembled' (1992: 25).

Fan groups are forms of neo-tribes: often resistant to the dominant culture, involving cosplay and identity play, they produce environments of belonging, centred on the star or celebrity that they are gathering around. As Lothian, Busse, and Reid comment in relation to slash fandom:

> Our experience in slash fan communities on LiveJournal.com (LJ) suggests that participation in electronic social networks can induct us into new and unusual narratives of identity and sexuality, calling into question familiar identifications and assumptions. Slash fandom's discursive sphere has been termed queer female space by some who inhabit and study it; we want to explore the function of this space in the lives of the people who occupy it, how it is structured, and what it can do.
>
> (2007: 103)

Of course, celebrity culture involves an engagement with public life, both through very public performances of identity and through commodified streams of connectivity.

Public celebrity identity

Celebrity culture shapes public life and private enterprise simultaneously. Public discourse is increasingly channelled through arguments and activities of famous people. People embody the politics of the public through encounters with famed and charismatic individuals, and these are increasingly commodified, given the synergetic connections they have to public relations, branding and advertising. Public life increasingly exists in the gestures and pronouncements of famed individuals and in the vortex of publicity that surrounds them. In this respect, one can read and understand contemporary public life through the lens of the mega-spectacle, whereby star-studded promotional events set the political stage (Kellner, 2003). The spectacle of fame-based public life threatens to seduce people, offers them only the logic of consumption and the neo-liberal ideology of supreme individualism.

As noted above, to be connected to these intoxicating layers of celebrity tribes and publics suggests commonality and group belonging, citizenship and active agency, while being denied access to such communities of engagement leaves one feeling isolated and alienated. The public nature of celebrity culture suggests open access for all but can be, in practice, exclusionary and discriminatory. Celebrity mythologises equality but carries on the same level of limits as previous forms of democracy entailed. As Graeme Turner (2006) reminds us, contemporary public life is not necessarily any more democratic but is more closely connected to the demotic, that is, to access without power or empowering representation. Celebrity culture is centrally involved in producing the illusion of greater democratisation, but in fact masks the truth that power remains in the hands of the select few.

The geopolitical landscape plays a part in this question of access since minority states are often rendered marginal or peripheral to the grand staging of major events. Celebrities play a key role in the organisation of public life in these interstitial global spaces, taking up causes, championing issues, joining forces with a range of public and state bodies to bring visibility to that which has been marginalised. The celebrity do-gooder or ambassador is central to this rainbow coalition since they make sacrifices on our behalf and call upon us to make sacrifices too, and to take up the response call. Through them we feel actively connected to the public life, to resistance politics, but we are also moved to take action ourselves.

We enter the messy politics of contemporary life through celebrity images and representations, and believe that we will and can make a difference if we act like them. Alternatively, and in contradiction to the reading just given, we may witness the gross orgy in which celebrity politics takes place and switch off, become disenfranchised and exit the politics of the public world as a consequence. One can see a strand emerging in this chapter: the forces of inclusion and exclusion played out, neither necessarily productive or enabling.

The gap that celebrities have helped fill is one arguably left behind by the collapse in religious faith and conviction, and in the authoritative frameworks that historically bound people together. As Ellis Cashmore suggests in relation to the celebrity of David Beckham:

> The Beckham fairy tale ... grew out of this fertile soil, a context in which people had lost trust in established traditional forms of authority, in which they no longer looked to monarchic, military, religious or political leaders for guidance and in which they found gratification in immersing themselves in the lives of glamorous and flamboyant celebs.
>
> (2004: 2)

In a similar vein, Chris Rojek suggests that celebrities, 'have filled the absence created by the decay in the popular belief in the divine right of kings, and the death of God' (2001: 13). Beckham, in fact, has been captured in religious style poses, has a well-publicised tattoo of *Jesus on the way to the cross* and has undertaken ambassadorial work that allows him to play the role of healer and life-giver. For example, in a headline that runs, 'Footie ace David is a winner with sick children', it is reported:

> Little five-year-old Amelia Ahlsrom beams as she chats with one of the world's favourite sportsmen, the pain of her recent operation temporarily forgotten. And it was the same with all the youngsters whom

David Beckham met on a visit to Melbourne's new Royal Children's Hospital. A few minutes with their idol and the young patients were soon smiling. Even the nursing staff and parents were not immune to the Beckham charm.

(www.hellomagazine.com/celebrities/201112066725/
david-beckham-australia-hospital/)

The hands (and feet) of Beckham are here given the miracle of curing pain, both physically and through the laughter and joy that he is bringing to the ward.

Digital celebrity identity

Contemporary celebrity culture takes place largely in the landscape of the digital age and the networks of social media. New online celebratised spaces emerge. The digital age has afforded contemporary life the opportunity to endlessly reproduce and represent itself so that the airwaves are full of public figures – so, so many public figures. In these new narrowcast spaces, micro-publics and micro-celebrities emerge: existing in contained electronic spaces if nonetheless available to all. According to Marshall, 'the symbiotic relationship between media and celebrity has been ruptured somewhat in the last decade through the development of new media' (2006: 634), with a shift from a traditional understanding of 'celebrity management', which is highly controlled and institutionalised, to 'one in which performers and personalities actively addresses and interacts with fans' (Marwick and boyd, 2011: 140). This is a shift that has been seen as both offering celebrities greater control in the management of their image (so responding to 'misleading' press representation or posting their own pictures of themselves) as well as becoming a site of risk in the way their images are controlled and maintained (celebrities courting controversy by posting opinions and comments that are not always vetted or shaped by a surrounding management team). At the same time, caution has been exercised with regard to the question of whether Twitter has easily 'democratised' the relationship between celebrity and audience. For example, Marwick and boyd observe that 'celebrity is by necessity a co-performance that requires fan deference and mutual recognition of unequal status to succeed' (2011: 155).

These niche networks create the appearance of carrying its own public life, with its own regulations and rhythms, but which ultimately sit within the wider fields of controlled and controlling political participation. New forms of star and celebrity images emerge from such sites and processes, not least the DIY celebrity who produces their own representational streams. The DIY celebrity perhaps best encapsulates contemporary public life: they take the ordinary and make it extraordinary, they have a skill they are able to self-promote or they develop a star image which people can lock onto, and which can be promoted. As we noted above, with regards to young children hungry for fame, the DIY celebrity embodies the sense that the modern world is more democratic and open to all, even if in reality their own status is demotic – their access to the media centre is limited and controlled and their power is measured in hits, likes and views.

Digital celebrity identity emerges in other ways: they can be reanimated, brought back to life through the digital hologram, as Tupac was for the 2012 Coachella music festival. Celebrities not only live beyond death through the recycling of their image, works, but in and through a digital media that can constantly return us to their living present. As Claire Perkins suggests,

> The star is 'born' upon their death, *as* their image: death is the pathway to immortality in a process that precisely encapsulates the way stardom abstracts a real person into a plastic figure. Edgar Morin sums this up best in his famous words on Dean: 'his death signifies that he is broken by the hostile forces of the world, but at the same time, in this very defeat, he ultimately gains the absolute: immortality. James Dean dies; it is the beginning of his victory over death'.
>
> (2014: 21)

Since his death in January 2016, David Bowie has appeared on screen in a different and particularly moving way as a type of fan wish-fulfilment and cultural haunting. For example, in the *Doctor Who* episode, 'Smile' (BBC, 2017), the Doctor faces an army of robots who are programmed to incinerate people if they detect that they are not happy. Retreating while smiling, the Doctor calls out, 'I'm happy, hope you're happy too,' linking the scene to the lyrics of the song 'Ashes to Ashes' (1980). Peter Capaldi's Doctor was also initially modelled on the Bowie star image, The Thin White Duke, and so Bowie is constantly re-materialised in the body of this alien time-traveller, who has the ability to resurrect or rejuvenate. Even after his death, then, Bowie lives on in screen culture. And in living on so strongly, if in part as an apparition, he perhaps points to the material thinness of how our cultural world is held together:

> Spectrality does not involve the conviction that ghosts exist or that the past (and maybe even the future they offer to prophesy) is still very much alive and at work, within the living present: all it says, if it can be thought to speak, is that the living present is scarcely as self-sufficient as it claims to be, that we would do well not to count on its density and solidity, which might under exceptional circumstances betray us.
>
> (Jameson, 1999: 28)

The most powerful example of David Bowie haunting a text comes with the latest series of *Twin Peaks* (Lynch, Showtime, 2017). Numerous interviews with key players involved with the series suggest that if not for his illness at the time of production, Bowie would again have taken on the role of Agent Jeffries as originally scheduled. The reporting of such facts stems from a longing to see him return, a nostalgia for what was once brilliantly there and an allusive way to presence him into the series. This hauntology has been compounded by 'readings' of the series by committed *Twin Peaks* and Bowie fans who have mined clues to suggest that Bowie, Lazarus-like, might return:

In one scene towards the end of the second episode, Bob Cooper believes he's talking to Jeffries, although his voice is distinctly different from the Southern accent Bowie used in *Fire Walk with Me*. In another scene, in Episode 4, Cooper tells Gordon Cole (Lynch) that he's been working with Jeffries, and, shortly thereafter, Albert (Miguel Ferrer) tells Cooper that he, too, has been in contact with Jeffries.

Return/remain he has, the light of his existence flickering through his fans' longing to see him living on – even if it is only on screen. David Lynch finally included Bowie's character of Agent Jeffries in a dream sequence, in Episode 14, 'The Return, Part 14', using footage of him shot for *Twin Peaks: Fire Walk with Me* (1992). This desire to see Bowie appear in *Twin Peaks* is three-fold: it is about the strangeness of a dead David Bowie giving animated life to the estrangement of the show; it is wanting to see an iconic, ghostly narrative foreshadow come to full apparition; and it is a loving, painful, wishing to see and hear the Black Star rise again, if only because our lives are painfully bare without him.

Global (local) celebrity identity

The idea that celebrity is global, found across the four hemispheres of the world, is a pretty much taken for granted assumption. When we examine the broadcast and narrowcast ecosystems from nation state to nation state, and when we look at the way the social media is interacted with, the cult and culture of celebrity clearly weave their way across outputs, schedules, formats, blogs, postings, gatherings, fandoms and spectacle event moments. From the back streets of Kabul to the markets of Morocco, from the crap tables of Macau, to the council estates of Coventry, and from the hipstervilles of Melbourne to the shrines and temples of Tokyo, celebrity is played out as entertainment, value, product and commodity, and as the way identity, community, nation and region are forged, cohered, re-imagined as stable and secure and sometimes powerfully resisted. Celebrity, then, sits at the heart of the myth of the global media centre, informing all the watery mediascapes and ideoscapes (Appadurai, 1990) of these liquid modern times.

There are two ways to read or unpack the meaning and influence of global celebrity. First, it can be read as central to the global proliferation and incorporation of neo-liberal values, processes and practices. Global celebrity involves the transmission of a homogenised and low-quality, individualist and commodity-driven Western culture that threatens, therefore, to flatten out all cultural distinctions and the very existence of what are argued to be rich and culturally diverse world cultures. For example, if we draw on Marie Gillespie's research on Asian teenagers in Southall, UK, we find:

> it is perhaps no wonder that they turn to a third, alternative space of fantasy and identification: they draw on utopian images of America to construct a position of 'world teenagers' which transcends those available in British or Indian cultures.

> (1989: 230)

Global celebrity involves the transmission of a dominant, Western ideology that both naturalises the Western way of life as the only life worth having, and fetishises its democratic structures, social relationships and lifestyles. When British Indians consume the Kardashians or the sweet life of Britney Spears, they are investing in the American Dream and the imagined possibilities it offers one.

It is also argued that global celebrity produces a deterritorialization experience where there is the perceived loss of the 'natural' relation of culture to its physical and geographical point of origin. This sense of borderless communication is speeded up by new media technologies and the social media, creating the impression of the erosion of cultural borders and national-cultural boundaries, and with it, arguably, national-cultural distinctiveness. Global celebrity colonises the airwaves, enters the production chain, monopolises media genres and shapes and bends the very 'content' of entertainment, politics and communication right down to the everyday discourses that dominate everyday life.

Global celebrity can be argued to involve the global imposition of commoditised Western media products over what are seen as the fragile and vulnerable traditional cultures, particularly in the 'developing' world. This can also be referred to as the 'core-periphery model' where information, news and entertainment are seen to flow from the West to the rest – 'the rest' being unable to resist or reply to this domination because of power and resource inequalities. When such a model is driven and energised by the poetics and politics of celebrity it is seen to have particularly enchanted capabilities, its demystification so steeped in spectacle and wonderment that it simply cannot be resisted. The global celebrity status of Barack Obama is one such example since he not only embodies the geopolitical power of the USA, but his 'change' and 'hope' message was easily translatable and sellable across the world (Redmond, 2010) (again, see Chapter 6 for a discussion of this).

Nonetheless, there is a second and alternative way to make critical sense of global celebrity, one that draws more fully on empirical data, ethnography and the close attention to exemplification and illustration. Arguably, when we actually begin to examine the impact of the global at the local level, rather than finding deterritorialization and cultural annihilation, we find the creation of a new global-local nexus, involved in 'establishing new and complex relations between global spaces and local spaces' (Robins, 1997: 36).

The subcultural theory of identity formation suggests that young people, in particular, through a process of *bricolage* or the conscious mixing and blending together of different and diverse cultural items, transcode or appropriate those cultural items, wherever they may come from, for their own localised identity ends. In terms of the consumption of global celebrity, famous figures are not simply digested without transformation.

In Japan, the subculture movement visual kei is focused upon Western musical and fashion aesthetics, particularly glam rock, characterised by the use of varying levels of eye and face make-up, elaborate hairstyles that call forth British and American bands from the 1970s and 1980s, flamboyant costumes and androgynous aesthetics. The movement included bands such as X Japan, Buck-Tick and Luna Sea, heavily influenced by artists and bands such as David Bowie, Japan, The Cure, Kiss, Twisted Sister, Hanoi Rocks and Mötley Crüe.

Another subcultural group, the ganguro girls, are in part defined by their dark, golden tans and blonde hair, reminiscent of 'Californian girls'. However, it can be argued that Ganguro is a form of revenge against, and a rejection of, traditional Japanese social norms, hierarchies and values. These subcultural groups form close bonds and transcode global celebrity culture, offering up an alternative to the isolation and constraint of Japanese society.

Global celebrity of course exists at a local level: local stars are born and make sense at the regional and national level. They sit within the flows of national cultures, and media landscapes calibrated by regulations and processes 'unique' to that space. That said, the global, transnational, glocal and local operate in complex inter-relationships: the modern landscape means that sheets of connections are constantly being made and re-made. A local television personality can be suddenly thrust into the national and international limelight, can find their name becoming a meme on Facebook, or their 'activity' turned viral via YouTube hits and shares. Such was the case when Charlo Greene, a reporter for Alaska's KTVA, resigned live on air to fight for marijuana legalisation. She told viewers:

> I – the actual owner of the Alaska Cannabis Club – will be dedicating all of my energy for fighting for freedom and fairness, which begins with

> legalizing marijuana here in Alaska. And as for this job, well, not that I have a choice but ... fuck it, I quit.
>
> (Gorton, 2014)

Celebrity ambassadors also work in the inter-connectedness of the global-local-global space: they are global entities whose images are tied to the national and international causes in which they register an interest. If, at the national level, they internationalise the issue, and if, at the international level, they authenticate the issue, that needs to be resolved. Josh Hartnett and 'Global Cool' (a charity that is trying to encourage 1 billion people to reduce their carbon footprints over the next 10 years); Brad Pitt and 'Make It Right' (an adopt-a-green-home campaign that he hopes will help to restore the Lower 9th Ward of Katrina-ravaged New Orleans); and Jay-Z, the founder of the United Nations' 'Water for life' programme (aimed at giving people world-wide access to clean drinking water) are all examples of this global-local-global interface. But celebrity ambassadors also localise the issue in the sense that their endorsements and on-the-ground trips resonate in the very spaces where that crisis is being played out. People who are hungry, fleeing a despotic regime, or who are trying to resist an outbreak, are given 'hope' by the appearance of the celebrity (and news teams) at their front door – even if ultimately this is always inescapably a false dawn. As Pramod Nayar suggests, a country can be infused with the vernacular of charity and benevolence when it is connected to star and celebrity branding. Brand Bollywood Care (BBC for convenience) helps reframe India as a global nation state suffused with benevolent ethics,

> retaining yet subtly erasing racial, national and geopolitical identifications by merging with, in distinctive fashion, transnational organizations like the United Nations or People for the Ethical Treatment of Animals, BBC is a marker of India's coming of global age by inserting its – India's – most recognizable, i.e., celebrity, faces into a global humanitarian project and semiotic universe filled with signs of benevolence.
>
> (2015: 273)

However, Pramod is also at pains to express that a certain amount of legitimacy accrues to BBC due to its *vernacular* origins and roots.

He uses the term 'vernacular' fully alert to its racial and imperial roots, and to signal a binary with the 'global' interface. As he suggests, 'care and charity work are technologies of global citizenship for the Bollywood star. They are conduits of hope and bring hope wherever their benevolence travels'.

Transnational stardom occupies a similar position in the global-local space. Film stars can operate both as national and nationalist figures of identity – types of 'social glue' – and as international 'de-nationalised' forms that speak to global audiences. As the case study on Russell Crowe suggests here, identity is forged around racial, class, national and internationalist lines. His film star images touch upon all the identity tropes and issues that this chapter has so far outlined. The case study also exists as a powerful juxtaposition to the reading of the alien whiteness of Scarlett Johansson that closed out Chapter 2, Celebrity Representations.

CASE STUDY

White manly beast: Exploring the star image of Russell Crowe

Russell Crowe occupies a fascinating cultural space when it comes to Australian film stars who are successful both in mainstream Hollywood and American auteur cinema. The longevity of this career and the range of Hollywood and auteurist films he has appeared in suggest a star-actor who can straddle popularist and niche, commercial and artistic terrains. That Crowe is also a national and transnational actor also points towards a mutability and semiotic transferability that allows them to cross cultural borders with relative ease.

Crowe is a remarkable example of the star-actor import and export business: home-grown Australian talent, crafted in part out of national archetypes and identity tropes; and an internationalist figure, able to transcend (de-odorise) his Australianess in the USA and global marketplace. He is touched by the glitz and glamour of tinsel town and yet is able to be re-rooted and uprooted to make meaning in nationalist and transnational terms.

What is equally fascinating, however, is how Crowe's international success is also 'imported' back into Australia both to validate his talent and the value of Australianess, and to carry forward the signifiers of white-centric Hollywood stardom. Crowe re-enters Australian screen culture as a transnational fusion figure, simultaneously national and international, Australian and American, brute and cultured, ideally white and ordinary and successful at home and abroad. In essence, he is shown to cross national borders while perhaps ensuring a hegemonic space is reserved for the ontological power of whiteness and the glamour and artifice of the Hollywood cinema machine and its auteurist leanings. Crowe's Australianess is 'here' and 'there' and this embodied fusion speaks to the way contemporary white masculinity plays out in contemporary Australia.

In terms of Hollywood, Elizabeth Ezra and Terry Rowden (2006) argue that star actors such as Russell Crowe, Kate Winslet, Jude Law, Penelope Cruz and Antonio Banderas function or operate as transnational stars, engaging in a 'performance of Americanness', which is 'increasingly becoming a "universal" or "universalizing" characteristic in world cinema'.

Nonetheless, Crowe also embodies a certain performance of unease, where the characters he plays (and the way he plays them) are full of doubt and insecurity, or, because of the semiotic weight or surplus value (Dyer, 1988) that his star-actor images carry into the film destabilises its integrity. This is particularly true of the independent auteurist productions that Crowe is cast respectively in, such as *A Beautiful Mind* (2001). As an Australian star-actor, then, Crowe 'unsettles' the art(istic) films he appears in.

As importantly, Crowe also enables a mythical white national identity to hold its cultural space in Australia's mediated imaginary. Crowe's beast is decidedly an Anglo-white, neo-settler mythic construction. With Crowe, however, such racialised markers begin to collapse and the very notion of (whose or what) national identity is called into open question and contestation.

White manly beast

Crowe is a star-actor whose name can lead a Hollywood blockbuster; whose meaty and unstable performances can drive an artistic film; and whose borderless identity position can seemingly speak to hyper forms of masculinity, gendered liminality and to mythical Australian national identity. The beast that this case study alludes to, then, is one at war with itself, struggling to hold at bay qualities and behaviours that might undermine its cohesiveness. The beast of Crowe is a mass of contradictions and tensions, yet which in part enable him to move easily (if complexly) across the films that we find him in. These clashes mirror or rather embody the very tensions that mark out a masculine and heterosexual identity in an age of globalisation, and they show how stardom and celebrity is made manifest in globalised media arenas.

Blockbuster Crowe

There is a near perfect symmetry between the Hollywood blockbuster aesthetic and Crowe's star image: the spectacle and action juggernaut that drives these films are also matched by his physicality, corporeal size and portentous – if surface level – sermons and announcements that he gives as the (often) titular hero. He is a body of action and a man of few (if significant) words. In *Gladiator* (Scott, 2000), for example, Crowe/Maximus delivers these heroic and prophetic lines to both locate his loyalty and to herald the avenging angel motif that runs through the film's subtext and subsequent star image:

> My name is Maximus Decimus Meridius, Commander of the Armies of the North, General of the Felix Legions, loyal servant to the true emperor, Marcus Aurelius. Father to a murdered son, husband to a murdered wife. And I will have my vengeance, in this life or the next.

Whether as Maximus, Robin Hood, or Noah, Crowe is a force of nature, whose active and hard body drives the narrative forward, while his words encapsulate an ethical and moral centre that enables his acts of killing to be seen as just and necessary.

There is always an inherent vulnerability, an aching softness, beneath Crowe's hard exterior. In the same way that action spectacle justifies its desire for destruction with victory for the common good against a Machiavellian force, so Crowe's violence is made sensible because it is done to protect the family, community or the wider body politic under attack. As DeAngelis argues, 'when aggression is added to the mix, as in *Gladiator* and *Cinderella Man* (Howard, 2005), it is motivated entirely as an obligatory act committed in the interests of family or the larger community' (2008: 50).

When asked, in *Cinderella Man*, why he would enter the boxing ring to face the brute force of Max Baer, he says, 'milk'. Milk to feed his family in depression-hit America; milk that should flow from a mother's breast; milk the Oedipal substance that compels this soft man to fight hard.

Gladiator is a particularly interesting example since the action spectacle in the film is mostly of one-to-one mortal combat played out in the theatre of the Coliseum. Not only does the *Amphitheatrum Flavium* provide the size and scale of event cinema, but also the fighting draws one in to the ferocious dance of death that has been relentlessly choreographed and subject to CGI. The play with scale – monumental and corporeal, epic and intimately personal – works *through* the star-character actor image of Crowe, who registers as both animal and civilised man.

In a very real sense, the character's evolution is Crowe's also: his star-character actor image is a perfect fit (Dyer, 2002) for the role since his off-screen history and (what was then) contemporary behaviour matches the brute and yet searching masculinity of Maximus. This is an authenticity and a real-ness that underlies the star and the starring roles that he plays. This is all played out through the marketing and promotional work that accompanies his appearances, of course.

For example, *Entertainment Weekly*'s description of him as a 'thinking man's animal' closely aligns with his own autobiographical statements; what we 'publicly' know about his upbringing in Australia (his father was a publican, he went to the school of hard knocks); how he handles the press, the paparazzi; his quick temper; and his eloquence in interviews.

Crowe is a Hollywood outsider but an Australian insider; he is brutish but cultivated; he is an artistic visionary and yet likes the simple, the ordinary, things in life. One can see how Crowe's star image draws upon Australian archetypes, and Australia's mythic status as a frontier nation, and how he is also able to transcend these through determination and 'unprecedented (star) power'.

Crowe's star image is rooted in nationalist characteristics and yet transcends national borders through the way it encapsulates a monomyth easily digestible and translatable across the world. One can read his blockbuster roles as, on the one hand, de-odorised performances, in which he embodies a pan-masculine selfhood. On the other, one can see how they are underpinned by his ocker authenticity.

Australian Crowe

Crowe seems to be the personification and carrier of one of the dominant forms of Australian masculine identity: 'He is perceived as an "authentic man", a model of traditional values, a pre-feminist, anti-commodified or anti-metrosexual "man's man" (Gottschall, 2014: 863). For example, his involvement with the rugby league football team, the South Sydney Rabbitohs, connects him to a range of Australian signifiers and again places him in a male environment in deeply homosocial and parochial relationships. The widely circulated photograph of Crowe in an intense embrace with team captain Sam Burgess, after the Sydney Rabbitohs won the Australian NRL, places him within mateship-type scenarios.

Connected to this, however, is the story of the underdog, played out in multiple ways: Crowe was the underdog actor who made it big in Hollywood; the Rabbitohs were the underdog footy team, on the verge of extinction, who Crowe helped re-build and resurrect, his own rags to riches story cementing the low to high mythology of the team. Setting this fable within settler and foundation myths, one can see how Crowe is a national icon, capturing the qualities of white Australia and the battlers and achievers who make their way.

In this frame, Crowe exists in two cross-connecting representational streams: he is a Hollywood star who lives out the American Dream, and he is the Australian boy next door who is safely one of us. Crowe is in the ideological import/export business: his star image seamlessly moving across divergent national and international spaces. In a contemporary setting, where migration and immigration and indigenous identity unmake this myth, Crowe becomes a form of nationalist social glue. And yet again, not quite.

Crowe is an outsider, born in New Zealand, with a residence in Beverley Hills, whose left-centred politics is well known (he supported Julia Gillard in the 2012 'spill' vote). Crowe's ideological and cultural allegiances are full of fault lines and tensions, in the same way that his star image is. In a very real sense, he embodies the complexities of modern global relations. *Cinderella Man*, for example, while being set in depression-hit America, clearly speaks to the coming GFC and the austerity politics it unleashed across the globe. Crowe's James J Braddock, a labourer by day, is everyman set against corporate greed and an uncaring social system. This is a political message that is easily if vexedly imported into Australia.

Crowe's first directorial feature, *The Water Diviner* (2014), perhaps best sums up his contradictory and unravelling ideological function within this contemporary nationalist maelstrom. In an interview about the film he responds,

> Growing up in Australia, you tend to see the battle from only one point of view ... I wanted to have the audience realize from the first take, 'Oh, this is not my grandfather's Gallipoli.

(Hammer, 2015)

The Water Diviner tells the story of an Australian farmer, Joshua Connor, played by Crowe, who loses his three sons at Gallipoli and travels there four years later to find their bodies. On one level, the film draws upon all the masculine qualities of the Crowe star-character image: he is a 'paragon of manhood' (D'Addario, 2015), wanting to return his sons to their rightful resting place and honour their sacrifice.

Crowe's character is given the power of insight: he can find water in the desert and this clairvoyance also enables him to find his sons, as if it his manifest destiny to do so. On another level, however, the film is critical of the 'masculinity' and nationalist fervour of the Gallipoli landings, one of Australia's foundational 'mateship' myths. The film in part characterises the Gallipoli campaign as an unprovoked invasion of a sovereign nation state and offers us access to the Turkish point of view, allowing audiences to also see the suffering they experienced. There are clear global markers here, not least the forced invasion of Iraq. However, one can also see the film as an allegory about the white settlers' invasion of Australia at the 'birth' of the modern nation state. Crowe, then, isn't simply a cohering national figure: as in the roles he plays, he is both nationalist beauty and international beast.

CONCLUSION

What then does Crowe's Beast reveal about transnational stardom and Australian national identity? Crowe's star image has begun to part question or undermine Australian masculine markers and the hegemony of whiteness. His transnational stardom enables him to be both extraordinary (Hollywood) and ordinary (ocker), and yet the delicate layers of his sexuality work against the grain of such representations.

What Crowe's star image reveals is probably the unstable state of the nation, blinded by its settler past, holding onto its foundational myths and yet forcefully aware of their limitations and of their past-tenseness. Australia is at a crossroads: the right wanting to set up borders and keep out undesirables and the left wanting to re-navigate and recast what the nation state is. Australia is very much set within the mirroring fantasy of Crowe's unstable beast. At the level of stardom, de-odorised star images work globally and yet they also retain and maintain their national(ist) inflections; as import and export exercises they move representations, dreams, ideologies across the globe and closer to home.

CHAPTER SUMMARY

The chapter outlines the ways in which celebrity culture effects and transforms identity formation, at the local, national and trans-national level. Celebrity informed identities are public and private and are shaped by questions of power, access and visibility. The case study on Russell Crowe draws on many of these themes as the analysis contends.

5

CELEBRITY EMBODIMENT

In this chapter, we turn our eye to the embodiment node on the circuit of celebrity affect. The position taken here is that celebrity and fan encounters are always of the senses born and that living the body is the vessel through which powerful feelings emerge. That is not to say that celebrity embodiment is always positively somatic. To the contrary, as the chapter will now go on to discuss, the affective bodies of celebrity culture are both cages and songbirds to be set free.

THE BODY IS A CELEBRITY CAGE

The study of the body has become increasingly central to identity analysis and sociological and cultural enquiry (Butler, 1990; Featherstone, 1995; Kirby, 1997; Bordo, 1993). First, this is because the body has come to be understood as central to identity formation and to the unequal power relationships that emerge, in part, from the shape, size, colour and musculature of the body. The body becomes 'the medium through which messages about identity are transmitted' (Benson, 1997: 123), both through the way that it establishes a concrete sense of a closed, boundaried, discrete self, and because of the way it 'maps' out *in flesh*, or brings into material being, the 'natural' evidence for the unequal differences that exist in and between people of a different gender, race, class and sexuality. As Mary Douglas observes,

> The body is a model which can stand for any bounded system. Its boundaries can represent any boundaries which are threatened or precarious. The body is a complex structure. The functions of its different parts and their relation afford a source of symbols for other complex structures. We cannot possibly interpret rituals concerning excreta, breast, milk, saliva, and the rest unless we are prepared to see in the body a symbol of society, and to see the powers and dangers credited to social structure reproduced in small on the human body.
>
> (1966/2002: 373)

In reading the body as a cultural or social text; the site of a society's signifying practices; or, as Douglas puts it above, 'a symbol of society', one gets to understand more about difference, the construction of Otherness, cultural domination and resistance and the way that nature is used to efface the ideological processes that are at work in body politics.

Pierre Bourdieu is particularly interesting in this respect since he sees the 'meaning' of the body produced in a dynamic nature/culture framework. Bourdieu contends that bodily practices, and rituals and behaviours around the body, such as eating, act as vehicles for transmitting dominant cultural values. This 'culture made body' plays out the actual social conditions and power relations of a society, and for Bourdieu this resonates in terms of class differences/antagonisms. However, because such body idioms are represented as natural, essential, innate, they appear to be 'beyond the grasp of consciousness' and so are understood to be as *nature intended* and therefore without contestation (1977: 94).

One can see how celebrity bodies work to transmit dominant cultural values about race and ethnicity, gender and sexuality, age and social class. As already noted earlier in this book, idealised white female stars are marked out by their light skin tone, natural blonde hair, perfected face and physique and by their 'rarefied and magnified emotions' (Ellis, 1982: 307). This is contrasted with the white trash star who is blotchy, has died blonde hair and whose manners and values are uncouth and untrustworthy. Pam Cook, for example, has explored the British actress Diana Dors through the way her body intersected class and racial lines: 'On the one hand unashamedly putting libido and conspicuous consumption on display ('spend, spend, spend'), on the other tightly encasing her voluptuous body in constricting whalebone and figure-hugging evening dresses' (2001: 174). Similarly, Diane Negra locates the articulation between class and whiteness in the controversy that surrounded Nancy Kerrigan/Tonya Harding as one example where:

> Performing female bodies can powerfully incarnate notions of classed whiteness as spectators worldwide were cued to revile the unruly 'white trash' Harding and revere the assimilated Irish-American Kerrigan.
>
> (2001: 101–02)

Celebrity bodies can, of course, cross borders, as Negra suggests is the case of Cher's ethnic corporeality, which shows how her 'body functions as the sign of her unstable class and ethnic attributes – the marker of her ability to complicate operative distinctions between white and non-white, and high and low cultural forms' (2001: 165/166).

The celebrity body can materialise as an intense sensory stereotype, where they are positioned to emit difference through the very pores of their corporeality. As Colemen-Bell has argued, Serena Williams has become a modern version of the vivacious 19th-century Hottentot Venus, identified and identifiable as embodying an innate sexual difference (enlarged labia, buttocks) to white women. She writes,

> The 'famous' black sporting body has been variously used as a means to signify racial difference (otherness), and to provide the evidential material out of which meritocratic success can be proven. The black sporting body is brought into racist discourse to either prove that all black people are physical creatures, that their vast black mass essentially connects them to primitive impulses, excessive desire and 'mindless' behaviour (all body and no brain); or to herald the athletic power of the body so that all Americans can be proud of 'it'.
>
> (Coleman-Bell, 2006: 196–197)

By contrast, white female sporting celebrities often are framed as having ideal bodies that are to be attained and attainable to those who work them into pictures of health and slender fitness. These thin, toned, white celebrity bodies are centrally involved in reproducing the 'tyranny of slenderness' (Chernin, 1983) that haunts popular media culture more generally.

A whole set of power-saturated, binary oppositions are constructed around the differences between white and black celebrity bodies: differences that continue, to varying degrees, in contemporary 'racialized regimes of representation' (Hall, 1997). Generally, the connotations of the white celebrity body are positive, while those of the black celebrity body are negative (see Figure 5.1).

If one was to take as an example the 'feud' between Kanye West and Taylor Swift that began when West interrupted Swift's acceptance speech for the MTV Video Music Award (VMA) for Best Female Video in 2009, one can see how their bodies were constructed on racial and gender lines, set within the theatre of a 'racial melodrama'. West became the 'anti-Tom—violent, perverted, sadistic, black … what he called "the abomination of Obama's nation" on his 2010 track "Power" from *My Beautiful Dark Twisted Fantasy*, a role that was

Figure 5.1 The race and gender of West and Swift
Image courtesy of Kevin Mazur/WireImage/Getty Images

alternatively stifling and uplifting' (Cullen, 2016). Swift became the innocent bystander, whitely pure and illuminating:

> Depicted as the sweet, young innocent, undeserving of West's negative attention, who had perhaps even transcended racial boundaries during her frankly minstrel-like performance of 'Thug Story' with T-Pain just a few months earlier.

> (Cullen, 2016: 3)

The second reason that the body has been placed at the centre of sociological and cultural analysis is because of the way it is seen as 'directly involved in a political field; power relations have an immediate hold upon it; they invest it, mark it, train it, torture it, force it to carry out tasks, to perform ceremonies, to emit signs' (Foucault, 1977: 25). Michel Foucault's work is central here, positing as it does the notion that social bodies are trained or disciplined to be obedient by historically specific groups of people in related institutional complexes, such as doctors and teachers, in hospitals and schools. However, Foucault also suggests that the surveillance on/ of the body has been away from these more formal, external forms of bodily domination and control towards a system of surveillance that emerges from individual self-regulation, self-management and self-discipline.

In the modern world, according to Foucault, this body has become increasingly 'docile' because of the exhaustive amount of regulation imposed upon it from within. A body, then, is regulated and disciplined from the inside as much from external operations, as individuals turn the panopticon or their own self-surveillance mirrors on themselves, to become compliant citizens of capitalism and patriarchy.

In Su Holmes's moving reading of performer Lena Zavaroni, we see a normalising dualism in play: the media constructing her within a patriarchal script that denied her agency, alongside the scholarship on anorexia, which similarly marginalised the experience of the sufferer:

> In arguing that the voice of the anorexic female celebrity was either ignored in feminist work or positioned as simply commodified and politically 'inauthentic', I wanted to listen to what the star said about her own understanding of anorexia, while acknowledging that this

was inevitably shaped by, and was part of, popular and psychiatric discourse on anorexia at the time.

(2015: 105)

Both Iris Young (1980) and Sandra Lee Bartky (1997) have written on how women are 'taught' to move and use their bodies in typically limited, constrained postures, where reach and stretch actions are met by an invisible wall or boundary, which women literally feel they cannot reach or stretch beyond (best exemplified, Young argues, through the woman's body-in-sport). Such training occurs across a range of discursive practices but finds its most potent mode of transmission in etiquette classes and finishing schools, where young girls/women are trained to embody ladylikeness and to go unnoticed in patriarchal, polite society. As Bartky writes:

> Here is field for the operation for a whole new training: A woman must stand with stomach pulled in, shoulders thrown slightly back, and chest out, this to display her bosom to maximum advantage. While she must walk in the confined fashion appropriate to women, her movements must, at the same time, be combined with a subtle but provocative hip-roll. But too much display is taboo: Women in short, low-cut dresses are told to avoid bending over at all, but if they must, great care must be taken to avoid an unseemly display of breast or rump.
>
> (1997: 136)

Again, Serena Williams is interesting in this respect because of the way her body seems to transgress this regime: it is raced, overly 'sexual' and masculine. In the 2016 Pirelli Calendar series, shot by renowned photographer Annie Leibowitz, we see Williams photographed in an athletic pose, facing away from the camera, dressed only in cropped black shorts. Her arms are outstretched against a wall, and her legs are facing the same way, almost in an arrow-like composition. Her long hair flows or floats away in the other direction. The black and white shot emphasises her muscularity and femininity, seemingly breaking binaries as it does so, drawing attention to the performativity of the body. However, her hair is Westernised and the pose brings to mind Leni Riefenstahl's imagery for the 1936 Olympics: it is fascistic and fetishised and arguably brings to the fore the way the black body became a focus of western, scientific investigation in the early 20th century, put on display in countries such as France, to prove the excessive, essential sexual identity of the black woman (Gilman, 1985a, 1992). Such descriptions became 'the living evidence – the proof, the Truth – of an irreversible difference between the "races"' (Hall, 1997: 265). William's black body is being marked off as taboo-exotic, as a 'collection of sexual parts' (Gilman, 1985b), sexually different, although this difference is also contained, denied, since the signification process involves disavowal. The 'stranger' fetishism, the sexualised and racialised iconography that Williams is drawn into, works to, draw attention to and then displace, the fascination with this Other's sexuality. As Hall writes:

> Fetishism, then, is a strategy for having-it-both-ways: for both representing and not-representing the tabooed, dangerous or forbidden object of pleasure and desire. It provides us with what Mercer calls an 'alibi'. We have seen how, in the case of 'The Hottentot Venus', not only is the gaze displaced from the genitalia to the buttocks; but also, this allows the observers to go on looking while disavowing the sexual nature of the gaze.
>
> (1997: 268)

One can chart the boy's (white) body in a similar way, but here the boy's body occupies a position of real social power. Through many of the dominant scripts of the arts and popular media, including classical literature, folk song and folk story, children's books, poems, comics, adverts, cartoons, films, etc., the masculine body becomes the representational site that makes flesh those 'regimes of truth' (Foucault, 1977) that suggest that boys are hard-bodied, active, heroic, scientific, physical and protective. These heroic bodies are then taken into the world of 'play' and other informal and formal sites of social interaction. For example, Ellen Jordan's (1995) study of seven-year-old boys in Australian schools suggests that a 'warrior' discourse informs the fantasy play of most boys. Taking up the position of omnipotent masculine heroes, warrior boys re-enact the adventures of King Arthur, Superman and Ninja Turtles, in celebratory games of physical excess. One can clearly see how hard-bodied film and television action stars play this heroic mythology out: their bodies save the day, often in violent and uncompromising action. This is particularly true of Chris Evans and the Captain America franchise, which serves as 'propaganda for militarism and hyper-masculinity' (Lout, 2017).

Judith Butler (1990: 128–41) argues that gender 'is not passively scripted on the body', but 'put on, invariably under constraint, daily and incessantly, with anxiety and pleasure'. The gendered body, then, is a lived and living performance that both women and men 'enact' to represent and to give materiality to their masculinity and femininity. Such performances produce both a series of rewards, such as social status, ideological power and affirmation of the self, and a series of penalties, such as limited status and political and economic disenfranchisement. But such performances also manifest as a series of 'contests' about how the body should work and present itself to the social world. For example, anorexia is arguably one particular embodiment process where women wrestle with the material form of their body in a ritualised rejection of normalised notions of the thin, female body (Palmer, 1980; Orbach, 1993). As Foucault observes, assessing the historical trajectory of capitalism:

> The human body was entering a machinery of power that explores it, breaks it down and rearranges it. A 'political anatomy', which was also a 'mechanics of power' was being born; it defined how one may have a hold over others' bodies, not only so that they do what one wishes, but so that they may operate as one wishes, with the techniques, the speed and the efficiency that one determines. Thus, discipline produces subjected and practised bodies, 'docile' bodies.
>
> (1977: 138)

Eve Kosofsky Sedgewick (1992) writes that modern society is caught in the grip of what she calls 'epidemics of the will', where the fear of these bad habits taking root drives the will to control the body, in ever excessive regimes of surveillance. We are no longer alone with our bodies, rather we are always *with our bodies*, taking notice of its blemishes, spots, taking care of its tempos and energies; and *with others*; friends, family, doctors, councillors, who check out our bodies for us and remind us to regularly check our own bodies. Nicholas Mirzoeff captures this frenzy of the body well: 'Your body is not itself. Nor, I should add, is mine. It is under threat from the pharmaceutical, aerobic, dietetic, liposuctive, calorie-controlled, cybernetic world of postmodernism' (1995: 1).

Our bodies are of course centrally monitored and encultured by celebrities who through the way they embody gender, sexuality, class and race, and through the advertising and sponsorship regimes that promote body maintenance, offer us endless ways to track and train our flesh. In a powerful study by Gow et al. on the 'Representations of Celebrities' Weight and Shape during Pregnancy and Postpartum: A Content Analysis of Three Entertainment Magazine Websites', we find that:

> Relatively few articles about celebrities' pregnancies discussed weight (13%) or shape (30%), and an even smaller proportion (6.2%) included any discussion of postpartum body dissatisfaction. This suggests a gap between portrayal of celebrities' pregnancies and postpartum experiences and those of non-celebrity women. This disparity is concerning as it might lead to unrealistic expectations about pregnancy and postpartum for both pregnant readers and a more general audience.
>
> (2012: 172)

Similarly, in Maltby et al.'s study of teenagers and adolescents, they suggest that there is an interaction between intense, personal celebrity worship and body image between the ages of 14 and 16 years, in which celebrities that are perceived as having a good body shape may lead to a poor body image in female adolescents who identify with them (2005: 17).

That is not to say, however, that bodies are not also sites of resistance, contest, negotiation and performance. The body is often a place of both cultural dissent and aggressive agency, with individuals shaping their bodies in ways that counter the dominant practices of regulating or surveying the body. So-called 'body projects', such as body-building, tattooing, piercing and dieting may 'provide individuals with a means of expression, and a way of feeling good and increasing control over their flesh' (Shilling, 2005: 71). Similarly, through individuals 'performing' what might be considered transgressive gender and 'sex' acts, such as cross-dressing and drag, one may open up the body to a reading that recognises or acknowledges that all sex and gender scripts are in fact 'acted out' and that femininity and heterosexuality are, in this context, forms of 'masquerade' (Butler, 1990: 128–41).

Nonetheless, there is another type of body that is important and one that squarely sits in a circuit of affect that recognises its somatic and sensorial qualities.

THE PHENOMENOLOGICAL CELEBRITY BODY

Terry Eagleton has suggested that 'aesthetics are born as a discourse of the body', and that,

> In its original formulation by the German philosopher Alexander Baumgarten, the term refers not in the first place to art, but, as the Greek aisthesis would suggest, to the whole region of human perception and sensation, in contrast to the more rarefied domain of conceptual thought.

> (1990: 13)

Aesthetics represents the 'first stirrings of a primitive materialism – of the body's long inarticulate rebellion against the tyranny of the theoretical (ibid). Aesthetics, in this context, is carnal appreciation, albeit set against the higher-order forms of the linguistic. It contains a heady mixture of uncultured responses and affects, including delight, desire and disgust.

The senses, as Susan Buck-Morss argues (1998), maintain an uncivilised and uncivilisable trace, a core of resistance to cultural domestication and discursive positioning. This is not to devalue them, of course, but to see their potential as unregulated forces that are not simply placed within discourse but outside of it, with radical embodied possibility.

I suggest that sensory aesthetics and sensuous knowledge have the potential for the radicalisation of the body, or a type of liminal becoming that frees one's flesh from its cultural docility and ideological entrapment. That is to say, while we are 'trained' and 'regulated' to take up certain identity positions and inhabit them (Foucault, 1977; Young, 1980), our bodies do also experience the world through carnal appreciation, which can in turn lead to a radical form of resistant embodiment. As Vivian Sobchack puts it, 'our bodies escape' the cultural and ideological conditions in which they are produced (Bukatman, 2009). Further, the body in phenomenology is seen to contribute directly to the content of what is perceived; and the material presence of 'things' is considered a relational process (Welton, 1999).

> Material things are not phantoms floating between the material world and the mind, but rather have a relation to each other precisely because of the orientation they have to our perceiving and moving bodies. Phenomenology recognises individual bodily orientation as directly linked to perceptual processing; and recognizes our kinesthetic sensations as contributing to, and being created within, a necessarily intersubjective, intertwining of our physicality in the presence of the world.
>
> (Merleau-Ponty, 1964: 49)

This production of a radicalised sensory aesthetics can be best understood to be a cluster of affects or bloc of sensations (Deleuze and Guattari, 1998) waiting to be born. These intense affects are free of language and emerge out of the unregulated sensorium of the individual. As Simon O'Sullivan argues:

> Affects are ... the molecular beneath the molar. The molecular understood here as life's, and arts, intensive quality, as the stuff that goes on beneath, beyond, even parallel to signification.
>
> (2001: 126)

As I have argued earlier and elsewhere (Redmond, 2006, 2014), celebrities are first and foremost embodied individuals, intense molecular manifestations, and one of the key ways they affectively engage with fans and audiences is through the primary senses activated by sensorial-based aesthetics. This is not, however, a one-way mode of communication: these molecular manifestations occupy and move between celebrity and fan, between and across subjectivities and identities.

I have begun to define this celebrity/fan relationship as *celebaesthetic* or one in which the individual and famous person face one another as experiential beings in a dynamic, relational structure of reversibility and reciprocity. Feelings and (their) affects move backwards and forwards, in and out, within and without the two identifying figures. There is a systolic/diastolic rhythm about these exchanges producing an intensification of bodily awareness, singular and combined. In this relational, cross-modal exchange through which the senses are activated, the body is the organ through which a communion – a shared experiential relationship – takes place.

This exchange relies on 'both synaesthesia (or intersensoriality) and coenaesthesia (the perception of a person's whole sensorial being)' (Sobchack, 2004: 67). Put rather simply, celebrities and fans communicate with one another in and through the activation of powerful emotions and senses; shared, heightened and proximate embodied awareness; and intense molecular manifestations that fill the body with of rapture and delight.

One can also conceive of these sensory relations in terms of what Laura U Marks (2000) has defined as haptic visuality, where 'the eyes themselves function like organs of touch' (162) and 'move over the surface of its object rather than plunge into illusionist depth, not to distinguish form so much as to discern texture' (ibid). For Marks, film and video may be 'thought of as impressionable and conductive, like skin' (2000: xi–xii) and their visual landscapes can be heightened through the way they utilise sensory-based activity, and 'sensuous imagery that evokes memory of the senses' (Totaro, 2002). While Marks argues that visual sensoriality is found in experimental film and video, it is clear to me that the tactile vision of the celebrity works in similar ways (Redmond, 2014).

In the Natalie Portman advert for Dior (also see Chapter 1), the camera that captures her joy, in what is represented to be a love-struck Parisian summer, is often placed close to her body, or her body moves towards it in delicate movements of transition, opening and desiring glances. It is clear that this is a point of view shot (of her lover), or of an omnipotent camera that can narrate this journey in close and proximate detail for us. The advert begins with a close-up of her face, side on, smelling a pink rose that she moves across her cheek to her mouth, so close one can smell its/her bouquet in that synaesthetic relationship through which the senses operate. Portman dances in a waterfall, swims towards the camera, falls into a floating sea of pink roses and her and her lover's faces at different points are captured in fine, grainy black and white detail. The advert is sensuous and evokes the memory of sensation and erotic feeling. Portman's skin and the conductive qualities of the camera that captures *breathe* through one another. Portman's celebrity image is conducive to such haptic visuality because it is built on roles and performances that affectively position her as the embodiment of natural, floral beauty. The vibrant pink that runs through the advert also runs across the carnal textures of her celebrity image. Hers is a skin of a very particular quality, set within a feminine discourse, and is particularly both contemporary and yet recalls a Paris long gone.

Such moments and situations of celebrity abundance can and should be placed in particular historical and political contexts, as we have suggested before. Not only do audiences respond to celebrities differently depending on a whole set of personal, memorial and psychological circumstances, but the experience of the celebrity is culturally and historically specific. For example, Marilyn Monroe sensorially transmitted what it was like to be a perfected white woman in a 1950s America dealing with racial difference and growing female independence (Dyer, 1987). Monroe created the somewhat contradictory 'experience' of desirable white womanhood for an America undergoing radical social and political transformation. Her body moved freely, it registered as soft and appealing, the embodiment of girl-like optimism and white womanly sensuality. It was full and fecund, but vulnerable and fragile, always in corporeal tension with itself (Cohen, 1998). Monroe was cotton and silk, a voluptuous body, and yet inhabited space like she was a little girl in awe of what she saw and was confronted by (Young, 1980). Her smile was often captured in a close-up, an affect image, and she readily, sometimes knowingly, drew attention to her body through the way she moved it through space, touched it, and let it 'escape' its borders and boundaries.

There is that word again, 'escape'. I would suggest that those women who would be found identifying with Monroe would be doing so as celebaesthetic beings; sensing her as they sense themselves in a carnal exchange not reducible to words, not accountable simply to the operations of bourgeois capitalism or patriarchal discourse. While this liberation of the senses may be short lived, may ultimately be recuperated in the services of patriarchy and consumption, there are always moments in time and space where the body is free, and delirious affects escape.

There is though, to repeat and further develop the thesis of this chapter, a more general and positive phenomenological perspective from which to understand the concept that the celebrity is an embodied figure that needs to be *experienced* to be effectively understood. They require recognition of a level of intimacy or intimate engagement that is not reducible to the demands of representation or the artifice of performance. To engage with the celebrity requires the release of feelings, a primal awakening, the activation of the senses and the mobilisation of affects. The mobilisation of the celebrity senses touched by transgression may be best understood to take place through the *confession*.

CELEBRITY CARNAL CONFESSIONS

We live in the age of a confessional culture and celebrity is one of the key conduits for its transmission and revelatory sense-making (Redmond, 2014). The celebrity confession is often melodramatic in form; the revelation will often be tearful, there will be a degree of nervousness signalled by faulty speech patterns, body language, perceived awkwardness and its perceived heartfelt honesty will be essential to the way it registers as truth and legitimate feeling. The confession will often be set in a space that is meant to aestheticise the encounter and sensationalise the outpouring. It may be set in a darkened television studio, in the celebrity's own front room or in an 'accidental' public place that is rendered extraordinary by the very fact the celebrity has broken down in some way. Of course, the confession may be spontaneous, free of narrativisation or generic convention – it may just happen, undermining the 'script' that is taking place at that moment in time. Celebrities such as Tom Cruise and Lance Armstrong have used the *Oprah Winfrey Show* to confess love and guilt respectively, while Amy Winehouse has grieved publicly during the middle of her set.

The press conference confessional has its own particular experiential qualities: it will have been called because of some damaging media story, such as a drug scandal, alleged adultery or perceived wrong of some sort. The press will have gathered in great numbers and a stage will have been set, where the microphones and lectern will have been set centre stage. The celebrity will arrive, lenses will glare and shutters will click and click. This is a moment of pure spectacle, but it has phenomenological qualities also. The celebrity will approach the lectern/podium and will either read from a prepared script or will speak spontaneously. In either case, emotion will be seen to leak through, particularly in those cases where a 'truth' is being revealed rather than the artifice of performance to shore up a celebrity's image. The celebrity will cry, falter, shudder and will struggle to find words, language, to articulate what becomes sensory pain escaping their bodies.

Viewers or readers who identify with the celebrity confessing will feel or undergo a bodily response: they will emit the same signs; will be caught in the grip of their own bodies confessing a shared and simultaneous pain. Again, while the confessional can be read as manufactured, a public relations exercise to stop or assuage the flow of damaging gossip, it can also be read as a carnal moment that works against the constructed and the representational. The melodramatic excess of the confession cannot be easily or simply recouped in the service of the media industries or capitalist ideology. Celebrity and viewer/reader will experience an embodied, cross-modal coming together. Again, this is best expressed or understood as a celebaesthetic confessional encounter.

There can, of course, be a powerful gendered dimension to the celebrity confessional. When it is a damaged female celebrity, caught in the grip of a damaging patriarchal culture, confessing to female fans about their woes, an experiential doorway opens up between them involving a realisation and a sensorialisation of hitherto unseen (if not unfelt) governance. As already noted in Chapter 1, one can read Britney Spears's head-shaving act as a type of revelatory confession where she is not only rejecting her sexualised and erotic celebrity image, but also removing herself from reproductive femininity and motherhood. When Angelina Jolie revealed she had removed her ovaries and fallopian tubes in the *New York Times* op-ed piece in March 2014, she was using the confessional mode to tell something important about her own body and of those women who might have the same cancer concerns. She writes:

> the doctors I met agreed that surgery to remove my tubes and ovaries was the best option, because on top of the BRCA gene, three women in my family have died from cancer.
>
> (Jolie Pitt, 2015)

Here reproduction deficit is a health concern and the governance it is asking for is about longevity and women making decisions about their own body. One fan responded:

> It's incredibly scary to be open and discuss your health with your own doctor, let alone the entire world. Just ... you rule, Angelina Jolie.
>
> (Jolie Pitt, 2015)

The female celebrity confession, then, not only draws attention to a/their crisis in relation to their own manufactured and damaging celebrity image, but also transmits their pain through bodily affect. Their carnal body refuses external governance, senses its own unease, leaks a truth that cannot be spoken and that cannot be undone. This is a positive type of celebrity affect involving self-determination and active agency.

Sensing celebrities involves recognition of the way complimentary sensory-based elements come together to create, produce and transmit levels of affect and intensities. The approach recognises the cross-modal nature of identification, and the way the body readily escapes its own docility and entrapment. I see transgressive and positive outcomes from the way the celebaesthetic subject operates and have used the example of the confession and celebrity carnival to anchor the way resistance is brought into corporeal being. The chapter nonetheless recognises the ideological and discursive nature of celebrity embodiment, but refuses to see it as always determining meaning, since other forms of phenomenological truths escape.

We escape through, in and within celebrity, and not through some fantasy mechanism or parasocial fakery. We escape because our bodies and their senses are activated in intense and affecting ways that cannot be simply used up or be recuperated by dominant ideology. We escape because the conditions of our existence demand it of us, even as they attempt to regulate us and control us. In sensing celebrities, we can get beyond the constraints and impositions of ideology and discourse, finding new ways to be in the world.

CELEBRITY SUBLIME

In encountering celebrities, we occasionally enter a sublime state of being in the world. Drawing upon Deleuze, my overarching definition of the sublime is that imperceptible moment in life or art when reason is absent and sensation consumes one with an overwhelming and indescribably profound intensity, chaos or force (Deleuze and Guattari, 1988). The overriding effect of this experience is the inability to verbalize or rationalize the encounter since it exists as that which cannot be comprehended. The sublime moment may be felt as a flash of insight in which one re-sees something familiar as if seeing it for the first time; it may be the familiar rendered strange, uncanny, as less or more than the experience of it has previously registered. This feeling of 'firstness' may occur in front of a gesture, a look, an object or a spectacular event.

In terms of celebrity, the sublime will often be an experience that takes place at a 'live' event: where the fan is in close proximity to the figure of their idolisation. For some, the encounter takes place in the pure realm of the senses – outside, before or beyond language and representation, although strictly speaking affect and percept are coextensive (Deleuze and Guattari, 1988) (see the discussion of dancing with Ian Curtis in Chapter 3). The experience of the sublime, then, is always an endangering one since the ontology of the self is questioned, and the 'social' disappears before the wonder of the star or celebrity as they perform in front of the fan.

The celebrity sublime is very often experienced as a 'holding onto air' moment, where the body threatens to give way or the scream replaces language and discourse. So-called 1960s Beatlemania was defined as, 'The ecstatic audience, breathing deeply in its rapt enthusiasm, can no longer hold back its shouts of acclaim: they stamp unceasingly with their feet, producing a dull and persistent sound that is punctuated by isolated, involuntary screams' (Lynskey, 2013). Heinrich Heine identifies a similar phenomenon with the 19th-century composer, conductor and pianist, Franz Liszt:

> And what tremendous rejoicing and applause! – a delirium unparalleled in the annals of furore! And what is the real cause of this phenomenon? The solution of the question belongs rather to the province of pathology than to that of aesthetics. The electric action of a daemoniac nature on a closely pressed multitude, the contagious power of the extase, and perhaps a magnetism in music itself, which is a spiritual malady which vibrates in most of us, – all these phenomena never struck me so significantly or so painfully as in this concert of Liszt's.
>
> (May, 2011)

Similarly, at a Beyoncé concert in 2013, a fan danced in ecstatic delight as the singer performed close to where they were standing. When Beyoncé stopped to hug the fan, they fainted. This loss of the self before the star or celebrity dramatises the circuit of affect which contains its passions.

However, for the celebrity sublime to take place, one doesn't need the encounter to be 'live' – far from it. The phenomenological properties of the screen are already fully sensorial and embodied, so that a star appearing on screen can open up the film world to sublimity. For example, in the film *Sunshine* (Boyle, 2007), Cillian Murphy is the leading star narrative agent, Robert Capa, a physicist who operates the massive stellar-bomb device that will reignite the sun and save humanity from its cold annihilation. Near the end of the film, as the bomb explodes, Robert stares in awe and wonder as the sun re-ignites.

His state of sublimity is that of the extraordinary film star (Dyer, 1997) while our eyes are being lost in this double attraction; we are touched by and are touching the sun's heat and magnitude; and, like Robert, are rendered 'speechless'. However, fans of Cillian Murphy are also positioned (wanting) to focus intently on his/Robert's eyes as he gazes in an awe-struck manner at the force that slowly engulfs him, the screen (and fan/viewer). What this double sublime may produce is that in a fan's state of sublimity, they not only recognise (see into) the sublime as it manifests in this character, but his sublimity works its way back into the adoring fans' eyes. Cillian's eyes are in a very real sense a part of the spectacle, conduits for it, are transformed, as is the fan, by it.

Cillian stares at the sun in the same way the fan does, in the same way as the fan sees and touches the sun in their/his eyes. Him, I, us, are lost for words, as we search with our eyes (as organs of touch) for the origins of this natural spectacle. This is sublime endangerment not simply in terms of the instability in the fans' faces, but in the way borders and boundaries are breached and transgressed. Cillian becomes a part of the now reignited sun, is taken up into its liquid centre, becoming an extraordinary star in the process. He becomes a part of the living eye of the sun.

Cillian becomes *the* time-image, he is placed or places himself in a situation where he is unable to act and react in a direct, immediate way, unsure or uncertain of who he is now as the magnificence of the sun empties him of language. This disintegration leads to a breakdown in Cillian's sensor-motor system because – as Deleuze notes – time-image characters are caught deep in thought, can verbalise very little, instead expressing a great deal through non-representational or affective signs (1989). Cillian becomes an interior being pulled apart by an exterior force, or 'a pure optical and aural image', that 'comes into relation with a virtual image, a mental or mirror image' (Deleuze, 1989). According to Deleuze, the result of this pure optical image is the witnessing of a direct image of time (a time-image or crystal-image). Such images are themselves free now to express forces or 'shocks of force' (1989: 139). The liquid eyes in this scene – defined here as Cillian, the film star, the eye of the molten sun and the eyes of the fan – engage in an inexplicable coming together that becomes a profound mediation on stardom and the phenomenal, phenomenological body.

In the case study that follows, we look at how Kate Winslet embodies and endangers class and gender binaries. The case study highlights a number of films which show how her body is both unruly and regulated – sensorial and bordered. Through the body of Kate Winslet, we see how the flesh of stars shifts the way that celebrity representations can be understood. The body of Kate Winslet also stands in sharp comparison to the alienated body of Scarlett Johansson (Chapter 2) and the nationalist beastly body of Russell Crowe (Chapter 4) – providing the model articulations from representation to identity, to embodiment.

CASE STUDY

The body of Kate Winslet

Winslet's early star image emerges in and through the heritage film, a term taken from Andrew Higson (1995) and Claire Monk (1995), amongst others, and which applies to a group of 'backward looking', and white 'nostalgic' films that began to emerge in the 1980s. This is an emergence which, on one level, works to establish and to symbolically privilege Winslet as an idealised 'English Rose', the personification or embodiment of idealised white English femininity, but which on another level works to (deliberately) undermine such a 'constraining' or 'death-like' representation, since as an unruly performer, Winslet brings a critique or a rejection of such passive, controlled and 'absent' femininity to the heritage text.

Nonetheless, Winslet brings this rupturing force to the heritage film that is already filled with contestation and critique. This is because, as John Hill suggests (1999), gender, class and sexual conflicts are at the (implied) core of many of the heritage narratives, and as such, there are already present a number of potentially highly subversive narrative ingredients. Such narrative tensions, especially around desire and constraint, are visually played out in and through what Claire Monk

(1995) refers to as the excessive, and emotionally charged *mise-en-scène* – a *mise-en-scène* that draws attention away from the desirable/desiring nature of the woman, and which metaphorically stands in for the body-that-is-sexually charged but denied its detonation. In my understanding of the conflicts that circulate in these texts, it is idealised whiteness that is at the core of many of these contests and it is in and through Winslet that I want to explore the way (her) idealised female whiteness is seemingly scorned and savaged. The films I will look at are *Sense and Sensibility*, *Holy Smoke* and, very briefly, *The Dressmaker.*

Heritage Winslet

The character Winslet plays in *Sense and Sensibility*, Marianne, is initially presented as a translucent figure. The first shot of her in the film is in medium close-up, as she mournfully plays the piano. Bright, 'natural' light strikes her face, her neck, and because she is wearing little make-up, and her hair is a vibrant copper-red colour, she appears almost transparent – as if her white skin is indeed paper-thin. Her appearance, in fact, is just like a delicate English Rose figure, at 'home' in a sumptuous mansion-size music room. But there is also a degree of 'death' in this static shot, with very little character emotion being expressed. While Marianne is literally in mourning from the death of her Father, the blue, chalky form of her white skin here creates the impression that she is herself close to being a female corpse. The melancholy piano solo confirms the lack of life here as it is embodied in Marianne. In essence, in terms of Marianne's role in the film, this is an apt metaphor or filmic foreshadow: the constraints on/of her white femininity are killing her and this is what she will resist, a resistance that will be played out in a mind/body, present/absent dichotomy.

We quickly learn that Marianne is headstrong, independent, unconventionally daring and deeply passionate. She says to her mother (Margaret) that her sister Elinor's suitor is not right for her because he is too polite, and that 'to love is to burn, to be on fire ... to die for love ... what can be more glorious'. And yet for the most part, early on in the film, Marianne plays out these emotions in her *head* and in the 'classics' that she reads. She is petulant, but she is also kept under strict control, under restricting corset and full dress, so that her voluptuous body is (partly) hidden and her corporeal desires are all but denied to her. One powerful way that the terror of this constraint is played out is through the dining/food scenes.

In the film, Marianne simply does not eat. At the lavishly prepared dining table, familial and romantic contexts always seem to conspire to make her at her most repressed and this manifests itself in her not eating, as if eating food would be an outward sign of desire, a marker of flesh and body, something she/the ideal white woman is not supposed to possess. For example, in the first dining sequence in the film, Marianne is distraught at the behaviour of the new matriarchal 'owner' of her Father's house; but she sits totally silent, hardly moving and in the whole sequence doesn't attempt to eat any of the food before her. In short, her anger and resentment are channelled through the 'white female' expected behaviour of absence, of self-denial, of not eating.

Shannon R Wooden (2002) has noted that this 'not eating' phenomenon is carried across a number of 1990s Austen films, 'visually celebrating food while sharply disapproving of the vulgarity of eating'. Wooden then goes on to suggest that this type of cinematic anorexic nervosa is connected to 'physical beauty' and 'with the presence of romantic power and sexual pleasure'. For Wooden, then, the not eating and the *slenderness* of the (beautiful) central female protagonists work to confirm this as a positive: the feminine ideal not only textually but extra-textually connecting to wider discourses about what it means to be beautiful. This argument is in part unconvincing. Rather, the not eating seems to be an *enforced* activity in these films. An activity or performance that is literally and metaphorically killing the women, turning them into simulacra of female corpses, without life, body or desire. Marianne is clearly not happy when she is *not eating*; the absence of food makes her *visibly* upset. Marianne clearly wants life in her body: she wants to eat (to fall in love, to fuck) but the demands of/on idealised female whiteness cannot allow it. Marianne (Winslet) is also clearly not thin, not slender, but full-bodied. Marianne does or will eat, of that we can be certain. *We only have to look at her*. (For a discussion of food and disgust see also Chapter 10 and the case study on Shilpa Shetty.)

Of course, this is where the emerging star image of Winslet comes into play. The story of her body size and weight is scripted into the discourses that are found throughout her career. She has championed the philosophy that women can (should) be big and beautiful and, until recently, has resisted the media onslaught for her to be ideally thin. So, having Winslet as Marianne not eating adds an extra semantic or somatic dimension to the representation. We know Winslet likes to eat. We know that Winslet is herself also wrestling with the repressions put on her by the media at this time; and by the promotional mechanics of the star system that is trying to groom her as a quaint, spiritual English Rose figure, with her purity, innocence, morality and *thinness* championed as core values. Winslet's own articulations in this promotional work, by contrast, reveal an actress who wants to work outside, or subvert this persona: they reveal an actress whose independent spirit and unruly body will not be constrained within the parameters of idealised whiteness. She will be no English Rose.

Marianne will be no English Rose. She repeatedly resists, if not by eating, and not just through 'free spirit', but through unashamed and wanton desire for Willoughby. This is best illustrated in their wild carriage ride through the village, with Marianne screaming out in near orgasmic pleasure. The romantic fiction/poetry they read together; the open, 'public' affection they show one another; and the barrage of passionate letters that she sends him when he has moved away, are all traits of unruly behaviour for the ideal white woman. Marianne comes alive at this point in the film and it is the pulse of this behaviour that seems to carry the experiential weight in the film.

Christine Geraghty has written an interesting analysis of Winslet's performance, arguing that Winslet uses her body to signify emotional and sexual desire:

> Winslet ... gives the impression of needing to escape from the restrictions of the historical costumes and manners. The empire-line emphasises her full bosom, and her strong body is clear under the thin material of the dresses. Her hair is frequently dishevelled, escaping from ribbons or hats that attempt to restrain it. Her white skin colours easily, and Marianne is seen biting her lip and pinching her own cheeks to deliberately bring up the colour. More often though the blushing is the 'natural product of physical exertions or the pressures of emotion'.
>
> (2003: 109)

So, the more unruly Marianne becomes, the less white she literally appears to be. The more blood, life, in her veins, the unrulier the body and the more immoral the behaviour. The further away Marianne moves away from idealised whiteness, the greater an object of corporeal desire she becomes. Marianne rejects this form of English Rose femininity for something much more like (white) life itself and the audience are asked to identify with her, be more attracted to her the further she moves away from this repressive 'exterior' ideal.

Marianne can do this 'movement away' convincingly because it is Winslet who is playing Marianne, and she brings this dichotomy and resistance to the part. This then, on the surface at least, seems highly transgressive: in what becomes a supra-articulating critique, idealised whiteness in the form of the English Rose is being rejected and undermined by Marianne, the star Winslet and the heritage aesthetic. However, one can argue that the rejection of this type of ideal whiteness is one that will ultimately allow the star Winslet to be truly stellar – a borderless supericon. Once Winslet throws off, throws away, her nation-specific white identity, she can/will be an ultimate extraordinary/ordinary white star with international appeal above and beyond the specific constraints of the English Rose ideal found in this film.

Of course, there is a price to pay, a degree of moral retribution for Marianne/Winslet daring to be more than this idealised white, English Rose figure. Willoughby cheats on Marianne and abandons her for money, and the film ends with her marrying the man whom she had earlier spurned for Willoughby, and therefore probably does not love. However, this man (the Colonel) is himself a transgressive figure, who as a younger man had wanted to marry someone outside his class but was unable to; and so, her unruly freedoms are, it is suggested, largely safe with him.

Similarly, one could argue that there is eventually a degree of moral retribution for Winslet also, forced to become the slender ideal of modern media imagination in her most recent public incarnation, after years of jibes and commentary about her overweight body. However, to return to a point which is worth reiteration, the empowered oscillation between fat/thin, red/blonde, etc. may in the end confirm Winslet's exterior status as the ultimate white star who can make herself up as she pleases. Not retribution, then, but divine revelation, for an always absent/present star.

The unruly Winslet

If Winslet is unruly in her heritage incarnation by virtue of somatic and sensorial gestures, the later, post-Titanic, indie Winslet is, by contrast, *all* voluptuous body, curves and sexual urges. She is filmically and publicly free to be sexual, desirable and glamorous. Not only do we see Winslet's naked body on screen, but she advances the sexual encounters she is found in (*Titanic, Holy Smoke, Quills, The Dressmaker*). We see her dressed in low-cut, figure-hugging designer dresses at galas, premieres and 'cafe parties', often hand-in-hand with superstar directors, every inch the star. The unruly Winslet is an embodied white female star who *is* to be desired and desirable, if ultimately above and beyond racial classification.

However, the 'later' Winslet is unruly in another sense. As Winslet's body has become fuller – more publicly desirable and sexualised – her head/face has also, almost simultaneously, become more softly angelic, literally blonde(r). This is because Winslet's hair has also gone through a transformation over the years, from dark brown, to pre-Raphaelite red, to light brown, to high-lit blonde, to near total blonde most recently. It is as if the maturing Winslet has become a trans-Atlantic white star in/through the persona of the *modern* blonde 'bombshell' figure.

Modern, or 'updated', because this is an unruly figure who despite their sexual activity seems to remain free of moral retribution. In films, such as *Holy Smoke* (Campion, 1999), Winslet truly transgresses what it means to be a white woman by destroying the white patriarch in the film. Unlike Marilyn Monroe and Diana Dors, then, Winslet seems to be able to have an unruly white body without moral consequences. However, this is in part because she exercises her freedom in independent or European art films, where such transgressions are encouraged and generically or authorially expected. It is also because Winslet is ultimately above and beyond this or any (one) film fiction incarnation. She moves in and between image-spaces as if she is not-of-this-world – borderless, de-raced, like the material of ideal whiteness (see Figure 5.2).

In *Holy Smoke*, one of the most transgressive images of the film occurs during the opening credit sequence. Ruth Barron (Kate Winslet) makes her way along a vibrant, intoxicating Delhi street, and is mesmerised by the appearance of a group of young 'white' women

Figure 5.2 In-between in *Holy Smoke*

dressed in white saris worshipping, she soon learns, the guru, Baba. Ruth has left home to find herself, and has travelled to India, one presumes, to learn about and to experience different, more exotic cultures than her own: cultures that have a degree more life or vitality than the one she has left behind in white, suburban Australia. This opening is soon set in the narrative context of Eastern mysticism, and of Ruth's rites of passage journey into the heart of the Other: offering up a profound critical mediation on the nature of whiteness and of her own white identity. Ruth immediately sees, senses and experiences the energy, physicality and feminine power of these white women who are positively 'Othered' through their connection to the sari and guru worship. These are women who have, in effect, left holy and saintly Christianity, their dreaded suburbia and the 'death' of idealised whiteness behind. These are women who have left absence for presence, a dead (from the neck down) spirituality for a mystical force that rewards their physical and spiritual life on earth. Ruth is immediately attracted to this liberating Otherness and soon clothes herself in the white sari – a transgressive act against (her) idealised female whiteness and the repressive constraints of the white culture she has left behind. It is not just her family name that is 'Barron'.

The image of the white sari is a recurrently powerful one in the film. When Ruth is tricked by her worried family into returning to Australia, she arrives wearing it, deliberately displaying her spiritual and sexual conversion, and the rejection of her family's mores. When she dances wildly in the outback, she does so in the white sari, which offers glimpses of her flesh, her midriff, the outline of her breasts as she moves. Ruth is metaphorically bringing this Othered life, her libidinal corporeality, to this barren 'desert-white' homeland. When PJ (Harvey Keitel), the deprogrammer employed by her family to 'recover' her, tries to show her the error of her cultish ways, he takes away her white sari as if this will return her to the 'natural' state of her white femininity. The white sari is the textural symbol, then, of her embodied Otherness, of her rejection of idealised whiteness and it this touch-based symbolism that terrifies PJ as white patriarch and protector.

When Ruth removes even these floating textures, to leave her literally naked before the male gaze, we get to the see the thickness of her flesh, her full physical presence, where only symbol had been before. Again, it is important to highlight that it is the star Winslet who decides to wear the white sari, and whose curvaceous body we see stripped bare. Winslet is, as Kate Pullinger suggests, 'possessed of a full-blooded, amorous beauty' (1999: 8), a beauty that seems to be the very embodiment of a fleshed and confident sexuality. In short, the echoes of Winslet's unruly star image necessarily bring transgression to the part of Ruth.

Winslet gives Ruth a degree of textual power, then, that renders PJ ultimately impotent. He is no match for this fully embodied and young 'blonde' transgressor, whose spirit is not holy but revolutionary. Played by the ageing and flabby Harvey Keitel, PJ struggles to reason with her or reclaim her for white patriarchy. By the end of the film, although both have been wounded and brutalised, it is PJ's dishevelled masculinity that is shown to be inferior to the life-force Ruth is charged with. Ruth/Winslet is ultimately a triumphant white transgressor.

In the recent film, *The Dressmaker*, a similar scenario is envisaged as Tilly/Winslet seeks revenge for being wrongly accused of murder as a child. Tilly is a seductive dressmaker who designs dresses that empower the women who wear them. The fabric and colour of the dresses are sensorial signifiers, transforming the contours of the staid, rural town. The film ends with Tilly burning the whole town down, offering her own moral retribution to conformity and limp patriarchy.

Slender Winslet: Exterior Winslet

However, this is not the end of the story in terms of Winslet's star image-meaning. Winslet's full and sexualised body has been, and continues to be, rallied against, and her transgressive whiteness is, and continues to be, challenged. But this is not through textual exorcism or revelatory biography (yet), but through the extratextual tyranny of cultural slenderness. Throughout Winslet's career, the tabloid press and gossip magazines in the UK have focused on the size of her body, connecting it, in the most fascistic of discourses, to good/bad motherhood and morality. When Winslet is big she is lazy, slovenly (shots of her in jeans, sneakers, hair in a mess are used to suggest this). When Winslet is big she is a bad Mother who has 'cheated' on James Threapleton and who spends more time at galas than with her own child. When Winslet is big she is unhappy, unattached, lonely or 'fame' has got to her. In short, when Winslet is big something is wrong with her. The something wrong is that she is no longer ideally white.

Of course, the story of Winslet's more recent stardom is one of dieting, fitness and fat busting. She has now worked her body into a thinner state of ideal perfection and with her blonde hair and superstar lifestyle, she seems to be the personification of the idealised white female star that dominant culture favours. Winslet glows, she radiates, she lights up the night sky. Given that thinness can be read as a 'tyranny', however, this may not be a sign of compliance and conformity, so much as the ultimate statement of Winslet's own self-control and mastery.

Winslet's blonde thinness, nonetheless, has taken a different affective turn more recently: as the cold and deadly Jeanine Matthews in *The Divergent Series: Insurgent* (Schwentka, 2015), she hunts down Tris (Shailene Woodley) and Four (Theo James), two divergents, or people who don't fit perfectly into one of society's five factions, and who therefore threaten her corrupt control of a dystopian Chicago. Winslet's self-control and mastery of her body become a conduit for social surveillance and control.

In summary, one can begin to argue that Winslet is generally a rather 'problematic fit' in terms of the meaning of her white stardom. Regardless of timeline or film form, Winslet is a troubling, transgressively cohering force in her films: a transgression that bleeds over from the range of extra-textual texts that reveal her to be an unruly woman, especially in terms of her body size/weight and her independent mind. Across these media texts, across a great number of her films, Winslet constantly subverts what it means to be an English Rose, an ideal white woman, a blonde bombshell figure and an idealised white star. Winslet is on one level a transgressive white-fantasy figure, who through her unruly body and aggressive 'feminised' roles resists absence for presence, spirit for body, fat for thin, empowerment for docility.

Nonetheless, on another level, Winslet's shifting and contradictory form of white stardom may after all serve to shore it up as an extraordinary form of subjectivity. The superhuman qualities of her white stardom: extraordinary and ordinary, heritage-esque and independent, promiscuous and an 'English Rose', the 'blonde bombshell' who is unruly, too fat, too thin, make hers an *unearthly* corporeality that cannot be named as white at all. The meaning of Winslet continues to float as if she herself possesses the qualities of an extraordinary angel.

Winslet is a sign of the times: in a contemporary geopolitical landscape where national borders have never been so porous, national identity so unstable and white power structures so much under threat; Winslet's contradictory, transformative and oscillating form of white stardom may actually work to recuperate whiteness and to secure its place as the highest ideal available to man/woman. It is no coincidence that in a great deal of Winslet's later pictures, travel and movement across borders is a key motor of the narrative, as if whiteness itself were on the move, repositioning, renewing itself in the Winslet persona itself set in the global age. Winslet is a death star but with an awful lot of life-force at her/its core.

CHAPTER SUMMARY

In this chapter we look at the way somatic relations have a major impact on the way celebrities meet the social world and the activities of fans and consumers. Celebrity embodiment involves forms of fleshy governance, but it also found in the affective realm of the sublime. The case study on Kate Winslet stands as a fascinating contrast to both the analysis of Scarlett Johansson in Chapter 2 and Russell Crowe in Chapter 4: the three chapters use whiteness to analyse the stars in question but from alien, national and unruly markers. One can again see both the models working in consort and contestation but that the nodes articulate within and across cultures and affects.

6

THE LIQUID LIGHTS OF CELEBRITY PRODUCTIONS

This chapter is concerned with production as it is found on the circuit of celebrity culture. It recognises that celebrities are produced but also that there are cultures of production, shaping the products produced by the entertainment industries. The chapter explores the mass society thesis and the issues of late, liquid capitalist production and the dreams it manufactures.

CELEBRITY CULTURAL PRODUCTIONS

Culture is a term we use in a variety of ways, each definition laced with political and historical connotations and contestations. In fact, the meaning of culture has not only shifted over time but its present definition is bound up with these associative histories.

First, culture can be understood to be implicated in the process of human development, as if humankind is on a forward march to ever greater civility and enlightenment. Culture can be seen to be a state of intellectual refinement, separating the high from the low: to possess high culture is *to be cultured*. By contrast, to lack cultural capital traps one within particular disempowering structures of exclusion. Culture is not only a property of social class but gender, race and sexuality swim in its tides: some cultural forms, such as soap operas and rom-coms are considered to be feminine, while rap and hip-hop are entwined with black American culture. These sub-cultures can stand in radical opposition to dominant culture but are also positioned on the negative or lesser-side of power-saturated binary oppositions.

When it comes to celebrity culture these qualities and oppositions are apparent: celebrity is very often thought of as low-culture unless of course it is associated with higher art forms, such as literary figures, film auteurs and art-house performers. Celebrity is often associated with feminine forms of behaviour, such as gossip, hysteria and excessive drama, and yet privileges whiteness as its ideal type of embodied production. Celebrity is drawn into debates about the trivialisation of public affairs and dis-enlightenment as a consequence.

Mark Rowland (2008) suggests the moral malaise of the present is the fault of celebrity culture. Rowland terms this degenerate version of celebrification 'new variant fame', or vfame, a state in which 'we are constitutionally incapable of distinguishing quality from bullshit'. The metaphors that Rowlands uses throughout *Fame* repeat and solidify the notion that vfame is akin to disease or mental illness, and that Western culture has undergone a 'severe dementia'. Vfame is a symptom of a Western world cut adrift in a sea of obscene relativism, where Britney Spears can be considered to be 'just as good as Beethoven'. Rowlands contends that such comparisons are 'truly facile'. In fact, he considers that cultural relativism has led to a state in which ordinary people can no longer make critical sense of their lives, too busy are they with consuming empty celebrity signifiers and comparing the merits of, say, *Hello!* magazine and the *E!* entertainment channel.

Second, culture can be drawn upon to define and solidify national and ethnic identities: to be the fabric out of which imagined sovereign communities grow (Anderson, 1983) (see the discussion of Russell Crowe in Chapter 3). Here culture is essentialised: ideology is turned into the skin and bones of the people who embrace its over-arching values and beliefs, rituals and practices. Culture involves the transmission of shared meanings, where making sense of the world happens through representational exchanges and relays: through a series of *semantic networks* and *signifying practices*.

As we saw in Chapter 3, the relationship between celebrity and national identity is a very strong one, with key stars acting as forms of nationalist 'social glue'. Celebrities are increasingly the conduits through which ideology is produced and sanctified and the celebrification of politics ensures that it exists at the very centre of the corridors of state power.

Third, culture is also the story of ordinary, everywhere, everyday life-worlds. Culture is here defined as a:

> a description of a particular way of life which expresses certain meanings and values not only in art and learning but also in institutions and *ordinary behaviour.*

> (Williams, 1976)

Drawing upon storytelling and ethnography, the minutiae of micro-actions, and observable resistance strategies, cultural studies has moved to take in/on new research methods to capture the way cultures emerge at the local level. These everyday entanglements have been also taken up in celebrity research as the way to best examine the impact of celebrity on ordinary people and everyday habitus. For example, in Jackie Stacey's work on female fans' recollections of American female films stars of the 1940s and 1950s, we find how central the production of pleasure is to the fan-star assemblage:

> The memories I have analysed have highlighted the many levels at which escapism provided pleasures for female spectators: material, sensuous, emotional as well as psychic. For example, the cinema interiors provided a utopian space and numerous sensuous luxuries; the feelings of being in an audience offered a sense of belonging and togetherness; and the stars were enjoyed as utopian transcendent fantasies. Thus, it was not simply the visual pleasures of film texts that operated, but rather a whole range of appeals which encouraged the feelings of complete absorption into another world.

> (1994: 122–3)

THE CELEBRITY TURN

Historically, and particularly through the filter of the social sciences, culture has been allotted an inferior role when considering the determination of the outcomes of social and political processes. In crude Marxist terms, for example, culture is produced: the infrastructure or the material/economic base is seen as the engine that drives human action, social history and the cultural processes separately housed in what is termed the 'superstructure' (Hall, 1997). Culture broadly reflects the material conditions of any society and supports the continuation of those conditions through processes and practices of ideological mystification. As Dominic Strinati suggests,

> Dominant groups in society, including fundamentally but not exclusively the ruling class, maintain their dominance by securing the 'spontaneous consent' of subordinate groups, including the working class, through the negotiated construction of a political and ideological consensus which incorporates both dominant and dominated groups.
>
> (1995: 165)

However, with the so-called 'cultural turn', culture comes to be understood as the very matter that shapes and influences human action and the forces of social history. The cultural turn recognises that human experience has become increasingly *mediated* and that the *everyday* has been '*culturalised*' or turned into arenas of commodification and pleasure domes. New cultural sensibilities and lifestyles are argued to have emerged in this theatre of possessive individualism. The aestheticisation, or 'fashioning', of an almost infinite number of goods, services, institutions and organisations means that people move around in a social universe where branding, imaging and specific representations have been produced by one form of cultural industry or another. According to Baudrillard, in fact, we have all become consumers, with our identities and our sense of a place in the world made up from our consumption practices. We are what we eat, drink, wear, buy.

Further, the cultural turn recognises that the economic organises and represents itself in a particular set of social references: there is a discourse of the economy which allows people to identify with and understand its manifestations. We increasingly use the language of culture to organise the economic and to employ cultural practices to better run workplaces and employee relations. The economic is thus considered to have become thoroughly 'culturalised', particularly because the rise of transnational *cultural industries* is argued to globalise and

Americanise world cultural forms. The cultural economy involves cultural intermediaries, operating between the interface of production and consumption, who re-fashion cultural goods in the light of consumer feedback. In these new cultural economies, new types of service/media workers emerge, creating a new 'mythic' centre where notions of a good and productive life are seen to emerge.

Celebrity is implicated in all these cultural-economic intersections: the aestheticisation of the everyday very often occurs through the commodities and dreams of famous people; and the role of cultural intermediaries is centred on the connection between celebrity relations and the consumer goods and services they are seeking to promote. Beyoncé:

> is less a human being, more an ambulant brand, an advertisement for a new gilded age when commodities overpower everything – including race – and in which some black people are able to exercise a right that is afforded almost sacramental status in modern culture: to make consumer choices. One of the effects of the Beyoncé brand – the physical appearance, and name associated with the abundant products she dispenses or endorses – is to undermine the age-old belief in racism and racist discrimination by reducing hitherto insoluble problems to the dimensions of the market. In the Beyoncé narrative, racism is merely a vestige of a bygone age when black and other ethnic minorities were outside the consumerist economy. Now, as Beyoncé incessantly reminds anyone who has ever listened to her music, seen her movies or bought an item of the numberless pieces of merchandise that bear her imprimatur – and that probably means all of us – black people are on the inside.
> (Cashmore, 2010: 138)

Famous people are not only the obsessive subjects of the media but are employed to enunciate from its centre: to offer counsel, impart wisdom, comment on all manner of issues and themes; and to make linkages between their fame, wisdom and commodity and consumer purchase. As Tania Lewis suggests,

> What lifestyle programming sells to the audience then is not just products but ways of living and managing one's private life. The celebrity lifestyle expert takes this process one step further – embodying and enacting

models of consumer citizenship through their own much publicized and idealized domestic and personal lifestyles, which are played out across their various personae as experts, celebrities and private selves.

(2010: 587)

In the workplace, gurus and inspirational figures are employed to energise the workforce and to self-brand the institution as particularly favoured. The cultural and economic world seems to be very much in the productive service of celebrity. Nonetheless, there are different and competing ways to engage with the liquid lights of producing celebrity culture, which this chapter will now work through.

PRODUCING MASS CELEBRITY CULTURE

According to Adorno and Horkheimer, proponents of the Frankfurt School, once a cultural text is produced within a capitalist industry, it is immediately corrupted or polluted because it will have been produced solely with profit-making in mind: and with profit-making central, the processes of production will inevitably be rationalised and standardised to ensure that profit is maximised. Replication, repetition and product and service reinforcement are the indicators of mass culture, resulting in the relentless production of genre films, reality television, pulp fiction, pop music and the tabloid press. In drawing upon such a massified framework, Adorno and Horkheimer linked,

the idea of the culture industry to a model of mass culture in which cultural production had become a routine, standardised repetitive operation that produced undemanding cultural commodities which in turn resulted in a type of consumption that was also standardised, distracted and passive.

(Keith Negus, 1997)

For Adorno and Horkheimer, in a capitalist economy cultural forms take on the following characteristics and qualities. First, cultural items are produced in the same way as goods and services are: there is in fact a 'culture industry'. This means that films, records, television programmes, and film stars and celebrities have assembly-line characteristics and are subject to the same 'rationalised organisational procedures' that befalls the production of washing machines and auto-mobiles. Cultural forms are standardised products, mass-produced, and therefore work at the 'lowest common denominator' so that the widest number of people can consume them.

Second, through the consumption of these texts, people imagine themselves in terms of a 'pseudo individuality' in which,

> the individual is an illusion not merely because of the standardization of the means of production. He is tolerated only so long as his complete identification with the generality is unquestioned. Pseudo individuality is rife: from the standardized jazz improvisation to the exceptional film star whose hair curls over her eye to demonstrate her originality. What is individual is no more than the generality's power to stamp the accidental detail so firmly that it is accepted as such. The defiant reserve or elegant appearance of the individual on show is mass-produced like Yale locks, whose only difference can be measured in fractions of millimeters.
> (Adorno and Horkheimer, 1997: 154)

Culture is loaded with a particular (dominant) ideology, which works upon the passive and obedient audience. Culture effects and shapes in a one-way causal relationship those that it comes into contact with – defined as the mass audience. One case study will help illustrate these points.

Manufacturing boy bands: BTS

The example of manufactured boy bands is particularly insightful here: put together by pop music 'gurus', individual members are chosen on their shared physical characteristics, ability to dance and harmonise (see Figure 6.1). Each band member embodies a certain type of safe and sanitised masculinity, their difference to one another minuscule: hair colour, clothes and persona type – cheeky, shy, overt, innocent. Their music is built upon recognisable musical leitmotifs, riffs, harmonies, with high-tempo songs matched against slow burn romantic numbers: their songs are formula-based and mass-produced. As Sullivan suggests,

> Boy bands reproduce the sounds and harmonies of others in cover versions, a musical mode that emphasizes safety, stability and the repetitive reliability of tried and tested formulae – factors as important

as tax-breaks, low-cost labour and a highly educated workforce for overseas, especially American, investors.

(2007: 190)

Sell-out tours and merchandising are crucial to the mass-marketing boy bands undergo. Their songs and performances are synergetically connected to a range of consumer goods and services, to live video streams, television and magazine interviews.

The seven-member South Korean boy band BTS, formed by Big Hit Entertainment, is an interesting case in point. Each band member went through a series of auditions and the make-up of the band went through different iterations until they got the combination of personality types right. As Bang Shi Hyuk, CEO of Big Hit Entertainment, explains, 'once he saw Rap Monster rap, he thought a hip-hop group should be created. Hyuk then set out on the task of looking for members to join the proposed group. He targeted members who could not only be idols but would also be able to tell their own stories' (*Koreaboo*, 2017). Musically, BTS aims for transnational hip-hop pop songs based on a classic formula. They de-odorise the more radical qualities of the genre for notes and harmonies that can be (re)exported, particularly to the United

Figure 6.1 Manufacturing boy bands: BTS
Image courtesy of Shutterstock

States and Europe. BTS employ such writers as Matthew Tishler, a Canadian-born multi-platinum songwriter and music producer who has written and produced songs for teen pop artists such as Ashley Tisdale, Dove Cameron, Olivia Holt and Ross Lynch, as well as popular K-pop/J-pop artists like EXO, Taeyeon, Namie Amuro, Kumi Koda and EXILE Atsushi. In 2017, their latest album broke into numerous international markets, including the Billboard Top 100 (see Table 6.1), and they were invited to play on the *Ellen DeGeneres Show*.

Table 6.1 BTS album chart position by country

Chart (2017)	*Peak position*
Australian Albums (ARIA)	8
Austrian Albums (Ö3 Austria)	17
Belgian Albums (Ultratop Flanders)	18
Belgian Albums (Ultratop Wallonia)	51
Canadian Albums (*Billboard*)	3
Chinese Albums (Billboard V Chart)	2
Danish Albums (Hitlisten)	34
Dutch Albums (MegaCharts)	19
Finnish Albums (Suomen virallinen lista)	11
French Albums (SNEP)	83
German Albums (Offizielle Top 100)	57
Hungarian Albums (MAHASZ)	40
Irish Albums (IRMA)	19
Italian Albums (FIMI)	56
Japanese Albums (Oricon)	1
Japanese Digital Albums (Oricon)	1
Japan Hot Albums (*Billboard*)	4
New Zealand Albums (RMNZ)	9
Norwegian Albums (VG-lista)	16
Scottish Albums (OCC)	17
South Korean Albums (Gaon)	1
Spanish Albums (PROMUSICAE)	33
Swedish Albums (Sverigetopplistan)	13
Swiss Albums (Schweizer Hitparade)	26
UK Albums (OCC)	14
US *Billboard* 200	7
US Independent Albums (*Billboard*)	2
US World Albums (*Billboard*)	1

Thanks to an active social media presence, BTS took home the 2017 Top Social Artist at the Billboard Music Awards, and was the most-talked-about artist/group on Twitter. With 502 million retweets and likes, BTS were number one in both the 'Top 10 most tweeted-about music artists in the US' and the 'Top 10 most buzzed-about celebrities around the world'. This highly responsive set of communication channels has resulted in BTS having one of the largest fan-bases, ARMY, an acronym for 'Adorable Representative MC for Youth,' Their fan base arguably reinforces the para-social production of pseudo intimacy and attraction: turning feeling and emotion into conduits for the purchase of cultural texts and productions that reinforce the simulacra of individuality against the reality of the 'crowd' instinct.

NOT PRODUCING MASS CELEBRITY: AN ALTERNATIVE POSITION

One can offer up a number of criticism of the mass celebrity production position taken up by scholars such as Adorno and Horkheimer, and Mark Rowland. One of the sub-texts of this theory of massification is that authenticity and creativity singularly reside with 'high art' texts and it is only with 'low art' texts or 'popular culture' that commodification and ideological fixedness exist. Invariably, this low art culture is consumed by the working class (prime-time quiz shows) or 'women' (melodramas/soap operas) or people from different ethnic backgrounds (rap, drum and bass).

Celebrity exists in the maelstrom of this imagined relative emptiness. However, when we actually examine the 'value' of celebrity culture we find the complex interplay between high and low art, and the various threads of artistic practice. For example, Kanye's *Runaway* music video (2010) draws upon various high and popular art forms and idioms, as Nitsuh Abebe of New York summarises:

> In *Runaway*, the short film he released this fall, he uses a plinking piano to summon a ballet troupe, then sings about raising a toast to the douchebags and assholes of the world — in other words, he sticks a symbol of classical refinement next to a lyric about being toxic and acting ugly. (Ballet already does this, too: All that beauty is built on twisted toes, bloody shoes, deformed legs.) ... He's attracted to

these symbols of classical refinement and aristocracy — ballet, golden goblets, 'Persian rugs with cherub imagery,' Greek mythology, next-level luxury brands — and then he sits among them reminding us that it doesn't make him any different, or keep him from acting poisonous, or pissing the world off by grabbing people's microphones.

(2010)

Second, the mass society thesis denies that at the point of consumption people actively work on the culture that has been produced for them: appropriating it, shaping it, subverting it, modifying it as they do so. 'Culture' only really becomes meaningful when it is actively produced at the site of consumption. At certain key moments, consumption practices determine or shape production processes. The audience can affect production practices and procedures through fan engagement, activism and marshaling the media communication tools to ensure they have a say in the text's form. As Henry Jenkins argues:

Media producers can garner greater loyalty and more compliance to legitimate concerns if they court the allegiance of fans; the best way to do this turns out to be giving them some stake in the survival of the franchise, ensuring that the provided content more fully reflects their interests, creating a space where they can make their own creative contributions, and recognizing the best work that emerges.

(2006a: 173)

Third, the idea that people from differing cultures now consume a similar range of cultural texts, in similar contexts, with similar effects, denies the way local differences work upon the global. Globalisation, from this alternative perspective, is conceived in terms of a process of creative and conjoining hybridisation. Fans of celebrities actively transcode the meaning of the stars they admire depending on a whole range of local and autobiographical contexts.

the new global cultural systems promotes difference instead of suppressing it, but selects the dimensions of difference ... we are not all becoming the same, but we are portraying, dramatising and communicating our differences to each other in ways that are more widely intelligible. The globalizing hegemony celebrates particular kinds of diversity while submerging others.

(Wilk, 1995: 118)

The transnational is never simply a singular or static exchange; a fixed meeting or consumption point. The relationship between text and context, place and reception, translation and translatability is a myriad one, liquid in form, and always involves a matter of becoming. As Hunt and Wing-Fai note:

Trans denotes moving through space or across lines, as well as changing the nature of something ... (it) also alludes to the transversal, the transactional, the translational, and the transgressive aspects of contemporary behaviour and imagination that are incited, enabled, and regulated by the changing logics of states and capitalism.

(2008: 3)

We now turn to the central case study of the chapter: an analysis of Barack Obama's 2008 election campaign, in terms of liquid spectacle that spoke in transnational registers. Through the Obama case study, we get to see how political stardom is manufactured and how its cultural registers produce ripples across the international landscape.

CASE STUDY

Producing Barack Obama

Obama loves New Zealand

The ZMFM Breakfast Show with Polly and Grant is one of New Zealand's most popular radio shows. Irreverent, mainstream, topical and occasionally softly political, Polly and Grant provide the soundtrack to the start of the weekday. During the American presidential election campaign in 2008, which ran at the same time as New Zealand's general election, Barack Obama became a constant topic on the show, with Polly and Grant regularly playing snippets of his speeches, commenting on his extraordinary aura and charisma and championing his political message. During one show (22 October 2008), Polly re-tells the following story that she had been relayed: a New Zealand student on exchange at an American university had been on campus and part of the celebratory crowd when Barack Obama had come to envision their political future. The student, straining to be heard above the chants, whistles and applause of the 15,000-strong crowd, had shouted out: 'New Zealand loves Obama'.

On hearing this, he reportedly turned and responded, in what is read as that persona-defining mercurial voice: 'Obama loves New Zealand'. That Obama was valorised on this radio show (and much of the mainstream, virtual and social media in New Zealand), and that his key campaign themes of hope, change and transformation had travelled to New Zealand (as it had across much of the world), begins to locate him as a spectacular celebrity politician, who resonates profoundly and prophetically at a global level. That his auratic iconicity and message of hope and renewal are ultimately liquid or transient, as I will go on to explore, defines not only the condition of late modernity but the core quality of celebrity culture as it manifests itself today. For this chapter, I will contend that Barack Obama is the leading illustration of what is the expanded nexus of celebrity, spectacle and politics in the age of what Zygmund Bauman refers to as liquid modernity, or 'the era of disembedding without re-embedding' (Bauman and Tester, 2001: 89). This is the era in which a traumatic sense of fear, uncertainty and transience defines one's relationship to the nation state, and social centre, as they lose their economic singularity and cultural coherency and cohesiveness, in a world system ever interconnected and driven increasingly, incessantly by supra-corporate concerns and spectacle-based presentations.

In this world of 'togetherness dismantled' (Bauman, 2000: 119), the disenfranchised individual feels they cannot meet the trans-capital intensive, show reel-like, boundaryless world on solid ground. That love, or a liquefied definition of it, is key to this imagined and affective communion between Obama and those who adore him suggests that there is a terrible wanting and simultaneous waning to those who look for such rootedness and the promise of deliverance in the celebrity political figure. This is a charismatic authority figure, who promises this solidity yet streams in and out of material view, unable to fix or properly propagate their communion beyond triumphant spectacularism. Their 'lightness of being' (ibid, 123–9) is powerfully seductive and decidedly empty because it echoes the instantaneous (instant) way in which all lives are increasingly led. I will suggest that liquid celebrity is one of the cornerstones of liquid modernity, and Barack Obama is the epitome of this 'runniness'.

What is this love of which the Kiwi student speaks, that Polly and Grant cherish and share and which Obama requites? It is love high on the oxygen of the media event; a love born of uprootedness and a longing for connectedness; a love fashioned in promotional strategising and consumed in the glare of cultural intermediaries, bean counters and YouTube downloaders. When the post-human, shape-shifting avatar Obama (all things to all people, as I will go on to argue) uses the words 'love' or 'hope', or the words 'change you can believe in', he commodifies their sensibilities and extends their connotations into the folds and flows of transient commodity possession, and to the self that self-loves. While this is a love that seemingly knows no bounds or acknowledges no boundaries, it is also one that knows no bounds and has no lasting ties, as it is created and consummated virtually; furnished by deep-seated needs that cannot be met on these para-social terms; articulated through hard-nosed politicking; made on unequal but effaced power geometries; and mobilised to serve ever-shifting consumption needs.

Consequently, this love is a watery love, an absence of love, even if it is love imagined to be fulsome, liberating or 'blindingly intense' (Bauman, 2000: 62). This is, in the end, a hopeless love, one that will eventually return the devotee to existential anguish and dissatisfaction, because the love interest (Obama) cannot commit or consummate, except in cliché symbols, commodity signs and grand gestures, or through higher-order claims to be beyond simple earthly love (to be a man of destiny, a God-man). When this love perishes – when destiny fails or does not live up to the prophecy mandated – the Obama devotee moves on to the next higher-order celebrity figure, never fully re-embedding, as this relationship will also inevitably liquefy. Obama, too, will be consumed by liquid capital and the routinisation of political life, brought back down to Earth, so to speak. Similarly, the socially conscious celebrities who currently invest in his divinity (Oprah, De Niro, Damon) will find other personages, causes or movements in whom to believe.

To summarise, then, in this case study it will be my contention that Barack Obama is the epitome of the liquid celebrity, embodying the floating nature of capitalism in the global age, commodifying

the concept of hope and offering the disenfranchised devotee/fan/
worshiper – albeit fleetingly – the chance to embrace change and to
live fully again in a world that has been found hitherto to be cut free
from meaning and belonging. It is through Obama that I intend to find
the fluid pulse of celebrity culture today; its arterial like qualities that
emanate from the social centre and which promises each and every
one of us (so 'inclusive' is its imagined reach) solidity and belonging,
but which ultimately confirms our recurring or returning alienation
from the modern world.

This case study focuses upon the publicity and promotional material
created by Barack Obama's presidential campaign team, and on the
news reports, interviews and blogs produced in the mainstream media
and the virtual social networking sites. My central critical framework
will be Zygmund Bauman's concept of liquid modernity (Bauman and
Tester, 2001), mapped onto the figure of Obama and celebrity culture more generally. However, I will also be drawing upon and fusing
together Doug Kellner's work on media spectacle (2003, 2008); Nick
Coudry's myth of the media centre (2003, 2009) and the celebrity as
the privileged point of access to its glittering and empowered arena;
and Emile Durkheim's theory of charismatic authority (1968). The
concept of liquid celebrity will run into all these articulating positions,
so that it (and Obama) emerges as contingent upon a watery modern
landscape where, to appropriate Marx and Engels (2002), all that is
solid melts into liquid.

While, for the most part, my position equates liquid celebrity with
existential lack, a crisis in political authority and late capitalist commodity dreaming, I conclude by assessing the potentiality of what might
also be understood to be the sublime nature of its embodiment. The case
study will finally, if briefly, turn to phenomenology to re-engineer its
negative approach to this sticky concept called 'liquid celebrity'.

Liquid celebrity spectacle

According to Doug Kellner, the cultural world is organised around the
production and consumption of media spectacles, or:

> Those phenomena of media culture which embody contemporary soci-
> ety's basic values, serve to enculturate individuals into its way of life,

and dramatize its controversies and struggles, as well as its modes of conflict resolution. They include media extravaganzas, sports events, political happenings, and those attention-grabbing occurrences that we call news – a phenomena [sic] that itself has been subjected to the logic of spectacle and tabloidization in the era of the media sensationalism, political scandal and contestation, seemingly unending cultural war, and the new phenomenon of Terror War.

(2003: 2)

A media spectacle has aesthetic and technological dimensions: it utilises special effects, costume, set, setting, music, graphics, pyrotechnics, consumer goods endowed with special significance and exaggerated, binary storytelling arcs to present the event as awesome, overpowering, easy to comprehend and consequently essential to emotional pleasure or self-centredness. Media spectacles are also highly public social events, ritualistic in form, hierarchical and require certain types of act and action by those taking part (Dayan and Katz, 1992) One is asked to take part in the 'show' that one is watching in a celebratory or condemnatory manner. There will often be VIP areas, celebrity hosts, compères and guests, and event triggers or signifiers (music, fireworks, conflict, dancing, a limousine arriving) for the type of behaviour required at any particular moment (boos, whistles, clapping, awe, wonderment, silence, applause). Spectacle events build to a crescendo or defining sublime moment, in which the orchestrated, collective response is seen, felt to be breath-taking. This response is itself presented to be spectacular: images of the spectacle are cross-cut with planning and tracking, aerial and close-up shots of the mesmerised or enrapt crowd, in a dizzying alignment of celebratory participation and spectacular excess. One has only to think of the megaspectacle rock/ pop concert by a band such U2, or a solo artiste such as Madonna, to gain a sense of this imagined wonderment captured in the close-up shot of the desiring, star-truck or joyfully screaming face.

As Kellner suggests in the above quotation, there is an ideological dimension to media spectacle. It tries to seduce the individual and efface or naturalise its own architecture so that the spectacle seems non-political while it depoliticises its consumers. A media spectacle is very often a fun-filled, decidedly consumerist, leisure-based culture of attractions, which asks for a purchasing/purchaser mentality, and attempts to shape or effect identity formation so that it hinges upon the belief that one is a possessive individual who lives in a Show Time universe (Pateman, 1988). This is an ideology, then, wedded to an 'entertainment economy' and, more broadly, consumer culture, as the spectacle is produced to sell itself and selling and buying in general, in a high-octane 'vortex of publicity' (Werneck, 1991). As Kellner suggests, this structural shift 'to a society of the spectacle involves a commodification of previously non-colonised sectors of social life and the extension of bureaucratic control to the realms of leisure, desire, and everyday life' (2003: 3).

Celebrity spectacle is a particular and perhaps over-determining version of this mediated, culture of attractions. When in the public sphere, celebrities exist in heightened states and they appear at events that are televised, orchestrated and designed to exhibit, to show off, their glamour and status and the range of ancillary products or services to which they are tied, or which have made the event possible. The celebrity sells their image, the goods and services to which they are connected, the event itself and spectacular culture more generally. As Kellner argues:

> Media spectacle is indeed a culture of celebrity who provide dominant role models and icons of fashion, look, and personality. In the world of spectacle, celebrity encompasses every major social domain from entertainment to politics to sports to business.
>
> (2003: 4)

It is Oscar night. Crowds of fans scream their pleasure at the arrival of their favourite film celebrity. The celebrity exits their sleek black limousine, and begins the walk up the red carpet, cordoned off to everyday people. Their Yves Saint Laurent or Versace dress shimmers in the wall of warm lights that surround them, and a multitude of Nokia mobile phones click and click, relaying images, videos and the sights and sounds of the awesome event to friends and fans through interfaces and portals global and instantaneous in reach. This is a space/venue endowed with special significance (Couldry 2003). The paparazzi crowd around frenetically, jostling to capture the authentic shot of the night, to sell on to celebrity-spectacle-obsessed magazines such as *Hello!* (who will then devote a spectacular special edition to the event). Lights flood the immaculate, reflective entrance area, and immaculately dressed TV hosts (from all corners of the world) clamour to interview the bejewelled celebrity in an imagined intimate one-to-one moment, in a special section of the foyer. Channel- or CNN-sponsored helicopters fill the night sky, gathering panoramic shots to visualise metonymically the enormity of the event. This 'entrance' event is followed by the truly spectacular Oscar night show where the dreamscape of Hollywood is recreated in the staging of the awards ceremony. Lights. Camera. Spectacle.

I would like to argue that media spectacles such as these are also particularly liquid modern in form. They are transient, a part of a must-see, must-interact-with, schedule of spectacle events that structure the media/public calendar, demanding of the audience that they passionately invest in it (as if it is the event to end all events) and to then move on dispassionately once it is finished, so that they can get ready for, and welcome in, the next spectacular on the social horizon. This, in essence, is the motor of spectacular commodity consumption. Such transience, such a constant switching of one's affections, such incessant cultural movement, based on seemingly surface-level attractions and purchase-based driven interactions, is one of the fear-inducing terrors of the age, to paraphrase Bauman and Tester (2001). The social centre cannot hold in terms of principles of faith, rationality and economic certainty, and while its liquidity paradoxically sustains it as a symbolic centre, its impact on the individual is felt as one of watery loss.

In this age of transient spectaculars, the social centre becomes filled with what Karin Knorr-Cetina calls media-produced 'unfolding structures of absence' (2001: 527–9) in which the void at the centre of mediated life is filled with the disposable, the frivolous – the wasteful events and personages presented as higher forms of social life. Celebrity spectacle sits at the kernel of this conundrum. There is a further double-bind to this symbolic centre-without-a-real-centre fissure. In the liquid modern one only matters, one only really exists, if one finds oneself in a media spectacular – a part of the show. This is the myth of the media centre, or as Nick Couldry argues:

> the claim that 'the media' are our privileged access-point to society's centre or core, the claim that what's 'going on' in the wider world is accessible first through a door marked 'media'. The myth of the

mediated centre enfolds another myth, 'the myth of the centre', the idea that 'societies' nations have not just a physical or organisational centre – a place that allocates resources, takes decisions – but a centre in a different sense, a generative centre that explains the social world's functioning and its values. Both myths obscure other realities and sources of value, other scales on which communications might connect us.

(2009: 2)

The liquid modern individual is asked not only to believe and invest in the transient nature of the spectacle, which never quite fills them up, but to accept its higher-order status while exiling them to the banality of 'ordinary' life if they are not actually a part of the show. The figure of the celebrity is at the apex of this lack-filled paradox: they head the attraction and are the gateways to life in front of the lens, to the power it affords, or else they are the constant reminder that one is powerless if one is not a famous person in a famous show. There may well be a triple bind in operation here: the celebrity spectacle, endlessly scheduled and re-packaged and re-played becomes the epitome of banality, but a banality that nonetheless is compulsive/repulsive viewing.

Media spectacles are also often nationalist creations, bringing the positive histories and meta-symbols of the nation state into one supercharged media event. This is a spectacular gathering designed to bring together and validate the imagined community of the country in question. In England, for example, there is the pomp and circumstance of the Last Night of the Proms; in the United States, the Super Bowl; and in France, Bastille Day. Such nationalist events appropriate the iconography and histography of the homeland and they are framed within a closed, discursive register that essentialises and universalises participation (everyone in the country is in tune, and always has been, with the event).

Nonetheless, their aestheticisation and commodity appeal transcends national borders and territories. In fact, the nationalist spectacle is always simultaneously internationalist, because its sense of cohesion and collective communion has global appeal (to its own diaspora, to the disenfranchised across the world); and its branding of the nation state is for tourists and commodity investors world-wide. In a very real sense, this multiplicity in purpose and reception render the spectacle porous, polysemic, and contributes to the sense that it is a transient thing that cannot be rooted or rooted into, particularly in terms of a national identity that appears fleetingly, and as nothing more than seductive symbolisation within the overall 'show' that is taking place. This 'suspension of disbelief' (Dayan and Katz 1992) in which, lost nostalgically in the spectacle of the nation, one forgets that the symbolic centre of the/a nation no longer exists, is coupled with a near-simultaneous subjunctive awakening that what one is consuming is already gone or is past tense. This is nationalist/internationalist spectacle that is always on the verge of disappearing and then re-appearing as phantom without substance.

The Beijing 2008 Olympic Games offered a global, broadcast audience of some one billion people a spectacular feast of Chinese history and culture, ending with a closing ceremony where 'Heavenly drums, silver bell dancers, light wheels and flying men took centre stage to greet guests at the National Stadium Sunday for the closing celebration of the Beijing 2008 Olympic Games' (http://en.beijing2008.cn/). Modern, confident, commodity-driven China appeared in the guise of its spectacular historical past, effacing, among other things, its human rights atrocities, and re-imagining its global capitalist reach as hyperbolic, intensified picturisation and ritualisation into which local, national and global audiences can buy. The spectacle of Brand China is conjured-up, but the very liquidity of such a presentation/representation loses its hold as meaningful communication, if not its power to hold one in its sway.

Nationalist spectaculars are, of course, often hosted by (trans)national celebrities, or they are given a prime slot within the event, or they are involved in its construction and marketing. The Beijing 2008 Olympic Games' opening and closing ceremonies were directed by star-auteur Zhang Yimou, while Jackie Chan starred in a promotional movie about successful Chinese athletes. At the Super Bowl XLIII (1 February 2009), Bruce Springsteen and the E Street Band played during the game's half-time show. In a post-Bush era, with Barack Obama's presidency ushering in an age of hope, healing and transformation, Springsteen's appearance is particularly symbolic of new nationalist sentiments. A spectacular stage performer, who performed spectacularly at Barack Obama's inauguration, Springsteen gives musical truth to the New America being reborn in 2009. He also gives commodity truth to the album that has been released and the tour that will take place. In 2010 (2011, 2012, ...), of course, a different performer will headline, with a different performance style and pop-political mandate, and with a different (but similar) range of products to be sold. This is liquid celebrity in the age of liquid capitalism. As I will now go on to argue, this is how one can and should make sense of spectacular Obama.

Spectacular Obama

Barack Obama's presidential campaign was full of spectacle and spec-tacular campaign events, presented particularly through the mass rally and the key 'speech' moment, which anchored such tumultuous gath-erings. The Obama presidential campaign was played out spectacu-larly on talk-shows, magazine front covers and numerous other sites that gathered around him. For example, auratic photographs of Obama were found on the front covers of *Vanity Fair* in July 2007 (called the 'Africa' edition), *Rolling Stone* in March 2008 (the first time the magazine came out in favour of a particular candidate), *US Weekly* in June 2008, *Ebony* in August 2008 (the 'Black Cool' issue), *GQ* in December 2008 and *Time* in December 2008 (named Person of the Year, and analysed below).

Collectively, these front pages offered the reader a metonymic and cohering representation of Obama as one who could or would lead the nation, so seemingly perfected and refreshingly honest was the man imaged before the reader. His face, presented generally in close-up, was in fact often more than enough to suggest the visionary and the enlightened: the man of and for these troubled, liquid times. This was a solid, human face that one could directly access and in which one (was told through various 'framing' mechanisms) could believe. This was a celebrity face: ideal, affective and inclusive, not least because it was also a blank, de-raced face, an argument I will also develop fur-ther below. Obama's was a spectacular face, blown up to be larger than life and any identity politics that might get in the way of its affecting signification.

The spectacle of Obama did not simply emerge, however, through such hyper-iconic settings, broadcast live or tracked in news bulle-tins and written about in the mainstream media. Obama's spectacular campaign colonised the internet and social networking sites and interfaces such as YouTube, Facebook, My Space and Twitter; and it sent (around the world) live text messages and updates to subscribers/devotees, via their mobile phones, about upcoming speeches, rallies or as a call for donations or active support. Obama posters, art prints, videos, t-shirts, mugs, books and transcripts of speeches were visible across all these sites and often re-engineered or transcoded by fans who would spread Obama graffiti and poetry and who produced short internet advertorial trailers that were a homage to him and which called on people to join the communion. As Kellner summarises:

> There has also been an impressive Internet spectacle in support of Obama's presidency. Obama has raised unprecedented amount money on the Internet. He has over two million friends on Facebook, and has mobilized youth and others through text messaging and emails. The YouTube (UT) music video 'Obama Girl,' which has a young woman singing about why she supports Obama with images of his speeches interspersed, has gotten over 5 million hits and is one of the most popular in history.
>
> (2008: 4)

It is 2 August 2008, and from my New Zealand home I am watching the spectacular YouTube footage of Senator Barack Obama accepting the Democratic nomination for President of the United States, at Denver's Invesco Field at Mile High. Set in a coliseum-type sports venue, where the Denver Broncos' National Football League team plays, the suite of cameras cut between wide, panoramic shots of the immense crowd and medium shots of Obama smiling and waving: returning the affection that he has been bestowed. Photography flashbulbs light up the night, as 85,000 people chant his name and his campaign slogans and, with absolute delight, wave American flags and 'Change' banners. Obama delivers his speech from an elaborate columned stage, resembling a miniature Greek temple. The plywood columns are also reminiscent of Washington's Capitol building or the White House. Two giant plasma screens relay images of Obama as he delivers his speech. Shots of the adoring crowd are rhythmically inter-cut as awe and wonder 'response moments' to an important truth he has touched upon, or to a piece of rhetorical flourish he has countenanced. The public ritual inherent in such events as, for example, clapping spontaneously, is a cultural known, but embodied as if it is not known but instantaneously 'lived'. The circular stage on which he stands is neon-lit and encircled by mounted cameras, and gently raised steps lead from its raised centre down into the crowd, or the VIP area (where his wife, children, running-mate and dignitaries sit).

This is as much television quiz-show aesthetics and theme-park iconography as it is political theatre. The setting pastiches and mixes together ancient history, key US governmental institutions and Disneyland imaging to create this liquid entertainment environment. A neon CNN advertorial is placed conspicuously in one of the prominent structures, confirming the commodity and infotainment-based (Kellner 2003) nature of this event. The key commodity is of course Obama: Brand Obama or liquid celebrity Obama. This runniness can be found in the slogans that ran across his campaign, repeated by the crowd and in the speech he made that night. Slogans such as 'Change we can believe in', 'Yes we can', 'A new beginning' and 'We must pledge once more to walk into the future' are self-referential, without content, ideographs or higher-order abstractions, 'representing commitment to a particular but equivocal and ill-defined normative goal' (McGee 1980: 12). Consequently, these worked well 'because they were empty boundary objects – different groups could project their own concrete hopes for a better future on the signifiers offered' (Knorr-Cetina 2009: 132). Such slogans were above or beyond class, ethnic, religious and gender lines and attempted, therefore, to create the sense of a national cause – a mythical imagined centre – in which all Americans had an investment.

However, the purchase in these slogans of aperture, their 'glittering generality' as intangible nouns that embody universal ideals, meant that groups from across the world could find their selfhood embedded in them. Their liquidity in form and content met or mixed with the watery nature of modern life so that, for example, Kenyans could appropriate and transcribe them as, 'Sing Obama', 'Obama for Africa', 'Walk thinking Obama' and 'Obama for families'. In New Zealand, John Key's right-wing Nationalist Party was able to riff/rip off such slogans, aligning themselves with the mantra of 'Change' (after 10 years of a Labour government) that Obama was prophesying. That New Zealanders could be seduced both by the liberal politics of

Obama and Key (who won the election by a sizeable margin) confirms the liquidity of the message and the looseness of attachment in the liquid modern world.

The slogans are also advertorial or shaped in the shadow of commodity advertising and celebrity endorsements. They mimic or take place alongside the metaphoric, playful, heightened language found in advertisements for everything from weight-loss products ('a new you') to fizzy drinks. In fact, Obama's campaign slogans resemble or replay Pepsi Cola's 'Pepsi. The choice of a new generation' (1984–91), and 2008/09 'Something for everyone' and 'Every generation refreshes the world'. In terms of the social networking sites Obama was intent on hitting, the slogans not only fit the reduced format perfectly but echo the way in which celebrities write themselves online and through mobile technologies. For example, Miley Cyrus sloganises: 'Find ur voice; take action; change ur world' (www.mileycyrus.com/get-ur-good-on/). This is a spectacular commingling set of articulations.

Obama's campaign slogans tap into the way in which celebrities communicate increasingly with their fans through hyperbole, suggestion and allusion and transformative rhetoric. Celebrities with a social conscience, for example, will often lend their names to green campaigns, organised around a worthy slogan: Josh Hartnett and 'Global Cool' (a charity that is trying to encourage 1 billion people to reduce their carbon footprints over the next 10 years); Brad Pitt and 'Make It Right' (an adopt-a-green-home campaign that he hopes will help to restore the Lower 9th Ward of Katrina-ravaged New Orleans); and Jay-Z, the founder of the United Nations' 'Water for Life' programme (aimed at giving people world-wide access to clean drinking water). Such endorsements and campaigns are also envisioned spectacularly as they will be accompanied by forums, conventions, launches and trips or visits to the affected area, with the press, broadcasting and publicity teams present to capture the celebrity-healing now underway.

The celebrity ambassador (Littler, 2008) will be seen trying to help, assist and transform the degradation (of whatever kind or magnitude it is) into something hopeful. However, again, the incongruity between this persona (the hands that will get dirty, do-gooder, who can do good things with their fame and wealth) and the glamorous celebrity life from which they have come and to which they will return, are decidedly liquid in form. While celebrities have always combined the life of glamour with visits to see a sick child at a hospital or to support the troops, and so on, the self-reflexive and ironic ways in which celebrities view themselves and are viewed today (Gamson, 1994) mean that there is a spilling-over and constant shattering of persona. For a celebrity (politician) to rise above such a tide they need a charismatic authority that effervesces, and the rooted (even if temporary or transitory) adoration of devotees.

Charismatic Obama

If we return now to the ending of Obama's acceptance speech, we can see a desire on his part to create a mythic or symbolic centre or social union in which all Americans (and hopeful people from across the world) can access, invest and belong to:

> But what the people heard instead – people of every creed and color, from every walk of life is that in America, our destiny is inextricably linked. That together, our dreams can be one. 'We cannot walk alone,' the preacher cried. 'And as we walk, we must make the pledge that we shall always march ahead. We cannot turn back.' America, we cannot turn back. Not with so much work to be done. Not with so many children to educate, and so many veterans to care for. Not with an economy to fix and cities to rebuild and farms to save. Not with so many families to protect and so many lives to mend. America, we cannot turn back. We cannot walk alone. At this moment, in this election, we must pledge once more to march into the future. Let us keep that promise – that American promise – and in the words of Scripture hold firmly, without wavering, to the hope that we confess. Thank you, God Bless you, and God Bless the United States of America.
>
> (CNN, 2008)

In the first paragraph (cited above) Obama calls upon the mythos of America's manifest destiny and the American Dream to create a sense of a shared past and a collective trajectory of becoming (although he also making an allusion to Martin Luther King's 'I have a dream' speech, on the 45th anniversary of its delivery). In the second paragraph he alludes to a religious parable and the idea of looking forward and forward momentum, conjured-up in the idea of the union march that leads to progress, change and renewal. In the third paragraph he offers his devotees not only a literal picture of the problems they face on a day-to-day basis but a (symbolic) way out of the crisis based on collective belief. This path is again one to be marched, shared and interconnected, religiously sanctioned and, ultimately, dependent upon him. This is his promise (to them) and the promise he wants his devotees to keep for him; action and an action in an abstract belief he has sanctioned. When Obama finishes this speech, when the fireworks begin to colour and heat the night sky, and as the country music sounds of 'Only in America' fill the stadium, one can still hear the ecstatic applause of the crowd and the chanting of Obama's name. As I will now go on to argue, this is a form of charismatic authority and collective effervescence in the age of the liquid celebrity and liquid modernity.

Weber defines charismatic authority as 'resting on devotion to the exceptional sanctity, heroism or exemplary character of an individual person, and of the normative patterns or order revealed or ordained by him' (Weber, 1968: 215). The charismatic leader is imagined to be supernatural, divine and/or superhuman, and to naturally possess exceptional powers or qualities – such as those of a religious prophet. Weber saw a charismatic leader as one who emerged in times of anomie or dislocation, heading a new or revolutionary social movement that promised respite from such woes. Although the charismatic leader may have a special gift, be countenanced with a particularly seductive oratory or performative style, the basis of their authority rests with the devoted conferring this status upon the leader. A charismatic leader is defined as such by those who utter their name, who express their belief and faith in their power over them, and who pour them into their hearts:

> If you watched Obama's victory speech on 4 November 2008, or download it now and look at the faces of those present, you can see what he meant. It was in their eyes and not in his – the love, the tears, the adoration.
>
> (Knorr-Cetina, 2009: 137)

Such adoration and devotion are markers, I would suggest, of liquid modernity and the emotional and ontological crisis it creates for the individual. In a world unstable in its relations, uneven in its distribution of resources, driven by spectacular presentations that mask commodity capitalism logic, figures who appear to be beyond such disintegration and capable of renewal draw one in completely. The relation is imagined or felt to be one-to-one and personal (he speaks to me and the issues that mark my life) and collective (he speaks to and for all of us). The collective sense of the relationship, of course, is felt as intensely (as it is as 'personal' as an individuated response) and holds powerful sway because it offers that sense of shared belonging lost in the liquid age.

The intensity emerges, to repeat but extend my earlier refrain, because it comes from the spectacle arena in which Obama is sited/ sighted, and because it/he operates from within the (myth of) the media centre. His symbolic calling to gather people together, to re-find themselves in the nation, takes place in front of the lens in all its fragmentary and multiple guises and so the access he has, and we have to him, is privileged.

That this devotional politics acts in symbiosis with celebrity culture, as I have suggested, profoundly deepens the affective connectivity, while lessening its ability to hold that connection for any length of time. Celebrity culture exists very often in the spectacle of emotion and confession, and the promise that self-expression, revelation and feeling is the route to happiness and security (Redmond, 2008). The adoration given to Obama (and his affecting mode of address for that matter) is a part of an 'emotional democracy' (Dovey, 2000) in which feeling is the currency of power. Of course, feeling does not pay the bills or stop capitalism expanding its networks. Feeling rises and falls, dissipates and is transferred. Feeling is lost. Similarly, the charismatic leader, once/if they are elected or assume power, finds they are 'routinised' and that political life demands rational-legal mechanisms (Weber, 1968). In effect, they find that liquid modernity cannot be solidified.

Nonetheless, it can be argued that Obama is a gifted speaker, one who because he orates through emotive symbolism lies outside the rationalist rhetoric of much of contemporary political communication in the West. He has a wonderfully deep but silk-like voice that gives gentle birth to the ideographs and glittering generalities from which he builds his speeches. He does not move like a politician; his corporeality has an air of grace about it (Knorr-Cetina, 2009: 135); but Obama also has superhuman qualities that take him beyond the everyday and the conventional rags-to-riches narrative that the American Dream prophesies. In fact, as Edward D Bacal suggests, Obama trades in superhero mythology. Society is weak, the economy is faltering, politicians are bankrupt, the police inept and corrupt and the world order is near collapse and it needs, calls upon, a superhero to intervene and save the day. Obama thus becomes SuperObama. Bacal suggests, however, that Obama's struggle to be accepted as a serious candidate is also racially inflected and mirrors to a degree John Hancock's (played by Will Smith, *Hancock*, 2008) struggle to be accepted as a superhero:

> to be elected into power and deliver change for the better, he has had to gain the trust and support of so much of an American population that still, on a conscious level or otherwise, typecasts blacks into the roles of an inferior other (which is to say not as their president).
>
> (Bacal, 2009)

Nonetheless, the superhuman qualities that Obama possesses render him more like an (alien) Messiah figure with a transcendental power to affect change. This is not the same type of healing power practised by television evangelists who miraculously cure followers of arthritis or cancer, but one who can rid the world of its political, social and economic ills.

Obama seems not to be of this world (hence the idea of the alien), even if his well-documented and read autobiography grounds him so. Such a figure necessarily needs to be beyond race, while being seemingly connected deeply to a raced history; to be both human and yet superhuman; to be liquid in form.

Avatar Obama

The liquidity of modern life can be read in terms of the crisis in subjectivity in a world in which binary and fixed subject positions have been called into question (Woodward, 2004) and where biotechnologies, cybernetics and information technologies question the parameters of the human, extending their reach into new post-human domains. For example, one can multiply and fragment oneself in online worlds (Turkle, 1995) or re-inscribe the body through transformative surgery. The experience of liquid modernity, then, can be read in terms of the way the body and mind have been rendered borderless and open, on a more apocalyptic note, to invasion and continual disorientation. The self in one reality, one time-zone, with one set of spatial coordinates has been torn asunder. One can place Obama in this framework in terms of how he seems to offer one self-security while being someone that repeatedly shape-shifts, and who plugs into those virtual technologies that are partly responsible for the deterritorialisation of the self.

According to Frank and McPhail, Obama experiences a 'twoness or double-consciousness of being both African and American' (2005: 572). This is a splitting of the self that haunts the African American imagination and one's sense of history and roots. During the campaign, Obama seemed to steer clear of politics that addressed the race issue, and yet he also drew upon his African ancestry to evidence the success myth: here I stand, he conferred, proof that in a multi-racial country colour is no bar to what one can achieve.

There seemed to be a degree of colour-blindness at key moments in the campaign, and a foregrounding of race when it could be used to validate America's present. In one sense, Obama functions in a similar way to super-icon Tiger Woods; 'a commercial emblem who makes visible and concrete late Modern America's narrative of itself as a post-historical nation of immigrants' (Cole and Andrews, 2000: 72).

The media were implicated in this present/absent representation of Obama as raced/not-raced. If one returns to the front covers of *Vanity Fair* in July 2007 and *Ebony* in August 2008, the issue of race is foregrounded and championed: the former unites Obama with other successful black Americans under the biologically essentialist union of descendants of Africa, while the latter brings together Obama and the 'coolest' black men on the planet. By contrast, the heavily reported campaign by 'birthers' such as Stefan F Cook, Philip J Berg and Jerome Corsi to discredit the legitimacy of Obama's birth certificate pointed to the Othering of Obama as Foreigner and not therefore a legitimate son/President of America. Obama was a non-American who was born in either Kenya or Indonesia, depending upon the conspiracy theorist promoting the story. Of course, conspiracy theories are a core part of the liquid modern; now rampant or dominant in terms of scope, they point to the sense that truth is elusive while a desire for truth (to be told) is all-consuming.

I think one can profitably extend the idea of Obama, and the media's double-consciousness, outwards into multiplicities or liquidities, where in the realm of the digital and virtual media it(he) exists as an avatar or a person with multiple identities not limited to a fixed corporeal self, grounded in one nation state or a narrow set of political circumstances. Obama's ability to connect globally with so many different and diverse social groups points to the fact that he was able to reach across porous barriers and borders – be they identity – or nation-based – and ground a relationship through being (and in spite of being) a liquid entity. The virtual and mobile sites, interfaces and portals he commandeered brought him to people in quick or real-time simultaneity, in designated 'social' sites, so that the context seemed intimate and personal, while also being clearly collective and shared.

Such activities connect him to contemporary celebrity promotion, where the internet and mobile virtual technologies are employed to provide the fan with immediate and proximate access to the (private) thoughts, (exciting, spectacular) activities and trials and tribulations of the celebrity. That 'mobile youth', often the most disaffected and disenchanted inhabitants of liquid modernity gravitated towards him (the celebrity) confirmed their need for fixedness and at the same time, perversely, the watery nature of the messenger and message. This liquid celebrity politician communicated through liquid technologies to liquid moderns in global sites – promising solidity, while washing away his truth through the very liquidity of his celebrity being (see Figure 6.2).

The December/January 2008/09 edition of *Time* magazine named Barack Obama as their Person of the Year. The full-page photograph of Obama is retro-scoped so that it appears animated. Obama is tinted red, white and blue, becoming the American flag, with the imprint of other key historical moments shaded in behind him. He is looking off into the distance (the future) in classical auratic pose: he has a vision and he intends to march us towards it. The image recalls pop-art and the celebrity portraits of Andy Warhol. This is a spectacular celebrity image, mass-reproducible and therefore a part of the Obama brand and the infotainment world to which he connects so readily; but the image also, and consequently so, conjures up the spectre of the avatar. Obama is all colours to all people, rendered blurry and

Figure 6.2 Retro-scoping Obama
Image courtesy of Chris Hondros/Getty Images

impressionistic, post-human, wet not dry and liquid not solid. He can only, surely, ultimately disappoint?

Loving Obama: Reprise

Doug Kellner has suggested (2003), although not explicitly in relation to the Obama campaign, that political spectacle can be progressive and lead to positive, transformative outcomes. Two recent examples spring to mind, both of them spearheaded by Twitter. The first involved an injunction against *The Guardian* newspaper from reporting on a leaked report that had suggested a link between oil-trading firm Trafigura and Ivory Coast toxic waste. *The Guardian* editor, Alan Rusbridger, posted a tweet referring to the injunction and the knowledge (and disquiet over the injunction) snowballed until it was lifted.

Following a ghastly homophobic case study by Jan Moir in the *Daily Mail*, in which she called Stephen Gately's death 'strange, lonely and troubling', adding 'Whatever the cause of death is, it is not, by any yardstick, a natural one', Scott Pack, publisher at HarperCollins's The Friday Project, launched a Twitter campaign to have the Press

Complaints Commission investigate. With tweet support by Stephen Fry, within 48 hours they had received more than 1,000 complaints, a record number (http://news.bbc.co.uk/2/hi/uk_news/8311499.stm). Both examples, reported in the wider media, show both active agency on the part of the celebrity and those who follow their lives.

If one was to re-engineer the reading of Obama's spectacular campaign, one might want to make a claim that while being a show of immense proportions it was borne out of progressive politics and a shared love of liberal values; not non-political, or depoliticised, then, but an example of progressive spectacle politics in the making (Kellner, 2003: 177). If 'progressive' is taken to mean the foregrounding or transmission of radical ideology or counter-hegemony, then I think that this would be a mistake for all the arguments presented in this case study. However, the progressive qualities of Obama's campaign, of his charismatic leadership, may be found in the sensuous connectivity of spectacle, although as I will now conclude these are decidedly liquid properties.

Media spectacle is a sensory and sensuous phenomenon; its appeal resides in the realm of the senses, in the moment of the experience as it takes place. One feels exalted, deeply touched, as those moments of splendour and special effects and, in the case of Obama, higher-order oratory, bombards the senses in an overwhelming or awesome tidal flood. One is put back in touch with the carnal self in the moment of the media spectacle, even while the body seems to (further) lose its materiality. One feels that one's entire sensorium is being re-charged and torn asunder. When this spectacle is led or is centred by a celebrity (hypersensory being), then the intensity or shock of the experience can be sublime (see the discussion also of the sublime in Chapter 5). The celebrity presented in a media spectacle produces hysteria, an uncontrollable outpouring (tears, screaming, fainting and chanting). The overriding effect of this sublime experience, then, is the inability to verbalise or rationalise the encounter, because it exists (at that moment) as that which cannot be comprehended. One is lost in the transcendental, overpowering 'show' as it takes one over.

The sublime moment may be felt as a flash of insight in which one re-sees something familiar as if seeing it for the first time; it may be the familiar rendered strange, uncanny, as less or more than the representation of it has signified previously. This feeling of firstness may occur in front of a gesture, a look, a movement, an object, a location or a site. It may manifest at a spectacular political rally in front of a charismatic leader whose abstract ideographs and glittering generalities (not rooted in concrete language at all), or whose voice, body movement and facial expression seem new or unique, and which in summation carries you away. Love is born in such sublime moments, as the intensity of the experience is of the highest degree. However, this was a love, to bring my case study full circle, created out of the liquid modern world. This was liquid love in a liquid celebrity show.

To end on a personal note, I cannot help but remember the intense and incommensurable level of affect that Obama's speeches and presentations had on me at the time. He moved me deeply, profoundly, and in watching others being moved by him in similar ways, I felt a belonging and a sharing that was politically orientated, or that manifested itself in the politicisation of the senses. I felt a sharing in the injustices of capitalism, the history of slavery and racism and the opportunity we had (that Obama said we had) to make the world anew again. One feels stronger, almost superhuman, when one is taken over by a belief or a conviction such as that. Surely, this sensorial transformation is something?

Surely, and to move the ground to active policy making, the liberal agenda he has begun to action is important and will positively transform ordinary lives? But such imagined strengthening of the self and of the consumerist world is the exact way in which liquid celebrity and liquid modernity manage to ensure that it holds the imaginary or mythical centre together. I, we, have to believe passionately in the glittering 'thing' we invest in, even while its effect/affect on us wanes, disappoints or ultimately confirms our status as isolates in a dislocated world. As I reflect upon my love for Obama now, as I re-watch his spectacles and speeches, the transient nature of the connection and the emotional seduction he once offered but no longer does is what I most feel. Avatar Obama, ultimately, will disappoint and it is time to move on.

CHAPTER SUMMARY

This chapter has explored the vexing arguments that greet the production of celebrity culture. But it also demonstrates how production involves cultures and these cultures are transnational in reach.

Again, the chapter demonstrates how the circuits of both models fire off one another: production and consumption, affect and embodiment are seen articulating through one another as the very forces of production move like synapses across the retinas of celebrity culture. Celebrity politics is a product of such liquid productions.

7

CELEBRITY TEXTURALITY

This chapter considers the importance of design and tactility to the production and maintenance of celebrity culture. In the circuit of celebrity affect, texturality refers to the fine-grain nature of the design work that goes into creating celebrity experiences. The chapter concludes with an analysis of celebrity enwaterment, taking the notion of liquidity, which has been running like a current through this book, into its rivers of connectivity.

DESIGNING CELEBRITY PRODUCTION

I want to be seen. I want to be watched and noticed as someone who deserves to be looked at. I want to be afforded that much attention in an age of the attention economy and within the agora of visual sensory overload. I want to be the subject of a gaze, glance or glimpse that admires and desires my commodity identity, my lifestyle-image, in a Western world where the frenzy of the visible is everything. To be a literal famous spectacle to other fashion spectators and lifestylers, through what I wear, eat, purchase and consume, is the key to my self-realisation. To be wearing that expensive label, to be caught drinking that valuable brand, out of that sculpted glass/bottle; to be seen eating in the finest of restaurants; or strolling down the glitzy spaces of the modern high street, is to be confirmed as meaningful, wanted, a glittering prize: a living spectacle of modern consumption. Who I am is what I buy (Baudrillard, 1988), or, as Celia Lury eloquently puts it:

> In general terms, modern Euro-American societies are characterized by the strongly rooted belief that to have is to be (Dittmar, 1992); this is related to the privileging of a relationship between individuals and things in terms of *possession*. The emergence and growth of this preference is tied up with the rise of individualism and mass consumer society, which are seen to have led people to define themselves and others in terms of the things they possess.
>
> (1996: 7)

The academic turn to culture is increasingly a turn to *designing affective forms of consumerism*. The everyday has been 'culturalised' (Hall, 1997), or fashioned, so that not only do the most glamorous and iconic of transnational commodities continue to have imagined identities inscribed, but the most mundane of (local) services also come to have emotionalised brand identities. Take the example of the UK Internet bank 'Smile'. Deposits, withdrawals, overdrafts and interest rates are eroticised, made chic and given a degree of cultural capital through a set of arty advertising images and ironic, self-reflexive sound bites. These include the use of Andy Warhol's 'Marilyn Monroe' painting on Smile's bank-books, web pages, letterheads and logos; an advertising campaign with an up-beat retro-sounding pop soundtrack and the sexy voice of a 'knowing' female commentator; and a selection of 'pretty young things' using its (high-tech, ultra-modern) services. Almost any organisation or business one can physically encounter will have branded interiors and exteriors, 'mission statements', logos and miscellaneous merchandising, which hail its customers and project its affective corporate identity to the world. One only has to *Smile*.

Celebrity culture is of course central and essential to the production of an emotionalised corporate identity: they will embody the values of the corporation in question, and the corporation is reified by their embodied presence. 'Oscar-winner Nicole Kidman' became 'the global brand ambassador for the UAE's national airline' in 2015, drawing upon the glamour and sophistication of her star image to connect with the prestige set of representations the air carrier promotes. Starring in the first 360-degree virtual reality film, titled 'Reimagine', it

> shows the actress speaking directly to the camera, as she rehearses scenes from the script of a film. The adventure on the twin-decked aircraft also gives the viewer the chance to interact with several characters, including Kidman's film director, an opera singer and even an Emirati guest with a falcon in the first-class cabin on the Airbus. The journey also provides personal interactions with the Savoy-trained butler in The Residence, the airline's private three-room cabin, plus the inflight chef in first class, the food and beverage manager in business, and the 'flying nanny'.

> (Bell, 2016)

Here we see how the body of the star and aircraft are aligned and fetishised, and through their point of view we glide through the glamour of the transnational flight, in consumption heaven. Textures, tastes, fabrics and touches are crucial to the emotional envelopes on offer: the film offers up refracted light, chiffon, saffron, steel buildings and soft fabrics to transpose both the modernity and intimacy of air travel. In an advertorial interview, Kidman waxes lyrical about the airline:

> The film is a culmination of Etihad's vision to tell the airline's story in an extremely innovative way and a commitment to engaging with the public as has never been attempted by an airline before. It was a great challenge but one which has definitely paid off and it was great to be part of such an exciting project.

> (Bell, 2016)

Kidman's endorsement highlights the visionary and participatory aspect of the film and the airline, collapsing the distance between consumer and brand as they do so, creating a veneer of demotic access and the sense that journeys lead to emotional awakenings. The endorsement of course denies the exploitation accusations labelled at the airline: Kidman was subsequently taken to task for her role by the Association of Professional Flight Attendants' national president Laura Glading. In an open letter to Kidman, Glading argued that the sponsorship was at odds with her role as a United Nations Women's

Goodwill Ambassador, since Etihad and other United Arab Emirates airlines 'are well-known in our industry for their discriminatory labour practices and deplorable treatment of female employees'. What is missing from the design of the advert is the sweat and toil of its air and ground staff and the 'emotional' labour put in.

Jean Baudrillard argues that in the Western world today the dominant mode of communication is in and through the affective language of consumption: 'marketing, purchasing, sales, the acquisition of differentiated commodities and objects/signs – all of these presently constitute our language, a code, in which our entire society communicates and speaks of and to itself' (1988: 44). While this is a contentious position to take, especially given the recent, often violent, backlash against the brand, one can see how the language and motor of the production of consumption have become increasingly central to the way the economy functions, and to how individual identities are experienced, taken up and resisted.

In the contemporary Western world, then, identity is increasingly purchased, and connected to consumption practices and consumption agencies. These commodity identities are connected to consuming culture, wearing culture, living in 'design culture' environments. Affective subject positions are produced through consumption practices and processes. The role of so-called 'cultural intermediaries' (Bourdieu, 1984), or those who are employed to positively represent goods and services, is central here.

CELEBRITY INTERMEDIARIES AND INFLUENCERS

Cultural intermediaries 'lifestyle' products so that they symbolically 'speak' to people about their place and position in the world. They are 'most frequently found in the media, fashion, advertising and design industries' (du Gay, 1997: 62) and attempt to give functional artefacts a symbolic, sensuous form. Through the emotive language of advertising and marketing, cultural intermediaries attempt to create 'identification between consumer and product' (ibid: 65). This identification centrally hangs on fantasy networks, where symbolic goods are imagined to transform the identity of the consumer in ways that enrich, empower or improve their lives. Cultural intermediaries fill functional goods with ideological meaning that both efface the 'reality' of how the product came into being (in a factory, for example) and the 'reality' as it is (and will be) really lived by the consumer.

Stars and celebrities very often take on the role or function of cultural intermediaries, and more typically or accurately, as 'influencers'. Famous people are given various roles where instruction, interaction and feedback are a central part of the branding and design network. Furthermore, they connect celebrity, brand and experience through a variety of textural signs, connecting the product or service to a form of embodied, everyday use. Helen Powell and Sylvie Prasad (2010: 111–12) suggest the celebrity expert functions 'to transfer knowledge of particular lifestyles to the lived experience of ordinary people at a time when objective and subjective class positions do not necessarily coincide. Celebrity experts gloss over and fill in the lifestyle cracks produced by inequalities in wealth by providing the means to have the "lifestyle" at an affordable cost'. For example, Candice Olson, 'one of today's most stylish and sophisticated interior designers', offers consumers insights and inspiration on the importance of fabric to home design:

> Textiles are the soul of a room ... I like to use textures and patterns that are visually captivating and texturally engaging. My branded fabrics are an extension of my colour preferences which are clearly inspired by my Canadian roots: the cool, fresh feeling of watery blues and greys set off by the warm comfort of wood tones.
>
> (Candice Olsen, Inc, 2015)

Olson's desire to animate and provide synaesthetic bridges between colour, texture, light and shade leads to what she defines as her signature look:

> My signature fusion of traditional form, scale and proportions are balanced by the simplistic beauty and crispness of modern design ... The marriage of contrasts—the old and new, sleek and lustrous—brings excitement and individuality to each piece and in turn, your home, because the look is current yet timeless, fresh yet familiar.
>
> (Candice Olsen, Inc, 2015)

The turn to 'your home' brings the design exchange together: the celebrity experts encourage you to adopt their textural suggestions, purchase their associated fabrics, to have easy access to that signature look. As McCracken argues, meanings that reside in the brand, and the celebrity who endorses it, are magically enchanted and aim to enchant the life of the consumer (1989: 313).

Celebrity influencers work in a similar way, but occupy the micro sphere of the social media. They are on the one hand 'everyday, ordinary Internet users', but they 'accumulate a relatively large following on blogs and social media through the textual and visual narration of their personal lives and lifestyles, engage with their following in digital and physical spaces, and monetise their following by integrating "advertorials" into their blog or social media posts' (Abidin, 2015). For example, Zach Lipson, 'a Chicago-based creative with a passion for all things visual', has sixty-one thousand Instagram followers. Lipson posts high-contrast, beautifully composed photographs of places and people, largely in the Chicago area. The photographs are often tagged advertorials, such as this one from 2017:

> Nothing beats a sunrise from up above this beautiful city. Also, excited to be partnering with @livenation for their #kingandqueenofheartstour that's rolling through Chicago tonight. Looking forward to a solid night!

Lipson's photographs are part tourist gaze, but the gaze here is a haptic one where his followers are asked to reach into the environments to capture the sensorial qualities of the places and people he captures. His advertorials combine brand with affect, product with design, in a sea of textural arrangements. Crystal Abidin suggests that the posts put out by influencers are more:

> amateur and raw, and allowed for immediate interactivity and response from followers. Stripped of bureaucratic negotiations and social distance, followers are able to view interactions with influencers as more personal, direct, swift, and thus intimate (boyd 2006).
>
> (2015: 17)

FASHIONING CELEBRITY

Lifestyle fashioning starts in design and production centres where the size, shape, materials and colours of the product to be used are decided upon, and a concept of use and an imagined consumer identity are nurtured. The fashioned product is then given literal and symbolic meanings in still and moving adverts and advertorials, in showrooms and shops where it is to be sold, and in the materials used to design the interiors and exteriors of these shops, shopping centres and design centres. Lifestyled goods are made a spectacle of, put on display, given stages/pedestals/shop window space to seduce and emotionalise 'the stroller' (Bauman, 1996) on the lookout for the next big fashion thing.

Donald A. Norman argues that design involves 'the choice of material, the manufacturing method, the way the product is marketed, cost and practicality and, how easy the product is to use, to understand. But what many people don't realize is that there is also a strong emotional component to how products are designed and put to use'. These decisions can be distilled into three different but interrelated aspects of design: the visceral, behavioural and reflective.

> Visceral design concerns itself with appearances. Here is where the Nanna teapot excels—I so enjoy its appearance, especially when filled with the amber hues of tea, lit from beneath by the flame of its warming candle. Behavioral design has to do with the pleasure and effectiveness of use. Here both the tilting teapot and my little metal ball are winners. Finally, reflective design considers the rationalization and intellectualization of a product. Can I tell a story about it? Does it appeal to my self-image, to my pride? The objects in our lives are more than mere material possessions. We take pride in them, not necessarily because we are showing off our wealth or status, but because of the meanings they bring to our lives.
>
> (2005: 5)

Coke is a supreme example of this design process. The iconic red Coke can; the soft, sexy calligraphy used to speak its global name; the cosmopolitan, multi-racial images of youth that are used in adverts to transfer its imagined set of one-world values; and the neon-lit, corporate/concession fridges, used to chill and house this funky drink, speak of a product designed, represented and displayed in an affective network of cool consumer experience.

Marie Gillespie's study of why young Asians in Southall, London, consumed Coca-Cola, confirms its fantasy message-system for this particular group:

> The consumption of Coke promises happiness, love, friendship, freedom and popularity. In the world promised by the ads, relationships are uncomplicated (unlike in real life); young people simply care for each other, everyone loves one another and socialises together (unlike in the peer culture where group boundaries are strong); life is fun and free (a teenage dream).
>
> (1995: 194)

In the 2017 Coca-Cola 'Elevator' video advert, a famous but unnamed DJ and a hotel waitress are together trapped in the lift. As the temperature inside the lift increases, she offers him an ice-cold Coca-Cola from her cart and he takes a sip. They smile, he shares his headphones and we hear the music that they begin to dance to. The doors eventually open and they are rescued, but just as they are, they pause and she takes a selfie with her 'new famous friend'. However, when the maid checks the selfie, as she pushes the cart down the lobby, she realises that his face is hidden by the Coca-Cola bottle. The advert draws upon the iconography of celebrity – the paparazzi and adoring crowd are captured at the beginning of the advert, as he enters the hotel, as well as the fantasy that they (via the maid) can enter his life, that he is attainable. The advert sets up the Cinderella myth – the DJ notices the ordinary girl's beauty – but the ending is not with a shared kiss and the transgression of class and role boundaries, but the shared effervescent bottle of Coke. The tag line is of course 'taste the feeling', drawing emotional synaesthesia into the constituency of the drink and the embodied dream networks it supposedly solicits.

The churches and cathedrals of consumption are the shops and shopping centres: glass housed and chrome reflected consumption sites, which are also, of course, products in their own right, with desirable identities to be 'consumed' by shoppers exercising their taste distinctions (Carter, Donald, and Squires, 1993). Shops are branded through the organisation and layout of their interiors, through the signage over the front door and through their branded exteriors. As Eight Inc. write of their design of Apple Stores:

> We have designed Apple's branded exhibitions for over a decade, using vivid graphic elements, intuitive space delineation and interactive product displays to encapsulate the essence of the brand ... Today, all of Apple's branded consumer experiences—retail stores, shop-in-shop, Apple Premium Reseller (APR), trade shows and point of purchase displays – are designed by Eight Inc. These environments are extensions of the Apple brand experience and design philosophy, constructed with straightforward materials and a spatial organization that reflects the consumer lifestyle.
>
> (http://eightinc.com/work/apple/apple-events)

When a consumer walks into a shop they enter a culturalised environment full of commodities that they are invited to buy. These commodities are lit, displayed and put-into-reach so that the consumer walks amongst them, rubbing shoulders with the commodities that call their names and position them as particular subjects (Bowlby, 1985; Ferguson, 1992). While each shop has its own walkway, the shopper and the commodity share the same space. In terms of clothes or fashion purchases, the consumer tries on the commodities to see what they look like, either publicly, in the aisle (making a spectacle of one's self) or in the changing rooms provided. A number of mirrors are provided and in the consumption environment of the shop the consumer imagines whether the lifestyle that this garment/shop offers them is one that corresponds with their desires. Consumers gaze in the mirror, recalling the identity promised, and they marry it with the identity they see in front of the mirror. Fantasy and role-play take over, and they buy or they exit, satisfied or disappointed. As Sean Nixon writes:

> Shop interiors direct us towards both the establishment of codes of looking and the interweaving of techniques of looking with other practices – handling the garments, trying on clothes, interacting with shop staff – which is integral to the activity of shopping. The interior space of shops and their windows thus represent one of the privileged places for the performance of techniques of the self.
>
> (1997: 325)

Given the relationship of stars and celebrities to fashion and the behavioural cues and routines that they offer fans and consumers, these techniques of the self are very much fame inflected and directed. The textural world is full of stars and celebrities performing in front of mirrors, in self-branding and self-presentation regimes of looking, seeing, sensing and touching. This is, of course, highly gendered and raced. Both Iris Young (1980) and Sandra Lee Bartky (1997) have written on how women are 'taught' to move and use their bodies in typically limited, constrained postures, where reach and stretch actions are met by an invisible wall or boundary, which women literally feel they cannot reach or stretch beyond (best exemplified, Young argues, through the woman's body-in-sport). Clothes are designed to complement this and to sexualise the self-presentations that emerge. As Stella Bruzzi argues, clothes 'become the very agents through which desire is made possible. It is the juxtaposition of clothes and the body upon which the fetishistic emphasis is placed' (Bruzzi 1997, 61).

The relationship between celebrity, fashion and fashioning the self has a long history in affective culture. For example, Edith Head, Head Designer at both Paramount (1931–67) and Universal (1967–82), 'leveraged her success to transcend the studio system and create new opportunities dispensing fashion advice for 'regular' women across print, radio and television' (Fortmueller, 2017: 1). Head's,

> savvy career management contrasted with her ideas about fashion and gender, resulting in designs and style advice largely espoused conservative values and advocated for domestic femininity. Advice columns, radio and television scripts provide evidence of Head's restrictive notions of respectable taste and femininity and help paint a complex picture of one woman's success in Hollywood.
>
> (ibid: 1)

Fortmueller (2017) goes on to illustrate how the Academy Award-winning costumes of *A Place in the Sun* were 'featured in the film's marketing material and reproduced for a mass market'. Elizabeth Taylor's dresses were both affectively innocent but suggestive of her sexuality, which appealed to young female consumers of the time. Contemporary stardom and fashion have similar engendered synergies, but the star can also transgress normative forms of embodiment. In this regard,

Tilda Swinton is an exemplary case study, a fashion and style icon who resists gender binaries and the trappings of the fashion industry:

> Swinton embodies a particularly European identity as fragmented and unresolved through her 'performance' as a specific persona, in this case, as a fashion icon, a role that she both embraces and denies.
>
> (Radner, 2016: 404)

Designer shops are fantasy and performance environments, designed to excite, entice and involve the consumer in meeting, greeting and buying the ideal images manufactured in advertising and re-imagined in the spaces of the shop floor itself. Shops (shopping malls) can be considered as 'total environments', which 'overload the senses' (Lury, 1996: 240). However, shops are also heavily regulated spaces, subject to surveillance and control. Hidden just behind the spectacle of consumption is a more repressive 'regime of truth' (Foucault, 1979). Through the watching, lurking security officer, surveillance camera, 'help' buzzer, commission-driven shop assistants and electronically tagged clothes, the shopping environment becomes a panopticon (Foucault, 1980; Langman, 1992), or 'electronic panopticon' (Lyon, 1993). Once the consumer enters a shop, they are under constant surveillance: if they look like they might buy then they are 'greeted' and asked to enter, to buy. If the consumer loiters for too long without buying, or if they enter with an identity that does not match with the 'brand' of the shop – if they look poor or are the wrong social type – then they are watched under the spectacle of Otherness. Affective design becomes synonymous with repressive consumption.

Of course, before a consumer enters a shop, in fact even before they leave the home, they are under surveillance in another sense: through database marketing whereby manufacturers and retailers collect, store and manipulate economic and 'lifestyle' information about customers/ consumers. As David Lyon suggests, 'Database marketing works by clustering consumers by social type and location, and by more and more tightly trying to personalize advertising and consumer advice' (1999:356).

The film *Pretty Woman* (1990) of course plays this out: hooker Vivian is denied entry to the high-end fashion shops on Rodeo drive, ticketed and docketed when she first enters the shop as without cultural or economic capital. It is only when she emerges as Cinderella (the 'star' Julia Roberts) with a credit card that she gains entry and permission to move and enunciate like a woman. A similar theme is played out in the film *Personal Shopper*, but here Maureen (Kristen Stewart) is a personal shopper in Paris for Kyra (Nora Waldstätten), a celebrity. She travels to European capitals to shop for her, buying clothes, accessories and jewels. Maureen is de-starred and yet embodies the unknown celebrity (Kyra, never witnessed) of the film when trying on clothes for her: she has to mimic the very movement of the celebrity that she already is. These are affective, sense-based scenes, that take on a stalkerish feel when Maureen tries on a dress in Kyra's apartment: fetishising and eroticising the mimicry.

New frontier technologies have come to play a role in these technologies of the self, since forms of virtual and augmented reality can create the 'trying on' and 'becoming' scenario, having the 'body' of the celebrity become your body as the trying on regimes take place. For example, Moosejaw X-Ray App:

> allowed consumers to virtually undress female and male models inside the pages who were otherwise covered up from by the latest offerings from The North Face and other outdoor purveyors.
>
> (www.highsnobiety.com/2016/07/25/augmented-reality-examples/)

Celebrity is caught up in surveillance regimes in another way: there are numerous companies, such as Sysomos, Radian6 and Bazaarvoice, that 'are "listening platforms", trolling the web in order to offer "real-time intelligence" about the reputation of their clients' product, brand or service' (Hearn, 2010). As Alison Hearn suggests,

> The goal is to foster a community of loyal consumers that will endure 'in between the points of sale'. Tactics may involve participating in chat room conversations, and identifying influencers, viral marketers, or brand fans. In this age of social media, then, the goal of online marketing involves far more than finding and targeting a specific consumer, but in 'fostering a community' of influencers and brand advocates from amongst already existing consumers and deploying them to do the work of brand enhancement for free.
>
> (2010: 432)

CELEBRITY TRIBES

The concept of emotional self-identity is also caught up in this regime of individuated ownership and consumer surveillance. The 'possessive individual' (Abercrombie, Hill, and Turner, 1986; Pateman, 1988) is concerned with not only the purchase of commodities, goods and property, but with the ownership of the self that becomes 'a kind of cultural resource, asset or possession' (Lury, 1996: 8). The possessive individual styles himself in the same way as goods and services are styled: he measures his self-worth in terms of the aestheticisation of the self. The loss of material possessions is seen as a loss to the self and is 'experienced as a personal violation and a lessening of the self' (ibid: 8).

However, aggressive and active agency is also important. People appropriate cultural forms: they 'fashion' themselves and their local environments; and they *produce* culture, not only in terms of the 'service' roles that they take up in what is increasingly a goods- and services-driven economy, but in the very act of consuming goods and services. As Hugh Mackay argues:

> Consumption is not the end of a process, but the beginning of another, and thus itself a form of production (and hence we can refer to the 'work' of consumption).
>
> (1997: 7)

An example of this can be found in Daniel Miller's work on council property in London. Miller (1997) explored the productive way that working-class people re-fashioned their council-owned flats through exterior work to the building, and through kitchen modifications such as installing new wall units, tiles, floors and ceilings. Miller argues that such designs were undertaken to take away the stigma of living in a council property. Similar examples can be found with ordinary families copying celebrity-inspired interiors in a process of affective value transference (see the example above) or through the way fans transform their bedrooms to act as shrines to the stars they admire. The fan bedroom is both an indication of intimacy and a public signal of devotion.

One can see how the consumption of goods functions as a classificatory system, driven by what Bourdieu (1984) argues is people's symbolic need to have social status and class identification represented through the consumption choices that they make. The cars people drive, the restaurants people eat in, and the food people choose to eat there, mark them out as particular social types, with varying degrees of social and cultural power. For the bourgeoisie, to be cultured and civilised and to have cultural authority in the social world is in part about making the right consumption decisions and representing these 'right' choices to other people: choices that establish and confirm bourgeois class allegiance and superiority over the culturally 'inferior' working class. Very often such debates go to the heart of celebrity culture, which is mapped and marked by such taste distinctions. There are value-laden markers made between stars and celebrities, gossip and real news, film stars and television personalities, high art artists and those working in the popular mainstream. Celebrity culture is enmeshed in notions of cultural capital.

Paul Willis has examined the way that working-class men consume/ produce motorcycle culture to transmit symbolic messages about their social class: 'the ensemble of bike, noise, rider, clothes, *on the move* gave formidable expression of identity to the culture and powerfully developed many of its central values' (1982: 299). Film stars and motorcycles are often drawn together, in this empowering hypermasculine equation. Keanu Reeves, for example, is associated with making and riding Arch motorcycles,

> Riding your bike is one of the greatest things you can do to clear your head and just feel the speed and the motion ... I don't have a sense of fear, it's just that I've had enough accidents, a ruptured spleen, a lot of scraped skin and road rash that I don't really feel the need to test the limits as much. I also don't use riding a motorcycle as a way of getting rid of anger or frustration the way I used to. When I was younger, I used to get out on the road with the bike and just go as fast as I could and basically let it all out on the road. But after enough wipe-outs, you begin to think that that's not a really good frame of mind to be in when you're riding a motorcycle at high speed [laughs].
>
> (Armleder, n.d.)

While Bourdieu is right to identify consumption as symbolic, a signifier of belonging to and different from other users of other goods, he locates these 'taste distinctions' solely in terms of social class. There are two problems with his position.

First, what is increasingly certain is that lifestyle groupings and consumption choices exist beyond and across class positions. Allegiances to and a conscious awareness of social class background have in part been eroded or superseded by allegiance to lifestyle enclaves or the cultural mantra that 'life-is-a-consumption' choice. People do not necessarily buy goods to symbolise their 'real' social condition, but to produce a 'new' and affecting/affective lifestyle (or to consciously mask, efface the old one) in and through the use of emotionalised goods. In this respect, Sahlins (1974) argues that commodity objects function as 'totems', symbols for belonging/not belonging to a particular 'tribe' or social group that can emerge out of such things as the display of clothes. Maffesoli extends this idea to what he calls 'neo-tribes', or new commodity and fashion enclaves that emerge simply to confirm and reaffirm 'sociality' (1991: 19), and the attraction and seduction of the brand, or cultural item, that binds the tribe together:

> It is no longer possible to say that any aspect of social life, not cookery, nor attention to appearance, nor small celebrations, nor relaxing walks, is frivolous or insignificant. In so far as such activities may provide a focus for collective emotions, they constitute real underground movements, demands for life that have to be analysed.
>
> (ibid: 8)

One can read fan groups and relations through the filter of neo-tribe sociality: as textural productions that happen at the local level, through sense and experience, and through celebaesthetic reciprocity. Fandom involves object, materials, mementoes and spaces and enclaves to gather in.

Nonetheless, social relationships are always aesthetic engagements: sociality and experience, conversation and embodiment, touch and texture, go hand-in-hand. Neo-tribes are populated with people whose identities are self-conscious, self-aware, affective and hybrid in form. This is particularly the case around what were once represented to be fixed and essentialised determinants of the human condition, such as gender roles and sexual preferences. The attraction of neo-tribes, then, is that they provide a spiritual home for the isolated, possessive individual of the modern age, who has no other social network to belong to, or no other ontological 'truth' to believe in. As Zygmunt Bauman argues, 'tribes are simultaneously refuges for those trying in vain to escape the loneliness of privatized survival, and the stuff from which private policies of survival, and thus the identity of the survivor is self-assembled' (1992: 25).

In relation to celebrity culture, fan-celebrity pathologies can emerge: in this culture of loneliness, alienated and atomised people find that they struggle to achieve or maintain positive social interactions. Their loneliness – real and imagined – becomes the gateway to look for companionship in and through celebrity culture. Celebrities are recuperating figures, enabling fans to feel wanted and connected (Rubin, Perse, and Powell, 1985). I have previously used the metaphor of the loneliness room to understand this phenomenon: the liquid modern condition produces an exasperating sense of the world as lonely, disenchanted, with the absence of close community ties as the relentless tides of commodity renewal and transformation are forced upon everyday life. Celebrity culture provides the spectacle to constantly re-enchant the world, to suggest connectedness and grant access to the myth of the media centre, while celebrities provide idealised versions of the individuated self to connect and bond with. Fans leave their own loneliness room to access endless shared rooms that they can move through, chat in and reside in. These open rooms grant them a degree of self-empowerment, of a fantastical sense of fixed-ness in the world, and they offer people levels of emotionality not otherwise present in their lives.

Bauman is critical of the supposed democracy of consumer culture. He argues that neo-tribes are themselves regulated by the market, which sets the conditions of entry. In modern society, in fact, Bauman (1987) suggests that people are polarised into two groups: those who are 'seduced' by the market, and those who are 'repressed' by it. The seduced are hailed by the consumer market, they are monitored on marketing databases and are asked to buy into its commodity dreams and to display or flaunt them. The seduced have money, disposable incomes, and this is spent on the acquisition of goods and services. The repressed are excluded from the market. They are those without work, capital or property, and so instead have to rely on the state provision of services. The seduced are 'free' and are encouraged to shop in the supermarkets of the modern world. By contrast, the repressed are hounded by the state, who subjects them to ever-increasing regimes of 'penal' surveillance and control.

Celebrity culture seduces and represses, admits and expels: although its embodied dream networks suggest only the former. The supposed democracy of celebrity culture is suggested by both its ubiquity – it seems to be everywhere and potentially 'in' everyone – and interactivity: one can actively participate in its affective streams. However, its cruel mythology actually falls short on its dreaming: access is restricted.

The second problem with Bourdieu's position is that race and ethnicity are increasingly important to the identities or lifestyles that people imagine they buy through the purchase of symbolic goods. In fact, Susan Willis (1990) suggests that there has been a generalised aestheticisation of race within consumer culture. No longer represented as a matter of natural or biological difference, racial difference is instead turned into a style, a style that one can consume like any other commodity of choice. Similarly, Sean Nixon (1997) has also considered this process in terms of new forms of commodified masculinity that was produced in Britain in the 1980s. For Nixon, a set of plural, ethnic inflected masculinities were packaged and promoted as wannabe lifestyle choices for young men. These included (black style) 'street style', 'Italian-American' and 'Conservative English' masculinities.

In Justin Timberlake's promotional short film for his new album, *Man of the Woods* (2018), we see him return to his native Canada to live freely in the mountains, streams and forests that we are told populated his childhood, which allows him and us to understand where he came from. Over tracking and close-up shots of empty roads, wheat fields, snow-covered tundra, lakes, woods and mountains, Timberlake tells us 'it's personal'. In the second half of the film, a voice-over provided by his wife Jessica Beal reveals that it is like we are in 'the Wild West but now', as shots of mountainous camp fires and enigmatic shots of Justin standing, staring or running weave his masculinist presence through the suffuse imagery. At one point in the film, wild horses and Justin are cross cut and dissolved so that the notion of masculine, primitive freedom is given representational weight. Justin is a wild Mustang, set free on the prairies of Canada. The promotional film carries songs from the album and ends with Justin in the studio, accompanied by the record's producer, hip-hop star Pharrell Williams, who says 'that will be a smash'. Here we see two representational arcs meeting: white primitivism and cultural appropriation. This is a post-colonial Wild West, where Justin remains empowered and in charge.

Alistair Bonnett has examined the mythopoetic men's movement that emerged in North America in the 1980s and 1990s as an example of white men's flight into the arms of primitivism. Bonnett argues that 'mythopoetic men are creatively reworking colonialist fantasies of non-Western societies and landscapes' (2000: 95), and, moreover, that mythopoeticism represents an attempt to reaffirm and reinstate white male power, in response to an increasing feeling of powerlessness in the modern world. Mythopoetic men venture into wilderness regions, not only because of the way they 'may experience freedom from social constraint, and a sense of liberation' (ibid: 103), but because of the 'cult of the primitive', who they imagine they can find there and can become like. The romanticised figure of the Native American is key here. Untouched by modernity, in tune with the land and in touch with the rhythms of nature, and as 'unchanging and spiritually potent as "untouched" Nature itself' (ibid: 103), the Native American comes to represent the life-affirming values of the wilderness. Bonnett argues that mythopoetic men 'act out' these primitivistic discourses in weekend 'retreat' gatherings, taking on roles in what is considered to be an 'authentic' environment, that mirror the (heroic) narratives of Native American culture. These discourses:

> Are also used to naturalise these experiences and to displace political and social engagement. The attendees' repeated allusions to tribal and wilderness 'ways of wisdom' are invariably designed to lead beyond, or leave behind, everyday concerns and enable the men to reach the dynamic yet timeless male spirit.
>
> (Bonnett, 2000: 106)

One can argue that central to this experimentation with and purchase of racial or ethnic identities is the increased mediation and simulation of human experiences, human relationships and communication: which Celia Lury (1996) refers to as 'prosthetic culture'. Through both old and new media and information technologies, and the appearance of ethnic products on the high streets, Other cultures, places and spaces, and a range of different identities, are brought closer to home: in fact, they are brought in *to the home* through the television, radio, Internet, advertising and commodity purchase. Ethnicity,

once a genie contained in the bottle of some sort of locality ... has
now become a global force, forever slipping in and through the cracks
between states and borders.

(Appadurai, 1993: 228)

Nonetheless, the purchasing of or the trying on of identities remains an
uneven encounter or project (Bhabha, 1993), especially for the racially
'repressed'. In Western terms, this is because the consumption of ethnic
goods is imagined to take place in an exchange that locates the consumer as white and Western, and the consumed as black, oriental or
non/off-white. This desire for the Other, for the 'strange', radiates out
from a cultural centre that is white, and stems from a 'white' need that
is about both owning the exotic Other and devouring or ingesting them.
Jackie Stacey defines this as the desire to (be able to) get closer to the
Other: to 'literally ingest otherness in consuming these exotic products'
(2000: 104). The 'strange' is imagined to give the white consumer a
more intense life experience, an experience that is hard to match within
white culture, and symbolic power over the Other. bell hooks argues that
this is why the 'commodification of otherness' has been so successful:

it is offered as a new delight, more intense, more satisfying than normal ways of doing and feeling. Within commodity culture, ethnicity
becomes spice, seasoning that can liven up the dull dish that is mainstream white culture.

(1992: 21)

hooks has read pop star Madonna as a plantation mistress who engages
in such Othering commodification:

White women 'stars' like Madonna, Sandra Bernhard, and many others publicly name their interest in, and appropriation of, black culture
as yet another sign of their radical chic. Intimacy with that 'nasty'
blackness good white girls stay away from is what they seek. To white
and other non-black consumers, this gives them a special flavour, an
added spice. After all it is a very recent historical phenomenon for any
white girl to be able to get some mileage out of flaunting her fascination and envy of blackness. The thing about envy is that it is always
ready to destroy, erase, take over, and consume the desired object.

> That's exactly what Madonna attempts to do when she appropriates and commodifies aspects of black culture. Needless to say, this kind of fascination is a threat. It endangers.
>
> (hooks, 1992: 157)

Mainstream white culture consumes the exotic Other in a process of exchange that Sara Ahmed (2000) refers to as 'stranger fetishism'. Ahmed argues that through consuming the commodity of the Other one is both making the 'strange' familiar and subordinate to the Western subject: since such consumption confirms the 'subject's ability to "be oneself" by getting closer to, and incorporating the stranger (a form of proximity which produces the stranger as *that which can be taken in*)' (2000: 133). So, while globalisation may seem to offer a democratic and enriching encounter or engagement between different cultures, what potentially takes place is the reinforcement of racial difference, and the re-centring of white culture in a master/slave relationship with the Other. Jackie Stacey suggests that:

> By consuming global products, the Western subject and the exotic other are thus reaffirmed even as such a dichotomy is apparently transcended by the appeal to a universal global culture.
>
> (2000: 104)

One can readily see how celebrity culture very often eroticises, fetishises and consumes the racial Other: very often through sensory stereotypes where the star in question carries the affective markers of their race and ethnicity. Sensory stereotypes are part of the designing of the star image: taste, sweat, temperature, colour and muscle mass are all used within the production of images to experientially 'fix' the race or gender of the famous figure (see the discussion of Serena Williams in Chapter 2 for an illustration of this).

Nonetheless, the texturality of celebrity culture is very often enwatered, something the chapter now picks up in the closing case study.

CASE STUDY

Celebrity wetness

> *I am swimming, swimming in a sea of liquid camera movements, dissolves, reflections, blue pools, deep oceans, lavish spectacles, messy births,*

intimate bodily exchanges, bad romances, trashy sex, bright lights, swirling colours, big windows, runny eyes, wet wounds, red blood, DNA, semen, salty tears, moist mouths, saliva and beads of sweat. I am experiencing the incredible tides of celebrity wetness.

Contemporary celebrity culture can be experienced as a wet technology, the celebrity can be felt through a wet aesthetic and the reception experience can be one defined by its wetness. It is not that other sensations and senses are not also being activated, or that celebrity wetness always prevails as sign, sense and sensation. Rather, the suggestion here is that when wet aesthetics and wet reception align, one feels as if one is watching celebrity liquidity, is immersed in liquidity and that one is wetted and revitalised by the experience.

This feeling of being 'enwatered' (D'aloia, 2010) is potentially liberating since the bodily borders of the star, the formal and thematic confines of the text, and the bordered body sensing the encounter, flow into one another, allowing one to float away, free of technological, aesthetic and carnal constraints. I imagine celebrity wetness emerging most powerfully in the context of the 'dry' domestic space, giving floating life to an environment that by and large represses a version of the wet experience. And yet, within this waterscape, wetness also emerges to confirm the liquid nature of modern life, to affirm gender binaries, and to secure viewers as bodily beings that (we are instructed to believe) need 'dry land' to function. Celebrity wetness, then, is a contested archipelago, arising out of or rather through two vessels: wet spectacles and wet bodies.

Wet celebrity spectacles

As outlined in Chapter 4, a media spectacle has aesthetic, technological, spatial and temporal dimensions: it draws upon special effects, costume, set design, marquee settings, triumphant music, graphics, binary storytelling arcs and pyrotechnics, at a 'special' time in the calendar, to affectively present the event as awesome and overpowering. Such events are charged with ensuring that an individual's emotional pleasure and self-centeredness are secured.

However, celebrity spectacles are also decidedly wetted and liquid. Wet celebrity spectacles are doused in watery metaphors, emerge on screens and in settings which appear fluid and dreamy. Wet celebrity aesthetics include the fluidity of the camera, rapid editing, liquid graphics, watery colours, water-based settings and the microscopic attention to watery details in the material matter found in the event's proceedings. Costumes are often watery in appearance, designed with 'flow' and 'ripple' in mind, or their colours and fabrics bring to mind liquidity, the ocean, a stagnating waterphilia. For example, in Beyoncé's Formation stadium shows (2015–16) we see her dressed in a Cavalli jumpsuit while dancing and cleansing herself in a rejuvenating 'lake' as she performs songs from her album, Lemonade. As Es Devlin, production designer on the tour, states:

> The stage also consists of a runway, which also acts as a treadmill leading onto a B-stage that fills with a pool of water. The treadmill on the catwalk was designed to be waterproof in order to withstand unpredictable weather found in outdoor stadiums. The B-stage stores 2,000 gallons of water inside of it and takes approximately 10 minutes to fill up, which occurs without the audience even realising. The inspiration for the water within the B-stage was inspired by the tour's supporting album Lemonade, in particularly the song 'Forward', as the song's message is described as a turning point from anger to forgiveness. The pool of water is the antithesis to the fire-spitting monolith; the most joyful, redemptive sequence of the show takes place here, from 'Freedom' through to 'Halo'.
>
> (Wong, 2016)

In 2016, the Italian label Fendi developed a couture show to celebrate its 90th anniversary that involved supermodels walking across a watery catwalk over the Trevi Fountain in Rome. As Lauren Alexis Fisher reports,

> For its 90th anniversary, Fendi staged one of its most breathtaking shows ever—a clear plexiglass runway stretched across Rome's iconic Trevi Fountain. The couture collection's theme was fittingly 'Legends and Fairytales,' as models walked on water–literally—across the backdrop of the famous fountains and pools from the 1960 film, La Dolce Vita. This marked the first-ever fashion show to take place at the Italian landmark.
>
> (2016)

In both the women's fashion magazines *Vogue* and *Harper's Bazaar* we find female celebrities imaged in liquid conditions. In the April 2016 edition of *Harper's Bazaar*, for example, we find Jennifer Aniston standing in a custom-made pool, designed by Paolo Benedetti. Aniston is imaged in long shot, at the point of the vanishing horizon, looking to the right of the camera, with her hand on her forehead, miraculously standing on the pool water she is reflected in. Wearing a Versus Versace dress, Tiffany & Co. rings and a gold Cartier bracelet, Aniston shimmers like a floating mirage. In the April 2016 edition of *Vogue*, Rhianna is photographed in a Tom Ford Dress, again seemingly walking on the water she is posed standing on. The front cover alludes to the 15th-century painting, *The Birth of Venus*, by Sandro Botticelli. The painting depicts the goddess Venus arriving at the shore after her birth, when she had emerged from the sea fully grown.

All three examples draw upon the qualities of water to eroticise the star: to create an affective 'stream' between image and consumer. The water is always haptic and immersive and washes over the celebrity within or on its ripples and flows. In these examples, of course, there is a biblical dimension: each of the stars gets to walk on water as if they are divine figures.

Award ceremonies very regularly play out the wetted celebrity spectacle: crowds of fans are captured in streams of liquid imaging, screaming their pleasure at the arrival of their favourite film celebrity. The celebrity exits their sleek black limousine, lights reflecting off its black and immersive liquid surface, and begins to the walk up the red carpet, cordoned off to everyday people. The frenzy of the lights and reflective surfaces, and the ripples found across the clothes, and faces, and expressions, creates a scene of an enwatered spectacle. One can also argue that those involved, fans and stars, are liquid technologies: made of water, blood, plasma, with a 'primordial sense of liquid or fluid and … an (unconscious) memory of the in utero state' (D'aloia, 2010), which the wetted spectacle activates, drawing upon our 'hydro-knowledge' (ibid) of things.

Award ceremonies occur in spaces/venues endowed with special significance (Couldry, 2003). Let me liquefy a media spectacle that I have mentioned before in this book. The paparazzi crowd around frenetically, jostling to capture the authentic shot of the night, to sell on to celebrity-spectacle-obsessed magazines such as *Hello!* (who will then devote a spectacular special edition to the event). The movement of the paparazzi and the movement of the cameras recall the currents of water and the eddy of fluctuations. Lights flood the immaculate, reflective entrance area, and immaculately dressed TV hosts (from all corners of the world) clamour to interview the bejewelled celebrity in what is televised as an intimate one-to-one moment, taking place in a special section of the event foyer. Television channel or CNN-sponsored helicopters fill the night sky, gathering panoramic shots to visualise the liquid enormity of the event. This 'entrance' event is followed by the truly spectacular award show where the dreamscape of celebrity success is recreated in the staging of the awards ceremony where wetted spectacle meanders.

Wet bodies

The bodily response to wetted celebrity is wetness itself. At the physical level, one cries tears, sobs, emits beads of sweat, one feels the blood pumping through the bodies and one gets aroused. One might term these celebrities as wet genres, and the viewing response watered embodiment, a decidedly liquid version, then, of the body genre (Williams, 1991). However, at the level of sensory experience, one also feels the water on one's skin; and one feels time and space as liquid phenomena that wash over the face, the skin and the hairs on one's body. When wet television technology and the wet celebrity text combine, the screen, television world and domestic space flow into one another, so that immersion is within one and all around. One feels wet in an environment transformed by watery imagery and liquid sensation.

In reviewing and classifying memorial fan letters from women asked to reflect on their relationship to female film stars of the 1940s, Jackie Stacey finds a type of spectatorship that is constituted out of religious love and devotion. In summarising their responses, Stacey argues:

> These statements represent the star as something different and unat-
> tainable. Religious signifiers here indicate the special meaning and

status of the stars, as well as suggesting the intensity of the devotion felt by the spectator. They also reinforce the 'otherness' of the stars that are not considered part of the mortal world ... Worship of stars as goddesses involves a denial of self found in some forms of religious devotion. The spectator is only present in these quotes as a worshipper, or through her adoration of the star.

(1994: 143)

Celebrity love is here constituted as a supernatural force conferred on a venerated individual, not thought or felt to be of this world. As a fan, one loses one's sense of self in the heady mixture of perfected beauty, glamour and sexuality that the film stars are imagined to be. This enchanted reverie is particularly sensorial, felt in one's body, a 'homoerotic bonding', that is not subjection before the figure, but potential transgression of normative desire. Love is transformative and potentially liberating in these memorial letters of devotion.

Water is crucial to these devotional letters and to this type of devoted fandom: it draws upon the significance of water within religious practice:

Water cleanses. Water washes away impurities and pollutants, it can make an object look as good as new and wipe away any signs of previous defilement. Water not only purifies objects for ritual use, but can make a person clean, externally or spiritually, ready to come into the presence of his/her focus of worship ... Water is a primary building block of life. Without water there is no life, yet water has the power to destroy as well as to create. We are at the mercy of water just as we are at the mercy of our God or gods.

(www.africanwater.org/religion.htm)

For Christians, baptism by water – itself a symbol of the grace of God – signifies spiritual rebirth. The word 'baptism' comes from the Greek word *baptizo*, meaning to plunge or to wash. Integral to Hindu religious practice are pure and sacred rivers, most notably the Ganges, which comes directly from a holy source in the Himalayas. In Catholicism, holy water is water that has been sanctified by a priest for the purpose of baptism, the blessing of persons, places and objects, or as a means of repelling evil. These qualities of water are very often transferred onto/into the celebrity: they purify, and one is involved in purification rituals through the practice of fandom. Celebrity allows one to wash away the detritus of everyday life.

In many respects the wet body response to wetted celebrity can be argued to be liberating, translating sense, opening up experience to beyond the border possibilities. The dry confines of the home, and the regulatory way that everyday life is normally orchestrated, is washed away, cleansing the body, setting one free, initiating a watery rebirth of sorts.

Nonetheless, one can also argue that watered embodiment matches the rhythm of contemporary life exactly and the ephemeral condition of liquid modernity. Rather than wet celebrity texts being liberating, they may channel the fluidity of existence into the home. The watery escape or voyage is transitory, wetting the home, the body, for a limited time, before normal (dry) service is resumed. Celebrity liquidity may work cathartically, allowing the repressed to rise before the tide goes out once more. Celebrity wetness may be an aquatic form of the Bakhtin carnival, allowing one to swim free for a while before returning to service the needs of liquid capitalism.

CHAPTER SUMMARY

This chapter has explored how the design textures found in celebrity culture activate the senses, create the conditions for an embodied type of possessive individualism and ultimately find its primary substance in wetted spectacle. The chapter draws on design theory, consumption politics and celebrity waterphilia to show how important texturality is to the twin engines of production and consumption.

8

IMPRESSIONABLE AUDIENCES
CONSUMING CELEBRITY CULTURE

In this chapter, the vexing question of how fans and audiences receive celebrity culture is addressed. It centres its reading of reception on the theme of impressionability and the argument that celebrity culture shapes people in the mould of neo-liberal ideologies and patriarchal discourses. In the circuit of celebrity culture, consumption is very often set within discourses that see power operating on people.

IMPRESSIONABLE AUDIENCES?

Consuming celebrity culture is often argued to be detrimental to social life and resistant and active social identity formation. From a conservative perspective, this is because celebrity is thought to be demeaning in some way, trivialises public affairs, and conflates art with popular culture, infecting or polluting all aspects of social life as it does so. From a radical, leftist perspective, celebrity culture is seen to offer up a system of messages that promote and reinforce neo-liberal ideologies and fantasies, cementing social inequalities, entrenching social stereotypes, carrying forward the fantasy networks of the consumerist or commodity dream. A third position sees resistant and affecting qualities in the act of celebrity consumption (taken up in the chapter that follows this). Regardless of the position that one takes, however, scholars agree that celebrity culture has effects: that it influences behaviour, group identification, lifestyle choices, consumption habits and political allegiances.

One of the worries that emerges with regards to the consumption of celebrity culture is its effects on children, in particular. As Uhls and Greenfield conclude:

> Now even children can and do achieve their 15 min of fame, in the words of Andy Warhol. In summary, our focus group findings indicate that watching fame narratives with young protagonists in popular TV programming, both fictional and real, playing in or posting videos online, and developing an audience of 'friends' on social network sites make the concept of fame highly accessible to children between 10 and 12 years of age, transforming fame into a key value and goal for children in this age group.
>
> (2011: 10)

Celebrity culture is very often drawn into moral panics about the values, beliefs and attitudes of society, with young people identified as particularly impressionable. Tweens and teens are in particular argued to be most at risk from its forms of sexualisation, possessive individualism and brand-directed instruction. Celebrity influencers (discussed in the last chapter) are very often young, attractive and draw on self-presentation techniques, which require a set of 'mirroring' responses from the young fans that gravitate to their blogs and websites.

Joshua Gamson's schema for identifying various audience responses to celebrities, however, offers up five different audience typologies, each with different degrees of acceptance and resistance reading strategies (1994). First, 'the traditional' audience responds to media information about stars and celebrities as if they are receiving accurate, value-free news, rather than promotional or branding exercises. Further, these audience members are seduced by the representations and immerse themselves in the fantasy networks they offer them. In Marsha Orgeron's work on fandom they find:

> Fan magazine contests enabled and encouraged women to re-evaluate themselves in response to the star system and to articulate their fantasies in tangible ways through their participation. Fan letters, which materialized when fans sought stars' studio addresses from magazine editors, also make material fans' desire to emerge from anonymity, to create a concrete existence for themselves in relation to the star system. In providing an outlet or means for such fantasies, the fan magazines were, of course, in no way subversive; rather, they were part of the mechanism of fandom that developed out of a spectatorial demand for information, created in part by the industry itself. But while fan magazines were thus imbued with Hollywood's market-driven ideology, they still offered a practical way for women to become actively involved with movie culture and, in the process, to negotiate their own identities beyond the limited realm of their day-to-day experiences.
>
> (2003: 79)

When it comes to the contemporary social media, authenticity is crucial to the production and consumption of stars. For example, Kanye West employs two main strategies in his usage of Twitter: first, 'to promote his celebrity commodity, increase his celebrity capital and create an elite network of fellow celebrities. The second strategy aims at creating an authentic and personal narrative that redefines and extends Kanye West's celebrity persona'. Kanye employs 'stream-of-consciousness' and 'prayer' tweets to suggest his authenticity and to signal his Apostle Paul status (Gloe, 2016: 2).

The second category of audience type is the 'second-order traditional', who negotiate their consumption of the celebrity news, understanding that elements of it are staged, while still engaging with its dreams and fantasies. The second-order traditional often read celebrity news through the filter of authenticity versus simulacra or fakery, investing in authenticity wherever it can be found or 'weeded out'. Strong identifications with authentic stars emerge and are countenanced. One case sees this type of authentic identification emerge with regards to celebrity conservationists, whose authority and appeal derives from their apparent authenticity:

> For just as sports, film and pop stars enable people to cope with diverse forms of social alienation, celebrity conservationists allow people to cope with the profound alienation from nature they experience in their day-to-day lives. Celebrity conservationists in action give their audiences the satisfaction of watching them actually being there in real wild places and interacting with real wildlife.
>
> (Brockington, 2008: 562)

Third, the postmodern audience are well aware that celebrities emerge in and through promotional streams and processes and their investment is marked by critically finding how, when and why such media constructions are realised. They are actively interested in 'the techniques of artifice in and of themselves' (Gamson, 1994: 147) and pleasure derives from the irony with which they engage with celebrity culture. With regards to celebrity endorsements of charity campaigns, such irony is often noted and contested:

> Charity causes are often about, or the product of, grinding poverty, whereas celebrities are the embodiments of personalised wealth: a contradiction that makes this relationship, to say the least, problematic. One particularly graphic example here was the outcry by senior UNICEF staff in South Asia over the organisation's involvement in celebrity campaigns and corporate tie ins. In 2006, UNICEF launched an "exclusive" Christmas gift collection together with Gucci, an initiative for which Hollywood actress Jennifer Connelly supplied the "face". Furious UNICEF staff in Pakistan and India pointed out that the owners of Gucci have strong links with sweatshops in Mumbai and Karachi.
>
> (Littler, 2008: 243)

Irony is not always thought of as a productive encounter, however: central to post-feminist media culture (Gill, 2007 159–61; Tasker and Negra, 2007: 171), it is seen as the 'weapon of the "cultural capitalist"' (Hermes, 1995: 136), addressing women with a 'knowing wink' that implies that the sexist tropes it invokes are ridiculous and outdated, while simultaneously perpetuating them (Gill, 2007: 161).

The 'pleasing' use of irony in post-feminist celebrity culture is a strategy to further patriarchal ideologies and power (McRobbie, 2004: 262).

Gamson defines the fourth and fifth type of audience through the framework of game playing and game player. The game player gossiper engages in the sharing of celebrity titbits both for entertainment and social purposes, while the game player detective mines and maps the media in the quest for celebrity authenticity. Celebrity is a rich source of entertaining material and a playground for discovery and self-disclosure. However, both types of celebrity 'gamer' can be argued to perpetuate surveillance and disclosure regimes, producing discourses around privacy that threaten ethical behaviour, whose supposed openness is actually about power and control:

> In every society the production of discourse is at once controlled, selected, organised and redistributed by a certain number of procedures whose role is to ward off its powers and dangers, to gain mastery over its chance events, to evade its ponderous, formidable materiality.
>
> (1994: 210)

CELEBRITY CONSUMER

The relationship between celebrity and commodity consumption is one of the central ways that interaction takes place. Celebrities are almost always involved in a chain of promotion whether it be their own star-authorship, a text they are connected with, or a cause or brand they are attempting to sell. When it comes to celebrity and advertising effectiveness, the relationship between brand awareness and increased sales is often linked to the 'source credibility' model, which suggests that celebrity endorsements are most successful when three elements are in strong alignment: attractiveness, trustworthiness and expertise. For example, in terms of attractiveness:

> When using a celebrity as the endorser, the advertisement seems to be more effective if it is also enhancing the attractiveness of the celebrity. If the physical attractiveness of the endorser is also congruent with the product that is being endorsed, consumers tend to develop a positive attitude toward both the product or brand and the

advertisement evaluation. Additionally, the endorser's attractiveness could also significantly enhance the brand perception image.

(Ilicic and Webster, 2015: 167)

Further, there needs to be a high degree of value transference, in which the celebrity's values and lifestyle are seen to fully embody the product they endorse. The products, goods and services they promote provide the consumer with a tangible connection to them that can be owned, cherished and displayed. Celebrity endorsements very often takes place through a tissue of inter- and extra-textual references: in women's magazines, for example, the endorsement may well be part of a fashion shoot, be connected to a revelatory interview and juxtaposed next to celebrity advice columns, where the imagined reader is encouraged to 'be like' the famous figure. Details of the fashion garments are included, their cost and where to purchase or accessorise them, enabling readers to experience a 'sense of celebrity membership' (Feasey, 2006: 181) and to 'buy into some of the glamour, self-indulgence and decadence of the charmed life of a star' (Jermyn, 2006: 67).

Celebrity consumption is here being built on emotional connectivity and accessibility: the appeal is one based on transformatory identification and the imagined relationship the reader has with the star. Such relationships are often defined as para-social in formation, or 'the way we think and feel about people we don't know and who don't know us but who sometimes ... move us to act' (Cashmore, 2006: 39).

Chris Rojek suggests that the last century has seen a decisive shift in the 'balance of social encounters, from exchanges based on character to those based on personality or appearance, and that we are currently living in a context where public interaction is best characterised by the metaphors of "screen", "stage" and "image"' (2016: 58). Public, mediated personal disclosure is increasingly taken to be a quality of good civility – but, at the same time, works to effectively shore up problematic structures of political and economic power. For example, for those who feel isolated and alone, 'a sense of intimacy with a celebrity [is] preferable to ... feelings of isolation' (Stever, 2011), while never solving the issues that lead to isolation and exclusion in the first place. Similarly, 'celebrity bashing' (Johannson, 2006: 354) where the relationship consists of vilifying celebrities, may be used as a way of coping with class inequalities and issues around negative identity arising from them (Johannson, 2006: 354–55). Johannson describes 'celebrity bashing' (2006: 354) as a form of celebrity gossip, in which anger and resentment are expressed rather than admiration (ibid). She notes that this celebrity discourse is used by readers to voice their anger about social and class inequality evidenced by the glamour and excessive consumption featured in the celebrity media (ibid: 355).

Fantasy is crucial to the conceit that celebrity audiences are impressionable. Fantasy functions as a 'way in which identity is sutured together' (Hinerman 1992: 607), and as 'a necessary dimension of our psychical reality … as the place of excess, where the unimaginable can be imagined'. Hinerman's small-scale empirical research with Elvis Presley fans found that the escapist fantasies he offered up enabled them to withstand the traumatic events in their 'real lives'. The celebrity imaginary becomes a way to gather strength and resilience in the 'real' world. By contrast, Kerry O Ferris suggests that fans often want to close the gap between fantasy and reality, which create power imbalances, creating scenarios and attending activities which result in impoverished face-to-face interactions with the celebrity they dream of:

> Fan-celebrity encounters reveal both the pleasure and the perils of radically asymmetrical relations. These encounters feature fundamental imbalances of knowledge (in which the fan can possess a vast storehouse of information about the celebrity, but the celebrity has limited knowledge of the fan) and of power (the power to control the interaction shifts between fan and celebrity depending on the type of interaction). When these imbalances favour the fan, she has the license to direct the interaction in a way that may fulfil her desires but may make the star uneasy. When the celebrity (along with his handlers) has more control, the interaction is generally structured so as to limit fan contact and shield the star from any excesses. The interactional imbalances of fan-celebrity relations distinguish them from most other types of encounters between the unacquainted and indicate that the character of stranger relations in public depends on what kinds of strangers are involved. Fans and celebrities are 'intimate strangers' (Schickel 1985), and that makes all the difference.
>
> (Ferris, 2001: 44)

The phenomena of intimate strangers can of course lead to harmful fan practices, such as erotomania, where the fan imagines a consensual sexual or romantic relationship with the star or celebrity and enacts it through stalking or excessive modes of communication. The erotomanic believes that the celebrity has given them a 'secret signal', that they have revealed their admiration for them through a song lyric, interview or film and television role. This erotomanic episode results in them 'returning' the affection through letter writing, texts, gifts, phone calls and house visits. The more the celebrity declines the offerings, the more the erotomanic believes it is a concealment device, not to be revealed in the glare of the media. The erotomanic passionately believes that the celebrity passionately loves them but, has to hide this truth from the watching world. The fuel of pathological love is constantly re-ignited and the celebrity is hounded into existential crisis.

South Korean Sasaeng or 'private life' K-Pop fans dedicate themselves to following their fans at every step of their lives. Sasaeng fans are usually females aged 13–21, going first through puberty and then through progression into adulthood. Their devotion to K-Pop stars involve serial stalking, technical surveillance and snooping and attendance at all public events. Their desire is to be noticed by the star, to have interactions with them, in the hope of love being requited and to share with other Sasaeng fans their tactics and successes. For example, it was reported in July 2012 that, 'Sasaeng fans install CCTV in the parking lot of Park Yoochun's home'. Park Yoochun is a member of Korean boyband JYC, who have been the main object of Sasaeng's erotomanic impulses. The Sasaeng fan exists in a dual realm of interactions: on the one hand, they communicate in and through blogs and forums which are secret and secretive, and they desire more than anything to get to know the secret (private) life of the K-Pop star they stalk. On the other hand, their acts are self-publicised, their reported devotion a badge of honour; and their appearance in the media confirmation of their selfless love. Their interactions mirror the dual way that a celebrity experiences their fame; set in both private and public realms, existing in tension with one another.

However, there is also a masochistic relationship being fostered here. The Sasaeng fan allows their K-Pop idols to dominate and abuse them. K-Pop stars engage with fans in aggressive and violent ways. In March 2012, the Korean news outlet, Dispatch, released audio footage of JYC band members, Yoochun, Jaejoong and Junsu, which shows the three abusing and acting violently towards Sasaeng fans. Yoochun can be heard swearing at a fan over the phone, while Jaejoong can be heard repeatedly hitting one of the female Sasaeng fans. This doesn't break the devotion of the fan to the star, but seems to reinforce it, and the patriarchal power inherent in much of Korean culture.

Of course, erotomania can have serious and detrimental effects on the stars who are subject to such extreme devotion and attention. Stars consume 'fandom' and this affects their sense of self and well-being. The K-Pop singer Kim Jong-hyun, better known as Jonghyun, lead singer of the boy band SHINee, recently highlighted the pressures facing young stars in the cauldron of fan-worship as it manifests in South Korea's intensely competitive entertainment industry. In a suicide note he confides that he felt 'broken from inside … The depression that gnawed on me slowly has finally engulfed me entirely. I couldn't defeat it any more' (McCurry, 2017).

GOSSIP?

Another way that fan and celebrity intimacy is created is through the practices, processes and rituals of gossip (see Chapter 3). In Joke Hermes study of women's magazine readers, she describes gossip magazines as a form of 'serious gossip' (20), enabling readers to learn about themselves while expanding their private world (ibid). Hermes identified two frameworks that gossip operates through: the 'extended family repertoire' (1995: 126), and the 'repertoire of melodrama' (127). One is immersed in the extended family repertoire through the cross-thread stories and revelations that are writ large across the mass and micro media, suggesting unparalleled knowledge access to the lives of celebrities. Correspondingly, fans feel they have intimate knowledge of their private lives and talk about them as if they are part of their social circle, extending its size and malleability (Hermes: 127; Turner, 2004: 116).

Gossip that circulates through the repertoire of melodrama is pre-occupied with 'misery, drama, sentimentalism, sensation and paying for daring to rise above other people' (Hermes, 1995: 128). This repertoire allows readers/audiences the opportunity to revel in the misfortunes of celebrities and it provides solace for readers experiencing similar issues, while permitting others to take pleasure in the dramas celebrities are involved in.

> On an imaginary level it helps readers to live in a larger world than in real life—a world that is governed by emotional ties, that may be shaken by divorces and so on, but that is never seriously threatened. Sociological realities such as high divorce rates, broken families, children who leave home hardly ever to be seen again, are temporarily softened. The world of gossip is like the world of soap opera: whatever happens, they do not fall apart.
>
> (ibid: 80)

By invoking celebrity as the object of gossip, there are no personal judgements about friends or family members (Feasey, 2008: 693), as stars are 'members of the community whom *all* can evaluate' (emphasis in original, Alberoni, 2007: 66). Evaluation is a central motif in celebrity gossip, as it is through evaluating the actions of celebrities against one's own morals and values that people construct their identity and discern what is deemed socially acceptable (Hermes, 1995: 132; Fairclough, 2012: 92). The information gleaned through celebrity gossip is used to form moral communities (Wilson, 2010: 29) through which women can collectively evaluate (Gamson, 1994: 178) and debate the actions of celebrities (Turner, 2004: 24). These debates provide opportunities to transgress social norms by identifying with stars who also challenge them (Redmond, 2006: 38).

There is a strong contra ideological and governance mandate to celebrity gossip, however: Julie Wilson suggests that through reading and partaking in gossip about celebrities, women are made aware of and actively debate the 'dos and don'ts' (Wilson, 2010: 35) of fashion, love, mothering, work and familial relationships. Wilson argues that gossip magazines establish an 'evaluative hermeneutic' (28) and by doing so, they function as a way of ensuring women constantly monitor themselves to ensure they conform to the approved patriarchal version of femininity. Rather than encouraging women to debate and play with identities, Wilson explains that these magazines work to discursively position women to sit in judgement of other women and the choices they make regarding what they wear, how they look and who they sleep with.

Many of Wilson's arguments are evident in the tensions which exist in the post-feminist discourse between celebrity, choice, empowerment and agency. Post-feminist discourse involves:

> the notion that femininity is a bodily property; the shift from objectification to subjectification; the emphasis upon self-surveillance, monitoring and discipline; a focus upon individualism, choice and empowerment; the dominance of a makeover paradigm; a resurgence in ideas of natural sexual difference; a marked sexualisation of culture; and an emphasis upon consumerism and the commodification of difference.
>
> (Gill, 2007: 149)

Post-feminist discourse argues that the terrain of sexual objectification and subjectivity shifts: from a dominant male gaze that objectifies women, to that of a self-directed, internalised, appraising gaze (Gill, 2007: 151–52). Gill states that the body is perceived as a key source of women's power and the 'sign used to judge their "worth"'. However, in order to signify power and worth, the post-feminist body must conform to a particular type. It is the 'sleek, controlled figure [and] alluring young body' (Gill, 2009: 99) which portray success and embodies power. It is also very often white and blonde and stands in for notions of a perfected identity.

This constant scrutiny is demonstrated most clearly in the media, where female celebrity bodies are proffered to readers as objects for evaluation. Not only are girls/women invited to assess and value their bodies, but to undertake what Wilson calls 'star testing' (2010: 32), resulting in a process of evaluation between celebrities and fans (ibid). Women are also asked to re-embody themselves by undertaking various dieting and beauty regimes to look more like the celebrity in question. One way this is played out, particularly through 'selfie' culture, is before and after shots of celebrity-fan make-overs. Here two amateur shots are placed side-by-side with the more recent one an evocation of star transformation. Of course, a whole genre of television programmes has emerged in which female fans undergo make-over regimes, emerging like the star they so admire.

Kirsty Fairclough argues that the 'primary function' of celebrity gossip magazines and tell-tale sites such as perezhilton.com, 'is the hyper scrutiny of the female celebrity', particularly in relation to their youth and the called for invisibility of ageing. Ageing female celebrities are caught in an impossible bind: they can fight the signs of ageing and remain forever young; and they can go 'too far', revealing the very processes of the make-overs they have gone through. It is the revelatory 'talk' involved in celebrating or ridiculing these celebrity transformations which demonstrates that:

> the locus of power and agency for women of all ages now resides within displays of hyper-femininity, where power of the spending and sexual varieties are inscribed as the only ones' worth striving for.
>
> (2008: 103)

It can be argued that the consumption of celebrity is intimately caught up in the 'sexualisation of contemporary culture' (Gill, 2007: 150), enacting a form of social control under the guise of greater sexual choice and freedom. Duits and van Zoonen argue that 'porno-chic' (2006: 105) pervades a great deal of the output of the popular media. Music videos by artists such as Madonna, Rihanna and Britney Spears for example, feature the 'porno-chic' aesthetic while invoking notions of female empowerment. Overt displays of sexuality are equated with independence and 'liberation from repressive societal codes' (Duits and van Zoonen, 2006: 112). Miley Cyrus's recent incarnation as a young woman deliberately and provocatively revelling in her sexuality marked a distinct transformation from the wholesome character Hannah Montana she had played for years as a Disney starlet.

Miley Cyrus is a fascinating case study in relation to the main themes outlined in this chapter so far: the issue of gossip, effect and impressionable fans are bound up with her star image, as the following empirical research demonstrates. Miley Cyrus provides a rich discourse for understanding the gendered value of celebrity gossip for teenage girls.

CASE STUDY TALKING MILEY

The value of celebrity gossip

Introduction: The value of gossip

As outlined above, within the contemporary entertainment world the production and consumption of gossip has become a constant feature and is now found circulating across a wide range of media texts and interfaces. From legacy media formats including soap operas, chat shows and news bulletins, to the emergent digital forums via Twitter, Instagram and Facebook, gossip provides both an internal, narrative mechanism for the appearance of elevated drama, surprise and revelation, and an external forum for individual boundary testing and for shared and extended conversation to take place amongst reporters, interviewers, bloggers, fans and consumers. As Beer and Penfold-Mounce (2009: 2) argue, the:

> [C]hanging mediascape is populated by multifarious media forms that enable gossip to circulate through channels that are both organisationally lead, such as the print and online versions of magazines and newspapers, and also now, due to the rise of what might be thought of as participatory web cultures, are a product of ordinary users participating in constructing web-based content.

Gossip is also a sellable commodity in and of itself, and it energises the sales of media genres and forms such as magazines. Gossip entices people to be consumers, to purchase or download the media 'text' in question and to see themselves in a set of commodity relations and intertexts. Gossip specifically fuels the purchase of personalities, stars and celebrities so that they achieve, maintain or increase their status as valuable products in a chain of other synergetic goods and services. Gossip has become the contemporary currency of the media centre and the capital of consumption habitus.

Celebrity gossip is more than the remunerable circulation of a cultural commodity, however, simultaneously affording for a number, a certain emotive/affective reception and response. Drawing upon Robert Lane's earlier sociological work in *The Loss of Happiness in Market Democracies* (2000), Daniel Biltereyst (2004) represented a view, with reference to reality television, that the simulation of intimacy with the audience circulated via this media form coincides with the breakdown of traditional communities and families in the Western world. Echoing Lane, Biltereyst (2004: 119) acknowledged that: 'Western society struggles with a fundamental paradox: despite high material prosperity people more than ever experience personal unhappiness and unease.' What might be gleaned from this research and applied in the present context of how individuals engage with celebrity gossip, is that there appears to be an increasing desire by individuals to have a sense of 'connectedness' or 'intimacy' with others, whether through identifying with 'reality TV stars', celebrities or through social media more broadly. Moreover, Biltereyst (2004: 119) states that:

> [the] lack of warm interpersonal relationships and of solidarity in family life is reinforced (especially in the US) by the erosion of basic structures of societal solidarity since the 1980s, as well as by the growing work pressures in contemporary liberal market economies.

An important narrative has arisen then around the affective role that celebrities play in the everyday lives of individuals. The argument here suggests a mutual relationship between the capaciously termed celebrity, together with their associated textual objects including gossip, and the receptive individual. Indeed, there exists, what can be called a 'productive intimacy', in which stars and celebrities feel they are an important and valued part of everyday life, and listening bodies employ stars/celebrities to extend and enrich their everyday world (see also Rojek, 2001). Colouring the intimate nature of the relationship, is the suggestion here, that it is 'consummated' when an individual uses the celebrity/star performer to gradually intertwine experiences of them into the individual's own process of developing self-awareness or 'becoming'. This is not unaffected 'playful' identity construction/ exploration because for a number, it is serious and painful emotional growing, wherein a teen for example, pushes against the ideological, financial, regulatory, gendered, class confines of their lived world. Important is what is learned through this process and it is this higher personal, experiential and significant learning that is deeper than 'playful' imaginings (Redmond, 2014; Frith, 1996).

One can see, then, that the value of gossip is multi-dimensional. Gossip provides individuals with ideas about the self and selfhood, offers up representations of emulation and derision, connects people to each other, and operates within and across the streams of entertainment capital. Gossip is cheap to produce (or falsely create), manufacture and market, and within the social world it enables people – women in particular, as we will suggest below – to speak up about, and take pleasure from, the trials and tribulations, secrets and revelations that embody the stories of a great deal of revelatory discourse.

Celebrity gossip, of course, provides a heightened or particularly rich form of intimate revelation since famous individuals carry deep modes of feeling and affect in their representations and images. Celebrities are to be gossiped about precisely because of the complex and uneven relationship between their private and public worlds; because they continue to live only in the oxygen of publicity; and because there is 'an incitement to discourse' about our celebrities in terms of what they do in the world and how that impacts upon, or in part shapes, the way we conduct ourselves in everyday life (Foucault, 1990: 17).

This relationship between celebrity gossip, everyday life and gender identity is a perplexing one. Very often patriarchal discourse suggests that gossip is a negative female trait, one tied to crude essentialist notions about speech, intellect and what women are 'naturally' good at doing. Gossip is frivolous compared to 'serious' news and the heavy matter of politics, which men are more interested in.

In this frame, celebrity gossip can be understood as a discursive strategy to position women unequally within patriarchy and to continue capitalism's heteronormative, ideological and economic operations. In this light, Julia A Wilson (2010) contends that celebrity gossip is both post-feminist and neo-liberal, helping to produce a new type of gendered body, one that functions or signifies in the service of late capitalism. The value of celebrity gossip here becomes both behavioural and monetary: it models itself on a particular type of heteronormative version of femininity, partaking in a particular socially constructed and commodified image of gender. Specifically, celebrity gossip reproduces endless rounds of beauty/fashion rituals, and its central concern is with finding and keeping the right heterosexual man within a 'moral' framework of monogamy within the nuclear family.

The pleasure in celebrity gossip thus becomes the way it allows one to commercially and ideologically play out the stereotypical roles of beauty, mother, wife and 'bitch'. As Kirsty Fairclough (2008) concludes,

> The key practice of gossip blogging is to police the physiological status, style and appearances of female celebrities – regardless of their association (or otherwise) with more 'meritocratic' notions of talent and fame ... Female celebrities have become accustomed to such policing of their bodies via the Bitch character in blogs and magazines. The audience consumes this policing as part of the apparatus of

contemporary celebrity culture, while being subject to interpellation as a consumer themselves.

Nonetheless, there is an alternative or oppositional understanding of the value of celebrity gossip; one where it is reasonable to argue that it works as a ritual of refusal to patriarchal norms. This approach to celebrity gossip suggests that it has productive value and is involved in creating and sustaining pleasures that liberate those who are entertained by it. Joke Hermes's empirical research on how women consume celebrity gossip finds that it is a serious business that revolves 'around fantasies of belonging: to an extended family or a moral community' (1995: 132). Similarly, Rebecca Feasey (2008: 690) suggests that celebrity gossip is a:

> form of knowledge that awards women respect, status, and a privileged position among their peers while using these self-same discourses to connect with other women, far removed from any sense of social hierarchy.

For 'sex-positive' suffragettes, epitomised by American feminist author and Professor of Humanities and Media Studies, Camille Paglia, critical examination of performances by singers such as Madonna afford opportunities to revel in modern sexual expression and female identity (Paglia, 1990). She claims:

> Madonna is the true feminist. She exposes the puritanism and suffocating ideology of American feminism, which is stuck in an adolescent whining mode. Madonna has taught young women to be fully female and sexual while still exercising total control over their lives. She shows girls how to be attractive, sensual, energetic, ambitious, aggressive and funny – all at the same time.

In this contemporary context, the changing mediascape and rise of social networks are essential to the circulation of gossip by teenage women. Beer and Penfold-Mounce (2009: 4) argue that the new media are central to the relentless circulation of gossip, producing what they define as a new melodramatic imagination which:

> [O]perates to draw strands together and assemble 'structures of feeling' amongst this dirge of information ... The new melodramatic

imagination then not only sensitively assembles the fragmented parts to interpret and understand the melodrama found in celebrity gossip, it is also active in shaping how these stories develop by participating in their dissemination for other melodramatic imaginations to encounter and interpret ... We can see here how the new melodramatic imagination may not just be limited to the interpretation of texts but may also now be active and even mobile in assembling together the bits from a variety of texts across a mediascape in order to follow, appreciate and perpetuate the melodrama.

What the research below attempts to investigate is the question of impressionability when it comes to fan interaction with Miley Cyrus's social media use.

CASE STUDY

The value of celebrity gossip: Miley Cyrus

With Toija Cinque

This case study examines the value of celebrity gossip for young teenage women. Through a case study of Miley Cyrus, it explores the ways by which gossip is sanctioned and produced, speaks to gender identity and gender relations, and is interacted with, shared and transcoded. Social media was selected as a key resource for data collection and analysis, because a number of sites are the primary spheres of engagement between teen celebrities and their adolescent fan base. The overriding research questions are, therefore:

1. What is entertaining about this gossip; why and how are teenage girls being entertained by it?
2. Is the gossip in the service of gender norms or does it, can it, have productive outcomes and if so, what gendered themes emerge in the gossip about Miley?
3. What 'value' emerges from or out of its production and consumption?

Primary data was collected from two key digital sources: Twitter and Facebook. First, Twitter data in the form of tweets and retweets (including those responses to Miley Cyrus's official Twitter account), was collected over a two-week period from 1 August to 14 August 2014, using Tweet Archivist. This period of the first two weeks of August 2014 was selected because Miley's world tour was underway in North America and is where her largest fan base is. Consequently, there was expected a significant rise in digital 'conversations' or media traffic about her performances and musical work at this time. Moreover, August is also the summer season in the Northern hemisphere and social media use and interaction peaks at this time.

Second, content analysis of the official and unofficial sites of gossip about Miley Cyrus was undertaken to determine the nature of the digital conversations taking place on Miley's official Facebook presence and the fan interactions with it.

Unruly desire, cathartic affect and the value of tweeting

Twitter has become more commonplace as a discussion tool across a number of nations. Recent investigation by Axel Bruns and Jean Burgess (2011: 1) has underscored the important role of the Twitter hashtag, a short keyword that is prefixed with the hash symbol '#', for the purposes of forming publics in the Twitter community around an event, topic or interest. Bruns and Burgess (2011: 3) argue that:

> In the early phases of adoption following its launch in 2006, Twitter had almost none of the extended functionality that it does today. Twitter users were invited to answer the question 'What are you doing?' in 140 characters or less, to follow the accounts of their friends, and little else ... Many of the technical affordances and cultural applications of Twitter that make its role in public communication so significant were originally user-led innovations.

Drawing on data compiled by Tweet Archivist (www.tweetarchivist.com) between the dates of 1 August and 14 August 2014, noted as the time that Miley Cyrus's Bangerz Tour was in North America, this section examines the volume of digital commentary about Miley Cyrus, via the use of the search term 'Miley Cyrus' and the hashtag #Bangerz, in the context of the start of the US leg of her 2014 Bangerz tour.

The diverse range of contributors from official media such as MetroTV (tweeting to 5,466,114 followers); *Rolling Stone* magazine (tweeting to 3,818,424 followers); MTVNews (tweeting to 3,238,588 followers) to celebrity blogger Perez Hilton (tweeting to 5,918,894 followers); to the teen fans and detractors alike (tweeting to a few hundred followers), indicates that the results of this research can be seen to be representative of a 'fan'-base interest in the life and work of Miley Cyrus: Twitter is a central conduit for the way gossip about Miley is circulated amongst fans and followers.

Data collated from the archive of tweets highlighted that during the sampled timeframe 'Miley Cyrus' remained topical with the total number of occurrences of tweets about her, and sent to the timeline for the purpose of this research, regularly exceeded 250, 000 impressions (see Table 8.1).

The specific volume of tweets sent during the nominated timeframe was plotted for the term 'Miley Cyrus' and #Bangerz and is outlined in Chart 8.1 and Chart 8.2.

Data collated from the archive highlighted that there was a considerable number of tweets on 4 August (15,927) and on 9 August (17,981), with the least sent on 11 August (6,012) when there was no scheduled concert. As a point of comparison, the official Twitter account of Miley Cyrus indicates that on 4 August, Miley posted a link via Twitter to a photo of herself and her mother on Instagram that was retweeted 5,540 times and favourited 8,446 times:

MAMA MADE IT tishcyrus http://instagram.com/p/rTNKMVwzJX/

Table 8.1 Number of impressions using #MileyCyrus (1 August to 14 August 2014)

#Miley Cyrus	
Data range	*Number of impressions*
1 August–3 August	276,999,707
3 August–7 August	326,004,728
7 August–11 August	312,190,639
11 August–14 August	250,972,363

Note: Impressions are the total number of times that tweets were delivered to timelines with this search or hashtag in this archive.

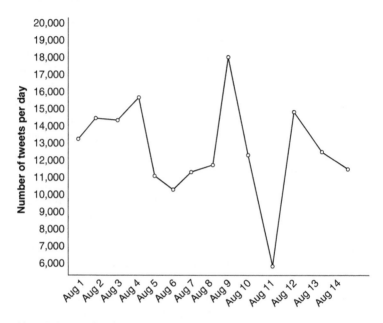

Chart 8.1 Use of 'Miley Cyrus' and volume over time (1 August 2014 to 14 August 2014)

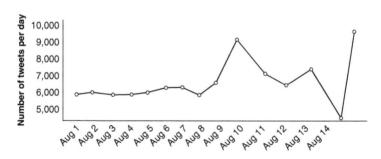

Chart 8.2 Use of #Bangerz and volume over time (1 August 2014 to 14 August 2014)

The tweet also became a Facebook post (see below for further analysis) and indicates a desire by Miley to create personal traffic about her family life and the emotional bonds she attaches to it.

Generating the greater traffic (more 'tweets') at this time, was probably her post of 2 August in relation to her forthcoming concert in Philadelphia that generated 12,621 retweets and was favourited 22,389 times:

> Excited for fucking Philly folks

In relation to the spike in posts on Twitter on 9 August, on this date, Miley posted a link via her Twitter account to her controversial parody on Instagram of Nicki Minaj's Anaconda:

> #dontwantnoneunlessyougotbunzhun @nickiminaj http://instagram.com/p/rgox2AwzFP/

Miley's meme incorporated her head on a version on Minaj's body, calling herself 'Hannah Conda' (see http://perezhilton.com/2014-08-11-miley-cyrus-nicki-minaj-anaconda-cover-art-booty-parody-instagram-angry-twitter#ixzz3CJFahJK5). The retweets alone occurred 5,540 times and the post was favourited 8,446 times.

One can see how Miley creates controversy through her tweets. Such controversy is a central part of her 'wayward' star image and produces 'gossip' that identifies her as someone who breaks rules; something we define below as 'misrule', when undertaking our analysis of her Facebook posts.

Data collated from the archive drew attention to the number of tweets between 1 August and 7 August, the first week of the Bangerz Tour through North America, that ranged between 5,705 tweets (August 3) and 6,398 tweets (August 7), with a considerable spike on 10 August (9,350 tweets) and on 15 August (9,564 tweets) respectively, the day after the North American concerts ended. Contributing to this traffic was Miley's own tweets. On August 10, she posted a photograph of herself with her father, with the post being retweeted 4,400 times and favourited 7,552 times:

> #creepyassfamilyphoto @noahcyrus billyraycyrus http://instagram.com/p/rhvqGvQzGk/

With one fan putting up a response:

> OMFG MILEY COMMENTED ON MY PICTURE IM LEGIT GONNA CRY ...

And, fans received news that she now had a piglet as a pet:

> newest member to the fam #bubbasue http://instagram.com/p/riojqrQzJZ/

Contributing to the volume of overall traffic, this post was retweeted 3,762 times and favourited 6,872 times. Again, during this reporting period we can see these tweets picked up on her Facebook posts, where they are interacted with in similar ways. The gossip that circulates around Miley involves a commitment to these familial longings.

Provocatively, however, the term #fuckingbangerz was used to reference the Bangerz tour by Miley herself and her publicity team:

> @MileyCyrus
>
> #FUCKINGBANGERZ
>
> One week til #BANGERZTour in Kansas City, MO! LOVE, MONEY, PARTY! #FUCKINGBANGERZ pic.twitter.com/b97sEFEzOC
>
> Miley Cyrus News, Miley Ray Cyrus, Official Miley Team and 7 others
>
> HOLY FUCKING SHIT!!! MILEY WAS AMAZING I LOVE YOU #fuckingbangerz @MileyCyrus

Overall, what emerged from the data was that the search term 'Miley Cyrus' was used frequently, with the tour-related term #Bangerz becoming subsumed by the 'official' hashtag #fuckingbangerz during the tour in North America. The most significant findings of the data analysis, however, are revealed in the intersections between this quantitative data and the qualitative data obtained from Miley Cyrus's own tweets on her official Twitter page relating to what is happening or important in her life on a given day. While the exact nature of access and use of Twitter, for example, cannot be surmised, it is evident that the vast majority of fans use the tool to reflect upon and gossip about the daily activities, thoughts and impressions left by Miley Cyrus.

The face that can't be tamed

According to Foster (2004), gossip fulfils four important social functions. First, it involves information flow and exchange, and is a type of individual and collective mapping of the social world that takes place outside of the official and formal lines of communication. Second, gossip is a form of pleasurable entertainment involving the joy of gossiping with one another, in spaces not public, and in conversations where someone is being deliberately omitted. Third, gossip is about friendship bonds and the trust and intimacy that is generated from revelation and disclosure – it creates a sense of closeness. Fourth, gossip is implicated in the power of influence, the shaping of opinion, and in changing the behaviour of the supposed 'sinner'.

With regard to celebrity gossip, there are necessary inflections to the way it functions and is transmitted. First, celebrity gossip is a central or official part of the mainstream media communication flow. Celebrity gossip is readily sanctioned and openly trafficked by media commentators and bloggers, by the public relations personnel, and by famous people themselves. Celebrity gossip is very much a public activity even if it also migrates to private conversations between fans, friends and consumers. Second, given the gossip that is being circulated is on an individual whom one does not know directly, the level of pleasure may be heightened because there are less real-life consequences, and one can increase the range and frequency and 'bite' of the whispers when it involves someone who is famous. As Turner (2004: 176) suggests, paraphrasing Gamson, 'celebrity gossip is a much freer realm, much more game-like than acquaintance gossip: there are no repercussions and there is no accountability.' Third, any sense of influence is set within a flow hierarchy. The media generally set the gossip in train with fans and consumers' 'speaking' only after the opinion has been set (up) by the media frame.

One can see these social functions of celebrity gossip being played out in both Miley's official Facebook page and the fan Facebook page dedicated to her. However – and remembering the questions we set ourselves in the introduction – we will suggest that not only is there a gendered dimension to the gossip circulated and commented upon, but that it very much sits within a teenage framework: Miley struggles to come to terms with her own wayward sexuality and fans wrestle with this 'becoming' identity. We find the 'gossip' circulated on Miley's page both speaks to patriarchal norms and challenges them, opening up channels of communication where normative borders around teenage female identity are breached.

Miley's official Facebook page was activated on 8 November 2007 and as of 5 September 2014 had a total number of 49,481,803 fans, with the United States providing the biggest share of likes with 7,898,486 or 16.0 percent of the total (www.socialbakers.com/facebook-pages/5845317146-miley-cyrus).

With regards to Miley's 'official' Facebook page, five themes emerge in and across her posts during the time of the reporting: (1) family and nostalgia; (2) mothering and nurturing; (3) promotion and publicity; (4) self-depreciation and self-reflexivity; and (5) misrule. Fans comments in response to these posts can also be grouped in terms of the following themes: (1) love, adoration, and desire for Miley; (2) rejection and dislike of the 'new' wayward Miley (and nostalgia for the old Miley); (3) hating, trolling Miley; (4) demonstrating prestige knowledge; and (5) empathy and understanding of Miley's trials and tribulations. Nonetheless, there is a degree of inter-textuality and cross-referencing across the themes that suggest gossip and interaction emerges in a plasma-like way. We would like to take each theme in turn, and the comments generated under the highlighted posts, to consider the value of gossip in each case.

Family and nostalgia

Miley's posts during this reporting period included directed references to her family life, family pictures and auto-ethnographic memorial work. For example, on 5 August, Miley posted a photograph of her mum and her, with the comment, 'mama made it'. The selfie captures them in suffuse light and there is a mirroring through their positioned closeness to one another. Posted comments included, 'mama is sexy'; 'she really got her eyes from her mama'; 'HER MUM LOOKS LIKE A DRUG ADDICT!!!!!' and 'See It isn't much hard to keep your tongue inside XD'.

The latter comment is a recurring sub-theme across the posts that contain photographs of Miley – a discussion emerges about Miley's beauty, maturity and sexuality through the way she poses. Similarly, one finds hateful trolling across the themes as anti-fans attack her looks, familial life and behaviour. These are generally gender-encoded, misogynist posts by both girls and boys who follow her. It seems as if the ideology of gender binaries seeps into the way that Smilers (Miley refers to her fans as Smileys; her own (now legal) name is a sobriquet given by her father) and anti-fans talk about her, with both sexes being as loving and hateful as each other.

On 8 August, Miley posted a photograph of her childhood cuddle toy with the comment: '#beenafreak this was my bf as a kid #snickerswasthename'. We get a sense of the memorial work being undertaken by Miley, and nostalgia for a childhood long gone. In a clear sense, Miley mourns the passing of her innocence, something her fans also do in relation to her transformation from good-girl Hannah Montana to the vamp who cannot be tamed. Comments on all these memorial and nostalgia posts include 'look at you and your happy and pretty family before being illuminati. shiit!!!!! illuminati changes from good to bad' (posted 8 August); 'Back when Miley was wholesome. A girl you could take home to mom'; and 'The gd times, Miley what happend do you cry at night?' (both posted on 11 August). There is an emotional and psychological alignment in operation here, one where Miley's star-life trajectory mirrors her fans as they grow up. Love, loss and longing circulate in interesting and competing streams at the time of this reporting.

Mothering and nurturing

On Miley's Facebook page, mothering and nurturing manifests in the following ways. First, Miley refers to her fans as Smileys and communicates with them as if they are family members or loved ones she cares for. Second, Miley adopts a piglet during this period and, along with her dog Emu, is shown caring for it, loving it. They are her 'babies' and she adopts a maternal relationship to them. For example, on 11 and 12 August respectively, Miley introduces her Smilers to, 'the newest member to the fam #bubbasue'. Miley is seen cuddling and holding her new piglet. Fans comments include; 'Wellllllll helllllllllllllo!! Little pretty Bubba Sue xoxo you are a doll, what a lovely pig^^!'; 'Awww i want 1 love u Miley'; and 'So sweetie'.

Miley hashtags most of her posts creating the context for cross-media pollination, as her stories are tweeted and shared. A number of posts carry on the theme of supporting Miley, no matter what she does, including:

> I support u no matter wat ... It's been my dream to see one of ur con-
> certs and meet u ... Ur my hero and im glad u dont care wat haters
> think ... Hey haters make u famous ... stay you and peace girl!!!
>
> Love, Emily (Flower Power)

Smilers readily take on trolls in the threads of the comments section, adopting or challenging 'bitch-like' identities to trade blows with one another. The discourse is heavily gendered, then, focusing on looks and appropriate female behaviour. However, the discourse is also challenged as comments revel in the rebellion that Miley offers up as empowered and empowering behaviour. Miley's Facebook page carries out the contestations of gender and age as they manifest in the neo-liberal age of hyper-individualism and collective uncertainty.

Promotion and publicity

Miley's Facebook page includes promotional posts for her concert tour, associated marketing and invites, and encourages Smileys to vote for her in competitions such as the MTV Music Awards for Best Video. Of course, all of the posts can be considered to be forms of publicity and promotional since they contribute to Miley's star image and maintain the currency of her celebrity. On 3 August, Smilers are encouraged to: 'Smilers! Show your support for Miley and vote for "Wrecking Ball" for Video of the Year at the 2014 MTV VMA's!! http://bit.ly/MileyVMA2014'; and on 9 August, 'Last chance to get your votes in for "Wrecking Ball" to win Video of the Year at the 2014 MTV VMA's! Voting ends Aug. 11! http://bit.ly/MileyVMA2014'. Smiler comments included, 'I voted for you my queen'; 'Turkish Smilers love you Miley'; and 'Omg one of my favourite songs !!!'. The promotion and publicity strand encourage gossip, invites Smilers (and Trolls) to talk Miley up (and down), creating the oxygen of publicity that sustains and nourishes her fame.

Self-depreciation and self-reflexivity

During the two weeks of reporting we also discerned the theme of self-depreciation, where Miley would mock or lampoon her own celebrity status. This ironising was combined with a clear sense of reflecting on one's success, of commenting upon one's life journey. For example, on 7 August, Miley posted a photograph of herself with baggy eyes, with the comment, 'dem eye bagz'. Again, this created a contradictory set of responses, from 'Still looking cute girl', to 'I like the other Miley Cyrus because you are a crazy lady'.

On 9 August, Miley posted a photograph of herself in a derelict house, with overgrown weeds and plants surrounding it. Holding a water bottle, dressed in shorts and a hoodie and looking away from the gaze of the camera, she looks lost and deep in thought, perhaps troubled by her celebrity status. Comments posted included, 'You are beautiful, thanks God for his perfect creation like YOU!'; 'why have u changed miley..........??????????'; and 'we miss you hannah'.

This fan desire to see Miley return to her Hannah roots suggests that Smileys are also full of nostalgia for a time they once lived in and through Miley. It also suggests an uncertain relationship to woman-hood and femininity, as if they are all touched by the ambiguity they face within patriarchal culture.

Misrule

One of the clear themes to emerge across the posts was that of mis-rule and transgression. These posts would either refer to rule breaking, celebrate rule-breakers or would include photographs of acts of trans-gression and hedonism. For example, on 4 August, Miley posted the comment 'always the best fucking time in NY', with the accompanying polaroid 'snaps' of Miley and friends partying. The photographs show Miley revealing the breast of a friend, and play 'fingering' another through her clothes. Comments included, 'party in the usa! hell to the hell yeah', and this extended one from a mother:

> She used to be my daughters favorite person ... But she doesn't watch or listen to her anymore ... She asked me what happened to the old Miley ... What happened to Hannah Montana? Think Miley ... You are setting a bad example ...

Miley's embodiment of misrule is of course connected to the wider controversy that surrounds her current star image and such incidents as the 'twerk' and the sexual explicitness of the Wrecking Ball video. Miley embodies the gender controversies of the times. On the one hand, she can be seen as the post-feminist girl who takes power through her looks and active sexuality. On the other, she can be seen to reinforce gender normativity, serving to discipline girls into the act of womanhood.

Gossip is central here – it either gives voice to young girls to discuss these issues or creates the conditions for talk that works in favour of patriarchy. We can see both in operation during the time of this reporting. The value here is a confused or ambivalent one since it reads like a rite of passage for Smileys as they go through their own trials and tribulations. Value is, of course, about market-value, and one can see how her Facebook promotes her star image in numerous ways. It helps give 'birth' to the neo-liberal individual who uses talk to secure his or her own empowered ontology in the marketplace.

CONCLUSION

The research here presents findings illustrating broadly that contemporary screen culture and engagement with new media technological innovations, Twitter, Instagram and Facebook as exemplars, by teenagers is considerable. Further, a number of activities such a posting to Facebook or sending tweets via Twitter for the purpose of celebrity gossip in the everyday lives of teenagers seem to be 'naturalised'. During the select time of the first two weeks of August, this research found digital 'conversations' about Miley Cyrus being actively circulated, with five emergent themes across new media posts and tweets. These include (1) family and nostalgia; (2) mothering and nurturing; (3) promotion and publicity; (4) self-depreciation and self-reflexivity; and (5) misrule. Moreover, fan comments in response to such posts were classified further into the following themes: (1) love, adoration, and desire for Miley; (2) rejection and dislike of the 'new' wayward Miley (and nostalgia for the old Miley); (3) hating, trolling Miley; (4) demonstrating prestige knowledge; and (5) empathy and understanding of Miley's trials and tribulations. Indeed, there is an emotional and psychological alignment in operation wherein Miley Cyrus's star-life trajectory mirrors that of her fans as they are growing up or 'becoming'. Indeed, key life events across developing feelings of love, loss and longing flow in interesting and competing streams. The pleasure of celebrity gossip toward an economic value is its considerable influence on the way that celebrities are mediated across the contemporary mediascape. The positive moral evaluation of the pleasure to be found in celebrity gossip for the teenager (teen woman), be it actively posting comments, retweeting, creating tweets, and the subsequent opportunities for shaping opinion, is that it affords them with intimate connections to likeminded others, thus providing opportunities for friendship or developing community bonds. Here, in this context, celebrity gossip is presented as but one of a number of types of human communication.

CHAPTER SUMMARY

The chapter has explored the way celebrity culture is consumed by fans and audiences: it has analysed the relationship between the talk of celebrity and the effect such talk has on the values and beliefs of people. The chapter has drawn on audience studies, theories of consumption and post-feminism to critically engage with the ideologies and values produced by celebrity culture. The closing case study on Miley Cyrus has shown how complex fan reception is, opening the doorway for the discussion of affective agency that happens in the next chapter.

9

CELEBRITY AGENCY

This chapter takes an active approach to the way fans and audiences consume celebrity culture. It draws upon a number of arguments and illustrations to demonstrate the affective and empowering way that stars and celebrities, fans and audiences, create spaces of cultural activation where new intensified relations are forged.

VOICES AND STRUGGLES

Meaning, Stuart Hall suggests, happens at the precise moment a cultural text is received and consumed: the text may well be loaded with dominant ideology and will have been shaped to elicit a 'preferred reading', but its essential polysemy, and the wide-ranging nature of reception contexts it will be met in, makes activation and agency crucial (1997). Cultural texts are not 'fixed' and their meaning shifts over time. Further, audiences and consumers bring their own 'texts' to the 'text' in a constant process of mediation and remediation. Cultural texts are struggled over, their ideologies not simply worn but refashioned in the unpredictable moment of the lived experience. As Duits and van Zoonen suggest, in relation to their empirical research on how female fans respond to pop stars:

When asked which type of appearance promotes success, they argued against the beauty ideal, yet were aware of how celebrities 'manipulate' their appearance to comply with impossible standards. For instance, in talking about pop singer Pink they reflected on how she changed her image under pressure of the music industry. The focus groups testified to an understanding of how commercial culture and media stories work and how girls themselves are hailed by MTV's celebrity discourse ... This is not to suggest that all girls are feminist theorists in disguise, although they are remarkably media savvy, but that it is imperative to examine which tactics girls use in their everyday lives to 'make do' (de Certeau, 1984) with all the forces that bear on them.

(2007: 166)

Too often a top-down framework is applied to both understand how celebrity culture impacts upon everyday life, and to the interpretation of voices when they are indeed called upon to speak. Very often, when empirical research is carried out, the very responses that have been called upon are marginalised and re-framed, given a new theoretical 'voice' to capture what was supposedly there in the first place. While reading or making sense of audience responses is crucial, the tendency to dismiss the agency that is so palpably there, in the first place, is one of the failures of the work being carried out in this field. It is the relationship between the individual, the social and the cultural that calls for better alignment.

Further, too often audience research exists within the circuit of culture schema: rarely do the power of affects take centre stage when it comes to understanding the way people actively receive culture. Not all reception contexts are representational, linguistic, and neither are they housed in the streets of ideology.

One method that enables us to hear and see the voices of the people we interview is the storying the self-approach which recognises that:

At an elemental level we have a need for stories, to organise and transmit our experiences to others and to help form meaningful connections ... as information is indexed, stored and retrieved through stories, the process of telling a story is episodic, cathartic and pleasurable for both the teller and the listener. Stories, how we tell them and how we transmit them, are therefore pivotal to understanding behaviour.

(Rooney, Lawlor, and Rohan, 2016: 147)

This emphasis on 'writing the personal' (Probyn, 2011) has also been central to the epistemological and political interventions of popular culture theorists and those interested in 'hearing' the stories of the marginalised and politically disenfranchised. Connected to this approach is the recognition that researchers also have stories to share and in a way that democratises the empirical process – no one story is more important than the other – and through shared storytelling, experiential equivalences and 'clusters' emerge. Through storying the self, we find out about how people directly experience their own, often marginalised, subject positions. Autoethnography is also crucial here: it 'requires that we observe ourselves observing, that we interrogate what we think and believe' (Carolyn Ellis 2013: 10). Within the context of autoethnography, reflection on the process and experience of writing creates what has become known as a 'writing story' (Wall, 2008: 40).

FAN ACTIVATION

Active celebrity fandom involves two, sometimes interrelating, forms: one that is individualised and individually sanctioned; and one that takes place in fan communities, defined as 'the shared social contexts within which fan reading and creative practices occur' (Jenkins, 2006b). Those celebrity fans who individualise their active participation also often share and partake in communities, involving themselves in both a 'private' form of intimacy with the celebrity and a 'public' one, where the sharing of knowledge, readings, desires and the creation of homages and transcodings of existing texts takes place. According to Henry Jenkins (2010b), fandom is a key facet of participatory culture, where:

> [f]andom refers to the social structures and cultural practices created by the most passionately engaged consumers of mass media properties; participatory culture refers more broadly to any kind of cultural production which starts at the grassroots level and which is open to broad participation.

The participatory culture that builds around celebrity fandom can be argued to be regenerative, affecting the production and reception of the figure, as fans creatively transcode their meaning, produce and transmit new ways of understanding the celebrity, and engage in new forms of collective interaction. As Charles Soukup suggests in relation to online fandom communities:

> On the Chris Carter Web sites, fans analyzed the themes and symbols of *The X-Files* episode by episode. In these situations, the fan appears to be actively constructing meaning and refusing to 'accept' the dominant interpretation of the media text. Rather than (relatively) passively reading the text as 'intended' by the producers or interpreted by mainstream critics, these fans offer unique, alternative, and sometimes quite elaborate readings of the text. By actively reinterpreting the text, the fan is creative and empowered. Perhaps in the most dramatic example, a fansite dedicated to the musician Moby had a page of remixed songs (originally recorded by Moby) posted by fans. In a number of similar examples, fans rewrote or wrote new versions of songs by artists like David Bowie and Bob Dylan.
>
> (2006: 327)

For a number of scholars there is an understanding that in certain productive circumstances, fandom affords an individual with a sense of empowerment and, in relation to pop stardom, that some musical experiences can be responsible for indescribable, unlocatable sensations. For example, Ken McLeod (2003: 338) has argued that music is of fundamental importance because it,

> creates an embodied but imaginary space that mediates our internal space (feelings, desires, dreams) with external space (the physical, experienced) ... Music takes us outside our bodies and place while simultaneously reminding us of our location and what it means to live there.

Such forms of material transcendence have also been termed encounters of 'enchantment' (Bennett 2001: 5), whereby heightened musical connections can be seen to occur in the presence of the performer, or in their absence, as in the case of recorded music. As Mark Duffett's (2012) empirical research on Elvis Presley demonstrates, fandom can provide a vehicle for powerfully sensorial encounters:

> If I actually name the day I became an Elvis fan, the moment I became an Elvis fan was at the Leicester convention ... They played American

Trilogy. Some guy grabbed my hand and pulled me up to my feet. I felt this adrenaline go through from the top of my head to the bottom of my feet and it was just an astonishing feeling of brotherhood, almost, in the room. Just this family, you were in amongst this family.

(Duffett, 2012: 4–5)

Within the Japanese context of fandom, fans are not satisfied with the 'formal performances, with the mediated and staged glimpses of stars. Rather, they seek to get behind the curtain, to know more about the performers, to possess them through tokens like autographs and handprints and bootleg tapes' (Kelly, 2004: 9).

Racial identity can also be crucial to the way celebrity fan activation occurs. Through establishing an affective chain of communication, where difference and Otherness are highlighted but overcome, celebrity fandom resists, rejects and opposes the wider cultures that seek to oppress and repress it. Such affective interaction followed the death of Michael Jackson:

'I remember the time very well when I saw the first moonwalk, thriller, [sic] and all of your videos' (TM1-290); 'I [sic] grew up listening to his music. he [sic] was the first record i [sic] listened to, first song i [sic] danced to, first time i [sic] tried to imitate someone when I was three' (FB1-149).

(Sanderson and Cheong, 2010: 333)

Stars can act as affective machines where their embodiment speaks to the outsiderdom the fan may experience.

In the following migrant fan case study, we see how David Bowie was a figure of recuperation and renewal. Specifically, the case study focuses upon the ways that 'migrants' in Melbourne use David Bowie to story and make sense of their immigrant status in Australia, often as first-generation migrants coming to terms with their 'difference'. As the research has found, Bowie's alternative and outsider status resonates keenly with people who find themselves 'strangers' in a new land. Lyrically, musically and in terms of star representation, Bowie becomes, then, the figure through which migrants navigate themselves through new cultural and social environments. Here we also find that migrant identity readily intersects with sexuality, gender, class and age concerns.

CASE STUDY

Lazarus rises and the migrant fandom of David Bowie

With Toija Cinque

For this research, we adopted the focus group method for these various reasons: we intended for it to be a participatory space, where participants could openly share their stories. However, our focus on migrant identity in relation to the fandom of David Bowie sets the discussion in a cultural and social context that has not been explored by other fan scholars, or through a story-framed empirical method. This pilot study is unique in both focus and method.

Migrant method

By way of background to this study, Australia until the 1950s had defined itself largely as a 'new Britannia', emulating the 'empire' in the Southern Hemisphere (Langer, 2001). With post World War II immigration, however, the 'monoculture' of Australia changed toward an official notion of 'multiculturalism' or multi-ethnicity (Jupp, 1996). The terms 'multiculturalism' or 'multi-ethnicity' are now frequently referred to in policy documents as 'cultural diversity'. Moreover, the terms 'multicultural' and 'ethnic' become imprecise when they are only associated with people from non-English-speaking backgrounds (NESBs) because English speakers in Australia form various ethnic groups, for example, the English, Irish or Welsh, but so do the many Aboriginal communities. According to Gillard (2002), the term 'multiculturalism' was first used in Australia under the Whitlam-led Labor government (December 1972–November 1975), as part of its policy for Australia to move beyond its 'White Australia' heritage and beyond the assimilation policies which had governed the initial years of post-war migration. The constitution of Australia's population was changing, with migrants coming increasingly from non-English-speaking nations such as Italy, Greece and Germany, rather than from the English-speaking countries of England, Scotland, Ireland and Wales as had occurred in the past. By 1976 the national census revealed that one in five persons in Australia was born overseas and at least another one in ten had parents who were born overseas (Ethnic Television Review Panel, 1980: 10). The most recent 2011 Australian

Bureau of Statistics (ABS) Census recorded data indicating that where initially most migrants were born in countries in North-West Europe, followed by a number born in Southern and Eastern Europe, the proportion of the overseas-born population originating from Europe has now been in decline in recent years, from 52 percent in 2001 to 40 percent in 2011 (ABS, 2012). Moreover, recent arrival data reflects the increasing number of people born in Asian countries:

> Recent arrivals accounted for 47% of the total Indian-born population in Australia and 35% of the total Chinese-born population. In contrast, only 11% of the total United Kingdom-born population were recent arrivals.
>
> (ABS, 2012)

Data reveals that the Country of Birth groups which increased the most between 2001 and 2011 were India (up 200,000 people), China (176,200) and New Zealand (127,700). The largest decreases were seen in the birth countries of Italy (less 33,300 people), Greece (16,500) and Poland (9,400), according to the ABS (2012). Almost half (49 percent) of longer-standing migrants to Australia and 67 percent of recent arrivals spoke a language other than English at home. New migrants to Australia came from almost one hundred countries and, in one way, a multicultural society can be understood to be one which is based on mutual respect and recognition of difference, having a commitment to the core values of Australian democracy and a desire to maintain harmony in the wider community (Jakubowicz and Newell, 1995: 130–31). An alternative argument posed by Rex (1996: 15), however, sees multiculturalism as the means by which society is organised so that ethnic groups are incorporated and dominated by others; where these ethnic groups would otherwise be separate societies not bound by the state.

For the purpose of this study, clarity around the term 'migrant' is justified, in due consideration of its complexity. We in no way want to create another work that might be seen to commodify 'the Other'. On culture and cultures, and the notion of 'Otherness', the important work of Edward Said (1978) presented the argument that the (postcolonial) West writes about and describes a version of the East in order to dominate it. In the Australian context, Seneviratne (1992) has argued that the Special Broadcasting Service (SBS) – a media organisation established initially for new migrants to the country – pursued an elitist and monocultural outlook as demonstrated in news and current affairs programming and employment policies marked by cultural superiority. As a consequence, 'serious viewers' or 'cosmopolitans' (usually the well-educated in upper-income brackets) are able to enjoy, indeed revel in, 'ethnic' culture – but from a distance. This act, Hage (1995) claims, supports ideological domination within the nation.

What is not distinguished in the argument above, however, is that the term 'cosmopolitan' can refer to a group which, in Australia, includes people from various ethnic backgrounds because they too are often with secure socio-economic status, having come to Australia for 'the better life', and also curious about the activities and interests of other communities. Our intention with this paper is not to 'revel in' a version of 'ethnic fandom' and popular-music culture, but to allow fans to story their own 'becoming'. In undertaking the primary research, our aim was to discover the important ways that participants use(d) David Bowie to 'story' and make sense of their identity within Australia's particular cultural and social circumstances. Our aim was to learn how the fans feel (or felt) about the work of David Bowie and move toward a richer understanding of how they have negotiated their own identity amidst a contemporary Western media culture that largely marginalises the 'alternative'.

As a pilot study, four Melbourne-based adult participants, who self-identified as recent migrants to Australia or from post-war migrant families, and as fans of David Bowie, formed the first Fan Reference Focus Group in Metropolitan Melbourne. Our findings here are based on this first focus group session.

Fan Reference Focus Group participants were recruited from the researchers' network of peers. This was to ensure that individuals had appropriate interest in the research topic and were willing to participate. The Fan Reference Focus Group included the researchers themselves, who were active in the discussions that took place. The focus group was composed of two males and four females, with a modal age of 40 years, and lasted for approximately one hour. Five of them are quoted here, each from a family with a different ethnic background: ID (Chinese), MP (Italian), AN (Greek), NN (Irish), AP (Greek). The participants were invited to respond to open questions and visual stimuli (laid out on the table) about David Bowie's music and the role it plays (has played) in their lives. Participants were also asked to bring a special piece of memorabilia that they were invited to speak about, but not compelled to discuss. All interviews were audio-recorded and transcribed.

The focus group was organised around questions designed to enable the participants to 'story' their fandom in relation to migrant identity and identity politics more generally (given the way that subjectivity is always involved in intersectionality). The session began with asking each of these participants why they were here today and what it was about David Bowie they so identified with. The conversation then continued with specific framing around how Bowie helped them each to navigate their migrant identity, with each participant drawing upon a memory, event or series of events to story Bowie's impact on their lives. During the session, we played softly a compilation of Bowie's music and introduced visual stimuli – colour photocopied images of David Bowie from various decades and periods – and asked our participants to choose one that they felt they most identified with and to talk through their choice. The participants were then asked to story their self-chosen piece of Bowie memorabilia, linking it to their own (migrant) identity. Finally, we asked participants about how Bowie's recent death impacted upon them and why they felt he was such an important figure (for migrants).

We listened to the transcripts four times, and made notes on each occasion, looking for clusters of themes that repeated themselves and which were drawn upon by all respondents, either directly or in terms of supportive commentary and affirmative gestures. We found that there were five clusters of articulating or intersecting stories in relation to migrant identity and we have structured this chapter accordingly. We note that migrant identity was understood or addressed not simply in terms of: (1) identity difference, (2) ethnicity or nationality; and (3) family or community, but how it connected to questions and notions of (4) gender and sexuality; and ultimately an overall sense of (5) 'resurrection'.

The difference in me

> [s]ubjectivity includes our sense of self. It involves conscious and unconscious thoughts and emotions which constitute our sense of 'who we are' ... We experience our subjectivity in a social context where

language and culture give meaning to our experience of ourselves
and where we adopt an identity.

(Woodward, 1997: 39)

As Woodward notes directly above, we come to take up an identity
position in situational and temporalised contexts, which involve conscious and unconscious processes and yet which are actively enacted
within language and culture. Identity is never fixed (Hall, 1990) and is
involved in a range of intersections including class, sexuality, gender,
ethnicity, age and nationality. Often identity 'is most clearly defined by
difference, that is by what it is not' (Woodward, 1997: 2) and becomes
of importance 'whenever one is not sure of where one belongs [or] is
not sure how to place oneself among the evident variety of behavioural
styles and patterns' (Bauman, 1996: 19).

For our focus group participants, the question of difference and not
(quite) belonging was central, and centrally tied to their migrant status
and the role that Bowie had in both mitigating their sense of ethnic
and cultural 'Otherness' and providing an audio-visual arena in which
they could validate their 'alien' identity through song, lyric and performance. Bowie made 'weird cool' (ID), and:

> In Adelaide, as a little working-class migrant girl, I was on the outside
> to the Anglo private school thing, but also on the outside to my own
> Italian community ... he spoke on the border, through ambiguity ... and
> enabled me to cherish not fitting in.
>
> (MP)

The sense that migrant identity involved alienation and exclusion from
White Australia, as well as providing a conformist and claustrophobic
environment to grow up in, was an often-repeated position. Our participants were caught by and yet resisted a number of cultural binds, as
outsiders within outsider migrant families; outsiders within conformist and religious migrant families; or as outsiders to Anglo-Saxon,
white embodiment. As AN revealed:

> I was very against the Greek upbringing, I didn't have any Greek friends,
> it was really conservative and oppressive. I hated being dragged to
> these fucking Greek dances ... Bowie, his music, was a way of opening

up a different path for me which said creativity, I didn't want to be the same as everyone else ...

Similarly, ID reflecting on his own perceived oriental features and sense of ethnic Otherness, as a child at school, shared:

I already felt weird. I was already the 'Chinese Kid' in a private primary school where everyone else was white ... and yet there was no race I felt I belonged to, no race I identified with, I was expunged from other races, I was having weird sexual thoughts because of my abuse, and I was also escaping into the grotesque and there was Bowie who encapsulated all that.

In different ways, each of the participants made reference to being (like) matter-out-of-place – their migrant status a signifier of mutancy, detritus and dirt. The Italian community, for example, considered MP's father effeminate and his own perceived border crossing resonated with Bowie's androgyny. The common word drawn upon was 'alien', both in relation to their sense of self and to Bowie's star images. This alien Otherness was felt to be a pejorative, a not-belonging and also a lived experience to be embraced and championed. For AN, the alien became the comforting norm, and the everyday became their version of alien living. Bowie was the regenerative force that enabled the reversal of these normative binaries – he gave the participants a way of experiencing what idealised counter-cultural life could be. As Frith (1996: 123) writes:

But if musical identity is, then, always fantastic, idealizing not just oneself but also the social world one inhabits, it is, secondly, always also real, enacted in musical activities. Music making and music listening, that is to say, are bodily matters; involve what one might call social movements. In this respect, musical pleasure is not derived from fantasy – it is not mediated by dreams – but is experienced directly: music gives us a real experience of what the ideal could be.

Ghassan Hage (1997) argues that migrant home building is an active and conscious process of re-settlement, centred on the production and consumption of food and associated design and cultural practices. This home building combines the cultures of origin with the new setting and is as much about making the place as remembering the space that one came from. For our participants, the migrant home was a haven or a prison, and sometimes both, its duality comforting and confronting. For AN, her Greek parents supported her desire to resist conformity, the strictures of Greek culture – and so Bowie's music filled the house and was welcomed. Similarly, for AP, her Dad shared with her cultish figures such as Bowie and embraced the transgressions that he embodied. Their 'home building' together involved horror-film nights and music video binges, away from the traditional Greek community she/they were also connected to.

For ID, the home he remembers is his own private hell. Conforming and relatively strict, the space was also the site where he suffered sexual abuse. Bowie was played to both hide the fact that this was taking place and it was also the music that allowed our participant to soar beyond its earthly terror:

> There was this weirdness emerging in me that was actually imposed by external sexual forces and no form to discuss it ... All my drawings became very creepy. I drew monsters, hairy beings and I drew a lot of aliens. Escaping to the aliens is exactly what Bowie did and was an escape past his abuse.

Bowie is very often considered to be an artist one escapes in and through. His music reaches towards the stars, is engaged in alternative universes and grotesque histories, and his own liminal and transgressive images enable him to be written on and over. In terms of identity, he allowed our participants to both find alternative selves within and in opposition to migrant identity, and to rise above the damage they encountered within everyday life.

Family matters

Controversial social commentator and knight-errant, David Bowie, struck a chord with fans who were growing up and becoming dissatisfied with the prevailing established narratives. For those feeling isolated or oppressed or closed off from wider society, Bowie afforded a portal to possibilities unknown. Imaginings garnered from the screen and sounds of 'the seductive' presented a desirable visual and sonic 'other' world; a tapestry consisting of the alluring *leitmotif* of (post)modernity. Bowie was a vehicle for social influence (Cinque, Moore, and Redmond 2015; Devereux, Dillane, and Power, 2015) and a central means by which our focus group participants, as young teens growing up in Australia, observed and evaluated themselves. Moreover, in the bosom of family (variously understood and experienced), Bowie provided a means to 'new' thinking at critical junctures, adding shape to their world-views. For AN:

> Bowie was a way of processing all the other shit that was considered 'norm' and that was oppressive around me. He became my way of putting stuff together and saying 'no! *this* is my world; *this* is the stuff I love and if that is "grotesque", then so-be-it!'

Many fans came to Bowie's work very early in their lives and the same was found to be true within the Fan Reference Focus Group. Bowie 'reached out' to them, shrewdly expressing 'life-threatening ideas' (ID) – what it might mean to exist 'outside' certain norms – so that they came to an understanding of their particular distinctiveness being challenged by the (then?) dominant oppressive characterisations of gender, race and ethnicity (see Cross, Klein, and Smith, 1983) that they were being faced with, and 'Bowie made it OK' (ID). In parts of a society where they might not 'fit', Bowie provided a space for them to inhabit, where they were content to be different, and even able to push back upon the accepted culture around them. For MP:

> I found Bowie at 12 or 13 and he was just the epitome of masculinity, the way I thought it was amazing, softly spoken and elegant – and here, I had also grown up with an uncle and a father who were similarly very different to the mainstream masculinity whether 'the typical Italian' or 'man's man' and for me, Bowie just spoke of ambiguity, of never knowing quite where you fit ...

And when 'seeds are planted the vine flourishes' (NN):

> My parents emigrated from Ireland to the UK. I grew up initially in an Irish community; a Catholic upbringing and quite a masculine one too. My Dad was a masculine man, not a 'bruiser' in any way but quite tough and I had this conservative, forceful upbringing. But for me, Bowie

presented a figure beyond this sort of doctrine – a heavenly embodiment that I loved; I absolutely adored it. I didn't know at the time what it was, no idea, but the visceral connective response to Him I have kept all my life and it has steered me right in terms of my identity politics.

For the participants in the Fan Reference Focus Group, 'Bowie-inspired' creative activities were also important to their emerging personal identity and to their well-being growing up in a family and/or community with which they were, at times, at odds. While sometimes creativity can be negative when 'darkly' motivated, for example, a torturer might be creative, but his/her creativity makes the world a worse place (see Gaut, 2010), this facet was not found to be the case for participants in the Fan Reference Focus Group – indeed, participants' own creativity was personally valuable and instrumental. Noted above, ID, as a young teen trying to 'escape the grotesque' originating from his abuse, would draw aliens personified by Bowie as Ziggy Stardust and later Thomas Jerome Newton in *The Man Who Fell to Earth* (Roeg, 1976). AN hand-sewed outfits inspired by the Diamond Dog, Halloween Jack, to enrage her family, especially her Greek father (who was disowned by her grandfather for not having a son), but that enthralled her sisters:

I introduced my sisters to non-Greek music and I always went for the non-traditionally Greek things in music and fashion for example. I was very against the conservative and what I saw then as oppressive Greek upbringing.

Encouraging and fostering their creative spirit was understood by participants to be imperative to making sense of the world into which they had emerged, or, in certain situations, the events forced upon them. For years growing up, MP crafted scrapbooks that she filled with images taken from popular music magazines of David Bowie:

I always felt like I was on the outside of the prevailing 'Australian' culture *and* the Italian community both. My parents were anti-Catholic [Italians are commonly Catholic], not homophobic [Catholics are required, by biblical decree, to be homophobic] and they encouraged me to be a strong, strident, feminist, and; I was brought up differently to the 'typical' nuclear family. I had two Mums and two Dads and

I was brought up in a community. I had a gorgeous childhood – and then I went to school where I found that my life was considered 'different' or 'alien' and everyone else was living the so-called normal life. I was given labels like 'neglected' and even 'abused' which certainly was not the way I was brought up. Then at 12, I found David Bowie and I keenly remember a picture of him and Angie holding their son Zowie [MP finds the image in one of her scrapbooks]. And I thought 'WOW', you could get families that were queer, that you could get families that don't live up to the norm and that this was another possibility.

What became apparent from participant comments was that in mainstream Australian society growing up, there was a seeming lack of overt 'vision' for the ways in which people might live together harmoniously in the larger community, while simultaneously being able to maintain, rather than dilute or lose, a strong sense of personal core values or identity. They did not, however, 'give in' to this. For our participants, the use of key rituals, symbols and articles of belief allowed the then dominant cultural 'norms' and/or practices to be resisted through drawing on an alternative, an 'alien', so that they might question and explore the validity of the representation of lifestyles and values circulating at the time. As noted above, this was especially true for participants resisting the stereotypes of 'family', 'masculinity' and ethnic identity. For three of the participants, Bowie and his music afforded the cultural means of functioning effectively within their communities without feeling required to necessarily change their cultural allegiances or personal identities. For AD and MP, Bowie was an exploratory foray into new possibilities that moved in tandem or journeyed alongside other media of personal cultural significance, rather than a retreat into a separated enclave. What is at stake, then, for the individual, is far more than supporting imprecise notions of unrestricted freedom of choice (to rock and popular music for instance) and the personal significance of such that lies therein. It concerns nothing less than how (and by whom) our dreams have been shaped.

Grieving and healing

There is no binary division to be made between what one says and what one does not say; we must try to determine the different ways of not saying such things, how those who can and those who cannot speak of them are distributed, which type of discourse is authorised, or which form of discretion is required in either case. There is not one but many silences, and they are an integral part of the strategies that underlie and permeate discourses (Foucault, 1990: 27).

The focus group method is in one sense 'an incitement to discourse' (Foucault, 1990: 17), organised to reveal the unspoken and to hear the silences that may remain. It is also an intervention into dominant discourse: a way of cracking open the capillaries of power nodes that circulate within everyday life. Celebrity culture is itself a discursive set of practices and processes involving confessional and gossip modes and modalities of communication. On the one hand, celebrity talk can be argued to reinforce the politics of the neo-liberal self and commodity culture. On the other, it can be argued to reveal inequalities and to challenge and counter-normative behaviours and relations. Joshua Gamson sees celebrity gossip as involving an audience who reject the vertical (top-down) relationship between celebrity and consumer for a horizontal one, involving a collective or shared evaluation of the famed figure under the spotlight (Gamson, 1994: 177–78).

This was very much the case with our focus group – we found participants commenting on each other's responses, offering words of encouragement and support and using 'echo' and reinforcement strategies to align their thinking and emotional investment. Words and phrases such as 'icon', 'alien', 'elegant', 'liminal', 'boundary testing' and 'border-crosser' were the most often used phrases, becoming a way of not only defining Bowie but also the shared investment in him. A collective and empowering 'voice' emerged through this celebrity talk, one that in its sharing and hearing became a liberating tool of identification, and a form of progressive social cohesion. As previously discussed, migrant identity became a shared badge of resistance and transcendence. However, we not only found that in talking about Bowie – in sharing stories about how he impacted on the participants' lives – was he a figure of 'togetherness', but that in the 'conversation' that took place, a healing processed emerged or was sought. As AP shared and AN responded:

AP: I was always a Bowie fan, like my first record was a David Bowie record, which my Dad bought for me when I was two. It was 'Let's Dance'. And my Father passed away really recently, and he was a really big Bowie fan. A month ago, like a couple days before David Bowie. There was this weird thing that kind of happened with the mourning, that kind of fused to the point that the song was playing on the radio when he took his last breath was 'Space Oddity' ... weird sense of symmetry. And I thought my Dad would have really liked to come along.

AN: well he is here.

The sense that AP (and AN) re-materialises her father is a powerful one: we are party here to a ritual of grieving for both a loved one just lost and the shared subject of their affection and bonding. This is grieving and healing emerging in the same collective place – a place of new communion. AP is in part dealing with her grief by being here; a mechanism to deal with her Dad's death; it may ultimately work to support social cohesion. However, one may also see celebrity mourning as anti-structural and grieving as a carnal response to loss, and which open up mourners to doubt and confusion, rather than closure and cohesion. This can be seen as a ritual of philosophical questioning and phenomenological experience.

Each of our participants used and uses Bowie at crisis or critical points in their lives. Bowie embodied a particularly transgressive and transcendent form of agency, which was drawn upon to both garner support for the identity positions they were seeking to take up, or which offered a life-affirming way of overcoming obstacles. Both AN and MP turned to Bowie to normalise and ratify their difference. MP revealed how as a child at school she struggled to talk in public and so used David Bowie to overcome her shyness and sense of strangeness and alienation from other children who would mark her out as different: 'nah, you don't have a TV, we know your house'. For MP, Bowie was a gateway to self-actualisation:

> By the time I got to year 10 I still couldn't read out loud properly, couldn't do a presentation ... The first time I ever did a presentation at school and managed to get through it was speaking about David Bowie. Such a strategy of diversion.

For ID, the question of grieving and healing was connected to the sexual abuse he suffered. Bowie was employed to hide the abuse, but also became the voice, the melody and the star image that allowed him to escape his abuse and abuser and overcome the deep traumas he faced. Nonetheless, for ID, Bowie was also the vehicle through which a darker side of self-realisation emerged:

> [Holding up an image of Ziggy] I was in a psychiatric hospital, under observation, at the age of 17 ... thank God for David Bowie ... personally speaking, the staring, insanity of the man ... there is no other escape than madness ... I spent my 18th birthday in a psychiatric hospital.

For our participants, Bowie embodied a particularly transgressive and aggressive form of active agency and self-empowerment, and yet was also a conduit of/for understanding suffering in the face of conformity and abuse:

AN: For me, it wasn't an escape ... he became a way of processing all the other shit that was norm and oppressive around you ... this is my world, the stuff I love, and if it means it is grotesque or horrific or alien or whatever the hell it was, then bring it on.

ID: That in itself became a kind of anchor.

One can argue that celebrity talk also works as a ritual of refusal to patriarchal norms, it offers one an 'anchor' in a sea of complex, messy and unequal identity positions. Bowie acts as a nautilus for our participants – a sacred shape, perfect symmetry, ultimately capable of resurrection ...

Lazarus rises

> Now a man named Lazarus was sick ... 'Our friend Lazarus has fallen asleep: but I am going ... to wake him up' ... 'Did I not tell you that if you believed, you would see the glory of God?' ... When he said this, Jesus called in a loud voice, 'Lazarus, come out!' The dead man came out [of his tomb], his hands and feet wrapped with strips of linen, and a cloth around his face.

(John 11: 1–44)

The biblical story of the death of Lazarus is about demonstrating publicly the wonder and power of God through the miracle of a dead man raised to life. In his video for the song Lazarus, created during a time in which he faced his own sickness (cancer), Bowie linked spiritual belief and death by depicting the metaphoric Lazarus bearing linen superposed around his head, perhaps pitting his faith upon his own spiritual and/or physical resurrection – or, is he in fact '*The Exile Symbolised*' on Earth, with his covered eyes replaced by useless plastic buttons:

> Son of man, you are living among a rebellious people. They have eyes to see but do not see and ears to hear but do not hear.
>
> (Ezekiel 12: 2)

If read in this way it is certainly an important religious statement, but it is also one with implications for being far from 'salvation'. We might present the provocation then that while seeking his own (our) 'resurrection' through grappling with the esoteric, David Bowie acted concurrently to restore belief (life) to those suffering. One participant found accord in the Fan Reference Focus Group with this statement:

> After everything that has happened I've been thinking a lot about how one person can have such an incredible impact on society in their life. I haven't been able to stop thinking about his death and because of that, his life and what he did.
>
> (AN)

While David Jones ('Jones' remained his legal surname) pursued a single dictum of exploring life's depths, he did so via the mercurial 'Bowie' and associated characters, using different metaphors and metonyms at various times for different purposes (Cinque, 2015). Throughout a rebellious biography, involving resurrection moments, his rise and fall and rise again trajectory acted as a contextual frame. As Redmond (2013: 377) argues: 'his process of renewal means that Bowie constantly kills himself, an artistic suicide that allows for dramatic event moments to populate his music, and for a rebirth to emerge at the same time or shortly after he expires'.

Reflecting upon his final expiration, when asked about the profound response to his death by people of all ages from around the globe, across popular culture and the avant-garde, AN commented:

> On one hand it was the music and also how he performed as a musician – it really tested boundaries. So there was the message (for want

of a better word) that was sent out that reached people that way (his music and his persona), but beyond that he was a cultural presence in cinema. He represented things in terms of identity in the media, testing sexuality, individuality, and creativity. So his impact crept out beyond the music – it wasn't like he was a great musician alone and that was the end of it.

For a number, *his* struggles suffered (depicted in his art) help(ed) to create an existential understanding. An important study undertaken by Stever (2011) found that fandom could assist individuals to overcome difficult life events by reconnecting with their feelings allowing them to: 'rejoin … the social world' (2011: 3) after long periods of isolation (ibid) – much like Lazarus emerging from the tomb, or Bowie 'living on' in digital form, or the individual finding purpose anew:

> My Dad came to Australia from Greece when he was 15. He was actually helped to learn English by listening to Bowie albums because Bowie's diction was very, very good. He bought me my first Bowie album. So, he was a big Bowie fan. When he passed away and where the song playing on the radio was 'Space Oddity', that was weird and a kind of symmetry that is always something that I have associated with Bowie.
>
> (AP)

> I am so glad that we did this today [refers to the focus group]. After the news of his death it brought everyone together and has opened up another whole dimension for me.
>
> (AN)

One participant found great joy in great loss:

> When Bowie died, my little ones who live overseas were coming to visit the very next day. Normally, I would be pretty morose and down about it, thinking about Bowie's death and what it meant and I would have locked myself away – but my children arrived at 8 O'clock the morning following his death – this let me forget not Bowie, but to live on. In a sense his death (a perfect death) came at a perfect time for me.
>
> (NN)

In a heightened ideological sense, with regular recurrence David Bowie's works have engaged with the suffering of everyday life, while synchronously tendering renewal so that the pain of living unequally in the world might be evaluated, worked through and extinguished. Through his body, whether his intent or not, our own life events are explained or justified in ways that let us keep going.

CONCLUSION

> identities are never unified and, in late modern times, increasingly fragmented and fractured; never singular but multiply constructed across different, often intersecting and antagonistic, discourses, practices and positions.
>
> (Hall, 1990: 223)

In this study we have demonstrated the way David Bowie has positively impacted upon migrant identity and how notions of the self and self-hood move across sheets of belonging and estrangement – themselves connected to age, gender and sexuality. What we have seen emerging from these conversations – from this ship of stories – is not only the way stardom impacts upon everyday life, but also the way identities are forged, shaped and layered in dynamic points of intersection. As we have suggested, Bowie's own shape-shifting identity and liminality became the art, sound and the flesh that our participants were able to utilise to empower and enrich their own lives. Lazarus rose and continues to rise within them.

While in this chapter we have extracted clusters of themes, the talk that emerged merged them – so that in one 'story' from one participant, the themes of family/community; sexuality and gender; ethnicity and difference and personal renewal or 'resurrection' rose up together like the most beautiful song, like the most liberating sounding. That our participants deftly, unconsciously, wrapped the complexities of their lives around Bowie, tells us the way in which memory is enacted and active agency manifests in the world. Our work demonstrates the way fandom is decidedly private and continues to be beautifully communal. The talk of David Bowie not only allowed our participants to share how, why and when he mattered, revealing secrets and privacies rarely shared before, but in the telling and the hearing new understandings emerged – the participants saw their histories and herstories in a new light. Further, in the sharing, friendships emerged as stories aligned.

Of course, in a contemporary Australia, where certain 'types' of migrant are left to waste away in detention camps, these stories of migrant belonging are particularly relevant and important. These ships welcome those who arrive on boats.

For the authors of this case study, who are two lifelong David Bowie fans, the organisation of the focus group and its running happened only a few weeks after his death. Our participation in the focus group, then, was not only to do with exercising our preferred research method, but also so that we could share our stories with everyone else – at a time of great sadness and some personal need. This case study is for everyone who took part and it is for David Bowie. Lazarus rises.

CHAPTER SUMMARY

This chapter has examined the way that agency in the consumption of stardom and celebrity is a powerful enterprise and connects to affective and embodied states of being in the world. Through the migrant fandom of David Bowie, the chapter has shown how Bowie fans utilised his music and star image to resist their ethnic identities and to find new ways of creating 'home'.

10

CELEBRITY REGULATION IN BODY AND SPACE

This chapter addresses the regulation node on the circuit of celebrity culture. It examines the processes and practices through which celebrity regulation enters the social world. It draws upon themes of teen celebrity liminality to examine the way regulation is policed and sometimes challenged. It then examines a series of *Celebrity Big Brother* to demonstrate how celebrity culture regulates identity and body through food taboos and ethnic transgressions.

CELEBRITY RULES AND THE CIVIL BODY

As outlined in Chapter 1, regulation is 'inescapably bound up with cultural politics and policy'. Nothing stands outside of regulation, and its scope extends into areas such as work, leisure, religion and education. Regulation is composed of formal and informal rules and is both an external and internal set of processes: people are regulated by convention, ritual and rule, and, at the same time regulate themselves in unconscious patterns of behaviour. Each item in Table 10.1 demonstrates a form or character of regulation, and how celebrity culture becomes a part of controlling regimes.

Table 10.1 Celebrity rules

Activity	External regulation	Internal regulation	Celebrity rules
Clocking in: clocking out (day in, day out)	Neo-liberal and liquid capital discourses of work ethic	Body clocks and self-motivation	Hard work and effort pays off. The 'dream' is always in reach
Dieting	Health and educational discourses on body management; the fetishising of slender celebrities	Body monitoring through calorie intake, food choice, abstinence The docile body needs regulation	Attraction and thinness go hand-in-hand. The healthy body is a thin, taught body: it is the body of the celebrity
Buying clothes	Fashion and beauty discourses on identity The celebrity dress and suit as ideal and idealised costumes	Possessive individualism and the cult of narcissism (I am what the celebrity wears)	To be noticed equals success and validates the individual. Buying fashion is a valuable resource. You can be a celebrity too
Pumping iron	Health and educational discourses masculine body management Male stars and body fascism	Body as a 'project' to be re-made and kept tightly and hardly bound	Hard, masculine bodies are perfect(ed) You can have the body of a star, too
Attending a pop concert	Para-social fandom and 'tribe' belonging; the discourses of marketing and the rules of devotional 'participation'	Possessive fandom: Imagined as both 'counter' regulation (enchanted time) And scarce 'me' time	Pleasure is liberating but don't stray too far
Reading a celebrity magazine	Identity ideologies and the discourses of consumerism and fantasy wish-fulfilment	Gender, race, ethnic, class and sexual self-monitoring. Dreaming that one is a star	We can be who we want to be but stars are born not easily made
Taking a selfie	Discourses of objectification and persona building	Self-censorship Self-management Gaze management	Ritualisation of the media celebrity centre
Gossiping	The will to truth and the power of revelation and disclosure	The gendered self: speaking like a and for 'woman'	The morals and ethics of good and bad behaviour and redemption
Romantic encounter	Patriarchal and heterosexual script	Behaving like a boy or a girl	The spectacle of romance brings rewards

Regulation is (also) about resistance and counter-regulatory practices, while it is often found in a dialectical relationship with its opposite: de-regulation is often followed or accompanied by re-regulation. Public service broadcasting in the UK in the 1980s, for example, involved this type of regulatory oscillation. One of the regulatory practices played out by celebrity culture is through the body: the ideal celebrity body is civil and compliant, while the toxic celebrity body is uncivilised and needs regulating, training, disciplining, as a consequence (see Chapter 5 for an extended discussion of this).

The idea of the 'civil body' as the desirable norm is a relatively recent historical invention. According to Norbert Elias, up until the Pre-Renaissance period, and before the later development of Court Societies, in Western European countries in the 17th and 18th centuries, the 'uncivilised body' existed as the dominant form of embodiment. This 'uncivilised body' was driven by immediate, sensual gratifications and desires and was a type of body that practised little self-constraint. The uncivilised body was a public, explicitly material body, that farted, spat, burped, fucked, defecated and which engaged in violent, bloody acts in order to survive in what were less regulated and more brutal times (Elias, 1978: 192).

Elias argues that it was only with the advent of Court Societies that the uncivilised body comes to be increasingly regulated and disciplined, with an emphasis on self-restraint, self-reflection, emotional control and a higher degree of passivity. In Court Societies a range of accepted practices, unacceptable taboos and constraints develop around the body. For example, people's bodies became more sensitive to smells, to nudity, to the private spaces between people and to their own private, bodily actions. As Elias contends, this is explicitly true in the case of the use of brute force:

> As the structure of human relationships changes, as monopoly organisations of physical force develop and the individual is held no longer in the sway of constant feuds and wars but rather in the acquisition of money or prestige, affect-expressions too slowly gravitate towards a middle line.
> (1982/1939: 238)

Elias argues that this refinement in the use and display of the body is a necessary pre-requisite of Court Society's need for a symbolic map to represent the differences in social standing and position between court members. The civilising of the body, then, came about because of the development of particular power relationships that needed/demanded representational or embodied form. In Court Societies, the more civil the body, the higher the social status. As Elias writes, 'Court people developed an extraordinarily sensitive feeling for the status and importance that should be attributed to a person in society on the basis of his bearing, speech, manner or appearance' (1983: 55).

Elias (1983) also considers the civilising process in terms of the way it attempts to distance the body from the animal and the natural. Civil embodiment becomes a rational desire to advance beyond and to overcome those behaviours and actions that are seen to be closest to nature. The developments of taboos around bodily functions, then, results in the internalisation and privatisation of those bodily functions deemed as ugly-natural. The body becomes civilised because it becomes cultured, has manners, understands etiquette, recognises and adopts boundaries about acceptable and non-acceptable behaviour and because it removes itself from those savage impulses and carnal desires that drove the uncivilised body. In short, the civilised body is a constructed body, moulded to not only distance itself from the supposedly natural impulses, noises and desires of the body, but to also embody social difference and validate social hierarchy.

THE GENDERED CELEBRITY BODY

Gender is particularly important in this respect. Women, particularly middle-class women, are made up to be the most civil of people; restrained, quiet, passive, cultured, if never fully 'intellectual' (supposedly unlike their male counterparts). And yet women are also closely aligned with the natural, since 'the identity of woman has traditionally been associated with the essential stuff of the body and nature' (Kirby, 1997: 67). It is through Woman's prescribed or essentialised role as Mother, involving the capacity for biological and social reproduction, that she is chained to the 'uncivil', to the abject; to noisy and leaky bodily practices, and which places her firmly in the domain of the natural. However, this civil/nature 'confusion' is continually effaced because of the way 'nature' is itself managed and disciplined within civil culture. In this respect, one can read star girl-becoming-woman narratives as civil stories about how to manage and discipline a young girl into controlling/repressing her 'natural' instincts. If we take the example of Taylor Swift, she:

> represents a nostalgic longing for a piece of Americana in which women's sexual desires were kept under wraps. Swift's music implicitly and explicitly insists that race and gender no longer matter; yet, it privileges 'traditional values' such as monogamy, propriety, and abstinence—values which are historically and inextricably tied to whiteness, heterosexuality, and normative femininity. The idealisation of American girlhood, which Swift represents, constantly and implicitly privileges a vision of 'authentic' girlhood that is invested in whiteness, heterosexual monogamy and romance, and middle-class propriety and consumption.
>
> (Brown, 2012: 162)

Elias argues, however, that one of the consequences of this cultural-isation of the body, of forcing it to behave in a way deemed civil or civil-natural, is that the body is always at war with itself, is always wrestling with those contradictory forces which it suppresses. The body struggles to contain those impulses and desires, which threaten to man-ifest in overt, unruly body behaviour. In effect, the body struggles to keep up its appearances; it struggles to maintain its gender differences.

In fact, one can postulate that the civil, gendered body is all about struggle and performativity. Judith Butler (1990: 128–41) argues that gender 'is not passively scripted on the body', but 'put on, invariably under constraint, daily and incessantly, with anxiety and pleasure'. The gendered body, then, is a lived and living performance that both women and men 'enact' to represent and to give materiality to their masculinity and femininity. Such performances produce both a series of rewards, such as social status, ideological power and affirmation of the self and, where this bodily corruption, a series of penalties, such as limited status and political and economic disenfranchisement.

But such performances also manifest as a series of 'contests' about how the body should work and present itself to the social world. For example, the mental illness, anorexia nervosa, is arguably one particu-lar embodiment process where women wrestle with the material form of their body in a ritualised rejection of normalised notions of the thin, female body (Palmer, 1980; Orbach, 1993). Such representations of celebratised thinness of course frame much of the representational regimes of female stardom and celebrity. Health, food and dieting are the key ingredients in the way the body should be managed; often advocated by celebrities through a range of health-led discourses. Food becomes both 'friend' and 'alien' in this scenario – necessary to a healthy life but also the reason that people are not found attractive if they get too fat. As Bartky summarises,

> The current body of fashion is taut, small-breasted, and of a slimness bordering on emaciation; it is a silhouette that seems more appropriate to an adolescent boy or a newly pubescent girl than to an adult woman.
>
> (1990)

Ideals of contemporary motherhood are caught up in this tyranny of slenderness with celebrity mums being encouraged to quickly return to their slender, bikini-ready body, 'to re-establish both mothering and beauty as the most important components of femininity, while reinforcing the domestic division of labour that continues to persist between women and men in the private sphere, despite the fact that unencumbered (without children) men and women's lives are much more similar today' (O'Brien Hallstein, 2011: 111).

GIRL-WOMAN CELEBRITY BODIES

Celebrity culture very often or perhaps inevitably re-enacts and re-plays this move from the uncivil to the civil society, using betwixt and between stars to represent the struggle that goes into making them civil-natural. The performance of liminality and gender transgression by such star figures as Miley Cyrus and Britney Spears is not only about their own struggle to suppress or regulate their wayward female bodies, but patriarchal society's struggle to teach them, and of course their young fans, the self-surveillance techniques that she/they will need to tame, or make docile, to use a Foucauldian term, her/their wayward body/bodies in future life. For example, Miley's pole dance (see Figure 10.1) at the 2009 Teen Choice Awards:

> Took place in a context of increasing attention to celebrities as well as the sexualisation of adolescent celebrities. Sexualization is a word that

has recently replaced objectification in feminist discourse, and refers not only to making women into objects for male viewing and the valuing of women primarily for their attractiveness and sexuality, but also the tendency to sexualize aspects of a person or an event that are not inherently sexual and to represent children and adolescents in increasingly sexual ways. Gill (2007a: 151) describes sexualisation as 'the extraordinary proliferation of discourses about sex and sexuality across all media forms ... as well the increasingly frequent erotic presentation of girls', women's and (to a lesser extent) men's bodies in public spaces'.

(Lamb, Graling, and Wheeler, 2013: 163)

As such, Miley Cyrus and Brittney Spears fit within instructionist paradigms of knowledge and behaviour transfer: as they wrestle with their desires and appetites, as they break rules and engage in misdemeanours and as we witness their journey to womanhood, young fans are drawn into these discourses of sexualisation while being 'warned' against them.

Assessing the historical trajectory of capitalism, Foucault observes,

The human body was entering a machinery of power that explores it, breaks it down and rearranges it. A 'political anatomy', which was also a 'mechanics of power' was being born; it defined how one may have a hold over others' bodies, not only so that they do what one wishes, but so that they may operate as one wishes, with the techniques, the speed and the efficiency that one determines. Thus, discipline produces subjected and practised bodies, 'docile' bodies.

(1977: 138)

Celebrity female bodies are subject to this 'mechanics of power'. When they fall from grace, ingest too many drugs or drink too much booze, they are subject to forms of therapy. When they have breakdowns they are subjected to forms of *psychiatry*. When they commit crimes, they are incarcerated and their bodies become objects and subjects of surveillance. They are treated to doses of *liberal law*, a form of 'just deserts' and a moral retribution of order for their embodied waywardness. Celebrity female bodies experience many of the remedies, sanctions, intrusions and behaviour calculations that mark out the modern behavioural and penal sciences. Once the celebrity body has been signified as Other, monstrous, as gender transgressive: and

Figure 10.1 Miley pole dancing
Image courtesy of Kevin Mazur/TCA2009/WireImage/Getty images

once it threatens to destabilise the rules and regulations of modern institutions like the family and school, it is subject to and the object of body discipline measures. The message here to young fans is: do not transgress, or rather, do not transgress too far.

The key narrative moment for the instigation of these disciplining/training regimes very often occurs when the celebrity's uncivil and abject behaviour threatens to 'infect' their fans. As role models and figures of idolisation, the cultural fear being imagined here is contagious imitation. In this totalising moment, the wayward celebrity comes to represent not only the horrors of the unruly, sinful body, a body that threatens the moral order of civil society, but the horror of the toxic body – more 'natural' than civil, more abject than contained – which, since it spills out, disrupts the 'normal' gender relations and the differences between girls and boys. This was the case with Miley's above-mentioned pole dance (also see Chapter 8): in empirical research carried out by Lamb, Graling, and Wheeler (2013: 17) they found that:

> Rather than blaming adults around her alone, these comments also blame Cyrus for self-sexualizing at too young of an age and in some cases for using her sexuality for secondary gains. The position here is not that the self-sexualisation is in itself the problem but rather Cyrus's choice to do so at the wrong age or for the wrong reasons.

In contemporary Western society there currently exists a moral panic about the 'nature' of children; and an interconnecting set of training, disciplining and surveillance regimes that are designed to keep the child in check, free from harm and committing harm; and parents, significant others, the police and teachers in control of their children. In fact, since the 1980s, there seems to have been a collapse in the belief (representation) of the innocent child, fuelled by heinous 'real life' crimes and murders by children (the Jamie Bulger case being the most high-profile). What has emerged in this 'children-are-risky' and 'at-risk' culture, is a rash of self-help and instructional texts on how to 'nurture' a child and 'how to be a child'.

A new discourse 'of increased public and professional anxiety about the safety of children has emerged' (Scott, 1998: 11), which can be found in television programmes such as *Little Angels* (ITV, 2004), where a 'trained' psychologist is employed to help teach parents to banish their children's bad behaviour; and 'Parent, Adolescent and Child Training Skills' manuals, such as *Banish Bad Behaviour: Helping Parents Cope with a Child's Conduct Disorder* (Herbert, 1996), which tells parents:

> Failure is costly for parents, and, in the long run, emotionally bankrupting for their undisciplined children. While disobedience and defiance are fairly common problems as children grow up ... if they persist and intensify, they can sometimes prove dangerous.

(3)

In contemporary society children have become a 'horror' story and horror is central to the telling of the wayward celebrity body. Not only is the celebrity contagion narrative the very material out of which childhood nightmares grow, but it provides a space for the playing out of the 'return of the repressed' (Wood, 1978), or what Sarah Gilead calls 'the return as narrative repression' in relation to closure in children's fantasy fiction (1992). *The wayward child celebrity* becomes a 'classic' horror story, with the premise that this terrifying child-monster lurks within all children. The uncivil celebrity body is meant to act as a barely coded personification of those collective, unconscious desires, fantasies and fears that 'civil children' have to repress to live 'normal' lives.

However, this enactment of the unconscious is meant to be both cathartic and message driven. Young fans are initially encouraged to revel in the carnivalesque display of the wayward celebrity body. They are shown to be having such rebellious fun. However, as the celebrity wayward body becomes more dangerous, and as the consequences to the social order becomes graver, young fans are ultimately being asked/told to reject and repress such wayward body antics. With the eventual metaphorical death of the wayward celebrity body, when they eventually tame their behaviour (or die as a consequence if not) those demons are returned to the unconscious, in what is then transcribed as the inevitable 'happy ending'. Fans are meant to both acknowledge the need for the restoration of the civil body and to warmly welcome its arrival. Tween celebrity culture connects to the position that all children are born fallen, and 'it was only through nurturing and divine teaching that they could be transformed from "little devils" into "little angels"' (Macdonald, 2003: 109).

The regulatory practices so far discussed in this chapter have principally been external techniques: things done to the body and with the body; impositions on the flesh that require submission, obedience and compliance. Very often externality needs to be combined with internal self-regulation: the wayward celebrity needs to willingly recognise and comprehend how disgusting their body habits are, to others, but most importantly, in that *anticipated moment of self-directed clarity*, to herself. If wayward celebrity body is to be tamed, then, it needs to be taught to *see* and *monitor* the error of her ways for *herself.*

As Eve Kosofsky Sedgewick (1992) writes, modern society is caught in the grip of what she calls 'epidemics of the will', where the fear of these bad habits taking root drives the will to control the body, in ever excessive regimes of surveillance. We are no longer alone with our bodies, rather we are always *with our bodies*, taking notice of its blemishes, spots, taking care of its tempos and energies; and we *with others* – friends, lovers, family, doctors, councillors – who check out our bodies for us and remind us to regularly check our own bodies. Nicholas Mirzoeff captures this frenzy of the body well:

> Your body is not itself. Nor, I should add, is mine. It is under threat from the pharmaceutical, aerobic, dietetic, liposuctive, calorie-controlled, cybernetic world of postmodernism.
>
> (1995: 1)

This story of the bad or fallen or abject woman, running amok, polluting borders, can of course be found as a recurring trope across Western culture; Eve biting the apple of desire in the Garden of Eden; the loose, immoral Mary Magdalene tempting Jesus; the deceitful Delilah wooing/destroying Samson; Medusa turning men to stone with just one awful look; the Song of the Sirens luring sailors to their deaths; the monstrous feminine of film horror, castrating the narrative agent; the bio-medical discourse about the meaning and risk of woman's menstruation (to men) and the whole set of explicitly racialised images and narratives about white trash women and licentious, primitive black women, fucking wildly and spreading diseases. In the case of transgressive female rock stars, one can see how, in the case of Amy Winehouse, most newspaper articles treat her as a victim, expressing concern regarding her 'poor health'. Put simply, women who have lost control of their sexual bodies bring death and destruction. The wayward celebrity body, written/scripted from within a patriarchal discourse, and operating within the regime of a civil society, shows young girls the path away from such madness, such monstrosity. Taylor Swift's star image perhaps best sums this up:

> Swift has cultivated a visual image of sweet wholesomeness by wearing soft dresses and pastel colours—often white—in real life, in images on her website, and in her music videos, bolstering her image of demure white femininity, frequently in opposition to other girls.
>
> (Brown, 2012: 166)

The case study that now follows picks up on the main themes of the chapter so far: through Shilpa Shetty's filthy hands we get to see how regulation shapes celebrities' bodies and spaces.

CASE STUDY

Shilpa's filthy hands

The 2007 *Celebrity Big Brother* race row centred, in part, on the preparation, handling and consumption of food. While formal and informal dining is a key symbolic ritual in the series – a place of communal gathering, gossip and competition 'end games' – in this instance it was employed to establish racial difference and to construct the racial Other as unclean. White and British-born Jade, Jo and Danielle deciding to eat/not eat Indian became a symbol of bordered, racialised self-identity and a site of potential corporeal pollution – if one tasted, touched, consumed the food prepared by foreign Shilpa's 'filthy hands'.

If one ate Indian one was consuming the Other, taking it in, letting it become the fuel, the very dark matter of one's white, female self. Shilpa was being imagined, then, as possessing an essentialised dirtiness, or perverse inner 'spicy' vitality, that lurked beneath her glamorous exterior. In the series Shilpa came to stand for a complex and contradictory mix of Eastern/Oriental gender stereotypes: primitive and debased, unclean and carnal (tactile), exotic and sexual. She became a liminal stranger in the Big Brother home.

However, at the same time, this Othering of Shilpa actually drew attention to the 'trashy', docile, white bodies that name-called and bullied. Jade, Jo and Danielle's uneducated and spiteful abuse of Shilpa opened up a discursive space for an interrogation of British-ness and of white racism. As fallen B-list celebrities with limited 'artistic' talent and, at for least for two of them, existing as mere eye-candy objects of Western sexual attraction, they became pale ('dull-dish') sexual and racial signifiers, particularly in comparison to Shilpa's Bollywood star signification. Shilpa's auratic quality and her educated and sensitive demeanour enabled her to transcend the stereotypes put on her by her racist co-contestants. In so doing, she registered as a 'surplus value' figure, a super-iconic sign that could not be penetrated by the name-calling.

In this sense the *Celebrity Big Brother* race row may well be a text that makes a 'home' for the Other in the new transglobal community of multi-racial British-ness, where Chicken Tikka Masala is a national dish and Bollywood blockbusters regularly make the box-office top ten (Redmond, 2009). Nonetheless, the comparative version of white-ness (white British-ness) that emerges in the series is a class-inflected one. Jade, Jo and Danielle stand-in for the lower orders of white iden-tity formation and ill-educated opinion formation (Hegde, 2007). As such, Shilpa's upper-class, Raj-like iconicity is constructed on the bor-ders of class and postcolonial national identification. As I will go on to conclude, her transcendence may very well reinforce hierarchies of class and race in a new world order of consumption hegemony.

We are what we don't eat

The preparation and consumption of food is an incredibly powerful form of symbolic exchange and meaning-generation. As Mary Douglas (1966/2002, 1972) argues, food choice and cultivation is structurally indic-ative of social rules, dominant norms and values, existing taboos around desire and need, and identificatory boundaries concerned with gender and race. When and what one eats involves inclusionary and exclusion-ary decisions and the employment of imbedded classificatory systems that designate certain food groups and dining rituals as normal or civil – as constituting good self/group cultivating practice.

Douglas suggests that one key aspect of food consumption is the avoidance of pollution, of not ingesting or digesting something that will spoil, sully or make unwell the self that is taking it in. Powerful food taboos consequently emerge in which the transgressive food act is placed on the margins of cultural acceptability. For example, Showlater notes that in the Victorian period many girls refused to eat red meat because they associated it with heavy menstruation and sexual activity and because they believed that a carnivorous appetite ultimately lead to nymphomania and insanity (Showalter, 1985: 129). According to Fischler (1988), food consumption involves the often-conscious act of incorporation, or 'the action in which we send a food across the frontier between the world and the self, between outside and inside our body'. Food consumption is not just the act of ingestion, then, but the symbolic construction of self-identity. As Jean-Paul Sartre suggests:

> To eat is to appropriate by destruction; it is at the same time to be filled
> up with a certain being ... When we eat we do not limit ourselves to

> knowing certain qualities of this being through taste; by tasting them
> we appropriate them. Taste is assimilation ... The synthetic intuition of
> food is in itself an assimilative destruction. It reveals to me the being
> which I am going to make my flesh. Henceforth, what I accept or what
> I reject with disgust is the very being of that existent.
>
> (Sartre, 1966: 23)

In Western society, food classification and taste distinction are very often gendered. For example, milk, eggs, seeded vegetables, sweet tasting products, chicken and fish are considered to be feminine, and femininity inducing. Red meat, of course, is masculine, and supposedly contributes to the fashioning of the prototypical hard body. Similarly, the eating/not eating regime that many Western women put themselves through to ensure they have slender bodies is a part of what Chernin (1983) terms the 'tyranny of slenderness' produced by a patriarchal, heterosexist culture that demands a certain type of female body size. Low-calorie, low-carbohydrate diets become a form of gender inscription in which the thin body speaks of not just culinary abstinence but embodied compliance for the male gaze.

One can usefully extend the inner/outer dichotomy of ingestion and digestion to racialised 'us' and 'them' binaries, in which difference is constructed out of what the Other eats, how they eat and how they prepare and handle food (Lupton, 1996: 25–6). In this respect, one can profitably apply Lévi-Strauss' (1975) culinary triangle to the construction and maintenance of racial difference, particularly in terms of the Eastern/Oriental Other.

For Strauss, culture in general involves fundamental structural oppositions, which get represented in food myths through two polarities: nature/culture and elaborated/unelaborated. When and how one cooks food determines its transition from the raw (natural) into the cooked (culture) and its place in a hierarchy of civility. Food that isn't cooked, or which is only partially cooked, as is the case with roasting, is closer to nature and is as a consequence more primitive in its culinary preparation (although Strauss suggests that this isn't always an indicator of lower order sensibility).

In relation to dominant racist myths that exist in relation to South Asians eating their food with fingers, undercooking food and adding spices and condiments to excite the palette, one can see how Western food preparation and handling can be diametrically opposed to the 'raw' and 'primitive' rituals of the Other. In terms of the implements for eating – sharp, penetrating cutlery in the West; fingers, spoons and chop-sticks in the East – one can see from a Western-centric perspective the construction of a civilised/primitive dichotomy in which the Other's lower order appreciation of food is based on mauling, chewing, biting and fingering. Connected to this 'savage' food aesthetic is what is represented to be the over-determination of sensation, texture and taste, with the exotic foods, flavours and culinary practices of the East. Eastern cuisine resides in the belly and bowels, in the primordial part of human nature. Obviously, to consume this food, to partake in both the raw handling and ingestion of Eastern food types is to not only invite the stranger in but to be transformed in flesh.

Sara Ahmed (2000) has written persuasively on how the proximity of the stranger simultaneously produces and confirms difference and causes anxiety. When the stranger gets close (when they move into our neighbourhoods, schools, workplaces, when we consume their food) we are able to recognise (and expel) our difference to them:

> Others become strangers (the ones who are distant), and Other cultures become 'strange cultures' (the ones who are distant), only through coming too close to home, that is, through the proximity of the encounter or 'facing itself'.

> (Ahmed, 2000: 12)

Jones suggests that the establishment of ethnic difference also occurs through food-based slurs which, 'not only denigrate others but also dehumanize the Other ... as in such ethnophaulisms for Germans, French, English, and Indochinese as Krauts, frogs, limeys, and fish heads' (Jones, 2007: 129–77). Economic power and status are inscribed through food choice, cooking method and dining ritual (Bourdieu, 1977, 1984). Meal combinations, the cut of the meat and the size of the spread can indicate social class as well as economic success. For example, Jones has suggested that the fat or plump body size for black American women has been read as an indicator that they had overcome poverty and racism. By contrast, the image of the starving African, unable to propagate the land, unable to cultivate their own food, unable to feed their own mouths, suggests a first world/third world binary in which the West's success is measured by its ability to feed its populace. Ethnic identification through culinary practice can have empowering effects, however. For example, Beoku-Betts (1995) suggests that diaspora groups use traditional cooking methods and 'handed down' recipes to keep memories and traditions alive. The immigrant keeps a connection alive with their homeland through the practice of preparing, and the act of tasting, traditional cuisine.

Nonetheless, in the global age of the trade and traffic in world goods, trinkets, electronics, fashion, tourist destinations, foodstuffs and recipes, the taking in, or the 'tasting', of the stranger is much more of a common occurrence. Susan Willis (1990) suggests that there has been a generalised aestheticisation of race within consumer culture. No longer represented as a matter of natural or biological difference, racial difference is instead turned into a style that one can consume like any other commodity of choice. Pieterse (1995) terms this transformation the 'creolization of global culture'. In fact, consumption hybridisation, the folds and flow of regional, ethnic, national identities, may suggest in part that 'home' and 'away', 'us' and 'them' have been brought together in a complex if uneven and contradictory fusion of cultural material. For example, 'British-ness' today includes a whole range of diaspora practices, including food and entertainment signifiers, and the very spaces and locales of shopping, worship and festival. Britain's national imaginary is composed of stranger-now-friend, Other-now-me symbols and signs, with food/cooking/eating one of the central places of this transformation – although, as I will go on to argue, multi-racial Britain 'pimps' only that which it can easily digest (the safe, home-grown aspects of the stranger) and expels or transcodes that which threatens the nation (the foreign-foreigner). The culture of food, then, is a powerful way in which a society communicates its power geometries, identificatory systems, taste distinctions and national and ethnic divisions and relations. In the contemporary age, television has become one of the key sites for its representation.

Television food

One could divide the myriad of current food, cooking, tasting and eating programmes into a number of thematic and ideological divisions. There is the food programme that invites us to cultivate our senses in relation to the choosing of the finest fresh and natural ingredients. In these programmes – which would include Rick Stein's *Mediterranean Escapes*, BBC TV, 2007 – the viewer sees and hears spices, condiments, vegetables, fruits, breads and meat being touched, smelt, weighed and tasted, as if the senses are a direct way to a more cultured appreciation of food. But this natural food, which we are encouraged to buy in open markets and which we subsequently cook (turn into culture), is particularly important, it is suggested, in an age of processed food, genetic modification and large-scale industrial production of crops. The raw can only be found outside of culture but then needs to be brought back (cooked) into culture for it to sustain us fully and help make or keep us civil.

The healthy food programme is concerned with nutritional balance, calorie intake and cooking and handling measures. Its concern is with shaping the perfect body, or with reducing, reshaping it from an imagined obese state. Such programmes encourage the viewer to eat healthily as a way out of a society that eats too much, and yet it promotes consumption and body surveillance as necessary and productive modes of behaviour. In the healthy food programme meat is lean, chicken skinned and grilled and the chosen ingredients are low in fats and high in nutritional value. The viewer is asked to shop for lean cuisine and to regulate their intake accordingly. The healthy food programme offers the viewer a sleight of hand in their examination of cooking, then: seemingly anti-consumption and pro the self/free choice, these programmes in fact attempt to instil a more disciplined purchasing regime and to create a more disciplined eater, one who will be fit enough to work and who will subsequently work to consume. Programmes such as Food Detectives play out this practice of dietary surveillance, putting shops, restaurants and eaters under the lens, prophesying on good and bad food habits.

By contrast, the celebration and ritual food programmes, such as Jamie Oliver's *The Naked Chef*, encourage hearty eating, communal and public get-togethers where food is to be enjoyed. Images and aesthetic sequences of prepared food steaming, dripping, crumbling, melting, is meant to activate the senses (the juices) of the viewer. The star chef revels in the eating and tasting of the produce, often re-enacting the public ritual of shared and celebratory dining when the meal has been cooked. In this bawdy, carnival-like, pleasurable celebration of eating, cooking becomes a relief, or an escape from normal, everyday routine. Cooking becomes a sensuous doorway into community exchange.

In the home food television programme, cooking is timed and spatialised in terms of the work/school/domestic sphere. Food preparation and cooking is carried out with speed and accuracy. And yet meal/family time is meant to be distinct from work and school, which is defined by the segmentation, routinisation and commodification of time. Home food television programmes prepare family meals that are quick and convenient to produce in the domestic kitchen. The nuclear family are the imagined diners and the dining table the venue (although there are those programmes that 'cook' TV dinners, or prepare meals for those 'on the run'). Implicitly, there is a gendered division of labour implied in these programmes, with the woman/mother located as the cook and the home a feminine refuge from the woes of the day.

In the food and travel programmes, cooking involves a literal and metaphorical journeying process. In the company of an experienced chef, the viewer travels to far off destinations to see, taste and smell the food and cooking rituals of (an)other culture. On the UK Food channel in 2008, two programmes invite such cuisine travelling:

Kylie Kwong: My China

Join chef and restaurateur Kylie Kwong on a personal and inspirational odyssey as she returns to the land of her ancestors.

Antonio Carluccio's Southern Italian Feast

A gastronomic odyssey with the convivial Italian. On the menu in Puglia are sausages with roasted pepper sauce, and fresh bread with salami and baked cheese.

In *My China*, the diaspora chef returns to her homeland to find the cuisine and the origins of her Chinese identity, amongst tourist images of her 'homeland'. Food, chef and cuisine are fetishised and packaged for the viewers watching and distance and proximity are established through its home/away binary. In *Southern Italian Feast*, 'Italian-ness' is a part of the mythological landscape of the programme. We can taste Italy by eating the food prepared for us by the authentically-named Antonio.

While there is often a welcome embrace of cuisine difference in these programmes (the chef revels in the conventions they stumble upon), there is also a degree of 'stranger fetishism' (Ahmed, 2000). The different ingredients, cooking methods, food handling and preparation rituals are seized upon to both designate the other as Other and to consume them in a devouring manner. Nonetheless, the spicy/rich/hot/exotic/hyper-natural qualities of the cuisine are also seen as positively transformative – by ingesting and digesting this food it is suggested one gets the longevity (of say, the Japanese) or the sexual vitality (of say, the Indians) imagined to reside in the Other's cuisine. The 'tourist gaze' here becomes the food gaze, but this gaze is a haptic one, where we touch-taste with our eyes. Practically, it manifests as an embodied, incorporative way in which one internally experiences cultures through the eating of their cuisine. The 'strange' is imagined to give the consumer both a more intense life experience, an experience that is hard to match within Western culture, and symbolic power over the Other. As Jackie Stacey suggests:

> By consuming global products, the Western subject and the exotic other are thus reaffirmed even as such a dichotomy is apparently transcended by the appeal to a universal global culture.
>
> (Stacey, 2000: 104)

The food competition programme involves a flexible format in which the best amateur or professional cook or chef wins, or in which food is itself the prize on the way to greater glory. Depending on the programme, the cook/chef will be given limited ingredients and limited time with which to prepare a meal (*Ready, Steady, Cook*), or they will be asked to prove themselves over a longer period, with the weekly prospect of elimination if they don't make the grade (*Hell's Kitchen*). These formats herald the success myth, that hard work, talent and perseverance will be rewarded (with a prize, an accolade, a restaurant of your own at the end of the competition), and they propagate the ethos that competition (for/over food) is a natural motivator and selector.

In terms of those formats in which contestants go through competitive trials and tribulations with food the prize if they succeed, the survival instinct is called upon to motivate them, with the primordial message, 'compete or go hungry'. At the same time, this format taps into the crisis over the artificial and industrial production of food and our relationship to it. One is reminded of food's relative scarcity and what it means to have to 'hunt' for it in the 'wild'. One is asked to understand food in raw/cooked, fresh/rotten, dead/alive, elaborated/unelaborated polarities, but with a degree of confusion over where the eater should place themselves. Raw/rotten and dead/alive foods are represented as 'trial' and as ethnic or tribal 'delicacy'.

This dichotomy is particularly foregrounded when celebrities are asked to compete for food (as is the case with the Bush Tucker Trial in *I'm a Celebrity Get Me out of Here*, and the 'tasks' in *Celebrity Big Brother*). Notionally wealthy, uber signifiers of conspicuous consumption, the celebrities' race for food turns them from plastic icons into natural (authentic) survivalists. The celebrity appears stripped bare of artifice, and this stripping away of the manufactured ego extends right into the phenomenological self where what they eat determines how real they are. Those celebrities who refuse the challenge, who resist taking in the raw and the rotten, or the dead and the live, often fail in the eyes of other contestants and voting viewers. The 'fake' celebrity shows their true colour when they refuse to take in natural/ordinary/uncooked food. When they refuse to be animal/human in this game of high stakes they get voted off (with the ironic prospect of a fall in celebrity status).

According to Mary Douglas (1972), anxiety around food and consumption, and the body's weight and size, occurs at a time of social change and crisis. Food, cooking, diet and dieting take on an increasing sense of importance when identity is in flux or its borders under threat. In the contemporary world where global capitalism has changed the nature of how one defines or experiences the nation state, and the cultural material out of which the national imaginary is fashioned, the *Celebrity Big Brother* scandal of 2007 draws attention to the way food preparation, handling and cooking are key markers in this crisis of self and nation.

Shilpa's filthy hands

Celebrity Big Brother organises its daily routines around two recurring, key events: cooking and dining; and the fulfilment of the designated task (which is often connected to 'shopping' and the granting of comfort foods if one is successful). Shopping, cooking and mealtimes are important social and narrative events in the *Celebrity Big Brother* home. House stars use it to socialise, gossip, flirt, reminisce, joke, argue/bitch, engineer a party or drinking session, form allegiances and alliances and to (naturally) perform their celebrity personas for the cameras/viewers (who also get to vicariously cook and eat with the famous few).

Narratively speaking, the ritual of shopping, cooking and eating creates a series of storylines and story arcs, develops 'characters' and character interaction and presents ethical and moral dilemmas. In fact, the dining ritual creates a context in which the house stars become a (dysfunctional) family unit, with hierarchical roles, divisions and archetypal role traits (such as peacemaker, sulker, outcast and attention-seeker), which may be race, class and gender inscribed (Jade Goody as 'the bitch' would be a case in point).

The daily task also works narratively. Given a difficult quest to complete, that may involve direct competition, and with a prize granted for its successful completion, the house stars are placed within a narrative pattern in which they are asked to 'work' for a living. Those celebrities who refuse to work, or who don't work hard enough (because, by implication, they are too removed from the ordinary world), incur the wrath of the other house stars. Success with the task is akin to a 'happy ending', and key protagonists in the success or failure of the task are labelled as heroes and villains. In a different sense, success in the completion of the task enables them to have their celebrity personas confirmed and they undergo a re-celebrification.

Nonetheless, in *Celebrity Big Brother* the home/work division that normally structures everyday life is decentred. While the task fulfils part of the function of (rewarded) activity, its more open-ended nature (its loose employment of the capitalist clock) means that there is more empty time (even for a 'celebrity') than in the real world. Given that leisure opportunities are limited and one cannot freely consume, cooking becomes a double-edged activity. On the one hand it productively fills up this time, allowing the celebrity to show their hands as good cooks. On the other, it designates the celebrity a cook, a servant in the *Celebrity Big Brother* home. Of course, when the task itself involves a Master and Servant dichotomy (as was the case in 2007), the dining ritual itself takes on an added significance.

A celebrity generally arrives at the *Big Brother* home with a dominant persona or iconic signification that the public know or knew well. They arrive with an intertextually mediated history, with one strand often involving a fall from grace or favour – the reason, although generally not stated, for them 'arriving' in the Big Brother home in the first place. The house stars are meant to be an eclectic mix of personalities, chosen in part because their differing personas will make good TV. The conventional format is that they will clash and conflict – warring, damaged celebrities are one of the central reasons that the programme does so well (in fact, in 2007 its ratings were at its highest during the Shilpa affair). *Celebrity Big Brother*, then, involves a conflict-driven, personality-centred narrative, in which cooking and dining become one of the key arenas for disputes and differences to emerge.

In 2007, of course, the programme's rhetoric of damage and rancour was complicated and amplified through the appearance of Shilpa Shetty. Not a celebrity but an Indian film star; privately educated; of upper-class background; and largely unknown to both her fellow house stars and the wider British public (although in the Asian communities she was a household name), her 'difference' is of immediate and notable significance. For Jade, Jo and Danielle, Shilpa came to represent the Other as threat and contagion. On the one hand, she was, and supposedly 'lauded' in being, the image of Indian feminine perfection, the personification of a Raj Princess and the embodiment of a new self-confident India. She was a global star next to their 'domesticated' celebrification. On the other, she was disease and virus, an embodied threat to Jade, Jo and Danielle's white British selves. Of course, both the fetishising and defilement of Shilpa drew attention to Jade, Jo and Danielle's racism, and to their working-class, uneducated, 'lower order' femininity. In almost every respect, cooking and dining became the battleground for the soul of British femininity, the national imaginary and the trade and traffic in global consumption.

In one sense Shilpa became foreign food, for the most part embodying its raw and rotten state, or else she became the cook or the dog (a different type of lower order animal, and one that gets cooked and eaten according to the racialised mythology of the East). Jade's name-calling repeatedly connected Shilpa to food, service or colonial slavedom. Shilpa was 'Shilpa Poppadom', 'Shilpa Fuckawallah',

'Shilpa Daroopa' and 'Shilpa Papadum'. Jade's mother, Jackiey Budden, repeatedly referred to Shilpa as 'the Indian' because, according to her, she was unable to pronounce her name. On Days 11 and 12 of the series, Jo and Danielle mocked Shilpa's accent. Danielle referred to Shilpa as a 'dog', commented that she 'can't even speak English properly anyway', and told Jo that she thought Shilpa should 'fuck off home'.

In a conversation with Danielle, kick-started because she believed that Shilpa had undercooked the chicken she had been preparing, Jo generalised that all Indians were thin because they were 'sick all the time' as a result of undercooking their food. Danielle generalised, 'they eat with their hands in India' and 'you don't know where those hands have been'. The most ferocious example of Stranger-as-Other was, of course, the Oxo incident – in which a row emerges between Jade and Shilpa over the use of Oxo cubes in a pasta dish, it being the key ingredient to a meal Shilpa is subsequently preparing.

What is of interest in this nearly eight-minute row is the way the verbal assault that Jade unleashes on Shilpa oscillates between revulsion of her body as foreign-fake, as fantasy-foreign heroine and as foreign-primitive. Near the beginning of the row Jade taunts, 'not only are you fake but you are a liar', a refrain she repeatedly picks up again during the course of the attack. The idea of performance, of Shilpa being something else, was a slur initiated by Jade earlier in the series when she suggested that Shilpa (after bleaching her facial hair) '... wants to be white ... she makes me feel sick ... she makes my skin crawl'. This idea of passing, of the stranger becoming like me, haunts Jade's Indianphobia, as it has done in much of the Western imagination. Jade 'suspects' that the real Shilpa is dirty, that she is 'matter-out-of-place', and so the interrogation that takes place in the Oxo row is an attempt to reveal the dirty Indian that lies beneath the glamorous mask. Jade is charging, summoning, questioning and finding guilty the 'real' Shilpa as if she is the embodiment of white law.

Historically, as Vera and Gordon suggest, 'white privilege includes the privilege to temporarily change one's colour, to masquerade as non-white' (2003: 120). Vera and Gordon use the example of 'racial masquerade' by whites in American film to explore what they see as an impossible fantasy solution both to the 'lack of life' at the core of whiteness and to the racial guilt experienced by whites in relation to the Other. According to Vera and Gordon:

> The fantasy played out in most white race-switching movies is an adult male fantasy of reversion to boyhood or adolescence, when the white self was free to play Indian or black. These white male heroes temporarily descend into an exotic racial underworld and assume the imagined qualities of the racial other ... only to return at the end to the security of the white bourgeois world. The white passing for another person of another race is, in effect, indulging in voyeurism, liberal slumming, and cultural tourism.
>
> (117)

When the Other tries to pass as white, however, the journey is very often a tragic one – the racial passing text very often requiring an inquisitor who finds out the 'truth' about she or he who is not racially pure. The outcome is violent and destructive. Jade is placing herself within this particular framework of meaning, hoping that in 'outing' Shilpa she will be banished (evicted) from the Big Brother home.

And yet, Jade also proclaims that Shilpa is a real Princess, but that she has to be ordinary (like her) while in the house. Jade shouts, 'You might have been some princess in fucking never never land but I don't give a shit … you're not no fucking princess here, you're a normal housemate like everyone else'. I think this ironic 'idealisation' of the Other works in complex ways here. First, it recognises the hierarchy that one finds existing in star and celebrity personas. Shilpa is an international movie star, her success based on merit, on being a 'talented actress'. By contrast, Jade is a minor or domestic celebrity, 'well known simply for being well known'. Second, it works on the fear of the Other as a national and international success, creating both a New Britain, and an international imaginary, in which India's Tiger economy, its diaspora children, its religion, culture and arts, lead the way, transforming the 'home' space in profound ways. Jade needs Shilpa to be ordinary so that the global/local threat she represents can be diminished or vanquished. Finally, it works to foreground the contradictions of femininity that may well transcend ethnic lines. Shilpa is ideally beautiful and an ideal woman who is mannered and compliant. In many ways, it is every girl's heterosexual dream to be like Shilpa – perfectly formed, thin and flowing in movement and gesture – a woman who will marry a Prince and live in a fairy castle. Jade is conjuring up a barely conscious cultural reading of the perfect female but this patriarchal fairy tale haunts and horrifies her because her own femininity – according to heterosexist culture – has failed.

Attacked by the British press for being fact, thick, uncouth and ugly, Jade reviles at this image of beauty that she can never attain. This is a fear also articulated by Jo: the thinness of Indian women, an embodied state she would like to attain if the patriarchal script writes her thinking, is dealt with through it being diagnosed as an illness brought on by inadequate cooking methods. Thin Indian women are not cultured as such, but raw and uncooked.

Jade's revulsion of Shilpa (a projection of her own revulsion of self) thus gets quickly articulated as shit, vomit and skin-crawling. Jade blazes, 'You are so stuck up your own arse you can't see anything … you are so far up your own arse you can smell your own shit … No, it don't smell of roses, it smells of shit'. Shilpa thus moves from being an object/subject of passing, to being the real feminine ideal, to the foreign-foreigner whose body and ethical centre resides in the manufacture of excrement. Jade tries to expulse the dog-like Shilpa through arguing that Shilpa shits through her mouth. Of course, for much of the media representation of the row, it is Jade that is talking 'shit'. Vilified and ridiculed in the press for her stupidity, ignorance and aggressive bullying, she quickly became the Other to Shilpa's embodiment of multi-racial ideals. Shilpa supposedly spoke for the contemporary age in which multi-racial assimilation is the key to a nation's success.

At the core of the primitivism and Easternisation of Shilpa, then, is a complex interplay of conflicting forces. While there is savage critique of the Other, there is also dissatisfaction with, and alienation from, the limitations of the white feminine self and a secret (shameful) desire to be like the woman that Shilpa is imagined to be. Britain's own sense of its national identity and its place in the global world is symbolically projected onto Jade, Jo and Danielle's crude and offensive musings. As Nandana Bose suggests, 'the nation's collective anxieties about racism, xenophobia and ethnic prejudice were displaced onto the figure of Goody who became the stranger-enemy' (Bose, 2007: 464). By contrast, Britain's identification with Shilpa becomes:

> The embodiment off its true national values, and its rejection of Goody as its unique self is a complex moment in the cultural politics of globalization, when the former empire must look for its 'real' image in its postcolonial subject.
>
> (Zacharias and Arthurs, 2007: 451)

This 'real image' though is as much an Othering one, helping to sustain the signifiers of difference. Shilpa's transportable and easily digestible Indian-ness was based upon her upper-class, passive femininity.

Jackie Stacey argues that a perceived lack of 'spirituality' in the West is also key to the way 'Eastern nature' functions 'as the source of potent fantasies of an Edenic nature' (Stacey, 2000: 122). Stacey suggests that this is best understood in terms of the growth in the new markets of self-health and in Eastern religions. They offer the Westerner a different vision of the 'meaning of life, death and God' (122) to the one offered up in Christian teaching and scientific rationalism. Stacey argues that Easternisation needs to be understood in terms of global culture and the process through which the subject is placed as part of a global order. Self-health philosophies and Eastern religions decree that 'all living things' are 'connected within one "natural-spiritual" system' (124), a system that embraces the whole planet. 'Read in this way, we might suggest that, according to an Easternised version of nature, the global is already within' (ibid: 125). In many ways, finally, Shilpa functions as a feminised Edenic ideal, not smelling or tasting of shit, then, but coming up roses. She connects herself to the global system in which the images, products and services of Otherness circulate and reverberate in both symbolic and hard cultural form. The national and international furore over the *Celebrity Big Brother* row led to a 'healing' process, ultimately culminating in Shilpa and Jade becoming friends. Shilpa's Easternisation then is a panacea for the lack of life in the West, and one that is easily purchased over the counter.

CHAPTER SUMMARY

The chapter explores the way cultural regulation shapes the way celebrities are produced, consumed and drawn upon in everyday life. Celebrity regulation is seen to affect the way bodies are gendered and lived. The Chapter ends with an intersectional analysis of how regulation functions in *Celebrity Big Brother*, and shaped the way one contestant, Shilpa Shetty, was signified an outsider because of discourses around food and disgust.

11

CELEBRITY DISRUPTION

This chapter explores the way anti-regulatory forces and messages operate in and through the politics of celebrity culture. Celebrity disruption manifests in forms of celebrity and fannish behaviour, which run free or counter to dominant ideologies, rituals and discourses. Examples drawn upon include celebrity toxicity, fan activism, disgust and the carnival. The chapter concludes with an unruly autoethnographic encounter where I chart David Bowie's disruptive star image on the wayward reaches of my life. This case study draws a series of disruptive threads together, highlighting how time, story and feeling navigate new paths to understanding celebrity culture.

DISRUPTERS

The history of cultural production and consumption is as much one of disruption as it is regulation: very often they exist in a symbiotic dance with an understanding that anti-regulation ultimately works in the service of routine and conformity, disrupters giving the impression of transformation when all that has occurred is tweaks in the armoury of power and control. Disruption, however, is not simply or singularly mechanical and macro-technologies of regulatory distance – but intimate and personal and formed by the irregular heartbeats of biography and embodied specificity. As Paul Booth argues in relation to Polyvore, a community-powered social commerce website, 'which disrupts the traditional e-commerce model by giving everyone everywhere a voice in shaping today's trends and influencing purchases', fans

> are using Polyvore both as a tool for consuming corporate images and industrial content from the web, but also organizing it in a particularly fannish, reflexive manner. This reflexivity connects the content to the user, reflecting the user's particular vision of his/her self, but using mainstream commercial media to do so. Importantly, generating this imagery and identity is an act of consumption, as it necessarily imbricates the media text. Yet, at the same time it is also an act of appropriation, pushing media into a specific contour.
>
> (2013: 2)

Forms of cultural disruption are carnal and storied: they emerge out of and from the habitus of the everyday and the resistant strategies that people make in the face of the forces of authority and the imbalances of power that is impressed upon them. Power resides not only in institutions, but in the ways people make sense of their world.

Antonio Gramsci (1985) argues that hegemony is necessarily involved in continuing cultural battles and that people readily engage in 'wars of position', where ideas and values are wrestled over. Counter-hegemonic culture emerges behind 'enemy lines', out of the experiences and consciousness of ordinary people, looking to resist and oppose dominant culture and to create new social and political relations as they do so. One way that resistant strategies emerge is through counter cultures and subcultures, which through various behaviour registers and group formations challenge the status quo. For example,

> Underground drag ball participants share a distinct set of meanings within their subculture. Underground drag balls are competitions that consist of individuals, mainly queer youth of color, who perform different drag genres and categories. The ball participants share their identities both as queer youth of color and participants in the ball scene. As part of the ball scene, they also have knowledge of certain values, rituals, objects, and slang that are unique to the subculture. For example,

the average person would not know what the term 'realness' means, however, when one enters the ball scene, every participant knows the meanings and intricacies of the term realness. Furthermore, the value of queering oneself and expressing one's sexuality at the balls, particularly in the 1970s, illustrates how the subculture deviates from mainstream norms and values surrounding gender and sexuality.

(Balzer, 2005: 115)

Forms of dynamic cultural activism occupy this space, also. For example, Melissa Brough and Sangita Shresthova have defined transmedia activism as creating 'social impact by using storytelling by a number of decentralized authors who share assets and create content for distribution across multiple forms of media to raise awareness and influence action' (2012: 14).

One example of this is Avatar Activism, involving various indigenous groups fighting against different forms of economic and political oppression, utilising the social media to share their stories. In 2010, the Avatar-themed demonstrations against the Israeli separation barrier in the Palestinian village of Bil'in involved Palestinian, Israeli and international activists painting themselves blue to resemble the Nav'i from *Avatar*, marching through the occupied village, translating the bio-politics of the film as they did so. They were met with fierce resistance from the Israeli military and the ensuing march and violence were recorded, edited with similarly themed shots from *Avatar* and circulated on YouTube. We hear the movie characters proclaim, 'We will show the Sky People that they cannot take whatever they want! This, this is our land!' Jenkins (2010a) suggests that the people of Bil'in:

have had to constantly innovate themes for their demonstrations and develop new props that can become the focal point for demonstrators and the media alike. What this suggests is that although the imagery used in the demonstrations is often simple and involves the reinforcement of crude binaries between oppression and freedom defined in terms of a contrast between the Israeli state and the Palestinian struggle, this mobilisation of simple imagery is the result of a sophisticated understanding of what resources politically weak agents can mobilise in a long-term struggle against the power of a sovereign state. The people of Bil'in have committed themselves to non-violence and consequently have had to turn to other media oriented means of resistance to the classic 'weapons of the weak' utilised in the armed struggles of guerrilla and national liberation movements.

Fan activism takes a central place in the disruption to the machinery and ideology of popular culture: 'understood as fan-driven efforts to address civic or political issues through engagement with and strategic deployment of popular culture content' (Jenkins, 2010a). For example, 'The Harry Potter Alliance Turns Fans into Heroes by making activism accessible through the power of story', and by being 'cultural acupuncture'. Their vision is to create a creative and collaborative culture that solves the world's problems. Their values are listed as:

- We believe in magic.
- We believe that unironic enthusiasm is a renewable resource.
- We know fantasy is not only an escape from our world, but an invitation to go deeper into it.
- We celebrate the power of community – both online and off.
- We believe that the weapon we have is love.

The Harry Potter Alliance include in their list of achievements a partnership with Walk Free that engaged over 400,000 fans and resulted in Warner Bros. changing the sourcing of their Harry Potter chocolate to be 100% UTZ, or Fairtrade, and raising over $123,000 for Partners in Health and sending five cargo planes of life-saving supplies to Haiti.

John Hartley has termed this growth in fan activism a form of DIY citizenship, involving active agency, social justice and the recasting of the self:

> DIY citizenship is a choice people can make for themselves. Further, they can change a given identity; or move into or out of a repertoire of identities. And although no one is sovereign in the sense that they can command others, there is an increasing concentration on self-determination as the foundation of citizenship.
>
> (1999: 178)

DIY celebrity citizenship can be argued to be a variant of this type of self-determination, in all its forms. First, ordinary people are increasingly visible and vocal in the arenas where celebrities are circulated or transmitted and take up positions as 'ordinary' celebrities, through the fame they get from appearing on reality TV shows, writing successful blogs and making notable appearances on YouTube. The 'accidental celebrity' (Turner, Bonner, and Marshall, 2000) would also fall into this category: thrust into the limelight because of an incident or event outside of their control, they become newsworthy for a distinctly limited period of time, but embody the very notion of democratisation. DIY celebrity citizenship is also closely tied to the emergence of micro-celebrities, which:

> is the result of various shifts and changes in technology, entertainment media, and labor conditions which enable and glorify celebrity while positioning self-promotion as a necessary skill for success. Micro-celebrity as facilitated by social media is one way in which the— cultural logic of celebrity and its emphasis on publicity and attention has affected self-presentation and interpersonal interaction. I describe micro-celebrity as a *practice,* and link it to social media and the celebrification of modern culture.
>
> (Marwick, 2010: 219)

Second, ordinary people now produce much of the content that defines a celebrity's output and they help shape and curate their celebrity image. The production of celebrity culture has very much undergone disruption as fan work spills out through the social media. Through blogs, fanzines, fanfilm, diaries, tweets, video footage and Facebook messaging, the 'story' of the celebrity increasingly happens in and through the micro communication channels of fans and consumers.

This content can be critical of the celebrity in question; can unpack the ideologies of the celebrity and the system that produced them. For example, the tragic suicide of Hong Kong star, Leslie Cheung, opened up fan responses to be critical of the patriarchal and surveillance regimes he was put under. His death initiated a 'collective mourning' and trauma that 'comes from the disruption, even exhaustion' in the way fans had to police their own lives.

Third, the media channels that celebrities can be accessed on has multiplied, and ordinary people can schedule their reception on their own terms, on mobile platforms and on sites that are not authorised by the celebrity. The low-cost entry requirements of much of the digital media have meant access to the means of production has massively increased, facilitating content generation by fans and facilitating inter-action in quick time. As Henry Jenkins (2010b) suggests:

> The rise of digital networks is facilitating new forms of 'collective intelligence' which are allowing groups of consumers to identify and pursue common interests. Alternative forms of cultural production, such as those surrounding fandom and other subcultural communi-ties, are gaining much greater visibility as they move through emerging platforms. Skills acquired through participation in popular culture are spilling over into education, politics, and religion, reshaping the oper-ations of other core institutions.

Nonetheless, Graeme Turner has cautioned against having such an enthusiastic approach to the idea of DIY celebrity citizenship, prefer-ring instead to use the term 'demotic turn' to describe the shift to ordi-nary people having greater access to the media, to celebrity culture. Demotic is a term that suggests in, of and for the people, but not nec-essarily with a corresponding increase in power and authority. In fact, much of the material that is generated by DIY celebrity citizenship may ultimately be in the service of media institutions, raw capitalist profit and contribute to the continuation in power inequalities (2004: 82). Nonetheless, Oliver Driessens contends that there has been a shift to greater DIY democratisation:

> more 'ordinary' people who could, through self-promotion on the internet, for example, take a first (and sometimes decisive) step to being well-known. In other words, the democratization of celebrity is the democratization of visibility—and again, relatively.
>
> (2013: 545)

The practice of celebrity trolling seems to warrant reading from both these democratic/demotic positions. On the one hand, trolling can be seen to be a critical engagement with the celebrity; a clever, considered interjection to create debate and to question their activ-ities and behaviours. On the other, trolling can be seen to be delib-erately inflammatory, destructive, a hate-filled polemic that intends to wound, which causes pain for pain's sake. The former arguably moves democracy forward, while the latter is democratic pretence, leaning on fascistic impulses, no more than a perverted will to power. As Tim Adams suggests (2011):

> Trolls aspire to violence, to the level of trouble they can cause in an environment. They want it to kick off. They want to promote antipathetic emotions of disgust and outrage, which morbidly gives them a sense of pleasure.

An example of this occurred over the announcement that Jonathan Ross was to host the Hugo awards in 2014. He received Twitter abuse from science fiction fans who complained that he had, in the past, made 'fat jokes' about women and was a misogynist.

Ross's 17-year-old daughter, Honey Kinney, tweeted in response:

> I'm Jonathan's overweight daughter and I assure you there are few men more kind & sensitive towards women's body issues.

This tweet was met with further trolling and abuse, leading her mother, Jane Goldman, Ross's screenwriting partner to tweet:

> You falsely accuse her father of sizeism, she gathers the courage to speak to a bullying adult with 12.5k followers ... and you ignored her and casually blathered on about the Oscars. Don't worry about the three real women whose weekend you ruined (me and my daughters).

Of course, the recent #MeToo movement shows the power of celebrity to utilise a social media (here Twitter) to share and collectivise stories of sexual abuse within the entertainment industries.

Nonetheless, there may be an alternative way of understanding DIY celebrity citizenship in this context: as a type of anti-citizenship and a rejection of the regulated borders of democracy. The desire for linguistic violence, the expression of rage and disgust found in fan trolling, in the hope that it will be requited and a public 'spat' will emerge, is a particularly anti-structural and carnal response to discourse. Trolling speaks against governance, regulation and conformity, and instead invites the carnival into the world. While the argument here is not to forgive or excuse misogyny, race hatred and homophobia, it calls to recognise the repressed forces that lurk in civilised society. DIY celebrity citizenship invites this type of extreme response since celebrities are very often anti-structural and carnal agents.

DISRUPTIVE CELEBRITY CARNIVALS

If there is a critical space in which sensory transgressions take place then it is the arena of what I would like to call the celebrity carnival (Redmond, 2013). This celebrity carnival is a wild and free space where 'actors and spectators' equally experience joy, sex, drugs, disinhibition and revelation, and where debauched self and collective renewal takes place and is countenanced. The celebrity carnival is one that stands in opposition to social hierarchy, everyday routinised life, the cultural and repressive constraints on the body, and which offers all under its marquee a version of the 'world upside-down'. According to Bakhtin:

> Carnival is not a spectacle seen by the people; they live in it, and everyone participates because its very idea embraces all the people. While carnival lasts, there is no other life outside it. During carnival time life is subject only to its laws, that is, the laws of its own freedom. It has a universal spirit; it is a special condition of the entire world, of the world's revival and renewal, in which all take part. Such is the essence of carnival, vividly felt by all its participants.
>
> (1984: 10)

The celebrity carnival takes place on a number of levels and diffuses itself through numerous settings and contexts. The celebrity carnival isn't formed on democratic principles and neither does it create the conditions for conformity or obedience to flourish. To the contrary, it is one crafted out of anarchy, involves a grotesque form of celebrity embodiment, one built on the logic of the chaos of the senses. The celebrity carnival is co-synaesthetic and draws on those qualities of the body that have been taken under control in civil society.

For example, there are those encounters where a devoted fan attends a live performance given by their favourite pop celebrity or band. Both in anticipation of the band appearing on stage and during the actual performance, the fan's bodies quiver, leak emotion, emit the uncontrollable signs of desire, longing and need. They scream, shriek, collapse, faint and frenetically jump up and down. The pop star and band can, of course, perform with equal hysteria, caught up in the frenzy of the intimacy before them. Celebrity and fan can create the conditions for the carnival to emerge and converge on the conventions of the proceedings at hand. In a 'live' Justin Bieber performance on the Australian version of the *X-Factor* in 2012, a teenage girl rushed the stage to hug and hold him. She brought misrule to the proceedings; she let her emotions take over as the erotic effects of Bieber took her over. For a few moments, the carnival entered the show and pandemonium broke out. While she was quickly ejected from the stage, her disruptive act of transgression lingers on as an impression, a bloc of sensation, as Bieber continued to play.

Ozzy Osbourne is one such carnival performer, at least in the heyday of Black Sabbath. He patrolled the stage like a cadaver, not quite living, not quite dead, using bodily fluids to wet the stage with his carnality. The famous 'bat' eating incident created the primal conditions for animal becomings, producing both repulsion, disgust in those present, as well as beastial desire. Subsequent concerts involved copycat activities, as animal blood seeped from the crowd onto the stage and back again. What Osborne is enabling here is the breaking of taboos and the hierarchies around water and saliva that permeate culture:

> Saliva – even one's own – is extremely defiling. If a Brahim inadvertently touches his fingers to his lips, he should bathe or at least change his clothes. Also saliva pollution can be transmitted through some material substances. These two beliefs have led to the practice of drinking water by pouring it into the mouth instead of putting the lips on the edge of the cup, and of smoking cigarettes ... through the hand so that they never directly touch the lips. (Hookas are virtually unknown in this part of India) ... Eating of any food – even drinking coffee – should be preceded by washing the hands and feet.
>
> (Douglas, 1966/2002: 156)

When it comes to the bodies of parastars we get to see and sense a different type of corporeality, far removed from perfected figures of mainstream fame. The parastar is often a transgressive and liminal figure who are defined by their excessive behaviour, both within the media texts they appear in and in public life. They are often excessively embodied and their bodies are exaggerated carriers of emotion and affect, set within hyperreal melodramas of action and reaction. These media texts are often experimental and gather cultish appeal, existing on the margins of the media centre. The parastar offers the fan a set of unruly pleasures, within 'a counter-aesthetic turned subcultural sensibility devoted to all manner of cultural detritus' (Sconce, 1995: 372). The parastar is often white trash, lowbrow, but they can also be the exact opposite: operating at the edges of high art, such as the performance artist, Stelarc. The parastar operates as border-crossing figures for the alienated, the marginal, the dispossessed, and, at the other end of the spectrum, the cultural elite.

The disgust that one finds in this type of celebrity carnival is sensory and cross-modal: smells, tastes, textures and environments can offend us; can turn our insides out, in synaesthetic union. Disgust is often met with 'vile' inner materials let out, or it transforms our palettes: we vomit, gas, shit, piss or we just experience the sense or feeling of having contaminants on our lips, caking the insides of our mouths. Disgust is related to survival, to the base instincts that reject things that might harm us. Disgust is also cultural and ideological: it works off normative and moralistic assumptions and conventions and helps construct power-saturated binary oppositions between insiders and outsiders (Menninghaus, 2003). Disgust creates an armada of taboos that arguably hold us in their corporeal and behavioural grip, or conversely, and this is my central point, they can be seen to bring into sensory existence the very essence of our animal beings, offering us transgressive experiences that momentarily wrench the body free from its civil docility.

Disgust can be understood as an anti-democratic force that opens up the body to new experiences and sensations that are usually repressed or denied expression. Disgust can be understood to be a border-crossing emotion, a particularly hyper-charged form of affect, a type of 'beyond' normal experience that cuts one free from language and a stable or simply known subjectivity. Such disgust can be located in/ with the figure of the toxic celebrity, usually associated with young female stars who exist in a world turned upside down: at night this manifests as all night partying and reckless behaviour involving an excess of sex, drinks, drugs and alcohol.

Celebrity toxicity, however, can be applied to any star whose image or behaviour which is seen to be a pollutant in some way. For example, the accusation that Woody Allen abused his adopted daughter, Dylan, has resulted in him being called a toxic star,

> Danny Deraney, a Los Angeles PR executive who does crisis communications for celebrities, said he would not advise clients to work with Allen at this time: 'It's extremely toxic, and why would you want to surround yourself and your career with potential damaging consequences?'

Here toxicity is given a double envelope: working with Allen would be 'toxic' to one's future career; toxicity resides in his disgusting pedophiliac behaviour.

A similar example emerges with USA gymnastics team doctor Larry Nassar, charged with the sexual abuse of nine female gymnasts under his charge. Nassar becomes an 'accidental celebrity' or a figure of heinous notoriety, implicated in disgust in two ways. Those he abused find his actions and violations disgusting and they express disgust in the victim impact statement they give as part of his sentencing hearing. Aly Raisman, an Olympic gold medalist says:

> Larry, you do now realise that we, this group of women you so heartlessly abused over such a long period of time are now a force and you are nothing. I am here to face you Larry so you can see that I have regained my strength, that I am no longer a victim, I am a survivor.

He also is a figure of cultural and social disgust for violating the trust of minors under his care: he becomes a figure with which to be disgusted at and which allows people to share their same values in respect to these acts. Disgust here is not a form of carnival for the victims and society at large, but a way to challenge and oppose unethical behaviour.

DISRUPTING TIME AND SPACE

The final way that this chapter will explore the way celebrity culture is involved in disruption is through the way it re-materialises time and temporality (see also the section on Affective Celebrity Time in Chapter 3). Celebrity culture very often opposes regulatory time with a version of spectacular time and, in so-doing, threatens the very nature of the neoliberal clock and its associated imaginary. One way of conceptualising this time and space disruption is by starting from the 'home' and working outwards.

Homes are very particular social and cultural environments; familiar and familial, lived in and encountered in the most ordinary but intimate of ways. They are a type of body, of skin, an emotional and belonging environment that allows or enables one to call them home (Bourdieu, 1990). From the middle of the last century, with the mass production of similarly designed and built houses, on parcelled up plots of land, many homes were themselves boxed shaped and placed on box-shaped grids with regulated and regular lines, roads, pathways and uniform green spaces (Harris and Larkham, 2003). In an experiential, closed-in sense, this is particularly true of high density, low socio-economic level housing, where conformity in design and planning is the norm for cost factors and where perhaps – in the context of the post World War II period – modernist utopian imaginings hoped that mass built, faceless homes would free society ('the masses') from property hierarchies (Rowe, 1993).

These were home-boxes, then, which framed one's entertainment and viewing experiences and which 'contained' one's everyday life. If one was to extend this concept of the boxed home, the actual institutional and commercial imperatives that operate in terms of the scheduling of entertainment is also boxed-in, with rules for timing, patterning and programming. One knows what is on 'the box' without really having to check the TV guide since, in approximate terms, soap opera is followed by situation comedy is followed by drama is followed by the nightly news. This concept of television flow (Williams, 1974/1992), or repeated and causal segmentation (Fiske, 1987) or of flow and seamless segmentation (Feuer, 1983), creates a framed viewing context in which elements, patterns, forms, segues and links are held together in an arresting chain-like gestalt.

These are thus home-boxes of regulation, mirrored by and connected with the strictures of capitalist work and school time, and with the regulated patterning of the everyday and the everywhere.

Routine existence, 'disciplinary society', to use Foucault's (1977) terms, is experienced from morning to night, in and through an articulating range of discursive practices and processes. However, when the box is turned on what can pour out of it is time re-imagined and spaces and bodies re-enchanted, particularly through the spectacle of celebrity culture. Celebrity spectacle gives time and space to what it might be like to exist *outside the box* while still being inside it.

At the level of celebrity spectacle, time is eroticised and space enchanted: we bear witness to the poetics of spatial movement, the dazzle of costume, the intimacy of perfected bodies and the tourist gaze that opens up the world to sight and vision. The boxed-in life is liquefied through the way celebrity spectacle affects the construction of time and space (see the discussion of wetted spectacle in Chapter 7).

One might term this form of intensified temporality a special type of 'heterotopia of time' or better still, a *heterotopia of celebrity spectacles*, outside or beyond the ordinary, through which a synthesis of 'special' irregular moments of time and space, conjoined with the wonder of idolised stars, recast the places in which one largely exists. The ordinary becomes extraordinary, and Other. Now, while it can and should be argued that these celebrity spectacles are a 'gift' to ease the limits of boxed-in life, and which one is returned too when the celebrity event closes, there is always a weight of surplus value in these spectacularly rendered celebrity events that cannot be contained by the force of closure. The box has been opened, its contents poured out, which offers the viewer a way out of the box and a greater understanding of its ideological and political limitations of regulation itself. This surplus value is also experiential, sensorial based, a body-centred phenomenon, where:

> We are able to be touched by the substance of images, to feel a visual atmosphere envelop us, to experience weight and suffocation and the need for air, to take flight in kinetic exhilaration and freedom even as we are relatively bound to our seats, to be knocked backwards by a sound, to taste and smell the world on the screen.
>
> (Sobchack 2000: 65)

The celebrity spectacle is a sensationally arresting encounter. One experiences a different type of life, through a heightened set of feelings, the value of which lives on and on and on. Life in the ordinary box is thus defamiliarised and the viewer left with the profound feeling that things, objects, time and space are limitless in potential. This is a sublime encounter, irreducible to ideology, to discourse, language and power, but rather initiated beyond it, in a sea of impressions and affects that cannot be boxed-in. Ultimately, in the context of celebrity spectacle, the ordinary becomes endowed with sublime properties and intensities that cast one free in a universe that has been chaotically re-ordered through the celebrity visiting your house, like an alien to the shore.

That said, there is a new tempo and rhythm to liquid modern life: the box feels open 24/7 and one finds oneself constantly available to communication, nearly always tuned into one electronic portal or another. Time has accelerated, is counted in tiny bits and one is given the impression of being constantly on the move in spaces constantly mobile and ephemeral. This is in effect the 'logic' of the age of liquid modernity, where one appears to be free of regulation and control and where one is asked or compelled to live lightly and instantly (Bauman, 2000: 123–29).

One might argue that this living lightly and freely produces an existential terror, as relationship security and situational stability are lost to free-networking and constant movement. I would like to suggest, then, that this living instantly and lightly produces a nostalgia for the past, for the certainty of the boxed-in life. Of course, this nostalgia for the stability of regulation, which holds its own repressive demons, does nothing to hold celebrity spectacle at bay. Nostalgia becomes merely a slip in time, a heterotopia indebted to memory and nostalgia, which will ultimately in turn be swept away in the great multidimensional corridors of time and space.

In the personal case study that follows I explore time, space and the carnival through my fandom of David Bowie, linking disruption to this unruly story of the self.

CASE STUDY

Feeling, story and time: An unruly life lived through David Bowie

Time is flying never to return

– Virgil

Introduction

Is it feeling?

I am a passionate man. I was raised to express myself fully and to feel things deeply. I bring passion's corporeal and exterior intensity to everything I do and I readily and willingly let these feelings be publicly known and affectively shown. This is no more so than with those stars and celebrities I am passionately connected to and who cast a net over the way I recall life events and the most cherished of memories. These feelings I have may relate to desire and attraction, empathy and longing, belonging and emulation, loss and memory, but they move me and I am moved by them – their recollection and reflection the plasma out of which I regularly orientate myself. These star-struck encounters always involve enchantment (Bennett, 2001) and are phenomenological, wet with expectation and experiential thickness (Redmond, 2014). My sense of my identity, then, is warmly wrapped up in the poetics and politics of stars and celebrities who have had a dramatic impact upon the arc and architecture of what is my wayward and uneven life.

A recent case in point was the death of Amy Winehouse. For me, she embodied a particularly transgressive and aggressive form of agency and empowerment, and yet she was also a conduit of/for suffering and loneliness in the face of betrayal and the pressures of patriarchal conformity. When she sang of, 'I cannot play myself again, I should be my own best friend; Not fuck myself in the head with stupid men', she draws attention to gender as performance, and romantic love as wasted on pathetic masculinity and the sexist impositions it demands of female lovers. Her passion, then, was one of chaos and dissolution as much as it was resistant to order and unity. Her confessional song lyrics and her confessing public appearances are the discourses out of which her opposition and refusal of patriarchy grow. Amy's resistance senses itself into corporeal existence, they sting my sense of rebellious self and they make me morally incensed too.

Is it story?

When I reflect on and memorialise over the stars and celebrities that have shaped my sense of self I do so through story: through narrative. Each story is in part classically constructed: there will be a narrative pattern, key minor and associated 'characters' drawn from my life will populate the re-telling, an event moment that holds the story together will be revealed and there will be an ending, generally happy, where all the loose ties of the story are bound tightly together. I share these stories with other story tellers, binding ourselves together through narrative in a shared storytelling universe (Turner, 2006).

One can understand the importance of storytelling as a means of exploring identity through Ruth Finnegan's sociological method (1997), and the affective turn within star and celebrity studies (see Redmond, 2014), whereby writing oneself into identification and desire is centred and encouraged rather than marginalised. The storying the self-approach to empirical research draws on a,

> Model of the self as 'storied' and of culture as both moulded and moulding through the personal stories of individuals … It extends the idea of 'culture' and media beyond the organizational structures of, say, the culture industries, broadcasting or the published media, into the everyday modes in which we express and construct our lives in personal terms, telling our own stories.
>
> (Finnegan, 1997: 69)

I can and do regularly story my life through my relationship with and to David Bowie's music, performances and film work. He is the figure that connects me back to friendship groups, a profound sense of alienation and loneliness, life aspirations and self-perceived failures. He is the 'hero figure' at the heart of my classic narrative (Propp, 2010), and yet he also offers me a way to understand my life story as one that undermines or unsettles the chrononormative time that most stories and narratives operate out of.

Is it time?

Stars and celebrities operate within and across two time continuums. In so doing, they actualise the way time is generally experienced and contested in what are the uneven liquid streams of the modern age. On the one hand, stars and celebrities exist as the embodiment of linear time as ordered, regular and sequential. This is time with a goal, moving forward with purpose, like the hands of an immaculate time-piece.

Stars and celebrities are central to what has been defined as the neoliberal temporal imaginary, which, as Claire Colebrook argues, is linear and spatialised; it is that of a subject 'for whom time is the passage towards complete actualization' (Colebrook, 2009: 11, 2012: 21). This 'chrononormativity' contends that we all share (Freeman, 2010) the same metered time, which we move through 'as though it were composed of successive points that drop away once we pass by' (Neimanis, 2014: 117).

On the other hand, stars and celebrities are constituted out of and constituents for what has been termed thick time heavy with a present-past (Colebrook, 2012). In this conceptualisation, time is always an embodied becoming, full of the memories and encounters of what once was. Thick time is not something we are simply 'in', or which we progress 'through', but is rather in action, a series of intersecting horizontal and vertical layers and sheets we are wrapped in, and shaped by and which is contingent on the spaces, things, objects we are in contact with. Thick time is space and place, thing and human, in dynamic and reverberating relationship – 'Thick time is made by material agents, including but not limited to us, in collaboration' (Neimanis, 2014: 118).

The conceptualisation of thickened time has been taken up by new materialist feminists and queer theorists (Freeman, 2010), for example, to demonstrate the possibility and potentiality of time unwound and being constantly remade, always lived and always becoming.

My relationship with David Bowie (un)hinges on both these conceptions of time: as I note above, he is the figure at the centre of the linear stories I tell when reflecting on my life and identity; and he is a figure that collapses and recasts the clock of chrononormativity because of the way his multitude of star images exist on top of one another and can be mixed and re-mixed in anti-narrational ways. Bowie offers me not just a fixed and forward moving linearity, but a way to experience my time in a myriad of contradictory ways. My time with Bowie is always thickened time, here/there and now/then.

Itisfeelinstorytime

Drawing upon feeling, story and time, in this case study I will make sense of my unruly life through the way David Bowie's musical and film work has impacted upon my sense of self and belonging in the world. I will remember and recall major life events and stinging memories through his songs and performances. David Bowie has provided me with what I have elsewhere defined as the star metronome, providing me with the psychological, existential and phenomenological rhythms out of which (my) bare life emerges, blossoms and sometimes withers – its beat not linear or singular but irregular and amplified (Redmond, 2014). I make sense of these wayward life stories through recall to the senses, and sensorial memory – remembering Bowie through touch, texture, sight and sound. My present and past, my here and now, this there and then, born out of the swimming tides of a remarkably fantastic voyage.

Voyage one: The dogs

My first fully intimate, meaningful engagement with Bowie occurred when I was aged 12. I had again been in trouble at school and had crashed on my bed, alone and lonely. It was in this mood of melancholy and introspective alienation that I put *Diamond Dogs* (RCA Records, 1974) on, while simultaneously running my fingers over the man-dog figure that spread itself over the gatefold album cover it came in. This aural–visual alignment – hearing Bowie strangely, while seeing and touching his animalised, hybrid self – allowed me to enter an enchanted world where his hybridity opened up new otherworldly spaces to exist in, and new liminal identity positions for me to 'try on' and embody (Frith, 1996; Bennett, 1999). I should note that here I am employing enchantment in the way defined by Jane Bennett, or that which:

> Entails a state of wonder, and one of the distinctions of this state is the temporary suspension of chronological time and bodily movement. To be enchanted, then, is to participate in a momentarily immobilising encounter; it is to be transfixed, spellbound.
>
> (2001: 5)

As I listened, my tiny room was filled with the uneven stylistic tones of the album, a mixture of the brassy chords and glam pop beats of his previous work, with the haunting, scratchy, apocalyptic tones of a future world gone terribly awry. I experienced *Diamond Dogs* as the sonic equivalent of glamorous artifice meeting the hard conditions of social realism – a musical odyssey at once familiar and strange, of-, and yet also, out-of-this-world. It was as if these Orwellian[1] sounds and pronouncements spoke to the dystopic elements of my life, while its futurism lifted me upwards and outwards.

I recall now that this produced an *'unheimlich'* (uncanny) feeling of being disrupted or torn out of one's default sensory-psychic-intellectual disposition' (Bennett, 2001: 5). I felt immobilised, enraptured, cut free from the physical and psychological limitations of place, space and body and I was exhilarated as a consequence. Bowie's music – the alien figure that created it – provided an escape from the limiting confines and regulatory conditions of my life, into a world that recognised the former while creating a space for the difference within me to be celebrated, extended, made into hopeful selfhood.

These enchanted tracks were supported by Bowie's deployment of 'cut-up' lyrics, inspired by William S Burroughs. This was his first attempt at cutting up complete sentences he had written and rearranging them into lines composed of allusive juxtapositions and oppositions, drawing on literature, cinema, pulp, science fiction and bohemian references and allusions as he did so. When Bowie sings his lines beginning with, 'This ain't rock n' roll, this is genocide!' one is drawn into a world of excessive consumption and bodily disintegration, the lyrics conjuring up the spirit of carnival (Bakhtin, 1993), set in a freakish public marketplace.

The enchanted world I experience here was far removed from the politics of my social life and allowed me to recognise myself in the outsiders who populate his songs, including, on this album (cover) his new star self, Halloween Jack, 'a real cool cat'.

Halloween Jack offered me a representation of Bowie as half man, half dog, as clearly male and yet neutered or suffering from penile and testicular agenesis. On the cover to *Diamond Dogs*, Bowie is positioned as if he is lying naked on a carnival stage, with two female-like empusae or vampiric demons either side of him – the famed creatures who folklore suggest seduce men in order to feed on their flesh and blood. Bowie's upper torso reveals the androgynous red hair and painted lipstick rock star of previous incarnations, including Ziggy Stardust and Aladdin Sane, and the lower part of the torso shows him to be a de-sexed dog. He is the embodiment of the text, 'the strangest living' curiosity, that runs down the side of the façade he lies underneath on this cover.

I hear and see Bowie/Jack, then, in a moment of pure animal and sexual liminality. Not only do I identify with such a representation, characterisation, but also, I let it take me over. I feel it (in my fingers) as a phenomenological, sensory transformation (Sobchack, 2000) where my self is hybridised, remade as animal, as dog. I am Halloween Jack, a real cool cat about town. Bowie's hybridity, androgyny, alien-ness, provides me with a space in which to border cross (Auslander, 2006).

Fans gather around Bowie as fellow border crossers, using his star image and music as a 'badge of identity' (North and Hargreaves, 1999) to mark out, and to share with one another, their difference to those who didn't act strange, who were not part of his alien universe. In my particular case, my fandom was a carnal one, made of the flesh, first properly cast in an enchanted space where I found the *sense(s)* to be someone else, someone more, a self-liberation that I subsequently took back into my everyday world, resistant and rebellious.

Stars and celebrities carry and are carried within discourses that suggest life is made up of a series of sequential stages – one after the other, which we all move through. These stages – child, tween, teen, youth, twenty-something, etc. suggest a deepening of experiences and challenges as one moves through the corridors of life's greater journey. These are also often signalled as moral stories, since if (when) a celebrity goes off the rail at a certain 'stage'; their transgressions are used to teach us a lesson about the need to keep on the straight and narrow. This rise and fall trajectory is contingent on linear time and creates the conditions for us to experience time as forward moving and with moral speed humps. Drew Barrymore, Macaulay Culkin, Miley Cyrus are all examples of this staged transgression.

Closely related to the stages of life trope, stars and celebrities undergo rites of passage (event) moments – where we see them at the prom, passing their driving test, getting married, having their first child, cheating, getting divorced. While these are often heightened and spectacular events, they nonetheless demonstrate the ordinariness of the ritual and of the naturalness of the moment in time it captures – these are rituals and events we all (must) pass through. While rites of passage events are more fluid in their actualisation they nonetheless become a point in time that dictates that which follows and eventuates.

Of course, my argument here is that while David Bowie can be seen to be pivotal to my stages of life maturation and is the crux at ritual-ised events, he does so to undermine the patriarchal and heterosexual script, and to offer bonds of communion which go against the grain of dominant ideology. He allows me to experience the stages of life through a resistant aesthetic – through rites and rituals that are simul-taneously enchanted and 'realistic'. Simon Frith (1996: 123) writes:

> But if musical identity is, then, always fantastic, idealizing not just one-self but also the social world one inhabits, it is, secondly, always also real, enacted in musical activities. Music making and music listening, that is to say, are bodily matters; involve what one might call social movements. In this respect, musical pleasure is not derived from fantasy – it is not mediated by dreams – but is experienced directly: music gives us a real experience of what the ideal could be.

The 'ideal' that I find in David Bowie is the counter-ideal: the one that celebrates the marginal, ignites the heart of the lonely and fuels the fires of counter-culture resistance and self-renewal and alien selfhood that is hopeful.

Voyage two: Changes (Lost in Dolymoch)

According to Henry Jenkins, fandom is a key facet of participatory cul-ture, where: fandom refers to the social structures and cultural practices created by the most passionately engaged consumers of mass media prop-erties; participatory culture refers more broadly to any kind of cultural production which starts at the grassroots level and which is open to broad participation (2010b). The participatory culture that builds around star and celebrity fandom can be argued to be regenerative, affecting the produc-tion and reception of the figure, as fans creatively transcode their mean-ing, produce and transmit new ways of understanding the celebrity and engage in new forms of collective interaction. As John Caughie suggests:

> The basis of most fan relationships is a social one. Fans have attach-ments to unmet media figures that are analogous to and in many ways directly parallel to actual social or public relationships.

(1984: 40)

While fandom is decidedly and deliciously personal and private, it is also the plasma through which friendships are made true and enacted in public settings.

We are on an Outward Bound trip to Dolymoch in Wales – a natural, rugged haven a million miles away from the concrete jungle (the city of Coventry, UK) we normally live in. The air is clean, the river water pure and the lush valleys and hills sing their own hopeful tunes. We are on a five-mile orienteering trek, the group thinly thread over the lost horizon. Jon, one of my good friends at the time, and I are weighed down with heavy rucksacks and are at the back of the group. We talk of violent presents and possible futures – his mean parents, my family's homelessness, his yearning to travel, my desire to act and write. We are two life-long Bowie fans and begin a game of matching which lyric to which song, followed by reciting our favourite Bowie lyrics.

The sky is black, the horizontal rain falls, the sodden sheep are nervous. We are caught in our own pathetic fallacy. We embrace, and we begin to sing, loudly and proudly – water on our faces – mud rising up our trousers – ch, ch, ch, changes...

This is an affective memory, enmeshed within a structure of feeling (Kuhn, 2010) – recalled upon when we are brought together, producing laughs and giggles and the return of the embrace; and or when we are separately hurting and needing to hold true. A life lived full of changes, a friendship held together by the singular memory of changes.

If I may momentarily draw upon string theory, if only to utilise the metaphors that Brian Greene uses to define it and to help me make sense of this story:

> If string theory is right, the microscopic fabric of our universe is a richly intertwined multidimensional labyrinth within which the strings of the universe endlessly twist and vibrate, rhythmically beating out the laws of the cosmos.

My identification work with David Bowie and the memorial work I undertake to story my relational selfhood, seems to be best understood as one cast and recast within this temporal labyrinth: my stages and stories seem to endlessly wrap around one another, bringing the present of today to the presence of yesterday and the present of yesteryear to the presence of today. My identification work with David Bowie is an accumulation of all that was, all that is and all that will potentially be. As a consequence, he becomes a site of endless possibility and a body that opens up time to identity that is always a matter of becoming (Hall, 2011).

When we search online for images and stories of our favourite star, the search engine throws up the many moments of their star images. These starry images are not ordered in a linear fashion at all but are subject to algorithms and real-time events that might change or affect what images are presented before us. Set in a sea of accumulations, the star or celebrity appears with all their stages and rituals set freely before us. This is not, then, linear time but all of time at once. All of time at once is the past meeting the present, the present visiting the past, and the past-present, present-past touching the hands of the future. Matter and materiality is of course important here. Karen Barad (2007) writes of 'intra-active becoming as indicative of a collaborative, productive, and open-ended relationship between time and matter' (178). In the here/now and there/then montage of celebrity faces the screens materially contain and maintain and sustain the 'living present'.

So is true of the photo albums I keep and the memories I store and the stories I share of David Bowie: each time I revisit them, re-tell them, something else is highlighted, remembered, lost or forgotten. Each time a new layer of me, my selfhood, sits upon the one before, and the layers before me weave themselves into my updated biography. When I think of David, Jon and Dolymoch, a whole interconnecting cosmos opens up before me. It changes every time.

Voyage three: Heart on my sleeve

Star and celebrity memorabilia are often types or forms of holy relics, invested with religious signification or higher-order iconicity, given surplus value by fans who purchase and consume them. An aura circulates around such memorabilia, a commodity exchange value is produced, an economy of the emotions is set in train. No more is this true than when the item or items in question have a personal connection to the fan – a ticket, poster or signed programme from a concert they went to, a drinking bottle flung from the stage with the star's own DNA wrapped around its opening. Such a precious thing in the fan's star-celebrity allegiance.

The word possession is crucial to this relationship; one is not simply possessing the star-struck thing but their essence, their being in the world. Their enchanted or charmed life is being co-located in the holy relic that is owned, cherished, touched and consumed. One can define this carnal and existential transference as celebrity contagion, or 'the belief that a person's immaterial qualities or "essence" can be transferred to an object through physical contact' (Newman, Diesendrock, and Bloom, 2011: 4). The material possession of a celebrity's personal item, then, captures their spirit and body, which through presence, touch, even/especially ingestion, possesses and changes or transforms the new you who now holds it. Here once public items become deeply private keepsakes and mementoes.

I saw David Bowie in 1983 at the Milton Keyes Bowl in the UK. I went with my sister Fiona, and her best friend Margaret. We got close to the stage and swooned and danced and sung for the entire concert. Although this was corporate Bowie, his difference, the carnival it became, lit up the boy-man within me.

Some months later I heard he was releasing a limited picture disc of a live version of 'Let's Dance' that would include a shot from the concert that day. I rushed to the HMV record store in Coventry to purchase the vinyl record.

The record is not just a memento, a memory of the day; it isn't another holy relic in my possession because there am I on the sleeve wearing my red fringe and blonde bouffant – more David Sylvian than David Bowie, perhaps. I have carried this vinyl record with me everywhere and through everything – all that life can throw at me; every adventure I have embarked on. It is a memory object, an interactive object, with the living me in reverie amongst the crowd. This is a happy object no less (Ahmed, 2008) and a private object I share in the public domain.

Such limited releases and wholesale merchandising are of course a part of an industry that works to grant certain stars and celebrities symbolic immortality; in which one's name, one's image, one's activities and art get written into history books, artistic canons and are carried across time and space, so that the famous figure lives on, way beyond the telos of the body. Virtual and digital stars do this living forever in a different way; with no mortal body to speak of, they cannot physically die, and so they live on without mourning or funeral, only beholden to archiving strategies and continued public interest in them. Their images float in virtual clouds that are eternally blessed.

Higher-order celebrities or supericonic stars, such as David Bowie, are already post-human, and divine: they have gone beyond the mortal limits of the body and their immortality grants them religious signification.

While this temporal deification might assuage our fear of death and create the condition for neoliberal life to flourish, the sense that there is no end game opens up the possibility of questioning the chrononormative script we have been blessed with ... It may in fact echo the 'monumental time' that Julia Kristeva (2002) rehabilitates from Friedrich Nietzsche, in that this time is larger than (our) life.

When David Bowie died in January 2016 he left behind him nest eggs and allusions and unpublished work that would ensure he would go on living beyond his death. As a supericonic star, of course, and one who had such a dramatic impact on culture and society, his immortality is granted. When I now hold the live version of 'Let's Dance' in my hands, however, I see my own mortality rise up like a ghost before me. These are ghosts I have met before.

Voyage four: Who am I now

I am watching for the first time the video to Bowie's new single, 'Where Are We Now?', released on the day of his 66th birthday (8 January 2013). Within seconds of hearing the first vibrato chords of this wistful song and of seeing the memorial images of the Berlin that Bowie did some of his finest work in, I find myself in a flood of tears.

The video has acted as a 'memory text', activated a 'structure of feeling' (Kuhn, 2010: 299) that has thrown up all sorts of nostalgic impressions, affects, and ultimately takes me right back to a heightened moment of personalised time, of enchanted plenitude, as this question begins to fall from my wet lips...

Who was I then?

'Where Are We Now' is a love song to the past, drawing on images and references to Bowie's own creative period in Berlin. As he conjures up his own memorial framework, composed of lyrics that recall his time there in the late 1970s, such as, 'Sitting in the Dschungel, On Nürnberger Straße', and shots of the places where he lived or travelled through, such as Potsdamer Platz, I am affectively positioned to do the same.

The objects, curiosities and mementoes that also fill the video – mannequins, a snowflake, a crystal, empty glass bottles, a giant ear – suggest Bowie's own memorabilia and again ask me to draw on them to memorialise my own affective investment in his work. It takes me back to the days of *Diamond Dogs*, to Dolymoch, to the Milton Keynes Bowl, to the sounds, sights, smells, textures and fabrics of my lost youth. A whole tsunami of tides rises up and sets me sail away on a sea of private and public ghost ships and liners. The melancholy of the song registers as a 'super expressive human voice' (Juslin and Västfjäll, 2008: 566) while the portentous images call on me to feel my way back into my past.

As Bowie asks, where are we now, I ask myself through an autobiographical framework, who am I now? I look back at the promise of my youth, at the hopes, aspirations, dreams I forged back then, and find the mismatches, the cracks, as well as some successes. There is an overwhelming awakening within me as I do so, a heightening of my senses, but also a deep and profound sadness as I experience my own mortality and newly experience the span of my life as it has been lived.

There is something of a 'cruel optimism' (Berlant, 2011) at work in this encounter with Bowie's new work; while I can longingly recall the enchantment I got from *Diamond Dogs*, from man-dog Halloween Jack, the encounter with his new songs registers as a disenchantment, or rather, it has led to 'the blow of discovering that the world can no longer sustain one's organizing fantasies of the good life' (Berlant, 2012).

When Bowie sings of walking the dead, I see myself in a crowd of zombies, indistinguishable from everyone else, crossing Bösebrücke, to an uncertain future. And yet Bowie and I are not yet completely used up, as the lyrics go on to suggest, we still live, we live with a remarkable fire burning within us. And I have you.

One last point, or is it my first?

The thick time of stars and celebrities ultimately exist as personal and intimate carriers and conveyors of dynamic temporality – this is not a temporal imposition, which clocks us in and out, but one fashioned out of the self as it is really lived in the world. Thick time is my time shared with, in, through and across places, spaces, people, memories, mementoes and keepsakes. In relation to stardom and celebrity, this thick time personalised involves memorial and material work, archiving and rituals, actions and reactions, talk and walking, hearing and seeing – rhythmically beating out the endless possibilities of the cosmos. The enchanted cosmos – where there is life on Mars.

It is time?

NOTE

1   A number of songs on the album had been initially written to be part of a theatrical production of George Orwell's novel, *1984*, but Bowie was denied the rights to use the material.

CONCLUSION

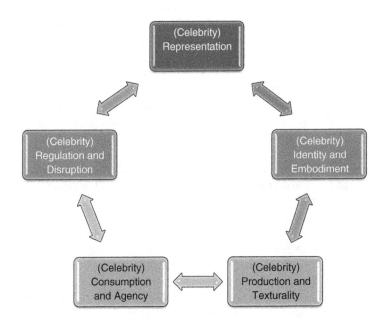

WHATYA GOT?

I fell in love with Marlon Brando at a young age, alongside George Best, Elvis Presley, Rita Hayworth and the Irish girl who lived next door. Brando was physically perfect, politically active, emotionally real and yet also mysterious, strange, Other. His own self-loathing – 'I have a face like a pig', he once remarked – was part of the attraction, the fandom, since Brando was so very extraordinary and so very real and realist.

In *The Wild One* (1953, Lásló Benedek), a film he didn't much care for, Brando is the leader of the black rebel motorcycle gang that rides into a small town to challenge cultural and social norms and to sweep the women – and perhaps the men – off their feet. In one seminal scene, in the town bar, the rigid conventions of courtship, drinking and dancing are being broken and Brando, or Brando's character, in what might be described as a perfect star fit, stands alone, surveying the bar from a position of power. He is able to express the nihilism and the promiscuity of his rebel-youth philosophy and of his star image, as they perfectly align. Standing at the back of the bar, with dancing couples around him, while tapping out his fingers to the jazz beat that anchors the scene, he is asked what he is rebelling against and answers, in a medium to close up shot, 'what ya got!'

The answer is itself electrifying, cutting through regulatory norms and cementing the idea of a counter-culture emerging through the weeds of civic society. The poetics of the image is at least as intense: dressed in leathers, a tight t-shirt and peaked cap, he radiates an embodied, powerful confidence. His movement across the scene – the short Brando walk with his hands in his pockets – the existential drifted translated and dirtied – is nonchalant, defiant, untouched, an immanent purity, so-to-speak.

Brando's face, of course, is also a mixture of the soft and feminine – painted seemingly – and the hyper-masculine, and as such forms itself against gender binaries. Brando's body moves in tune with the jazz soundtrack: the music enters him and he gives the music an embodied presence. These co-existences are carnally delivered – Brando, the dance, the music is meaty, fleshed, irregular and resistant. Brando isn't performing rebellion, he is *embodying* it, drawing on sensorial and synaesthetic qualities to do so.

For this fan, for a few brief moments, Brando's carnal being shatters the filmic narrative and ruptures or intensifies the star/actor/performance distinctions so that they seamlessly, symbiotically fold and flow into one another. This is brute matter before us. When the camera cuts to that medium close up and Brando delivers those now legendary lines, it isn't actually the words (language, signification) that carries the full power of his phenomenal, phenomenological being but his haptic look, pig face, curling lips and laconic voice.

For Deleuze and for Bergson, albeit in different ways, the face has the potential to free time and dislocate space, inviting or calling into being a suspension of normal motor activity, which allows other planes of reality to be perceivable. Brando's face and body are a brooding material that cannot be held in place or check by normative definitions of self-hood and masculinity. Further, Brando fills my body with a sensory aesthetics of rebellion; I feel my body rebel and I feel the rebel within me.

This example very much speaks to the intersecting nodes – the arteries and veins – of the two circuits that drive and structure this book. In Brando's performance we can see the registers of representation and affect, identity and embodiment, production and texturality, consumption and agency, regulation and disruption.

The circuit of celebrity culture and the circuit of celebrity affect are not linear devices, neither are they separate and fully separable. As the examples threaded throughout this book demonstrate, they fire off one another, extinguish one another, lay court and siege to one another. For example, we can see that celebrity spectacle takes its place at numerous points on the two circuits, like blood ebbing and flowing through a living, breathing body.

The book is at great pains to express the tussle that happens at the heart of celebrity culture, which is always involved in a 'war of position', and with hegemony and counter-hegemony in constant negotiation. On the one hand, it is clear that celebrity culture is very often heterosexist, patriarchal, racist and beauty and diet obsessed. On the other, it promotes bodies that resist and forms of fandom and consumption which are not simply agents of and for neo-liberal ideologies.

Too often, far, far too often in the study of celebrity, emotion, pleasure and affect are regulated to the margins, accused of being in the service of liquid capitalism, wanton consumption and parasocial relations that actually make docile those that it comes into contact with. What this book does is show how emotion, pleasure and affect produce intensities that cannot be tamed and subject positions that do more than stand in the mirror of self-love. This book centres the red heart of celebrity culture and does so with passion and conviction.

The book is deliberately full of productive tensions: it mirrors celebrity culture. The two models are in productive tension; nodes articulate in strings of tension and case studies are made out of material tensions. David Bowie in this respect is a gender and ethnic liberator, found in the stories of fans who use his work to both escape from and transform self and habitus in the process. But David Bowie is also caught in the hierarchies of whiteness and in the capitalist chains of music production which produce him and of which he is a product.

The celebrity body is everywhere in this book: a site of representation and affect, a fleshed form of identity and regulated and disruptive at the same time. Through Johansson, Swift, Beyoncé, Winslet and Crowe, amongst others, the body landscapes the two circuits under investigation.

The book draws on ethnography, autoethnography and small-scale empirical research to test the assumptions it and other writers make about celebrity culture. But its storied empiricism is also to let people *speak* and to *hear* what they have to say. Celebrity culture may be more demotic than democratic, but the research on its manifestations is at its best when we ask people to tell us their stories. The book is full of wonderful stories – made of feeling and of time.

Finally, the book draws upon both historical (and historic) examples and case studies from the contemporary moment. One of the criticisms of stardom and celebrity research, and of the area itself, is that it suffers from ephemerality: with a rapid turnover of the next big thing and famous people quickly forgotten. This is a position I readily and regularly resist. While official canons and canonical curators will have us believe that only certain stars and celebrities matter, the truth is that if they matter to someone, they matter, full stop. Every day in so many social contexts, memories are being born as fans and consumers meet and greet the star they so like at that time. These memories last a lifetime and at a sociological level should be the material we spend the most time with.

I will end with another short story – a recent memory that still holds me in its spell. I was seeing the Mass installation at Melbourne's NGV at the beginning of January 2018. The exhibition is composed of 100 different-sized human skulls and draws a gasp when you first see it. I was reading the title card and looked up to make direct eye-contact with Nick Cave (of the Bad Seeds) who was standing in front of me, less than three feet away. He could see that I had recognised him but he looked back at me as if to say, don't say anything, don't do anything crass, I am not the Nick Cave you are looking at and for. I quickly looked away and Nick drifted off. I am a massive Nick Cave fan so I was dizzy with excitement. That Nick wasn't 'Nick'; that he wanted to be not noticed and left alone speaks to the public/private dilemma that scars the field and those who are held in its frenzied grip. That I could feel this and that I could recognise his own contemplation in the work he was viewing, shows how fan encounters can happen on different levels, and that stars sometimes just want and need to be something other than their public selves. While Nick won't be recounting this no-story any time soon, I will carry it with me forever.

It is time.

References

Abe, Kashou (2000) *Nihon eiga ga sonzai sura [Japanese Films Exist]*, Tokyo: Seidosha.

Abebe, Nitsuh (2010) Filthy, Rich: Kanye West's Royal Fantasy, *Vulture*, available at: www.vulture.com/2010/11/filthy_rich_kanye_wests_royal.html; Accessed 22 March 2017.

Abercrombie, Nick, Hill, Stephen and Turner, Brian S (1986) *Sovereign Individuals of Capitalism*, London: Allen and Unwin.

Abidin, Crystal (2015) Communicative Intimacies: Influencers and Perceived Interconnectedness, *A Journal of Gender, New Media and Technology*, 8, 1–16.

ABS – Australian Bureau of Statistics (2012) *Cultural Diversity in Australia. Reflecting a Nation: Stories from the 2011 Census*, catalogue no. 2071.0, available at: www.abs.gov.au/ausstats/abs@.nsf/Lookup/2071.0main+features902012-2013; Accessed 18 February 2016.

Adams, Paul (1995) A Reconsideration of Personal Boundaries in Space-Time, *Annals of the Association of American Geographers*, 85, 267–85.

Adams, Tim (24 July 2011) How the Internet Created an Age of Rage, *The Guardian (The Observer)*, available at: www.guardian.co.uk/technology/2011/jul/24/internet-anonymity-trolling-tim-adams; Accessed 25 July 2012.

Adorno, Theodor and Horkheimer, Max (1997) *Dialectic of Enlightenment*, London: Verso.

Ahmed, Sara (2000) *Strange Encounters: Embodied Others in Post-Coloniality*, London: Routledge.

Ahmed, Sara (2008) Sociable Happiness, *Emotion, Space and Society*, 1, 1, 10–13.

Alberoni, Francesco (2007) 'The Powerless Elite: Theory and Sociological Research on the Phenomena of the Stars', in Sean Redmond and Su Holmes (eds) *Stardom and Celebrity: A Reader*, London: Sage, 65–77.

Anderson, Benedict (1983) *Imagined Communities: Reflections on the Origin and Spread of Nationalism*, London: Verso.

Appadurai, Arjun (1990) Disjuncture and Difference in the Global Cultural Economy, *Theory, Culture & Society*, 7, 2–3, 295–310.

Appleford, Katherine (2016) 'This Big Bum Thing Has Taken over the World': Considering Black Women's Changing Views on Body Image and the Role of Celebrity, *Critical Studies in Fashion & Beauty*, 7, 2, 193–214.

Armleder, Kirsten (n.d.) Keanu Reeves and His Love of Motorcycles. *Riderswest*, available at: http://riderswestmag.com/rideon/article/keanu_reeves_and_his_love_of_motorcycles; Accessed 16 April 2017.

Auslander, Paul (2006) *Performing Glam Rock: Gender and Theatricality in Popular Music*, Ann Arbor: University of Michigan Press.

Bacal, ED (2009) On the Obama-ization of Will Smith, *Cineaction*, available at: www.thefreelibrary.com/On+the+Obama-ization+of+Will+Smith.-a0200253752; Accessed 30 October 2009.

Bakhtin, Mikhail (1984) *Rabelais and His World*, trans. Hélène Iswolsky, Bloomington: Indiana University Press.

Bakhtin, Mikhail (1993) *Rabelais and His World*, trans. Hélène Iswolsky, Bloomington: Indiana University Press.

Balázs, Béla (1970) *Theory of the Film; Character and Growth of a New Art*, New York: Dover Publishing.

Balzer, Carsten (2005) *The Great Drag Queen Hype: Thoughts on Cultural Globalisation and Autochthony Paideuma: Mitteilungen zur Kulturkunde*, Bd. 51, 111–31.

Bann, Stephen (1998) Three Images for Kristeva: From Bellini to Proust, *Parallax*, 4, 3, 65–79.

Barad, Karen (2007) *Meeting the Universe Halfway*, Durham, NC: Duke University Press.

Barthes, Roland (1967) *The Elements of Semiology*, London: Cape.

Barthes, Roland (1972) *Mythologies*, 1st Edition, New York: Hill and Wang.

Barthes, Roland (2007) 'The Face of Garbo', in Sean Redmond and Su Holmes (eds) *Stardom and Celebrity: A Reader*, London: Sage, 261–62.

Bartky, Sandra Lee (1990) *Femininity and Domination: Studies in the Phenomenology of Oppression*, London: Routledge.

Bartky, Sandra Lee (1997) 'Foucault, Femininity, and the Modernization of Patriarchal Power', in Katie Conby (ed) *Writing on the Body: Female Embodiment and Feminist Theory*, London: Columbia University Press, 129–54.

Baudrillard, Jean (1988) 'Consumer Society', in Marc Poster (ed) *Jean Baudrillard. Selected Writings*, Cambridge: Polity, 29–56.

Bauman, Zygmunt (1987) *Legislators and Interpreters*, Cambridge: Polity.

Bauman, Zygmunt (1992) Survival as a Social Construct, *Theory, Culture & Society*, 9, 1, 1–36.

Bauman, Zygmunt (1996) 'From Pilgrim to Tourist – Or a Short History of Identity', in S. Hall and P. Du Gay (eds) *Questions of Cultural Identity*, London: Sage, 18–36.

Bauman, Zygmunt (2000) *Liquid Modernity*, Cambridge: Polity.

Bauman, Zygmunt and Tester, Keith (2001) *Conversations with Zygmunt Bauman*, Cambridge: Polity.

Beer, David and Penfold-Mounce, Ruth (2009) Celebrity Gossip and the New Melodramatic Imagination, *Sociological Research Online*, 14, 2, 1–15, available at: http://socresonline.org.uk/14/2/2.html; Accessed 8 August 2014.

Bell, Jennifer (2016) Etihad Airways Reveal 360-degree Virtual Reality Film Starring Nicole Kidman, *The National*, available at: www.thenational.ae/business/travel-and-tourism/etihad-airways-reveal-360-degree-virtual-reality-film-starring-nicole-kidman-1.198963; Accessed 16 April 2018.

Belton, John (2002) Digital Cinema: A False Reevolution, *October Magazine*, (Spring), 98–114.

Bennett, Andy (1999) Subcultures or Neo-tribes? Rethinking the Relationship between Youth, Style and Musical Taste, *Sociology*, 33, 3, 599–617.

Bennett, Andy (2017) Wrapped in Stardust: Glam Rock and the Rise of David Bowie as Pop Entrepreneur, *Continuum*, 31, 4, 574–82.

Benson, Susan (1997) 'The Body, Health and Eating Disorders', in Kathryn Wood-ward (ed) *Identity and Difference*, London: Sage, 121–66.

Beoku-Betts J (1995) 'We Got Our Way of Cooking Things'? Women, Food and Pres-ervation of Cultural Identity Among the Gullah, *Gender and Society*, 9, 535–56.

Berlant, Laurent (1997) *The Queen of America Goes to Washington City: Essays on Sex and Citizenship*, Durham, NC: Duke University Press, 5.

Berlant, Laurent (2011) *Cruel Optimism*, Durham, NC: Duke University Press.

Berlant, Laurent (2012) In a Nutshell, *Rorotoko*, available at: http://rorotoko.com/interview/20120605_berlant_lauren_on_cruel_optimism/; Accessed 5 June 2012.

Bhabha, Homi K (1993) 'The Postcolonial and the Postmodern: The Question of Agency', in Simon During (ed) *The Cultural Studies Reader*, London: Routledge, 189–208.

Biltereyst, Daniel (2004) Media Audiences and the Game of Controversy: On Reality TV, Moral Panic and Controversial Media Stories, *European Culture and the Media*, 5, 1, 117–37, available at: http://academic.csuohio.edu/kneuendorf/frames/phx/creativegeography/biltereyst_04.pdf; Accessed 26 August 2014.

Bogle, Donald (1973) *Toms, Coons, Mulattoes, Mammies and Bucks: An Interpretive History of Blacks in American Films*, New York: Viking Press.

Bogue, R (2004) *Deleuze's Wake: Tributes and Tributaries*, New York: SUNY Press.

Bonnett, Alastair (1998) How the British Working Class Became White: The Sym-bolic (Re)formation of Racialized Capitalism, *Journal of Historical Sociology*, 11, 3, 316–340.

Bonnett, Alastair (2000) *White Identities: Historical and International Perspectives*, Harlow: Prentice.

Booth, Paul (2013) 'Digital Cosplay as Consumptive Fan Labor', in Rethinking Resis-tance: Nonparticipation, Consumption, and the Recruitment of Affirmation in Internet Fandom, *Selected Papers of Internet Research* 14.0, 2013: Denver, USA, available at: https://spir.aoir.org/index.php/spir/article/viewFile/911/pdf; Accessed 7 October 2017.

Bordo, Susan (1993) *Unbearable Weight: Feminism, Western Culture, and the Body*, Berkeley, CA: University of California Press.

Bose, N (2007) Big Brother's Frankenstein: The Media Construction of Jade Goody as Object-Other, *Feminist Media Studies*, 7, 4, 463–67.

Bourdieu, Pierre (1977) *Outline of the Theory of Practice*, Cambridge: Cambridge University Press.

Bourdieu, Pierre (1984) *Distinction: A Social Critique of the Judgement of Taste*, London: Routledge.

Bourdieu Pierre (1990) [1980]. 'Structures, Habitus, Practices', in *The Logic of Prac-tice*, Stanford : Stanford University Press, 52–65.

Bowlby, Rachel (1985) *Just Looking: Consumer Culture*, Basingstoke: Macmillan.

Bradley, Peri and Page, James (2017) David Bowie – The Trans Who Fell to Earth: Cultural Regulation, Bowie and Gender Fluidity, *Continuum*, 31, 4, 583–95.

Brockington, Dan (2008) Powerful Environmentalisms: Conservation, Celebrity and Capitalism, *Media, Culture & Society*, 30, 551–568.

Brough, Melissa M and Shresthova, Sangita (2012) Fandom Meets Activism: Rethinking Civic and Political Participation, *Transformative Works and Cultures*, 10, 1–27.

Brown, Adriane (2012) 'She Isn't Whoring Herself out like a lot of Other Girls We See': Identification and 'Authentic' American Girlhood on Taylor Swift Fan Forums, *Networking Knowledge*, 5, 1, 161–80.

Bruns, Axel and Burgess, Jean E (2011) The Use of Twitter Hashtags in the Formation of Ad Hoc Publics, in *6th European Consortium for Political Research General Conference*, 25–27 August 2011, University of Iceland, Reykjavik, http://eprints.qut.edu.au/46515/1/The_Use_of_Twitter_Hashtags_in_the_Formation_of_Ad_Hoc_Publics_(final).pdf; Accessed 3 September 2014.

Bruzzi, Stella (1997) *Undressing Cinema: Clothing and Identity in the Movies*, London: Routledge.

Buck-Morss, Susan (1998) Aesthetics and Anaesthetics: Walter Benjamin's Artwork Essay Reconsidered, *October*, 62, Autumn, 3–41.

Bukatman, Scott (2009) Vivian Sobchack in Conversation With Scott Bukatman, *Journal of E-Media Studies*, 2, 1, available at: https://Journals.Dartmouth.Edu/Cgi-Bin/Webobjects/Journals.Woa/1/Xmlpage/4/Article/338; Accessed 6 April 2017.

Butler, Judith (1990) *Gender Trouble: Feminism and the Subversion of Identity*, London: Routledge.

Candice Olsen, Inc (2015) About Candice, www.candiceolson.com/aboutcandice.html; Accessed 16 April 2018.

Carter, Erica, Donald, James and Squires, Judith (eds) (1993) *Space and Place: Theories of Identity and Location*, London: Lawrence and Wishart.

Cashmore, Ellis (2004) *Beckham*, 2nd Edition, New York: Wiley.

Cashmore, Ellis (2006) *Celebrity Culture*, London: Routledge.

Cashmore, Ellis (2010) Buying Beyoncé, *Celebrity Studies*, 1, 2, 135–50.

Caughie, John (1984) *Imaginary Social Worlds: A Cultural Approach*, Lincoln: University of Nebraska Press.

Chernin, K (1983) *Womansize: The Tyranny of Slenderness*, London: The Women's Press.

Christensen, Clayton (1997) Disruptive Innovation, available at: www.christenseninstitute.org/key-concepts/disruptive-innovation-2/; Accessed 10 December 2017.

Cinque, Toija (2015) 'Semantic Shock: David Bowie!' In Toija Cinque, Chris Moore, and Sean Redmond (eds) *Enchanting David Bowie: Space/Time/Body/Memory*, New York: Bloomsbury, 197–214.

Cinque, Toija, Moore, Christopher and Redmond, Sean (2015) *Enchanting David Bowie: Space/Time/Body/Memory*, New York: Bloomsbury.

Clough, Patricia T (2008) The Affective Turn: Political Economy, Biomedia And Bodies, *Theory, Culture & Society*, 25, 1, 1–22.

CNN (2008) Obama: We Are Better than These Last Eight Years, http://edition.cnn.com/2008/POLITICS/08/28/obama.transcript/index.html; Accessed 11 April 2017.

Cohen, Lisa (1998) The Horizontal Walk: Marilyn Monroe, Cinema Scope, and Sexuality, *The Yale Journal of Criticism*, 11, 1, 259–88.

Cole, CL and Andrews, DL (2001) America's New Son: Tiger Woods and America's Multiculturalism, in D Andrews and S Jackson (eds) *Sport Stars*, London: Routledge, 70–86.

Colebrook, Claire (2009) Stratigraphic Time, Women's Time, *Australian Feminist Studies*, 24, 59, 11–16.

Colebrook, Claire (2012) A Globe of One's Own: In Praise of the Flat Earth, *SubStance*, 127, 41, 30–9.

Coleman-Bell, Ramona (2006) 'Droppin' It Like It's Hot: The Sporting Body of Serena Williams,' in Su Holmes and Sean Redmond (eds), *Framing Celebrity: New Directions in Celebrity Culture*, London: Routledge, 195–206.

Cook, Pam (2001) 'The Trouble with Sex: Diana Dors and the Blonde Bombshell Phenomenon', in Bruce Babington (ed) *British Stars and Stardom*, Manchester: Manchester University Press, 167–78.

Couldry, N (2003) *Media Rituals: A Critical Approach*, London: Routledge.

Couldry, N (2009) *The Media: A Crisis of Appearances*, Globalization Working Paper Series. Hamilton: McMaster University.

Cranny-Francis, Anne (2015) Robots, Androids, Aliens, and Others: The Erotics and Politics of Science Fiction Film, in Sean Redmond and Leon Marvell (eds) *Endangering Science Fiction Film*, New York: Routledge, 220–42.

Cross, Tia, Klein, Freda and Smith, Barbara (1983) Face to Face, Day to Day–Racism CR, in Gloria Hull, Patricia Bell Scott and Barbara Smith (eds) *All the Women Are White, All the Blacks Are Men, But Some Of Us Are Brave*, New York: The Feminist Press, 52–60.

Cullen, Shaun (2016) The Innocent and the Runaway: Kanye West, Taylor Swift, and the Cultural Politics of Racial Melodrama, *Journal of Popular Music Studies*, 28, 1, 1–18.

D'Addario, Daniel (2015) Russell Crowe's the Water Diviner Falls Short, *Time Entertainment*, April 24, available at: http://Time.Com/3833935/The-Water-Diviner-Review-Russell-Crowe/; Accessed 22 March 2018.

D'Aloia, Adriano (2010) Cinematic Enwaterment: Drowning Bodies in the Contemporary Film Experience, *Comunicazioni Sociali On-line*, available at: www.comunicazionisocialionline.it/2010/3/5/; Accessed 7 October 2017.

Dayan, D and Katz, E (1992) *Media Events*, Cambridge: Harvard University Press.

DeAngelis, Michael (2008) Cinderella Man: Russell Crowe as Il Diva, *Camera Obscura*, 23, 1, 47–67.

Deleuze, Gilles (1989) *Cinema 2: The Time Image*, trans. Hugh Tomlinson and Barbara Habberjam, London: Athlone.

Deleuze, Gilles (2005) *Cinema 1: The Movement-Image*, New York: Continuum.

Deleuze, Gilles and Guattari, Félix (1988) *A Thousand Plateaus*, trans. Brian Massumi, London: Continuum.

Denzin, Norman (2001) The Seventh Moment: Qualitative Inquiry and the Practices of a More Radical Consumer Research, *The Journal of Consumer Research*, 28, 324–30.

De Saussure, Ferdinand (2011) *Course in General Linguistics*, trans. Wade Baskin, Perry Meisel and Haun Saussy (eds), New York: Columbia University Press.

Devereux, Eoin, Dillane, Aileen and Power, Martin (eds) (2015) *David Bowie: Critical Perspectives*, London: Routledge.

Douglas, Mary (1966/2002) *Purity and Danger: An Analysis of Pollution and Taboo*, London: Routledge.

Douglas, Mary (1972) *Daedalus*, 101, 61–81.

Dovey, Jon (2000) *Freakshow: First Person Media and Factual Television*, London: Pluto.

Driessens, Olivier (2013) Celebrity Capital: Redefining Celebrity Using Field Theory, *Theory and Society*, 42, 5, 543–60.

Duffett, Mark (2012) Applying Durkheim to Elvis, *Transatlantica: Revue d'études Américaines*, 2, 1–7, available at: https://transatlantica.revues.org/6095?lang= en; Accessed 4 May 2017.

du Gay, Paul (1997) Introduction, in Paul du Gay (ed) *Production of Culture/Cultures of Production*, Milton Keynes/London: Open University/Sage, 1–10.

du Gay, Paul, Hall, Stuart, Janes, Linda, Mackay, Hugh, and Negus, Keith (1997) *Doing Cultural Studies: The Story of the Sony Walkman*, London: Sage.

Duits, Linda and van Zoonen, Liesbet (2006) Headscarves and Porno-Chic Disciplining Girls' Bodies in the European Multicultural Society, *European Journal of Women's Studies*, 13, 2, 103–17.

Duits, Linda and van Zoonen, Liesbet (2007) Who's Afraid of Female Agency?, *European Journal of Women's Studies*, 14, 2, 161–70.

Durkheim, Emile (1968) *The Elementary Forms of Religious Life*, New York: The Free Press.

Dyer, Richard (1978) Resistance Through Charisma: Rita Hayworth And Gilda, in E Ann Kaplan (ed) *Women and Film Noir*, London: BFI.

Dyer, Richard (1986) *Heavenly Bodies: Film Stars and Society*, London: British Film Institute/Macmillan.

Dyer, Richard (1997) *White*, London: Routledge.

Dyer, Richard (1998) *Stars: New Edition*, London: BFI.

Dyer, Richard (2002) *Only Entertainment*, 2nd Edition, London: Routledge.

Eagleton, Terry (1990) The Ideology of the Aesthetic, in P. Hernadi (ed) *The Rhetoric of Interpretation and the Interpretation of Rhetoric*, Durham, NC: Duke University Press, 75–86.

Elias, Norbet (1978) *The Civilizing Process, Volume 1: The History of Manners*, Oxford: Blackwell.

Elias, Norbet (1982) *The Civilizing Process, Volume 2: State Formation and Civilization*, Oxford: Blackwell.

Elias, Norbet (1983) *The Court Society*, Oxford: Blackwell.

Ellis, Caroline (2013) Carrying the Torch for Autoethnography, in S Jones Holman Jones, TE Adams and C Ellis (eds) *Handbook of Autoethnography*, Walnut Creek, CA: Left Coast Press, 9–12.

Ellis, John (1982) *Visible Fictions*, London: Routledge.

Ellis, John (2007) Stars as a Cinematic Phenomenon, in Sean Redmond and Su Holmes (eds) *Stardom and Celebrity: A Reader*, London: Sage, 90–8.

Ellsworth, E (1997) Double Binds of Whiteness, in M Fine, L Weis, L Powell, and M Wong (eds) *Off White: Readings on Race, Power, and Society*, London: Routledge, 259–69.

Ethnic Television Review Panel (6 February 1980) *Programming for the Multicultural/ Multilingual Television Service: Objectives and Policies*, Canberra: Australian Government Publishing Service.

Ezra, Elizabeth and Rowden, Terry (eds) (2006) *Transnational Cinema: The Film Reader*, London: Routledge, 1–12.

Fairclough, Kirsty (2008) Fame Is a Losing Game Celebrity Gossip Blogging, Bitch Culture and Postfeminism, *Genders*, 48, available at: www.genders.org/g48/ g48_fairclough.html; Accessed 20 August 20 2014.

Fairclough, Kirsty (2012) Nothing less than Perfect: Female Celebrity, Ageing and Hyper-Scrutiny in the Gossip Industry, *Celebrity Studies*, 3, 1, 90–103.

Feasey, Rebecca (2006) Fame Body: Star Styles and Celebrity Gossip in *Heat* Magazine, in Su Holmes and Seam Redmond (eds) *Framing Celebrity*, London: Routledge, 177–194.

Feasey, Rebecca (2008) Reading Heat: The Meanings and Pleasures of Star Fashions and Celebrity Gossip, *Continuum: Journal of Media & Cultural Studies*, 22, 5, 687–99.

Featherstone, Mike (1995) The Body in Consumer Culture, in Mike Featherstone (ed) *The Body: Social Processes and Cultural Theory*, London: Sage, 170–96.

Ferguson, Harvie (1992) Watching the World Go Round: Atrium Culture and the Psychology of Shopping, in Rob Shields (ed) *Lifestyle Shopping*, London: Routledge, 21–39.

Ferris, Kerry O (2001) Through a Glass, Darkly: The Dynamics of Fan-Celebrity Encounters, *Symbolic Interaction*, 24, 1, 25–47.

Feuer, Jane (1983) The Concept of Live Television: Ontology as Ideology, in E Ann Kaplan (ed) *Regarding Television*, Los Angeles: American Film Institute, 12–22.

Finnegan, Ruth (1997) Storying the Self: Personal Narratives and Identity, in Hugh Mackay (ed) *Consumption and Everyday Life*, London: Sage, 65–112.

Fischler, C (1988) Food, Self and Identity, *Social Science Information*, 27, 2, 275–93.

Fisher, Lauren Alexis (2016) Inside Fendi's Breathtaking Couture Show at Rome's Trevi Fountain, *Harper's Bazaar*, available at: www.harpersbazaar.com/fash ion/fashion-week/news/a16573/fendi-couture-show-at-trevi-fountain/; Accessed 16 April 2017.

Fiske, John (1987) *Television Culture*, London: Methuen.

Flaxman, Gregory (2000) Introduction, in Gregory Flaxman (ed) *The Brain Is the Screen: Deleuze and the Philosophy of Cinema*, Minneapolis: University of Minnesota Press, 1–57.

Fortmueller, Kate (2017) Gendered Labour, Gender Politics: How Edith Head Designed her Career and Styled Women's Lives, *Historical Journal of Film, Radio and Television*, [online], 1–21.

Foster, Eric K (2004) Research on Gossip: Taxonomy, Methods, and Future Directions, *Review of General Psychology*, 8, 2, 78–99.

Foucault, Michel (1977) *Discipline and Punish*, London: Tavistock.

Foucault, Michel (1979) *Discipline and Punish*, London: Peregrine, Penguin.

Foucault, Michel (1980) *Power/Knowledge: Selected Interviews and Other Writings 1972–77*, Brighton: Harvester.

Foucault, Michel (1988) 'Technologies of the Self', in L Martin, H Gutman and P Hutton (eds) *Technologies of the Self: A Seminar with Michel Foucault*, Amherst, MA: University of Massachusetts Press.

Foucault, Michel (1990) *The History of Sexuality, Volume 1: An Introduction*, Harmondsworth: Penguin.

Foucault, Michel (1995) *Discipline & Punish: The Birth of the Prison*, trans. Alan Sheridan, New York: Vintage Books.

Frank, D and McPhail, M (2005) Barack Obama's Address to the 2004 Democratic National Convention: Trauma, Compromise, Consilience and the (Im)Possibility of Racial Conciliation, *Rhetoric and Public Affairs*, 8, 4, 571–93.

Freeman, Elizabeth (2010) *Time Binds: Queer Temporalities, Queer Histories*, Durham: Duke University Press.

Frith, Simon (1996) 'Music and Identity', in Stuart Hall and Paul du Gay (eds) *Questions in Cultural Identity*, London: Sage, 108–27.

Gabriel, John (1988) *Whitewash, Racialized Politics and the Media*, London: Routledge.

Gamson, Joshua (1994) *Claims to Fame Celebrity in Contemporary America*, Berkeley: University of California Press.

Gaut, Berys (2010) The Philosophy of Creativity, *Philosophy Compass*, 5, 1034–46.

Geraghty, Christine (2003) 'Performing as a Lady and a Dame: Reflections on Acting and Genre', in Thomas Austin and Martin Barker (eds) *Contemporary Hollywood Stardom*, London: Arnold.

Geraghty, Christine (2007) 'Re-examining Stardom: Questions of Texts, Bodies and Performance', in Sean Redmond and Su Holmes (ed) *Stardom and Celebrity: a Reader*, London: Sage, 98–110.

Gerow, Aaron (2007) *Kitano Takeshi*, London: BFI.

Gilead, Sarah (1992) 'Magic Abjured: Closure in Children's Fantasy Fiction', in Peter Hunt (ed) *Literature for Children: Contemporary Criticism*, London: Routledge, 80–109.

Gill, Rosalind (2007) Postfeminist Media Culture: Elements of a Sensibility, *European Journal of Cultural Studies*, 10, 2, 147–66.

Gill, Rosalind (2009) Mediated Intimacy and Postfeminism: A Discourse Analytic Examination of Sex and Relationships Advice in a Women's Magazine, *Discourse & Communication*, 3, 4, 345–69.

Gillard, Julia (2002) From 'White Australia' to Whitlam: Migration and Multiculturalism in Australia. The Whitlam Government as Modernist Politics: 30 Years Later Conference. Canberra, 2–3 December 2002, available at: www.hnet.org/announce/show.cgi?ID=131218; Accessed 18 February 2016.

Gillespie, Marie (1989) Technology and Tradition: Audio-Visual Culture Among South Asian Families in West London, *Cultural Studies*, 3, 2, 226–39.

Gillespie, Marie (1995) *Television, Ethnicity and Cultural Change*, London: Routledge.

Gilman, Sander (1985a) *Difference and Pathology*, New York: Cornell University Press.

Gilman, Sander (1985b) Black Bodies, White Bodies: Toward an Iconography of Female Sexuality in Late 19th Century Art, Medicine, and Literature, *Critical Inquiry*, Autumn, 12, 203–42.

Gloe, Lucs (2016) The Life of Kanye a Qualitative Content Analysis of Kanye West's Twitter Practice, MA Thesis (unpublished), available at: http://lup.lub.lu.se/luur/download?func=downloadFile&recordOId=8872496&fileOId=8891938; Accessed 21 November 2017.

Gorton, Thomas (2014) News Anchor Quits Live on Air to Promote Weed Legislation, *Dazed,* available at: www.dazeddigital.com/artsandculture/article/21864/1/news-anchor-quits-live-on-air-to-promote-weed-legalisation; Accessed 11 April 2018.

Gramsci, Antonio (1985) *Selections from the Cultural Writings,* London: Lawrence & Wishart.

Gottschall, Kristina (2014) Always the Larrikin: Ben Mendelsohn and Young Aussie Manhood in Australian Cinema, *Continuum,* 28, 6, 862–75.

Gow, RW, Lydecker, JA, Lamanna, JD and Mazzeo, SE (2012) Representations of Celebrities' Weight and Shape During Pregnancy and Postpartum: A Content Analysis of Three Entertainment Magazine Websites, *Body Image,* 9, 1, 172–5.

Grosz, Elizabeth (1993) Merleau-Ponty and Irigaray in the Flesh, *Thesis Eleven,* 36, 1, 37–59.

Hage, Ghassan (1995) The Limits of Anti-racist Sociology, *UTS Review,* 1, 1, 14–21.

Hage, Ghassan (1997) 'At Home in the Entrails of the West: Multiculturalism, "Ethnic Food" and Migrant Home-building', in H Grace, G Hage and L Johnson (eds) *Home/World: Space, Community and Marginality in Sydney's West,* London: Pluto Press, 99–153.

Hall, Stuart (1990) The Emergence of Cultural Studies and the Crisis of the Humanities, *October,* 53, 11–23.

Hall, Stuart (1997) 'The Work of Representation', in Stuart Hall (ed) *Representation: Cultural Representations and Signifying Practices,* London: Sage, 13–69.

Hall, Stuart (1997) The Spectacle of the Other in Stuart Hall (ed) *Representation: Cultural Representations and Signifying Practices,* Vol. 2, London: Sage, 223–290.

Hall, Stuart (2011) The Neo-liberal Revolution, *Cultural Studies,* 25, 6, 705–728.

Hammer, Joshua (2015) Russell Crowe Takes a New Look at an Old Battle, *Simthsonian.com,* available at: www.smithsonianmag.com/arts-culture/russell-crowe-takes-new-look-at-battle-gallipoli-180954962/; Accessed 11 April 2018.

Hanlon, Karen (2006) Heavy Metal Carnival and Dis-alienation: The Politics of Grotesque Realism, *Symbolic Interaction,* 29, 1, 33–48.

Harper, Stephen (2006) Madly Famous: Narratives of Mental Illness in Celebrity Culture, in Su Holmes and Sean Redmond (eds) *Framing Celebrity: New Directions in Celebrity Culture,* London: Routledge, 311–28.

Harris, Richard and Larkham, Peter (eds) (2003) *Changing Suburbs: Foundation, Form and Function,* London: Routledge.

Hartley, John (1999) *Uses of Television,* London and New York: Routledge.

Hearn, Alison (2010) Structuring Feeling: Web 2.0, Online Ranking and Rating, and the Digital 'Reputation' Economy, *Ephemera: Theory & Politics in Organization,* 10, 3/4, 421–38.

Hegde, RS (2007) Of Race, Classy Victims and National Mythologies: Distracting reality on Celebrity Big Brother, *Feminist Media Studies,* 7, 4, 453–6.

Hellekson, Karen (2009) A Fannish Field of Value: Online Fan Gift Culture, *Cinema Journal*, 48, 4, Summer 2009, 113–18.

Herbert, Martin (1996) *Banishing Bad Behaviour: Helping Parents Cope with a Child's Conduct Disorder*, Leicester: BPS Books.

Hermes, Joke (1995) *Reading Women's Magazines: An Analysis of Everyday Media Use*, London: Polity.

Higson, Andrew (1995) *Waving the Flag: Constructing a National Cinema in Britain*, Oxford: Clarendon Press.

Hill, John (1999) *British Cinema in the 1980s*, Oxford: Clarendon Press.

Hinerman, S (1992) "I'll Be Here with You": Fans, Fantasy, and the Figure of Elvis', in LA Lewis (ed) *The Adoring Audience: Fan Culture and Popular Media*, New York: Routledge, 107–34.

Hobson, Janell (2008) Digital Whiteness, Primitive Blackness, *Feminist Media Studies*, 8, 2, 111–26

Holmes, Su and Negra, Diane (2011) *In the Limelight and Under the Microscope: Forms and Functions of Female Celebrity*, London: Continuum.

Holmes, Su and Sean Redmond (2006) Understanding Celebrity Culture, in Su Holmes and Sean Redmond (eds) *Introduction. Framing Celebrity: New Directions in Celebrity Culture*, London: Routledge, 1–25.

Holmes, Su and Sean Redmond (eds) (2006) *Framing Celebrity: New directions in Celebrity Culture*, Hoboken, NJ: Taylor & Frances, 27–43.

hooks, bell (1992) *Black Looks: Race and Representation*, Boston: South End Press.

Hunt, Kevin J (2015) 'The Eyes of David Bowie', in Toija Cinque, Chris Moore and Sean Redmond (eds) *Enchanting David Bowie: Space/Time/Body/Memory*, New York: Bloomsbury, 175–96.

Hunt, Leon and Wing-Fai, Leung (2008) *East Asian Cinemas: Exploring Transnational Connections on Film*, London: I.B. Taurus.

Ilicic, Jasmina and Webster, Cynthia M (2015) Consumer Values of Corporate and Celebrity Brand Associations, *Qualitative Market Research: An International Journal*, 18, 2, 164–87.

Jakubowicz, Andrew and Newell, Kerie (1995) 'Which World? Whose/Who's Home? Special Broadcasting in the Australian Communication Alphabet', in J Craik, J-J Bailey and A Moran (eds) *Public Voices, Private Interests: Australia's Media Policy Sydney*, Sydney: Allen & Unwin, 130–46.

Jameson, Fredric (1999) 'Marx's Purloined Letter', in Michael Sprinker (ed) *Ghostly Demarcations: A Symposium on Jacques Derrida's 'Specters of Marx'*, London: Verso, 26–67.

Jenkins, Henry (2010a) Avatar Activism and Beyond, available at: http://henryjenkins.org/blog/2010/09/avatar_activism_and_beyond.html; Accessed 15 December, 2017.

Jenkins, Henry (2010b) 'Fandom, Participatory Culture, and Web 2.0—A Syllabus', *Confessions of an Aca-fan: The Official Weblog of Henry Jenkins*, available at: http://henryjenkins.org/2010/01/fandom_participatory_culture_a.html; Accessed 23 June 2011.

Jenkins, Henry (2006a) *Convergence Culture: Where Old and New Media Collide*, New York: New York University Press.

Jenkins, Henry (2006b) When Fandom Goes Mainstream, *Confessions of an Aca-Fan*, available at: http://henryjenkins.org/2006/11/when_fandom_goes_mainstream.html; Accessed 1 February 2011.

Jenkins, Henry and Shresthova, Sangita (2012) Up, Up, and Away: The Power and Potential of Fan Activism, *Transformative Works and Cultures*, 10, http://dx.doi.org/10.3983/twc.2012.0435.

Jermyn, Deborah (2006) "Bringing Out the [Star] in You": SJP, Carrie Bradshaw and the Evolution of Television Stardom', in Su Holmes and Sean Redmond (eds) *Framing Celebrity: New Directions in Celebrity Culture*, London: Routledge, 67–86.

Jermyn, Deborah (2016) Pretty Past It: Interrogating the Postfeminist Makeover of Ageing, Style and Fashion, *Feminist Media Studies*, 16, 4, 573–89.

Johansson S (2006) 'Sometimes You Wanna Hate Celebrities': Tabloid Readers and Celebrity Coverage, in S Holmes and S Redmond (eds) *Framing Celebrity: New Directions in Celebrity Culture*, London: Routledge, 343–58.

Jolie Pitt, Angelina (2015) Angelina Jolie Pitt: Diary of a Surgery, *New York Times*, available at: www.nytimes.com/2015/03/24/opinion/angelina-jolie-pitt-diary-of-a-surgery.html; Accessed 11 April 2018.

Jones, MO (2007) Food Choice, Symbolism, and Identity, *Journal of American Folklore*, 120, 476, 129–77.

Jordan, Ellen (1995) Fighting Boys and Fantasy Play: The Construction of Masculinity in the Early Years of School, *Gender and Education*, 7, 1, 69–86.

Jupp, James (1996) *Understanding Australian Multiculturalism*, Canberra: Centre for Immigration and Multicultural Studies, Australian National University, Australian Government Publishing Service.

Juslin, PN and Vastfjall, D (2008) Emotional Responses to Music: The Need to Consider Underlying Mechanisms, *Behavioral and Brain Sciences*, 31, 5, 559.

Kellner, Doug (2003) *Media Spectacle*, London: Routledge.

Kellner, Doug (2008) Media Spectacle and the 2008 Presidential Election: Some Pre-election Reflections, *Mediascape*, available from: www.tft.ucla.edu/mediascape/Fall08_Kellner.pdf; Accessed 1 September 2009.

Kelly, William W (2004) 'Introduction: Locating the Fans,' in Willliam W Kelly (ed) *Fanning the Flames: Fans and Consumer Culture in Contemporary Japan*, Albany: State University of New York Press, 1–16.

Kirby, Vicki (1997) *Telling Flesh: The Substance of the Corporeal*, London: Routledge.

Knorr Cetina, K (2001) 'Postsocial Relations: Theorising Sociality in a Postsocial Environment', in G Ritzer and B Smart (eds) *The Handbook of Social Theory*, London: Sage, 520–37.

Knorr Cetina, K (2009) What Is a Pipe? Obama and the Sociological Imagination, *Theory, Culture and Society*, 26, 5, 129–40.

Koreaboo (2017) BigHit CEO Confessess BTS Was Created Because of this One Member, available at: www.koreaboo.com/buzz/if-it-werent-for-this-member-bts-wouldnt-exist-as-it-does-today/; Accessed 11 April 2017.

Kristeva, Julia (2002) *Revolt, She Said*, trans. by Brian O'Keeffe, Foreign Agents Series, Los Angeles, CA: Semiotext[E], 139.

Kuhn, Annette (2010) Memory Texts and Memory Work: Performances of Memory in and with Visual Media, *Memory Studies*, 3, 4, 298–313.

Lamb, Sharon, Graling, Kelly and Wheeler, Emily (2013) 'Pole-arized' Discourse: An Analysis of Responses to Miley Cyrus' Teen Choice Awards Pole Dance, *Feminism & Psychology*, 23, 2, 163–83.

Lane, Robert (2000) *The Loss of Happiness in Market Democracies*, New Haven, CT: Yale University Press.

Langer, John (2001) Media Democratisation in Australia: What Is It, Who's Got It, Where to Find It, How It Works (or Doesn't) – Part 2, *Screen Education*, 26, 27, 68–85.

Langman, Lauren (1992) 'Neon Cages: Shopping for Subjectivity', in Rob Shields (ed) *Lifestyle Shopping*, London: Routledge, 40–82.

Lévi-Strauss, C (1975) *The Raw and the Cooked*, New York: Harper and Row.

Lewis, Tania (2010) Branding, Celebritization and the Lifestyle Expert, *Cultural Studies*, 24, 4, 580–98.

Littler, Jo (2008) 'I Feel Your Pain': Cosmopolitan Charity and the Public Fashioning of The Celebrity Soul, *Social Semiotics*, 18, 2, June, 237–51.

Lothian, Alexis, Busse, Kristina and Reid, Robin Anne (2007) Yearning Void and Infinite Potential: Online Slash Fandom as Queer Female Space, *English Language Notes*, 45, 2, 103–11.

Lupton, D (1996) *Food, The Body and the Self*, London: Sage.

Lout, Jodie Nikole (2017) 'Agents of Global Armament: Analyzing Masculinity and Militarism in "Captain America" and the Marvel Cinematic Universe', MA Thesis, University of Texas at El Paso.

Lowe, Melanie (2003) Colliding Feminisms: Britney Spears, 'Tweens', and the Politics of Reception, *Popular Music and Society*, 26, 123–40.

Lury, Celia (1996) *Consumer Culture*, Cambridge: Polity.

Lynsky, Dorian (2013) Beatlemania: 'The Screamers' and other Tales of Fandom, *The Guardian*, available at: www.theguardian.com/music/2013/sep/29/beatlemania-screamers-fandom-teenagers-hysteria; Accessed 4 May 2017.

Lyon, David (1993) An Electronic Panopticon? A Sociological Critique of Surveillance Theory, *The Sociological Review*, 41, 653–78.

Lyon, David (1999) 'The World Wide Web of Surveillance: The Internet and Off-World Power Flows', in Hugh Mackay and Tim O'Sullivan (eds) *The Media Reader: Continuity and Transformation*, London: Sage, 353–64.

MacCormack, Patricia (2008) *Cinesexuality*, Aldershot: Ashgate.

Macdonald, Myra (2003) *Exploring Media Discourse*, Abingdon: Arnold.

Mackay, Hugh (1997) Introduction, in Hugh Mackay (ed) *Consumption and Everyday Life*, London: Sage, 1–12.

Maffesoli, Michel (1991) The Ethic of Aesthetics, *Theory, Culture and Society*, 8, 7–20.

Maltby, J, Giles, D, Barber, L and McCutcheon, LE (2005) Intense-Personal Celebrity Worship and Body Image: Evidence of a Link Among Female Adolescents, *British Journal of Health Psychology*, 10, 17–32.

Marks, Laura U (2000), *The Skin of the Film: Intercultural Cinema, Embodiment and the Senses*, Durham: Duke University Press.

Marshall, David P (2006) 'New Media – New Self: The Changing Power of Celebrity', in David P Marshall (ed) *The Celebrity Culture Reader*, Routledge: New York, 634–44.

Marwick, Alice E (2010) Status Update: Celebrity, Publicity and Self-Branding in Web 2.0, PhD Submission, available at: www.tiara.org/blog/wp-content/

uploads/2010/09/marwick_dissertation_statusupdate.pdf; Accessed 6 April 2017.

Marwick, Alice and boyd, danah (2011) To See and Be Seen: Celebrity Practice on Twitter, *Convergence: The International Journal of Research into New Media Technologies*, 17, 2, 139–58.

Marx, K and Engels, F (2002) *The Communist Manifesto* (Penguin Classics), London: Penguin.

Massumi, Brian (2002) *Parables for the Virtual: Movement, Affect, Sensation*. Durham, NC: Duke University Press.

May, Andrew (2011) Lisztomania, *Forteana Blog*, available at: http://forteana-blog. blogspot.com.au/2011/10/lisztomania.html. Accessed: 22 March 2017.

McCracken, Grant (1989) Who Is the Celebrity Endorser? Cultural Foundations of the Endorsement Process, *Journal of Consumer Research*, 16, 3, 310–21.

McCurry, Justin (2017) K-pop Singer Jonghyun's Death Turns Spotlight on Pressure of Stardom, *The Guardian*, available at: www.theguardian.com/world/2017/ dec/19/k-pop-singer-jonghyun-death-shinee-pressures-of-stardom; Accessed 16 April 2017.

McGee, MC (1980) The 'Ideograph': A Link Between Rhetoric and Ideology, *Quarterly Journal of Speech*, 66, 1–16.

McLeod, Ken (2003) Space Oddities: Aliens, Futurism and Meaning in Popular Music, *Popular Music*, 22, 3, 337–55.

McRobbie, Angela (2004) Post-feminism and Popular Culture, *Feminist Media Studies*, 4, 3, 255–64.

Menninghaus, Winfried (2003) *Disgust: The Theory and History of a Strong Sensation*, trans. Howard Eiland and Joel Golb, New York: State University of New York Press.

Mercer, Kobener (ed) (1994) *Welcome to The Jungle*, London: Routledge.

Merleau-Ponty, M (1964) *The Primacy of Perception*, Evanston, IL: Northwestern University Press.

Miller, Daniel (1997) 'Consumption and its Consequences', in Hugh Mackay (ed) *Consumption and Everyday Life* London: Sage, 13–50.

Mirzoeff, Nicholas (1995) *Bodyscape: Art, Modernity and the Ideal Figure*, London: Routledge.

Miyao, Daisuke (2004) Telephilia Vs. Cinephilia = Beat Takeshi Vs. Takeshi Kitano? *Framework: The Journal of Cinema and Media*, 45, 2, 56–61.

Monbiot, George (2014) The Age of Loneliness Is Killing Us, *The Guardian*, 14 October, available at: www.theguardian.com/commentisfree/2014/Oct/14/ age-of-loneliness-killing-us; Accessed 4 November 2014.

Monk, Claire (1995) Sexuality and the Heritage, *Sight and Sound*, 5 10, 32–34.

Nayer, Pramod K (2015) 'Brand Bollywood Care: Celebrity, Charity and Vernacular Cosmopolitanism', in David P Marshall and Sean Redmond (eds) *The Wiley Companion to Celebrity*, New York: Wiley.

Negra, Diane (2001) *Off-White Hollywood: American Culture and Ethnic Female Stardom*, London: Routledge.

Negus, K (1997) 'The Production of Culture', in P Du Gay (ed) *Production of Culture/ Cultures of Production*, Milton Keynes/London: Open University/Sage, 67–118.

Neimanis, Astrida (2014) Speculative Reproduction: Biotechnologies and Ecologies in Thick Time, *philoSOPHIA*, 4, 1, 108–28.

Newman, George, Diesendrock, Gil and Bloom, Paul (2011) Celebrity Contagion and the Value of Objects, *Journal of Consumer Research*, 38, 8, 1–15.

Nguyen, Sophia (2014) The Posthuman Scar-Jo, *Los Angeles Review of Books*, available at: https://lareviewofbooks.org/article/posthuman-scar-jo/#!; Accessed 15 January 2018.

Nixon, Sean (1997) 'Exhibiting Masculinity', in Stuart Hall (ed) *Representation: Cultural Representations and Signifying Practices*, London: Sage, 291–330.

Norman, Donald Arthur (2005) *Emotional Design*, New York: Basic Books.

North, A and Hargreaves, D (1999) Music and Adolescent Identity, *Music Education Research*, 1, 1, 75–92.

O'Brien Hallstein, D Lynn (2011) She Gives Birth, She's Wearing a Bikini: Mobilizing the Postpregnant Celebrity Mom Body to Manage The Post-Second Wave Crisis In Femininity, *Women's Studies in Communication*, 34, 2, 111–38.

Orbach, Susie (1993) *Hunger Strike: The Anorectic's Struggle as a Metaphor of our Times*, London: Penguin.

Orgeron, Marsha (2003) Making 'It' in Hollywood: Clara Bow, Fandom, and Consumer Culture, *Cinema Journal*, 42, 4, 76–97.

O'Sullivan, Simon (2001) The Aesthetics of Affect: Thinking Art Beyond Representation, *Angelaki Journal of the Theoretical Humanities*, 6, 3, 125–35.

Paglia, Camille (1990), 'Madonna – Finally, a Real Feminist', *The New York Times*, December 14, available at: www.nytimes.com/1990/12/14/opinion/madonna-finally-a-real-feminist.html; Accessed 28 August 2014.

Pallasmaa, Juhani (1996) *The Eyes of the Skin: Architecture and the Senses*, Chichester: Wiley-Academy.

Palmer, Rachael (1980) *Anorexia Nervosa*, London: Penguin.

Pateman, Carole (1988) *The Sexual Contract*, Cambridge, Polity, 291–330.

Perkins, Claire (2014) The Post-mortem Star Discourse, or, Loving Adrienne Shelly, *Celebrity Studies*, 45, 1–2, 20–31.

Pieterse, JN (1995) 'Globalization as Hybridization' in Featherstone, M, Lash, S, and Robertson, R (eds) *Global Modernities*, London: Sage 45–68.

Pink, Sarah (2009) *Doing Sensory Ethnography*, London: Sage.

Powell, Helen and Prasad, Sylvie (2010) 'As Seen on TV'. The Celebrity Expert: How Taste Is Shaped by Lifestyle, *Media Cultural Politics*, 6, 1, 111–24.

Probyn, Elizabeth (2011) 'Glass Selves: Emotions, Subjectivity, and the Research Process', in Stuart Gallagher (ed) *The Oxford Handbook of the Self*. Oxford: Oxford University Press, 1–10.

Propp, Vladimir (2010) *Morphology of the Folktale*, 2nd Edition, Texas: University of Texas Press.

Radner, Hilary (2016) Transnational Celebrity and the Fashion Icon: The Case of Tilda Swinton, Visual Performance Artist at Large, *European Journal of Women's Studies*, 23, 4, 401–14.

Rancière, Jacques (2004) *The Politics of Aesthetics: The Distribution of the Sensible* trans. Gabriel Rockhill, London and New York: Continuum.

Rayns, Tony (2003) Puppet Love, *Sight and Sound*, 13, 6, 18.

Redmond, Sean (2006) 'Intimate Fame Everywhere', in Su Holmes and Sean Redmond (eds) *Framing Celebrity: New directions in Celebrity Culture*, Hoboken: Taylor & Frances, 27–43.

Redmond, Sean (2008) Pieces of Me: Celebrity Confessional Carnality, *Social Semiotics*, 18, 2, 149–61.

Redmond, Sean (2009) 'The Power of Love: Popular Indian Romantic Comedy', in D Jermyn and S Abbott (eds) *Falling in Love Again*, London: IB Taurus, 65–78.

Redmond, Sean (2010) Avatar Obama in the Age of Liquid Celebrity, *Celebrity Studies*, 1, 1, 81–95.

Redmond, Sean (2013) Who Am I Now? Remembering the Enchanted Dogs of David Bowie, *Celebrity Studies*, 4, 3, 380–83.

Redmond, Sean (2014) *Celebrity and the Media*, Hampshire: Palgrave MacMillan.

Rex, John (1996) 'Transnational Migrant Communities and Ethnic Minorities in Modern Multicultural Societies', in John Rex (ed) *Ethnic Minorities in the Modern Nation State*, London: Palgrave Macmillan, 96–113.

Robins, K (1997) 'What in the World's Going On?' in Paul du Gay (ed) *Production of Culture/Cultures of Production*, London: Sage, 11–66.

Rojek, Chris (2001) *Celebrity*, London: Reaktion Press.

Rojek, Chris (2009) So You Wanna Be on Reality TV? *The Faster Times*, available at: www.thefastertimes.com/fameculture/2009/09/03/no-talent-reality-tv/#more-23; Accessed 3 April 2012.

Rojek, Chris (2016) *Presumed Intimacy: Para-social Relationships in Media, Society and Celebrity Culture*, Cambridge: Polity.

Rooney, Tara, Lawlor, Katrina and Rohan, Edward (2016) Telling Tales; Storytelling as a Methodological Approach in Research, *The Electronic Journal of Business Research Methods*, 14, 2, 147–56.

Rowe, PG (1993) *Modernity and Housing*, Cambridge, MA: MIT Press.

Rowland, Mark (2008) *Fame*, Stocksfield, UK: Acumen Publishing.

Rubin, Alan, Perse, Elizabeth and Powell, Robert A (1985) Loneliness, Parasocial Interaction, and Local Television News Viewing, *Human Communication Research*, 12, 155–80.

Ruppersberg, Hugh (1990) 'The Alien Messiah', in Annette Kuhn (ed) *Alien Zone*, London: Verso, 32–38.

Sahlins, Marshall (1974) *Stone Age Economics*, London: Tavistock.

Said, Edward (1978) *Orientalism*, New York: Pantheon Books.

Sanderson, Jimmy and Cheong, Pauline Hope (2010) Tweeting Prayers and Communicating Grief Over Michael Jackson, *Bulletin of Science Technology & Society*, 30, 328–340.

Sartre, JP (1966) *Being and Nothingness*, Washington: Washington Square Press.

Sconce, Jeffry (1995) Trashing the Academy: Taste, Excess and an Emerging Politics of Cinematic Style, *Screen*, 36, 4, 371–93.

Scott, Stephen (1998) Swings and Roundabouts: Risk Anxiety and the Everyday Worlds of Children, *Sociology*, 32, 4, 689–705.

Sedgewick, Eve Kosofsky (1992) 'Epidemics of the Will', in J Crary and S Kwinter (eds) *Incorporations*, New York: Zone, 582–95.

Seneviratne, Kalinga (1992) Multicultural Television: Going Beyond the Rhetoric, *Media Information Australia*, 66, 1, 53–7.

Shilling, Chris (2005) *The Body in Culture, Technology and Society*, London: Sage.

Shilling, Chris and Mellor, Patricia (1996) Embodiment, Structuration Theory and Modernity: Mind/Body Dualism and the Repression of Sensuality, *Body and Society*, 2, 1–15.

Shouse, Eric (2005) Feeling, Emotion, Affect, *M/C Journal*, 8, 6, available at: http://journal.media-culture.org.au/0512/03-shouse.php; Accessed 6 April 2017.

Showalter, E (1985) *The Female Malady: Women, Madness, and English Culture, 1830–1980*, New York: Pantheon.

Sobchack, Vivian (2000) What My Fingers Knew: The Cinesthetic Subject, or Vision in the Flesh, *Senses of Cinema* [online], 5, available at: http://sensesofcinema.com/2000/5/fingers/; Accessed 6 April 2013.

Sobchack, Vivian (2004) *Carnal Thoughts: Embodiment and Moving Image Culture*, Berkeley, CA: University of California Press.

Sobchack, Vivian (2008) Embodying Transcendence: On the Literal, the Material, and the Cinematic Sublime, *Material Religion: The Journal of Objects, Art and Belief*, 4, 2, 194–203.

Soukup, Charles (2006) Hitching a Ride on a Star: Celebrity, Fandom, and Identification on the World Wide Web, *Southern Communication Journal*, 71, 4, 319–37.

Srivastava, Lina (2009) Transmedia Activism: Telling Your Story across Media Platforms to Create Effective Social Change, *NAMAC*, available at: http://archive.li/8O1Rd; Accessed 7 October 2017.

Stacey, Jackie (1994) *Star Gazing: Hollywood Cinema and Female Spectatorship*, London: Routledge.

Stacey, Jackie (2000) 'The Global Within: Consuming Nature, Embodying Health', in S Franklin, C Lury and J Stacey (eds) *Global Nature, Global Culture*, London: Sage, 97–145.

Steers, Mai-Ly N, Wickham, Robert E and Acitelli, Linda K (2014) Seeing Everyone Else's Highlight Reels: How Facebook Usage is Linked to Depressive Symptoms, *Journal of Social and Clinical Psychology*, 33, 8, 701–31.

Stevenson, Nick (2009) Talking to Bowie fans: Masculinity, Ambivalence and Cultural Citizenship, *European Journal of Cultural Studies*, 12, 1, 79–98.

Stever, G (2011) Celebrity Worship: Critiquing a Construct, *Journal of Applied Social Psychology*, 41, 6, 1356–70.

Strinati, Dominic (1995) *An Introduction to Theories of Popular Culture*, London: Routledge.

Sullivan, Moynagh (2007) 'Boyz to Men: Irish Boy Bands and Mothering the Nation', in W Balzano, A Mulhall and M Sullivan (eds) *Irish Postmodernisms and Popular Culture*, London: Palgrave Macmillan, 184–96.

Tasker, Y and Negra, D (2007) *Postfeminism: Gender and the Politics of Popular Culture*, London: Duke University Press.

Taubin, Amy (1993) 'The Alien Trilogy: From Feminism to Aids', in Pam Cook and Philip Dodd (eds) *Women and Film: A Sight and Sound Reader* London: Scarlet Press, 93–100.

Telotte, JP (1990) 'The Doubles of Fantasy and the Space of Desire', in Annette Kuhn (ed) *Alien Zone*, London: Verso, 152–9.

Thompson, Kenneth (1997) 'Regulation, De-Regulation and Re-Regulation', in Kenneth Thompson (ed) *Media and Cultural Regulation*, London: Sage, 9–52.

Toba, Vikki (2016) Photographer Jonathan Mannion on the Making of Jay-Z's 'Reasonable Doubt', available at: www.contacthighproject.com/blog/photographer-jonathan-mannion-on-the-making-of-jay-z-s-reasonable-doubt; Accessed 11 April 2018.

Totaro, Donato (2002) Deleuzian Film Analysis: The Skin of the Film, Off-Screen, available at: www.horschamp.qc.ca/new_offscreen/skin.html; Accessed 1 August 2011.

Turkle, S (1995) *Life on the Screen: Identity in the Age of the Internet*, New York: Simon and Schuster.

Turner, Graeme (2004) *Understanding Celebrity*, London: Sage.

Turner, Graeme, Bonner, Frances and Marshall, David P (2000) *Fame Games: The Production of Celebrity in Australia*, Cambridge: Cambridge University Press.

Turner, Graeme (2006a) *Film as Social Practice*, London: Routledge.

Turner, Graeme (2006b) The Mass Production of Celebrity: Celetoids, Reality TV, and the Demotic Turn, *International Journal of Cultural Studies*, 9, 2, 153–65.

Uhls, Yalda T and Greenfield, Patricia M (2012) The Value of Fame: Preadolescent Perceptions of Popular Media and Their Relationship to Future Aspirations, *Developmental Psychology*, 48, 2, 315–326.

Vera, H and Gordon, MA (2003) *Screen Saviors; Hollywood Fictions of Whiteness*, Oxford: Rowman & Littlefield.

Wall, Sarah (2008) Easier Said than Done: Writing an Authoethnography, *International Journal of Qualitative Method*, 7, 1, 38–53.

Warner, Maria (1994) *From the Beast to the Blonde*, London: Chatto and Windus.

Weaver, Hilary (2017) Scarlett Johansson Doesn't Think Monogamy Is Natural, *Vanity Fair*, February 15, available at: www.vanityfair.com/style/2017/02/scarlett-johansson-marriage-and-monogamy; Accessed 15 April 15 2017.

Weber, Max (1968) *Economy and Society: An Outline of Interpretive Sociology*, New York: Bedminster Press.

Welton, D (ed) (1999) *The Body*, Malden, MA: Blackwell Publishers.

Wernick, A (1991) *Promotional Culture: Advertising, Ideology, and Symbolic Expression*, London: Sage.

Wilk, Richard (1995) 'Learning to Be Local in Belize: Global Systems of Common Difference', in D Miller (ed) *Worlds Apart. Modernity Through the Prism of the Local*, Routledge: London, 110–33.

Williams, Linda (1991) Film Bodies: Gender, Genre, and Excess, *Film Quarterly*, 44, 4, 2–13.

Williams, Linda Ruth (1999) 'Dream Girls and Mechanic Panic: Dystopia and Its Others in *Brazil* and *Nineteen Eighty-Four*', in IQ Hunter (ed) *British Science Fiction Cinema*, London/New York: Routledge, 153–68.

Williams, Raymond (1974) *Television: Technology And Cultural Form*, London: Fontana.

Williams, Raymond (1976) *Keywords*, New York: Oxford University Press.

Wilson, Julia A (2010) Star Testing: The Emerging Politics of Celebrity Gossip, *The Velvet Light Trap*, 65, Spring, 25–38.

Willis, Paul (1982) 'The Motor-bike and Motor-bike Culture', in B Waites (ed) *Popular Culture: Past and Present*, London: Croom Helm, 284–94.

Willis, Susan (1990) I Want the Black One: Is There a Place for Afro-American Culture in Commodity Culture? *New Formations*, 10, Spring, 77–97.

Wong, Karen (2016) How Beyoncé's Seven-Story Monolith Sets New Bar of Design Extravagance, *Artnet News*, available at: https://news.artnet.com/art-world/beyonce-formation-tour-art-551048; Accessed 16 April 2018 https://news.artnet.com/art-world/beyonce-formation-tour-art-551048; Accessed 16 April 2017.

Wood, Robin (1978) Return of the Repressed, *Film Comment*, 14, 4, 25–32.

Wooden, Shannon R (2002) "You even forget yourself": The Cinematic Construction of Anorexic Women in the 1990s Austen Films, *Journal of Popular Culture*, 36, 2, 221–36.

Woodward, Kath (1997) *Identity and Difference*, 3rd Edition, London: Sage.

Woodward, Kath (2004) *Questioning Identity: Gender, Class, Ethnicity (Understanding Social Change)*, London: Routledge.

Young, Iris (1980) Throwing like a Girl: A Phenomenology of Feminine Body Comportment, Motility and Spatiality, *Human Studies*, 3, 1, 137–56.

Zacharias, U and Arthurs, J (2007) Starring Race, *Feminist Media Studies*, 7, 4, 451–53.

INDEX

Note: Page numbers in *italic* refer to figures.

#MeToo movement, 281

Abebe, Nitsuh, 146–147
Abidin, Crystal, 176
accidental celebrity, 279
Adams, Paul, 48
advertorials, 176
aesthetics, 117
affect theory, 15–16. *see also* Circuit of
    Celebrity Affect model
affects; overview, 17–19; affective
    relations and, 57–61; case studies,
    62–82; sensory aesthetics and,
    62–68
agency; overview, 24–26; case study,
    231–247; fans and, 228–230;
    meaning and, 226–228
Ahmed, Sara, 190, 262
Alien Messiah figure, 43
Aniston, Jennifer, 193
Apple, 179
Appleford, Katherine, 37
Arch motorcycles, 184
Armstrong, Lance, 121
attractiveness, 201–202
attributed celebrity, 90–91
audience, typologies, 198–201
augmented reality, 182
authenticity, 146
autoethnography, 25–26
Avatar, 277
award ceremonies, 194

Bacal, Edward D., 164
baptism, 195–196
Barad, Karen, 297
Barthes, Roland, 33–34

Bartky, Sandra Lee, 113, 180
Baudrillard, Jean, 86, 174
Bauman, Zygmunt, 55, 91, 149, 186
Baumgarten, Alexander, 117
Bazaarvoice, 182
Beal, Jessica, 187
Beat Takeshi, 68–82
Beatlemania, 124
Beckham, David, 93–94
Beijing 2008 Olympic Games, 156
Benedetti, Paolo, 193
Bennett, Andy, 11
Bennett, Jane, 292
Beyoncé, 4, 59, 124, 141, 192
Bieber, Justin, 24, 283
Bihaku embodiment, 7–8
Bil'in, 277–278
Biltereyst, Daniel, 209–210
Black Sabbath, 283
blackness, 189–190
Blanchett, Cate, 7, 37
blondeness, 42–43, 131
body projects, 115. *see also* embodiment
Bonnett, Alistair, 188
Booth, Paul, 276
Bourdieu, Pierre, 109, 184, 187
Bowie, David, 8–14, 95–97, 231–247,
    291–301
boy bands, 143–146
Bradley, Peri, 12–13
Brand Bollywood Care (BBC), 100
Brando, Marlon, 303–305
bricolage, 99
Brough, Melissa, 277
Bruns, Axel, 214
Bruzzi, Stella, 180
BTS, 144–146

Buck-Morss, Susan, 117
Burgess, Jean, 214
Burgess, Sam, 105
Burroughs, William S., 293
Butler, Judith, 115, 252

Capaldi, Peter, 95–96
Carluccio, Antonio, 265
Cashmore, Ellis, 59, 93
Caughie, John, 184, 295
Cave, Nick, 305
celebaesthetic encounters, 21, 118
Celebrity Big Brother, 259, 268–273
celebrity management, 94
celebrity turn, 139–143
Chanel, 3
charismatic authority, 151
Cher, 110
children, 256–257
Christensen, Clayton, 28
cinema history, 61–62
Circuit of Celebrity Affect model;
    overview, 14–17; affects, 17–19;
    agency, 24–26; disruption, 26–29;
    embodiment, 19–23; texturality,
    23–24
Circuit of Celebrity Culture model; case
    study, 8–14; consumption, 4–5,
    11–12; equilibrium within, 8, 13–14;
    identities, 3–4, 9–10; production,
    5, 11; regulation, 6–8, 12–13;
    representations, 2–3, 8–9
civil body, 248–251
classificatory systems, 3, 84
close-ups, 17
Coca-Cola, 177–178
coenaesthesia, 119
Colebrook, Claire, 291
community, fostering, 182
competition, 90
confessions, 121–123
consumption; overview, 4–5; case
    studies, 208–225; case study,
    11–12; celebrity endorsements,
    201–205; gossip and, 205–208;
    impressionability and, 197–201

Cook, Pam, 109
corporate identity, 172
costumes, 180, 192
Couldry, Nick, 88, 154
Craig, Daniel, 26
creativity, 146
Crowe, Russell, 101–106
Cruise, Tom, 121
cultural diversity, 231
cultural intermediaries, 86, 174–176
culture, 137–139. *see also* production
Curtis, Ian, 64–68
Cyrus, Miley, 38, 213–225, 253–256

Daily Mail, 167
damage, 80–82, 122
Dams, Tim, 281
database marketing, 181
Deleuze, Gilles, 61–62
democratisation, 92
Devlin, Es, 192
Diamond Dogs (Bowie), 13, 292–293
digital celebrity, 94–97
Dior, 119–120
disgust, 284
disruption; overview, 26–29; case study,
    291–301; celebrity carnival and,
    282–285; vs. regulation, 275–282;
    time and space and, 285–288
disruptive innovation, 28
distinction, 90–91
DIY celebrity, 95, 279
Doctor Who, 95
Dolce & Gabbana, 42
Dors, Diana, 110
Douglas, Mary, 109, 260, 267
The Dressmaker (Moorhouse), 133–134
Driessens, Oliver, 280
Duffett, Mark, 229–230
Durkheim, Emile, 151
Dyer, Richard, 42, 69–70, 74, 77, 80

Eagleton, Terry, 117
eating, 128–129, 259–273
economy, 140–141
Eight Inc., 179

electronic panopticons, 181
Elias, Norbert, 250–252
Ellis, John, 68, 71
Ellsworth, Elizabeth, 43
embodiment; overview, 19–23; body as a celebrity cage, 108–117; body projects and, 115; case study, 126–135; confessions and, 121–123; phenomenological body, 117–121; sublime state of being and, 123–126; wetness and, 194–196
emotions, 14–15
enchantment, 28
endorsements, 5–6, 201–205
environments, 285–288
enwaterment, 191
erotomania, 204–205
ethnicity, 189
Etihad, 173–174
external regulation, 6
Ezra, Elizabeth, 102

Facebook, 63–64, 214, 220
Fairclough, Kirsty, 207–208, 211–212
fans; agency and, 228–230; celebrity encounters, 203; Sasaeng, 204–205; slash fiction work of, 5, 27
fashioning, 176–182
Feasey, Rebecca, 212
femininity, 37
Fendi, 192–193
Ferris, Kerry O., 203
Finnegan, Ruth, 290
Fisher, Lauren Alexis, 192–193
fluidity, 85
food, 259–273
Foucault, Michel, 7, 34–35, 112, 115, 254
franchises, 5–6
Frankfurt School, 142
Fry, Stephen, 168

Gamson, Joshua, 5, 198
Ganguro girls, 99
Garbo, Greta, 18, 19
Garland, Judy, 81

gender, 115, 251–253. see also embodiment; femininity; masculinity
geopolitical landscape, 92–93
Geraghty, Christine, 69, 129
Ghost in the Shell (Sanders), 52–55
gift economy, 27
Gilead, Sarah, 257
Gillespie, Marie, 97
girling, 7
Gladiator (Scott), 103–104
Glading, Laura, 173–174
global celebrity, 97–101
Goldman, Jane, 281
Gordon, Andrew M., 52–54
gossip, 36, 138, 205–211. see also consumption
Grace, Della, 21
Gramsci, Antoni, 276
green campaigns, 160
Greene, Brian, 296
Greene, Charlo, 99–100
grieving, 239–243
Grosz, Elizabeth, 20
The Guardian, 167

Hage, Ghassan, 236–237
Hall, Stuart, 2, 34, 85, 114, 226
Hamasaki, Ayumi, 7–8
Harding, Tonya, 110
Harper, Stephen, 76
Harry Potter Alliance (HPA), 29, 278
Hartley, John, 278
Hartnett, Josh, 100
Head, Edith, 180
Hearn, Alison, 182
Heavenly Bodies (Dyer), 69–70
Heine, Heinrich, 124
Hellekson, Karen, 27
Her (Jonze), 45–48
heritage films, 126
Hermes, Joke, 205, 212
Hill, John, 126
Holmes, Su, 59, 112–113
holograms, 95

Holy Smoke (Campion), 131–133
hooks, bell, 189
Hyuk, Bang Shi, 144

identities; overview, 3–4; case study,
    9–10, 101–106; celebrity and, 87–89;
    classificatory systems and, 84;
    consumption and, 86–87; cultural
    intermediaries and, 86; culture and,
    138; defined, 83–85;
    possessive, 89–90; types of, 90–101
impressionability, 197–201
individuality, 143
infamy, 91
influencers, 174–176
internal regulation, 7
intimate strangers, 204
irony, 200

Jackson, Michael, 230
Jacobs, Simon, 27
Jay-Z, 38–40, 100
Jenkins, Henry, 147, 228, 280, 295
Johansson, Scarlett; *Ghost in the Shell*
    (Sanders), 52–55; *Her* (Jonze),
    45–48; representation and, 40–45;
    Under the Skin (Glazer), 48–52
Jolie, Angelina, 122
Jones, David. *see* Bowie, David
Jonghyun, 205
Jordan, Ellen, 114
Joy Division, 64–68

Kardashian, Kim, 36–37
Keitel, Harvey, 133
Kellner, Doug, 151–154, 158, 167
Kerrigan, Nancy, 110
Kidman, Nicole, 172–174
Kim, Jong-hyun, 205
Kinney, Honey, 281
Kiss Justin app game, 24
Kitano, Takeshi, 68–82
Knorr-Cetina, Karin, 154
Kristeva, Julia, 67–68, 299
Kwong, Kylie, 265

Lane, Robert, 209
Langman, Lauren, 86–87
language, 33
Leibowitz, Annie, 113
Lewis, Tania, 141–142
lifestyle fashioning, 176–182
lifestyles, 87–88, 174–176
liminality, 253
lineage, 90
Lipson, Zach, 176
liquid celebrity, 149
listening platforms, 182
Liszt, Franz, 124
live performances, 16, 28
local celebrity, 99–101
loneliness, 67, 80
The Loss of Happiness in Market
    Democracy (Lane), 209
Lury, Celia, 54, 172, 189
Lyon, David, 181

MacCormack, Patricia, 78
Mackay, Hugh, 183
Madonna, 189–190, 212
Mannion, Jonathan, 40
Marchetti, Gina, 54
marketing, database, 181
Marks, Laura U., 119
Marshall, David P., 69
masculinity, 37, 102, 187–188
massification, 142–148
Massumi, Brian, 17
McLeod, Ken, 229
meaning; agency and, 226–228;
    generating, 69
media centre myth, 154
media spectacles, 151–154
Mediterranean Escapes, 264
melodrama, 205–206, 212–213. *see also*
    gossip
men's movement, 188
Mercer, Kobena, 85
#MeToo movement, 281
Miller, Daniel, 183
Minaj, Nicki, 217

Mirzoeff, Nicholas, 115, 258
misrule, 223–224, 283
Miss Dior, 23–24
Miyao, Daisuke, 70
Moir, Jan, 167
Monbiot, George, 48–49
Monk, Claire, 126–127
Monroe, Marilyn, 51–52, 74, 120
Montana, Hannah (fictional character), 38. see also Cyrus, Miley
Moosejaw X-Ray App, 182
motorcycle culture, 184
Murphy, Cillian, 125–126
music business, 11
musical experiences, 229–230
My China, 265
mythopoetic men, 188

The Naked Chef, 264
Nassar, Larry, 285
national identity, 105–106, 139
Native American culture, 188
Nayar, Pramod, 100–101
Negra, Diane, 59, 110
Negus, Keith, 25
neo-tribes, 91, 185–186
new variant fame, 138
Nixon, Sean, 179, 187
Norman, Donald A., 177

Obama, Barack, 58, 74, 98, 148–169
Oliver, Jamie, 264
Olson, Candice, 175
Olympic Games (Beijing 2008), 156
Oprah Winfrey Show, 121
Orgeron, Marsha, 199
Osbourne, Ozzy, 283
O'Sullivan, Simon, 118
otherness, commodification of, 189

Pack, Scott, 167
Page, James, 12–13
Paglia, Camille, 212
Pallasmaa, Juhani, 23
panopticon, 181

paparazzi, 194
Park, Yoochun, 204
Perkins, Claire, 95
Personal Shopper, 182
Pitt, Brad, 100
A Place in the Sun, 180
politics, 58
Portman, Natalie, 23–24, 119–120
possessive individual, 183
post-feminist discourse, 207
Powell, Helen, 175
power, 114
Prasad, Sylvie, 175
Pretty Woman, 181–182
private self, 90
production; overview, 5; case study, 11, 148–169; celebrity turn, 139–143; culture and, 137–139; profit-making and, 142–148
profit-making, 142–148
prosthetic culture, 189
Prudential Financial, 11
pseudo individuality, 143
public celebrity, 92–94
public discourse, 92
public self, 90
Pullinger, Kate, 133

race, 35, 110, 165, 189–190, 230, 268–273. see also embodiment; whiteness
Radian6, 182
Raisman, Aly, 285
Reasonable Doubt (Jay-Z), 38–40
Reeves, Keanu, 184
regulation; overview, 6–8; case study, 12–13, 259–273; civil body and, 248–251; vs. disruption, 275–282; forms and characters of, 249; gender and, 251–253; girl-woman bodies and, 253–259
Reimagine (film), 173
representations; overview, 2–3; case study, 8–9; corporeality in, 35–38; Cyrus, Miley and, 38; Ghost in the Shell (Sanders), 52–55; Her (Jonze),

45–48; Jay-Z and, 38; Johansson, Scarlett and, 40–45; *Under the Skin* (Glazer), 48–52; star success myth and, 41–45; theory of, 33–35
Reputation (Swift), 5–6
Rhianna, 193
Rojek, Chris, 79–80, 89, 90, 93, 202
Ross, Jonathan, 281
Rowden, Terry, 102
Rowland, Mark, 138
Runaway (West), 146–147
Rusbridger, Alan, 167

Said, Edward, 232
Sartre, Jean-Paul, 260–261
Sasaeng fans, 204–205
Saturn (Jacobs), 27
Sedgewick, Eve Kosofsky, 115, 257–258
self-branding, 180
self-worth, 88
Sense and Sensibility (Lee), 127–130
senses, 117
sensory aesthetics, 62–68, 117
sexuality, 36–37
shaping behaviour, 7
Shetty, Shilpa, 259, 268–273
Shilling, Chris, 3, 19–20
shop interiors, 179, 181
Shouse, Eric, 60–61
Shresthove, Sangita, 277
signs, 33
slash fiction, 5, 27, 91
slenderness, 128–129
Smile bank, 172
Sobchack, Vivian, 65, 117
Something Else (Joy Division), 64–65
Soukup, Charles, 229
Southern Italian feast, 265
space, 285–288
Spears, Britney, 21–23, 122
Springsteen, Bruce, 156–157
Stacey, Jackie, 139, 190, 194–195, 266
star success myth, 41–45
Stein, Rick, 264
Stevenson, Nick, 10

Stewart, Kristen, 3
storying the self, 25, 63, 227
stranger fetishism, 190, 204
Strinati, Dominic, 140
string theory, 296
sub-cultures, 138. *see also* culture
sublime state of being, 123–126
Sullivan, Moynagh, 36
Sunshine (Boyle), 125–126
surveillance, 182
Swift, Taylor, 5–6, 111–112, 252, 258
Swinton, Tilda, 181
synaesthesia, 119
Sysomos, 182

Taubin, Amy, 44
Taylor-Wood, Sam, 25–26
television, 286
texturality; overview, 23–24; case study, 191; cultural intermediaries, 174–176; lifestyle fashioning, 176–182; nature of, 171–174; tribes and, 183–191; wet celebrity spectacles, 191–194; wetness and, 194–196
Timberlake, Justin, 187–188
time, 285–288
Tishler, Matthew, 145
Tognozzi, Esther, 22
toxic celebrity, 284
transnational celebrity, 101
tribes, 91, 183–191
trolling, 221
Trump, Donald, 58
Turner, Graeme, 92, 280
Twin Peaks (Lynch), 96
Twitter, 94, 167–168, 199, 213–217, 281

Under the Skin (Glazer), 48–52
unfolding structures of absence, 154

Vera, Hernan, 52–54
vfame, 138
virtual and augmented reality, 182
visceral design, 177
Visual kei movement, 99

Warner, Marina, 42
The Water Diviner (Crowe), 105
West, Kanye, 111–112, 146–147, 199
wet celebrity spectacles, 191–194
wetness, 194–196
'Where Are We Now' (Bowie), 299–301
whiteness, 41–45, 128. *see also* race
The Wild One (Benedek), 302–303
Williams, Pharrell, 188
Williams, Serena, 110, 113–114
Willis, Paul, 184
Willis, Susan, 187, 263

Wilson, Julie A., 206, 211
Winehouse, Amy, 121, 258, 289
Winslet, Kate, 126–135
Wooden, Shannon R., 128
Woods, Tiger, 20
Woodward, Kath, 84
Wynne-Hughes, Emily, 22

Young, Iris, 113, 180
YouTube, 88

Zavaroni, Lena, 112–113